Praise for *Black Pain*

"Williams argues persuasively that Blacks are not alone. [She] is dedicated to convincing her fellow African Americans that assistance is readily available, whether through counseling, medicine, or self-help."

—*Publishers Weekly*

"A compelling look at depression in the African-American community."

—*Library Journal*

"As a young African-American male, you have to have your war face on at all times. It's all about maintaining your swagger. Some people like to run away from the uncut truth, but *Black Pain* is no slouch. It boldly confronts the reality of our pain head-on, flowing like hot lyrics over the perfect beat."

—Sean Combs, CEO, Bad Boy Records

"Terrie Williams is the grand freedom fighter of her generation in the realm of public relations within mass media. She has inspired me for decades. This book reveals the depth of her courage and compassion. Don't miss it!"

—Dr. Cornel West, professor of religion, Princeton University, *New York Times* bestselling author of *Democracy Matters*

"The issue of depression is more crippling than any of us want to admit. Many of us suffer from it ourselves, and part of the problem is our denial. Terrie dares to bring out what so many have not had the courage to confront, having learned that you can never heal until you expose what hurts you. *Black Pain* is an opportunity to reach your breakthrough moment. A lot of us will feel freer to realize that we are not abnormal or suffering alone in our pain and depression."

—Rev. Al Sharpton

"African-American leaders in particular face tremendous obstacles rising to the top and even greater challenges staying there. We are the face of the struggle and are expected to always show strength, grit, determination, and confidence, when the burden of depression is doing everything it can to pull us back down. *Black Pain* shows us that it is time we all talk about our depression and fight with the same vigor that we fight to achieve racial justice. We must reveal the darker moments and show, despite the pain that tries to bring us down, we realize that seeking treatment, talking through our pain, and taking the mask off our helplessness will not only make us stronger but will allow others to appreciate the fact that depression is indiscriminate and that we can fight back and win. It is hard putting on the public face as the tireless warrior. It is harder still to show our vulnerable side and our ability to work through the pain and depression, and come through with a sense of accomplishment despite the odds."

—Charles Ogletree, professor of law, founding director of the Charles Hamilton Houston Institute of Race and Justice, Harvard Law School

"As busy people, we've gotten used to juggling a million things at once—calendars, clients, bosses, home, and family—but when do we get to be our own client, giving ourselves the same level of care and attention? *Black Pain* is a wake-up call, helping us see what happens when we drop the ball on ourselves by neglecting our mental and emotional health."

—Iyanla Vanzant, *New York Times* bestselling author of *Yesterday, I Cried*

"We as a people have had to deal with so much pain just as a result of racism and prejudice. Add to that [the] tragedy and the problems we face in everyday life, and it's no wonder depression affects so many. African Americans haven't ever really been taught how to deal with those emotions. *Black Pain* shows us how to recognize that depression that may be hidden away and deal with it. It pushes us to give a voice to the pain without passing it on to others. Pain turns into depression when we keep it bottled up inside. Terrie teaches us how to let that pain go and turn it into peace."

—Patti LaBelle, musician, nationally bestselling author of
Pattie LaBelle's Lite Cuisine

"Living a closeted life, with part of you hidden behind a door of depression is a sad, fragmented existence. *Black Pain* not only unlocks this door of misery, it breaks it off its hinges and shows us a pathway toward whole, healthy living."

—E. Lynn Harris, *New York Times* bestselling author of *I Say a Little Prayer*

"Too many of us are in the dark about what depression is and how big a crisis it is in our community. *Black Pain* shines a spotlight on the issue, getting the message out that we must identify, understand, and seek the help we need to heal."

—Danny Glover, actor and activist

"Terrie has tapped into one of the universal issues in our community—pain. People from my generation are at a stage where they can admit some of it, but most are in denial. They don't know that they share a common story because they've never heard anyone else's. *Black Pain* is going to open up the conversation in a way that will be quite revolutionary."

—Geoffrey Canada, CEO, Harlem Children's Zone

"Terrie Williams has an extraordinary blessing that allows her to give us gifts of understanding about common problems that affect us all . . . she is a treasure we should value and support."

—Carl Bell, professor of psychiatry and public health,
University of Illinois, Chicago

"Like with a lot of Black men, depression is something that falls below my radar. The symptoms of depression are so ingrained into our daily lives that we accept these feelings as normal. The rage and anger we suppress is just another regular facet of our makeup. We have in many ways exchanged the shackles of slavery for the invisible shackles of depression. I think Terrie's book *Black Pain* will be a key to help unlock those invisible shackles that keep us enslaved in today's society."

—Butch Lewis, boxing promoter and manager

"*Black Pain* brings a new understanding to the widely held misperceptions and stigmas about depression. People around the country are now talking about the issue; many have been moved to start speaking about it publicly. It took extraordinary courage for Terrie to bare her soul, her pain, and her anguish. We should all thank the good Lord that she had the strength to share her story. By doing so she has helped countless fellow sufferers realize that they are not alone. It's a powerful thing to admit the pain, to seek help, and to move on to a more productive, healthy, and fulfilling life."

—Bebe Moore Campbell, *New York Times* bestselling author of *72 Hour Hold*

"I applaud Terrie Williams for standing up and addressing the issue of depression in *Black Pain*. It is a condition that is highly prevalent and misunderstood in the African-American communities. Statistics have proven that we all have a great chance of experiencing depression in our lifetime. It is time to welcome discussion in our circles. Do not turn a deaf ear, as a person experiencing depression needs friends and family. Stand up and talk!"

—Sampson Davis, *New York Times* bestselling coauthor of *The Pact* and *We Beat the Street*

"I think that in times like these, when the world is carrying a lot of grief on both the community and international levels, we need to talk about how we react to the challenges in our lives honestly. *Black Pain* starts the conversation so we can begin to heal ourselves and those around us."

—Farai Chideya, Host of National Public Radio's *News & Notes*

"Terrie has spoken directly to our issues and provided substantive and quality examples of how to shed our baggage. Now we act. So the real question is, What are you prepared to do now?"

—Roland S. Martin, syndicated columnist, CNN contributor

"I know so many Black men who walk with a black cloud over their heads. It's so real you can see it, but this darkness they cannot identify, so they refuse to acknowledge that it exists. In *Black Pain: It Just Looks Like We're Not Hurting,* Terrie Williams sheds light on the dark clouds and illuminates the road to healing."

—Jamie Hector, actor, HBO's *The Wire*

"*Black Pain* is a must-read book that shows each one of us how to stop hurting and start healing! Terrie Williams, like Harriet Tubman, Sojourner Truth, and other unnamed African-American heroines who endured the pain of the American slave trade and led others to liberation, has shown us how 'Black Pain' can be transformed into 'Black Power.'"
—Rev. Dr. Frank M. Reid III, senior pastor, Bethel AME Church, Baltimore

"While on tours with Run-DMC and [during] late nights while home, I would find myself watching ministers and evangelists on TV and think, 'What am I missing?' I found that I often hid my pain through the luxuries my celebrity afforded, spending money and smoking weed. For me, [it was] finding a mentor and developing a spiritual relationship with the Holy Ghost. My faith made me a better man, able to lead by example, serve God honorably, and help others find a light. Like me, Terrie answered God's call and He gave her the courage to expose her wounds through her groundbreaking book *Black Pain*—a guide that can help people heal."
—Joseph "Rev. Run" Simmons, Phat Farm executive, minister, and member of Run-DMC

"Nobody wants to admit to themselves that they are vulnerable and hurting inside, let alone confess to someone else. Walking around pretending that nothing's wrong won't make your pain and depression go away. We have gotten real good at pretending that everything is okay—so good at wearing the mask that it's suffocating us. *Black Pain* snatches the mask off, freeing us to take a deep breath of honesty and face our issues."
—Chris "Ludacris" Bridges, Grammy Award–winning rapper and actor

"*Black Pain* is a breath of fresh air. . . . This book serves as an eye-opener to many and an inspiration to all."
—Zane, *New York Times* bestselling author of *Addicted* and *Breaking the Cycle*

BLACK PAIN

---

*It Just Looks Like
We're Not Hurting*

Real Talk for When There's
Nowhere to Go but Up

TERRIE M. WILLIAMS

SCRIBNER
New York London Toronto Sydney

SCRIBNER

A Division of Simon & Schuster, Inc.
1230 Avenue of the Americas
New York, NY 10020

First Scribner trade paperback edition January 2009

SCRIBNER and design are trademarks of
The Gale Group, Inc. used under license
by Simon & Schuster, Inc., the publisher of this work.

For information about special discounts for bulk purchases,
please contact Simon & Schuster Special Sales at
1-800-456-6798 or business@simonandschuster.com.

Designed by Kyoko Watanabe
Text set in Minion

Manufactured in the United States of America

20 19 18 17 16 15 14 13

Library of Congress Control Number: 2007013049

ISBN-13: 978-0-7432-9882-7
ISBN-10: 0-7432-9882-9
ISBN-13: 978-0-7432-9883-4 (pbk)
ISBN-10: 0-7432-9883-7 (pbk)

For Lani, my beloved sister,
your guiding light and infinite faith sustain me.

Depression is rage turned inward

Contents

BLACK
PAIN

We Wear the Mask

We wear the mask that grins and lies,
It hides our cheeks and shades our eyes,—
This debt we pay to human guile;
With torn and bleeding hearts we smile,
And mouth with myriad subtleties.
Why should the world be over-wise,
In counting all our tears and sighs?
Nay, let them only see us, while
We wear the mask.
We smile, but, O great Christ, our cries
To thee from tortured souls arise.
We sing, but oh the clay is vile
Beneath our feet, and long the mile;
But let the world dream otherwise,
We wear the mask!

PAUL LAURENCE DUNBAR

Foreword

by Mary J. Blige

Everywhere I go I am moved by painful stories my people share with me. I look into their faces and I see myself reflected in their eyes. I feel their longing for comfort and their need for peace of mind. Women speak about how they are abused by men they love and the shame that comes with allowing it to happen again and again. I can relate, because I've walked in their shoes. I know the brothers' pain, too. I know that we're all bleeding internally, trying to patch up our own wounds with bandages, when we need healing from head to toe.

We need to love ourselves, and we can't love ourselves until we let God into our lives to help us heal and find our purpose. We find our strength and our truth through God's love. Sometimes, facing our truth is the hardest thing to do, because it means reaching out and asking for help. It means having the courage to tell your truth so that others can be healed. That's the way I try to live my life, even though it's not always easy. We have to make sacrifices because we are responsible for one another.

Terrie Williams knows this, too. As a woman in business, she put her career on the line by going public about her depression. I believe her when she says that she's a woman on fire. I know it's true when she says Black people are hiding their pain and dying every day because of it. I believe that Terrie is a woman who loves God as I do and that He is using her to do His work. As African-American women, we share a common bond by acknowledging that we know depression up close.

We've never had a book this personal to read that defines our feelings and helps us understand what to do to heal ourselves. I'm proud of Terrie for writing *Black Pain* so that everyone will finally recognize depression, as she puts it, what it "looks, sounds, and feels like." And I'm proud of all the people in the book who had the courage to share their stories with the rest of us.

Foreword

by Susan L. Taylor

In the June 2006 issue of *Essence* magazine, my beloved friend Terrie M. Williams bravely bared her soul by revealing her battle with debilitating bouts of depression for over half her life. The moment that issue hit the stands, a tidal wave of responses began pouring into the *Essence* offices. In an overwhelming reaction, thousands of men and women were moved to write to us not only to express their admiration of Terrie's courage but to break their silence and admit that they, too, are struggling with similar issues in their lives. Terrie's remarkable piece sounded the alarm, awakening our consciousness of Black America's deep secret. Even now, people are still talking, and the letters keep coming in, all reaching out to her. Terrie has heard you, feels your pain, and this book is her way of reaching back to you.

You are holding in your hands a true blessing. *Black Pain* was written with love straight from the center of Terrie's heart. Because she loves us so and knows that too many of us are silently suffering, she has thrown her net far and deep to bring together all of the information, resources, and inspiration she could muster to let us know that we can be better; that we can live healthier, happier lives. That is who she is and what she does naturally. *Black Pain* invites you to share in the raw, honest stories of other brave souls willing to speak about their emotional struggles. You will read about the well known, the everyday people, the health professionals, and Terrie herself, who finally put into words the sadness so many of us are suffering, yet never knew how or never had the courage to describe.

But what are we going to do about the emotional pain so many of us are hosting and holding on to? Too often we work overtime, hiding it behind a mask that makes us appear to be powerful, in control, and confident. The reality is that, privately, in the silence of our souls, we are dying because we simply don't know how to reach out for help. We barely exist, limping through each day under the weight of anxiety buried so deep and suffering so acute, it's made us lethargic, unable to cope with our angst. We hide our anxiety—even from family and friends, because we fear being judged as weak and ineffective. In doing this we're allowing and nurturing a state of emergency in the Black community, a state that twists the lives of those who need us most: our poor and our vulnerable young.

This is not who we are as a people. Since the beginning of time and throughout our history we have come through the fire and brought with us a powerful testimony of strength, creativity, and miracles that we seem to have reached up and pulled right out of the heavens. Yet, at a time when we should be soaring, we are floundering. And I know that, because of this, we won't do the larger critical work God is calling us to do—attend to the pain and suffering all around caused by lack in the land of plenty. Our people will remain shackled in the bondage of misery, unable to move forward until you and I free and heal ourselves. This is possible only if we come out of hiding, if we will be as brave as Terrie and tell the truth.

Our coming into the light needn't be a public declaration like Terrie's; it just needs to happen in our psyches and our souls. And we must commit to receiving the gift of therapy, which will help heal us. Terrie has opened the way; we just have to walk it. We have to admit that we bear the generational wounds caused by hundreds of years of slavery and abuse, the separation from family and culture and all that was dear and familiar to us. The heinous acts of violence are not forgotten. We remember that our beauty and our humanity were degraded, defiled, and devalued. The wonder is not that so many Black folks have succumbed. The wonder is *us*—that we have survived. We are the offspring of the people who refused to die.

But all is not well, and we don't have much time to secure our future as a people. We are in a deep crisis. In order for us to carry on in whole health and wellness, each of us, in his and her own way, must fess up to our weaknesses and lift one another up in collective support. We have to ask what work we are required to do to shine, and then get it done. Picking up this book is a glorious first step. *Black Pain* points the way to healing, teaches us that our hurting has a name, and shows us that we are not alone in our darkness. Along with Terrie, I encourage you to continue the journey toward inner peace. Your harvest awaits. Let the healing begin.

Introduction
Black Blues

I am a woman on fire.

I have two favorite pictures of myself as a little girl. One is of me at age three, naked except for my panties, standing on a large pillow, with a huge smile and my arms flung out wide. The other is of me about a year later dressed as Queen Esther from the Bible for a nursery school play. For the past year, almost fifty years later, I am more like the child in those pictures than I have ever been.

For much of my career I have spoken to diverse groups of thousands of people around the country about achieving success in business and in the field of public relations. In the last two years, I've begun dealing with major depression in my life, and when I give talks now, they're less about business than they are about this misunderstood disease. First I talk about how depression almost killed me; in other words, I stand in front of audiences of hundreds of people, naked and transparent, with my arms flung open. Then I talk about depression and Black people—how it is crushing our youth and destroying our lives—those who suffer from depression along with those who care about them. It is then that I think of Queen Esther, because she was called upon to reveal herself to save the lives of her people, *and she was scared to do it,* but she couldn't stand to watch her people be destroyed—she had to save them. I think of Queen Esther because depression is killing Black people by the thousands, and I have to talk about it no matter how much it scares me.

When I cast my eyes over the sweep of my life up to now, I see my whole adulthood in the long shadow of depression. The shadow starts right on the brink of my grown-up life. I was studying at Columbia University to become a clinical social worker. I worked like a maniac, doing everything required, everything optional, and even more work that I assigned to myself. The rest of the time I slept.

At first I didn't notice the change. Then things got worse. I always hated waking up, but slowly it was turning into something deeper; it was less like I didn't want to wake up, and more like I couldn't. I didn't feel tired, but I had no energy. I didn't feel sleepy, but I would have welcomed sleep with open arms. I had the sensation of a huge weight, invisible but gigantic, pressing down on me, almost crushing me into the bed and pinning me there.

The next second my heart would start pounding like crazy, and I would jerk myself upright and throw off the weight, heaving breath until the panic faded. And then I would get up and do what I had to do. I woke up with this terror every day—it felt like the universe was closing in on me. On top of that, I started isolating myself. Whenever I turned down an invitation to do anything, and got past the point where the person pressed me with "Are you sure?" and finally accepted my "No," I felt only one thing: relief.

And the panic got worse. By the end of my first semester I decided to see a therapist. I found a nice and well-intentioned white guy. Every week for nine months we talked, mainly about schoolwork and my daily routine, because I never once felt safe to talk about what was really bothering me: my obsessive working, my constant sleeping, and my chronic fear. Deep down I think I couldn't shake messages from childhood like "Keep your feelings to yourself" and "Don't air your dirty laundry (especially in front of white folks)." In the end my therapist described me as guarded but "on top of things"—and I'm sorry to say that his shallow reading of my symptoms satisfied me. I didn't know at the time that misdiagnosing depression in Black patients is routine—that our strong personal style, on top of beliefs that we can handle anything, often makes white professionals miss how much pain or anguish we're in. I was no exception: My therapist had misdiagnosed me by a long shot.

After a while my symptoms lessened, and I began work as a clinical social worker. The change, coupled with focusing on problems other than my own, started to make me feel more like my old self again. I still didn't understand the feelings I'd had in graduate school, but since that was behind me, I told myself, so were those feelings. I thought I was back on top of things, but you know the saying, denial isn't a river in Egypt.

After two years of social work I felt drained. God must have had a hand in leading me on a new path because within a year I had changed careers completely. Working at a breakneck pace, I became a public relations counselor, landing A-list celebrities like Miles Davis and Eddie Murphy. On the outside I was living the American Dream, but on the inside things still didn't feel right.

By the year 2000 I was the head of a public relations and marketing firm that was growing beyond my wildest hopes, but once again every day I was waking up with crippling anxiety. Once I was out the door, I was *on*: By 9:00 A.M. I had typically read five papers, placed twenty calls, and spoken with over a dozen people. My office was buzzing—clients were calling, news was breaking, I was doing promotion (like getting a celebrity on a magazine cover or getting the word out about a new CD or movie or book) *and* damage control (helping a client do media interviews after a DUI), and by 6:00 P.M. I was gearing up for that evening's movie premiere, fund-raiser, or book party. It was rare that I got home before midnight; when I did, there was nothing left—nothing left for me.

Here I had everything society tells us should make us happy: success, money, access, but not one thing in my life gave me pleasure. In the middle of all this action and all these people, I felt like I was in solitary confinement. And I began to cope with these feelings of emptiness and dread by numbing the pain with food—the only thing I looked forward to after a sixteen-hour day. On the way home I would pick up snack foods, ice cream, party mix, cheese . . . mix them with leftovers from restaurant dinners, and eat until I was beyond full. But my hunger increased week by week, until every half hour I would get out of bed and go to the refrigerator for a snack. I was gaining weight; the more weight I gained the more disgust I felt; the more self-disgust I felt the more I wanted to hide from the pain by eating and sleeping. Like every drug, the food gave me less relief each day, but I clung to it. It was the only thing in my life that could soothe me—the only crutch I had to help me limp around my intolerable feelings. But what started as a source of comfort became another prison.

The saddest thing about all this is that I was able to go so long without anyone really noticing or at least feeling like they could say something. Every shred of energy I could muster after a night of sleep interrupted by binge eating went into servicing my clients and doing my superwoman act: competent, together, single woman making it on willpower alone; I was the poster girl for ambition and achievement, the Strong Black Woman. Strangely, sadly, the façade held up. As far as my colleagues and clients were concerned, the work got done and got done well.

Sometimes I think about how things might have gone if I had been a less talented actress, less able to convince everyone around me of something I knew was false. The bottom line was that my success, the thing I had given so much of myself to, was a cover for what was killing me. I had reduced myself to two modes: my game face, the soul-destroying mask I wore to work, and the numbed-out shell of a woman who sat alone in her apartment eating and sleeping.

Finally, I reached a breaking point. I woke up one morning with a knot of fear in my stomach so crippling that I couldn't face light, much less day, and so intense that I stayed in bed for three days with the shades drawn and the lights out.

Three days. Three days not answering the phone. Three days not checking my e-mail. I was disconnected completely from the outside world, and I didn't care. Then on the morning of the fourth day there was a knock on my door. Since I hadn't ordered food I ignored it. The knocking kept up and I kept ignoring it. I heard the sound of keys rattling in my front door. Slowly the bedroom door opened and in the painful light from the doorway I saw the figures of two old friends. "Terrie, are you in there?" They opened the windows and I shielded my eyes against the light. They sat down and put their hands on me, gently lifting me to sit up. I don't think I could have done it myself.

They stayed for three hours. They did the dishes, got me into the shower, helped me pick out clothes, made me an emergency appointment with a therapist that afternoon, and somehow got me there—I honestly don't remember how. Fifteen minutes into the session, I was staring at the therapist, barely understanding our conversation, and feeling like I'd fall down on the floor any second when she said the words "clinical depression." I felt like I was outside my body, like I was seeing us on TV, but I knew something had finally given: I couldn't go on the way I was without hurting myself more. The therapist told me I was in an emotionally dangerous place, that I would probably need medication before any real work could begin. She gave me the name of a psychiatrist and called to make the first appointment for the next day herself. She gave me her cell phone number, telling me to call if I didn't think I could make it to tomorrow. I looked at her and the number. Tomorrow? Tomorrow was a million years from now. I wasn't going to make it to the next hour, forget about tomorrow!

My friends took me home. One of them stayed the night. Somehow I did make it to the next day and to my appointment with the psychiatrist. She asked questions, took my blood pressure, and began the long process of finding the right medication for me. Those six months were some of the hardest of my life. After two weeks the medication kicked in a little and I felt slightly better, and with it came an overwhelming clarity about what my life had become, a clarity that brought me a new kind of despair. I was in a pit so deep I didn't know if I could get out; and even though I was functioning, I was probably in a more fragile state than when I lay in bed unable to move. I was so low I couldn't fall off the floor.

When I think back on that time I'm stunned. There I was, a mental health professional, and I couldn't bring myself to admit that I was suffering from a major clinical depression. I had been too paralyzed by my feelings to recognize the whole range of symptoms. All my energy was going into just functioning, doing the work things I "had to" do; and because I was hiding my feelings the only guide to my well-being became my own confused perceptions.

Then I had a thought that began to change my life: If this could happen to me, with all my experience and knowledge and access, what was happening to other people? What was happening to people who didn't have any of my resources? That was when I realized that the only way I was going to get through this was to stop pretending, finally, that it wasn't happening. And the only way to stop pretending was to let people know how I felt every day.

The first time I did it God told me to. I heard his voice telling me it was time to share my story and I obeyed. I used to wonder when people would say, "God spoke to me," but now I know. It was just four months after my meltdown, when I was scheduled to give a talk at a conference with a good number of the best-known people in the world of business. I kept wanting to cancel the talk, telling myself again and again that it was too early, that I wasn't ready, and that, honestly, I might never be. But for reasons I couldn't understand I didn't cancel, and I forced myself to go. As I walked up to the podium my fear was so intense that I thought I was going to vomit. I made myself breathe deep and kept reminding myself that there's no way out but through—I knew that God put me there for a reason. Then I did something that shocked everyone in the room, including me: I told the truth.

Instead of the high-powered upbeat talk about self-marketing that we were all expecting, I told the audience straight out that I suffered from depression. That I was standing in front of them on sheer willpower, and that I was afraid that willpower would fail me at any moment. As I spoke I heard a voice inside me say "career suicide." To my surprise, I was relieved by the thought—if telling the truth was career suicide, then the sham I had been living for so long was about to end. But instead, something amazing happened. The powerful men and women gathered to talk business and do business seemed to be empathizing with me. I barely remember the talk, but I vividly remember that after it many people in the audience—men and women alike—came over and told me how moved they were by my courage and confession. They admitted to similar bouts of despair, how helpless and afraid they were, and how ashamed they were to have those feelings.

After that day, I began to discover that telling the truth is addictive— every time I did it, and survived, I wanted to do it again. The more I took off my mask, the more I shared my story, the more folks shared back with me. Slowly the clinical social worker woke up. It's a given that depression is all over the media, at least as a buzzword—you can hardly turn on the TV without seeing a commercial for an anti-depression medication, or pick up a magazine without seeing an ad for one—but what about the very particular ways it hits Black people and shows itself in us? Are we in the grips of an unacknowledged epidemic? I could rattle off our at-risk statistics by heart, but I found myself wondering about something much harder to quantify: How much does suffering from and living with addiction, incarceration, dirty neighborhoods, HIV, hypertension, violence, racism, and class discrimination make us vulnerable to depression in the Black community? How many of us are suffering from it and not able or willing to acknowledge it? Who *is* talking about it? What is our response? The silence is deafening.

I had spent my whole life helping other people, but for the first time I truly understood that I can't help others without helping myself. So I keep working on myself, trying to give myself the kind of attention and care I give to other people. But as essential as self-care is, it's not enough for me. As I understand my own depression, I realize that I am in a unique position to investigate the face of depression in Black America, the pain that keeps so many of us locked in unnecessary despair and isolation. Maybe we can't cure depression, but in the first decade of the twenty-first century we can certainly treat it.

Depression is a fact of Black life, but it doesn't have to be a curse. And we don't have to be ashamed to admit it. This book will speak openly about my own depression and share the experiences of other people, from celebrities to regular working folk, so that we can think in different ways about this condition—and about our options as Black people for dealing with it. More than anything, I want to open a dialogue. I want to give a voice to our pain and name it so we can make a space for our healing.

I also want you to know that writing this book was a struggle. So many days I felt weighed down and sometimes paralyzed by the pain I was writing about. I'm very sensitive to noise and light (so of course I live in New York City) and after days on the road giving talks, and hearing so much pain-filled testimony, it would be hard for me to come home and regain my focus on the book. Some mornings I would wake up with terrible anxiety and some nights I would slip back into old habits and raid the fridge.

But whenever I start to feel overwhelmed by this challenge I've taken on, this responsibility I've been given, I look at that childhood photograph of me as Esther. I remind myself that when Esther became queen, she thought things would be smooth from there on in—she didn't know she'd be called upon to reveal her Jewish heritage and sacrifice her own comfort to save her people. Once she decided to do it, though, she understood that she was not burdened with responsibility, but blessed with the opportunity to help the people she loved. I am inspired by Esther—the queen in the Bible and myself as a little kid. I *will* talk about depression because my people are dying. I love my people and I will not stop talking about it and I will not rest until we can freely speak our pain without shame, because I am a woman on fire.

Getting the Message Out

In writing this book I have drawn on my clinical background as a social worker, my contacts with the medical and scientific community, my access to the top African-American physicians and clinicians, and my connections to media, community organizations, and celebrities, to paint a compelling portrait of depression in African-American life. The book is not a self-help manual, because there is no "self-help" for depression—if you're suffering from something you can pull yourself out of by willpower or your bootstraps, it's not depression.

I have written *Black Pain: It Just Looks Like We're Not Hurting* as a resource to help us as a people identify, understand, and respond to the pain and depression in our lives and our communities. My hope is that by helping us name and recognize our pain and depression we can break the cycle of silence around mental illness that is hurting and killing so many of us— often through secondary symptoms like drug addiction, suicide, crime, abuse, obesity, and hypertension. My dream is that *Black Pain* will begin to undo the stigma of "crazyness" Black people often link with depression, that it will give us the space to talk honestly about depression in all its faces, and that it will inspire us to celebrate our stories and our achievements even as we do battle.

I will look at how depression affects men and women, as well as our young people, because there are important differences. I will look at how and why African Americans are so often misdiagnosed or not diagnosed at all. I will show the dramatic face of depression as we so often see it on the nightly news in the form of violent crime, drug addiction, suicide, and imprisonment. And I will tell the stories of people suffering silently, sometimes hiding behind their game face or caught up in patterns of helplessness and failure. I will talk about the role of community and specifically the Black church in helping and hurting progress in the treatment of depression. Maybe most important, I will share my own story as a fellow sufferer making daily sense of a condition that is crippling so many of us.

Far too little work has been done on the legacy of pain and depression left by slavery, and this book will not have the space to address this issue in the depth needed. I hope, however, that by creating a work made up of both personal testimony and solid information, I will inspire psychologists and other social scientists to do more research in this area. In so many ways, I see *Black Pain: It Just Looks Like We're Not Hurting* not as an end point, but as a beginning.

A Note to You

My life experience has taught me time and again that when you know better, you do better. I have written this book to help us know better. To know ourselves better, know our pain better, and know that there are paths to healing. It is my greatest wish that, as happened to those of us who read Price Cobbs and William Grier's now-classic *Black Rage* over thirty years ago, you will not be the same after reading *Black Pain*. That you will look differently at everyone you meet. That you will see those around you more compassionately, knowing that they, too, have a story. That the outer layer of people's lives never shows us how many holes the person has inside. That every meeting is filled with possibility—the possibility of touching someone in a way that may hurt their spirit, or of touching them in a way that helps them heal. We have the power to mend ourselves and others, simply by being true to our own feelings. Black pain may be a reality, but it doesn't have to be our destiny. Let's bring new meaning to "lift as we climb." Let's join hands to pull ourselves up, up from a long legacy of pain, and into the light of wellness.

Chapter One

DEPRESSION

Not Killing Us Softly

I'm Coming Out, I Want the World to Know
It's not just what we say, but what we don't say . . .

In June 2005 I wrote an article about my depression for *Essence* magazine. I was not prepared for the reaction it generated. I received over 10,000 letters, over half of them from people "coming out" for the first time about their pain and depression. Complete strangers wrote to me because I was the safest person they could share with. Not friends, not family members, but me—

> Our lives begin to end the day we are silent about things that matter.
> —MARTIN LUTHER KING, JR.

someone they didn't know! I also wasn't prepared for the intensity of my frustration as I came to understand how many Black women and men are suffering silently.

The folks who wrote to me were scared—some of them terrified—to breathe a word to anyone; they were paralyzed by the fear that no one would understand or accept them. Their fear was echoed in conversation upon conversation I had while traveling across the country giving talks about how we are doing—about waking up in pain each day—to audiences that ranged from CEOs to regular churchgoers. After my talks, person after person would come to me to confide that they, too, were "going through it."

Sometimes I would come home from these trips totally drained in my heart and soul, having heard stories like the one I heard from a man whose

1

two sisters are home suffering from major depression. He can't talk about it, nor can his family, even though he's a respected physician and his brother is a well-regarded man of the cloth!

If I'm honest with myself, and with you, the fact is that I'm more like these folks than I care to admit. If then *Essence* editor in chief Diane Weathers hadn't sensed what I was going through and asked me to write the piece, I don't know how much longer it would have taken before I really told someone I was depressed—or if I would *ever* have told anyone before the point where there was no hiding it anymore.

In fact, my mom, dad, and sister didn't know what I was going through until I mailed them a draft of the article and wrote a kind of offhand note saying, "I wanted you to see this before it came out." I didn't even ask for their responses!

My mom called immediately. "I'm so sad you didn't feel like you could come to me. Maybe there was something I could have done!" And my sister told me that she, too, had been through the fire. But I was so used to handling things on my own that I believed telling them would only make them worry. I knew I wasn't suicidal, even though I *was* dying on the inside. The pain I feel is so hard to talk about that my closest family still hears more about it when I'm in front of large groups than one-on-one.

> People should understand that depression is not an attitude problem. It's not a character weakness, it's not a spiritual weakness. It may reflect in those things, but depression is related to changes in the brain. It's related to chemical changes in the brain and what people should understand is that you can't just snap out of it.
>
> —DAVID SATCHER, MD, PHD, FORMER SURGEON GENERAL AND DIRECTOR OF THE NATIONAL CENTER FOR PRIMARY CARE, MOREHOUSE SCHOOL OF MEDICINE

> You can't fall off the floor. There's nowhere to go but up.
>
> —JAMES MTUME, RECORDING ARTIST AND MUSIC PRODUCER

These days I use my visibility to talk about pain and how we mask it. Every time I step up to the microphone I "out" myself as someone in pain.

I do it because I know that by sharing my story, my fragility, insecurity, frailty, and woundedness, I liberate someone else to do the same.

Sometimes the liberation comes through humor. In the months after the *Essence* piece came out, people would see me at events and shyly come over to me. I knew they wanted to mention the article and talk about depression, but didn't know how, so I would break the ice. "I can tell you read the *Essence* article," I would say. "Don't worry. I took my medication today. Everything's okay—and you don't have to whisper the word 'depression'!" That little bit of humor, that easy laugh, was usually all it took to open the gates to honest talk about something we think is shameful. And I'm telling you, there is not one among us who has not been touched by this!

This book is as much about identifying depression as it is about the power of testimony. Some of the people whose stories are in this book were willing to bare their souls for the record, in the name of a cause bigger than themselves—and that includes some of the most well-known names here. Others were willing and even eager to share their stories, but feared that giving their names could jeopardize their livelihoods or hurt their families, especially their young children; these are not famous people and I have respected their requests for anonymity because I believe their stories are the most valuable thing they have to offer. Finally, I have drawn on magazine and television interviews from a handful of famous people who have spoken publicly about their struggles with depression.

More important than anything else is that the thousands of people who have communicated with me about this in person, in writing, or on the phone have broken the silence that makes depression so lethal. In the pas-

---

Though whites experience depression more often, African Americans and Caribbean Blacks experience greater severity and persistence.

Depression is more disabling for African Americans and takes a greater toll on all aspects of their lives—including work, relationships, social and overall—than for whites.

Many African Americans turn to non–health care professionals for help, such as the clergy.

—THE NATIONAL STUDY OF AMERICAN LIFE

sages below Set Shakur, Mama DeBarge, Joyce Walker Joseph, and Diane Weathers come out to me about their depression.

Testimony

If you ever danced or sang along to the infectious music of the DeBarge family, you can thank Etterlene "Mama" DeBarge for bringing all those gifted artists into our world. Sadly, her marriage to their father was nothing like the sweet music her children made. A jealous, controlling man, he kept "Mama" pregnant for most of fifteen years—pregnant, lonely, and depressed. She shared with me a chilling excerpt from her forthcoming memoir:

> I lived every day in my own personal hell. I had noticed myself becoming more reclusive and despondent, and I spent every waking moment paranoid and afraid. I very rarely had visitors, and at one point I had even stopped answering the phone. The telephone was a luxury that I had learned to do without after my husband accused me of "talking to another man on the phone." It was actually a wrong number, and I had made the mistake of answering. It's a funny thing, depression; it's the only intangible thing I know of that can actually cause very real, very tangible changes in a person. The burden and the pain of my life weighed me down like a wet woolen blanket. I willed myself through every day by repeating to myself over and over again, *I can do all things through Christ who strengthens me,* and I would make it at least one more day.

"Mama" made it through many days, and helped bring her children to realize their gifts and share them, but how much richer would all their lives have been if only she had been able to get the help she needed when she needed it most?

Charles J. Ogletree, Jr., is the Jesse Climenko Professor of Law at Harvard Law School, as well as the founder and executive director of the Charles Hamilton Houston Institute for Race and Justice. This is what he told me about powerful Black men and depression:

> African-American leaders in particular face tremendous obstacles ris-

ing to the top, and even greater challenges staying there. We are the face of the struggle and are expected to always show strength, grit, determination, and confidence, when the burden of depression is doing everything it can to pull us back down. It is time that we all talk about our depression, and fight with the same vigor we bring to the fight for racial justice. We must reveal the darker moments and show, despite the pain that tries to bring us down, we realize that seeking treatment, talking through our pain, and taking the mask off our helplessness will not only make us stronger, but will allow others to appreciate the fact that depression touches us all. But we can fight back, and we can win.

His words were much on my mind as I talked with two other powerful Black men, Carl Anthony Foreman and Bill Lynch, about their own pain.

Carl Anthony Foreman, the sixty-two-year-old powerhouse real estate mogul and owner of radio properties, was diagnosed only four years ago as suffering from bipolar disorder. For most of his life he experienced mood swings, at times feeling like he could conquer the world and buying up tons of property. At other times he felt bone weary, unable to talk, staying in bed in a darkened room for two to three days at a time.

Despite the range of his achievements his depression led him to move away from his wife and three sons when his youngest was fifteen years old. Although he supported them and lived nearby, when he sent the family on vacation, he couldn't go with them.

In some ways Carl's resources buffered him because he didn't have to go to a regular "job" every day. He would call his office at 3:00 A.M. "so I wouldn't have to talk to anyone." Then he'd leave a message that he wouldn't be in the office for a day or two so nobody would call and he could stay home alone, in silence. He wouldn't answer his phone. He would respond to voice mails in the middle of the night so he didn't have to talk to people. This strategy also gave him the advantages of surprise and respect, since people assumed he was working 24/7.

For a while he tried Zoloft and Lexapro, but they had side effects that, for him, were worse than the symptoms. "Chemical imbalance in our brains is no different than any other affliction we might have in our bodies. It's just that when it happens to the brain, it affects how you act and how you communicate."

Diagnosis late in life was a blessing and now Carl manages his depression by putting less stress on himself and not overworking. He attends fewer events, not stretching himself so thin, and does much of his business by phone. He also calls his therapist when he starts to feel overwhelmed. He's been coming out about his depression person by person, and each time he does, it's a little more liberating.

Sekyiwa (Set) Shakur is a thirty-one-year-old high-powered fashion designer and sister of the late Tupac Shakur. She's a warm and open spirit, someone who is clear about who she is and who she's becoming. She's also a woman who uses her own pain and challenges to help others. At twenty-three she began mentoring girls at the YWCA, because she feels it's important for young people to "hear us speak our truth, so that they know healing is possible."

She remembers always being uncomfortable in her own skin. Often she felt angry and would argue endlessly with anyone around her. She describes the feeling in her body "like a tornado." "When I opened my eyes in the morning I'd wish the sun wasn't up. And I often felt like I was outside of myself. At times it got to the point where I felt suicidal." Her family always referred to her as "Crazy Set" because she always spoke her truth. As we talk she tells me something I've heard many times: "All I really wanted was somebody to hold me." So many women have told me that they wish someone in their circle could have recognized their pain and comforted them. Instead her pain took the form of sex addiction and addiction to diet pills. She knew she needed real help when she found herself in a dark, suicidal place. "I was at a point where I didn't even think God would be upset with me. But then one day I saw God and my two brothers turn their back on me. The vision was so powerful I knew they didn't want me with them. I knew I had to keep living."

When we speak about Tupac she tells me that "in his music he often spoke of feeling crazy and alone. I wish he could have lived to hear others speak about their pain so he could have realized that he wasn't alone. As for me, it was such a relief when I was finally diagnosed. I wasn't just a 'bitch' or 'crazy,' there was a reason for all these painful feelings. I'm not crazy, I have a chemical imbalance!"

These days Set takes better care of herself. "I monitor my triggers—lust and vanity drop me to my core, and so does the stress of overwork." She knows what she needs to do to stay sane, and once or twice a week takes some time for herself. She also nourishes her spirit by traveling as much as she can. "And I take antidepressants to control my depression and stabilize my mood."

* * *

I've known political strategist Bill Lynch for years. A longtime mentor, he has been the vice chair of the Democratic National Committee, helped get David Dinkins elected, and then served as his deputy mayor. An interesting fact that few people know is the role Bill played with *New York Times* bestseller *The Covenant with Black America,* edited by the amazing Tavis Smiley. Published by the small but mighty Third World Press, the book's demand grew way beyond initial expectations. In order to get the book on shelves Bill reached out to his close friend Len Riggio, chairman of Barnes and Noble, to help it find greater distribution streams. The result was the first time a small Black press made it to the *New York Times* bestseller list, and it was due in large part to Bill's caring intervention. What he does behind the scenes literally transforms lives! But Bill is, above all, a man who is unafraid of his feelings, a man I have seen weep openly in the face of human pain. He comes from humble beginnings and has stayed humble even as he wields tremendous political power. That quality is the thing that everyone who knows him treasures most in him. He is a man who lives his calling, to use his influence to help individuals and organizations achieve their highest goals, and that's what gives him his depth and capacity to feel. In recent years Bill had renal failure and needed a kidney donor to live. His son was a match and volunteered. As a parent it was very hard for Bill to see his son jeopardize his own life to save him. Surgery of any kind always bears a risk for the person who needs to have it, but needing to endanger his son's life in any way left him feeling helpless and depressed. These are feelings he's still working with and through, but that have made him even more compassionate.

Joyce Walker Joseph's pictures used to cover my walls when I was growing up. At nineteen, she had her first photo spread in a major magazine for a "Black Is Beautiful" article. In 1969, a year later, she was considered the top Black model in the industry. But her success had a dark side. At the height of her career she was also deeply depressed. For starters, her father didn't consider girls worth much of anything; her mother didn't have a much higher opinion. "My parents didn't think I was living up to my potential, so I didn't have their support. They told me I couldn't sing, they never came to see me on the Broadway stage, they kept saying I was wasting my education, and that I was just having fun. They had no idea how hard I worked or what I was going through. They weren't big fans of mine and at one point we were estranged, and during that time I was alone and got into destructive relationships."

Joyce entered the modeling industry so young, she had little choice but to grow up in the public eye. "It was a strain because it conflicted with my private life. I became addicted to drugs, but no one knew. I smiled for the cameras, but inside I was dying." Low self-esteem from her family's rejection, compounded by the isolation of a racist industry, led her to spiral downward.

"I found myself more alone and lonely on modeling shoots, always the odd Black girl with the Afro from Queens, who didn't fit in with the jet-setting cliques. The man I married was not there for me, physically or emotionally. We soon divorced, but I got into other relationships with men who kept me working in an industry that talked down to me. They also introduced me to drugs that they said would make me feel better, 'make everything all right.' I was too naïve to recognize their actions as manipulative and controlling. No one understood my pain and depression. My parents thought I was just being moody; I was a success, what did I have to be depressed about? My childhood friends put up a catty, jealous wall when I reached out to them. To the outsider, I had everything; to me on the inside, I had nothing—no love, no companionship, no meaning. I continued to numb my body with drugs and alcohol until I was trapped in a dark place where suicide and death seemed like the only light. If this was the best of life, I wanted no part of it."

> Surround yourself with meaning. Don't be stuck where you're merely tolerated—find that place where you're appreciated. Don't be afraid to talk and to share; we all deserve love and life. If you love what you do, you're a success!
>
> —JOYCE WALKER JOSEPH, AFRICAN-AMERICAN MODEL AND ACTRESS

Joyce's journey of self-healing wasn't short, and it wasn't easy. "There were no sister-circles of support in those days. And you know how talking to a counselor or a shrink was seen as a stigma to Black folks, as a sign of personal weakness. I was held out to be strong, a role model." So what did she do that brought her to the truly strong place she's at today?

"I got healthy by being still and reaching deep inside for my connection with God. I wrote in my diaries, I meditated and prayed daily. I changed my career direction and entered Rutgers law school. I found a life partner and created a beautiful family. I sought out a female therapist, who was a good listener and sounding board. I cofounded a creative arts and leadership training program for Harlem teens. Giving to children, my own and forty others, has turned out to be the greatest gift I could give myself."

Diane Weathers is a veteran writer and editor. She is also, as I've said, the woman responsible for my coming out about my depression in the pages of *Essence* after hearing me speak about it on C-Span. She shared with me this story of her own depression:

> Nights I could handle. I fell asleep easily, and sleep allowed me to forget. But my mornings were unmanageable. To wake up each morning was to remember once again that the world by which I defined myself was no more. Soon after opening my eyes, the crying bouts would start and I'd sit alone for hours, weeping and mourning my losses.
>
> During one six-month period in 2005, my marriage ended, I was asked to resign as editor in chief of *Essence,* and my daughter was threatening to run away.
>
> My spirit was shattered. I began to believe I must have been getting everything wrong. I feared I was cursed with some flaw that made me unfit as a wife, a mother, a magazine professional.
>
> My recovery has come in baby steps, and it is ongoing. The first smart thing I did was e-mail a couple of dozen friends and people in my network, letting them know what a hard time I was having handling the sudden upheavals in my life. In the subject line I typed in the word "help," and I asked for their friendship, love, and suggestions for coping. I had written too many stories on the tragic lives of men and women who kept their personal suffering private. I long ago decided that if ever I found myself adrift at sea and drowning, I'd never be too proud to ask for a lifeboat. At this point in my life, I felt I needed an entire flotilla.
>
> My next step was counseling. Initially, all I could do was sit on my therapist's couch and cry. Finally, I asked for antidepressants. Medication quickly helped quell the crying jags so that I could better tend to the business of my life. After a few months, I felt strong enough to

sort out the mess still crowding my plate, without meds and without falling to pieces.

I am grateful that my therapist encouraged me to make meditation a daily practice. She helped me discover that my chaotic thinking and inability to focus on the present had become part of my problem. I still marvel at how simply sitting still each morning for thirty minutes, concentrating on my breathing, helps clear my mind of the debris left over from all my yesterdays. Letting go of the mental clutter lets me think and see more clearly and this helps me live more skillfully.

This probably won't be the last time that I come down with a blues that brings me to my knees. I can be hypersensitive to the disappointments, dashed expectations, and losses that come with life. I hope that next time around I'll be able to handle it better and if not, just handle it as best I can. And if I can't handle it on my own, may I never be too full of false pride that I can't reach out and ask the universe for help.

Even mental health professionals aren't immune. Take Derek S. Hopson, a well-known psychologist who previously shared his therapeutic practice and work as an author with his ex-wife. After eighteen years together, despite sharing so much, they divorced. At one point, Derek couldn't seem to get his life or practice back on track. He began to avoid friends, to suffer from a sense of failure, and to feel a loss of pleasure in the research that had always been a primary joy in his work. Like for me, being a therapist didn't help him diagnose or treat his own depression. It wasn't until about his fifth visit to his own therapist, reconnecting with family, close friends, and receiving loving support from his new wife, Flora Allen-Hopson, that it became apparent he might be suffering from symptoms of depression.

Five Reasons We Hide Our Pain

- It would hurt my family.
- It will ruin my career.
- Folks will think I'm crazy.
- I can't afford to seem weak.
- I still have shame about it; I know I shouldn't, but I do and I can't help

And then there's the long legacy of secrets and lies in the Black family. Since slavery, Black families have felt the need to cover up a million things they thought shameful, starting with the fact that so many of us were born out of wedlock or as the result of rape. The true tragedy lies not in hard truths but in the shame that keeps generations of family members unable to talk about their pain and find comfort with one another.

Rande Thompson was a classical pianist and Columbia University graduate. His talents were amazing, but he spent a great deal of time alone and had only a handful of friends. After years of erratic behavior, of disappearing and resurfacing, he called two of his closest friends to tell them he was in the hospital. He had full-blown AIDS. His friends were stunned. They hadn't known he was gay, either. It turns out that he had led a shame-based double life for years, and that the denial of his sexuality mirrored his denial of being HIV positive. Ashamed of being gay, he could never come out and find a stable long-term partnership that would nourish his soul; instead, he had hundreds of anonymous partners and rarely engaged in safe sex. The depression brought on by his sexual shame drove him to a compulsion that cost him his life.

Joan Cartons is one of the warmest people I know. Petite and stylishly dressed, she always has a smile on her face. But she was only willing to share this story with me on the condition that I change her name. "Last year I attempted suicide. My daughters don't know, and I don't think they're ready to hear the story."

It happened to Joan very recently, but her pain started a long time ago. "My mother used to send poison pen letters. They were so cruel I think she may have had borderline personality disorder. I would call my sister and say, 'I got a poison pen letter today.' She succeeded in pitting us siblings against each other. One on one we're okay, but as a group we're a nightmare."

Joan felt that the distance she kept between her mother and herself in adulthood would be enough to insulate her against her mother's toxic ways, but you know what happens to the best-laid plans of mice and men . . . "When my mother became ill, I swore I wouldn't be the one to take her in because I knew it wouldn't be healthy for me. But I ended up taking her in for two months. I was in debt and under stress about my daughter's education, so as a mother, daughter, friend, and sister, I was being pulled in too many directions."

One day it all became too much. "I came home, sat down at the computer, and suddenly started crying. I ran outside because I couldn't breathe. My husband ran out after me, and my daughter brought a paper bag for me to breathe into. At 2:00 A.M. when everyone was asleep I went back to the desk and started writing about my feelings. I printed it, packed my bag, and decided I would kill myself."

This wasn't the first time Joan had had suicidal thoughts, but every other time she was aware of them, and felt a little crazy for having them. She had understood those thoughts, correctly, as a warning sign, as a cry for help, but this time was different—this was not a cry for help.

"The next morning I cleaned the house and took my mother to the doctor. My husband came home and read the letter on my desk, and he called, crying, saying 'Please don't do it!' In the middle of my talking with him the hospital fire alarm went off, so I had to take my mother out. My husband called my sister, she sent her son to the hospital, and he just missed me—I even saw him driving in. I dropped my mother off at home and drove to hotels until I found a room, ordered prime rib and baked potato, took out wine and pills, and spread out pictures of my husband and kids. It was the first time I had felt painless in a long time. I watched *Oprah,* and in between bites I would pop handfuls of pills."

Her husband and nephew drove all over town looking for her, stopping at every hotel they saw because her husband knew from things she had said that she would check into a hotel. He finally saw her car at one hotel and had to call the police to find out where Joan was and get into the room.

"I was awakened by police shaking me and slapping me, and I passed back out. I saw my husband in the corner crying. He saved my life, because I had taken enough pills to kill myself. I was hospitalized for seventy-two hours, and then moved to a 'crisis home' for a week."

But recovery was not smooth or easy. "At the beginning I told my hus-

---

CHECK THIS OUT

A lot of people report feeling greatly relieved when they are diagnosed as depressed. That's exactly what *I* felt when I was finally diagnosed with clinical depression—relief! It was a relief to know I wasn't crazy! Well, maybe I *am* crazy, but at least I know everybody else is, too!

band I was sorry he found me. He took six months off, because he was always worried about me. My therapist said it was a scary suicide because of how calm I felt.

"From a year ago March, up until January '07, I really had a lot of good days and bad days. In January I woke up and decided that I needed to try to help me as much as I could. It's like an alcoholic; you have to take it one day at a time. When I try to take on more than one day I can fall into a depression, because it's overwhelming to think too far ahead. I'm learning to say no. I need adequate sleep or I get depressed. And I've started exercising for my mental health. Now I have more energy and take my meds.

"I've learned that part of why I get depressed is that I have a lot of negative self-talk in my head and I diminish myself all the time. I think things like, 'I'm a bad mother, wife, friend,' even though people compliment me on being a good mother, et cetera, but when I'm depressed I can't feel any of that."

"Passing for Normal" at Work

The other day I was reading a study by the National Institute of Mental Health and I stopped short on this sentence: "Poor functioning while at work accounted for more lost days than absenteeism." That means those days when we're not effective at our jobs happen more often, and add up to more lost productivity, than days when we're not there at all! The study went on to say that some workers lose upwards of twenty-seven workdays a year this way. On top of this, they estimated that over 6 percent of workers in this country have major depression—in dollars and cents, that translates into $36.6 billion lost to depression every year!

So many of us are "walking wounded" in the workforce, yet most of us deal with it by putting the game face on tighter, afraid to let anyone see what deep pain we're in. I can't even count how many times I've done my job perfectly on the outside while on the inside I felt like I was falling apart. And so many men and women tell me they feel the exact same way day after day, week after week. That means thousands and thousands of people are sitting at their desks *not* working. Not working for themselves and not working for their employer. Now, if you ask me, that's a lot of waste— waste of human potential, and waste of corporate resources.

Listen to what Judge Nina Hickson, former chief juvenile judge of Fulton County Juvenile Court in Atlanta, who has struggled with clinical depression, has to say on the subject.

Although I had been in and out of counseling during my early adult life, when my counselor told me that she thought I needed to go to a psychiatrist because I seemed to be stuck, I resisted. She thought I might benefit from medication, but I was really afraid that it might cause me to be "a zombie," so I tried a variety of alternatives, including hypnosis. These alternatives would work for a little while, but eventually I would get in a rut. It took the intervention of my mother and my best friend from college to get me to a psychiatrist for an assessment and, eventually, a prescription for an antidepressant. At the time I was angry about the intervention, but I am eternally grateful to both of them for loving me enough to make me stop running from the help I needed.

My treatment initially consisted of 20 mg of Prozac a day and therapy once a week. After a few months the therapy was reduced to twice a month; after a few years, the antidepressant dosage was increased to 40 mg, which is normal because the body gets used to a certain dosage. Sometimes I increased my therapy sessions to weekly if there was a major life event I was dealing with, like the death of a family member, stress at work, or the end of a relationship.

I do my therapy with a psychologist and see a psychiatrist every few months for my medication management. This two-pronged approach is key to managing my depression. It is also important to me to read stories of other people who have managed depression and been successful in their careers.

As a judge I saw a great deal of depression in children and parents, often in the form of irritability and anger. Yet people are quick to label irritable or angry people as "bad children" or "bad people." But it's depression and it needs to be managed.

On the one hand, depression made me a good judge, but it also took its toll. The fact that I dealt with pain made me more empathic: When I saw kids acting out, my own depression made me look beyond the behavior that brought them before me. I would take the time to talk to each child, and I would try to find ways to have the child evaluated psychologically. Was there depression? Did we need to treat it?

My own experience with depression inspired me to go further to come up with meaningful interventions. I'd see children whose parents were addicts, so they weren't available to their children. They'd get clean and then come back and want to parent, but the kids were angry and acting out. The kids were dealing with the pain that addiction in a parent causes. So I tried to make sure they got the services they needed to deal with the emotional problems.

But at times seeing so much pain every day had a negative impact on me: It made my own depression worse. I tend to absorb other people's feelings, and some days I felt like I literally could not get out of bed. I would push myself to get up and go, but on weekends I would collapse and I couldn't move. I'd always had a low level of sadness, and at times even a hopeless outlook, but I'd cope by working so that I didn't have time to feel. I didn't tell people I was depressed, but it would have helped if I had. The people who worked for me would tell me I was getting irritable and short-tempered, which is not my nature, but it was part of how the pain manifested.

> You can have a PhD and be a second-grade dropout emotionally.
>
> —MARY PENDER GREENE, PSYCHO-THERAPIST, RELATIONSHIP EXPERT

There was a white male judge I knew in another jurisdiction. When I heard folks talk about him, I knew he was suffering from depression. I reached out to him. And because I did, he went for treatment—and he was grateful that I helped him seek help for himself. There is healing and help out there. We just have to not be afraid to ask for it in the workplace.

Then there's Jessica Martin, a beautiful and charismatic music industry vice president.

For most people the arrival of spring is a good thing. For me it brings on a series of questions: How am I feeling? Am I able to sleep through the night? But most of all, I wonder if spring will mean the return of "It." The Vise. The Grip. Depression.

For years I had made it through spring with my best "I'm a Black girl and I can get through this" face. Although I am a child of an attorney and I never wanted for anything, I do not remember having a carefree childhood, I was a shy and introverted child, racked with insecurity and worries too big for my young soul. But I made it through my childhood by escaping into a world of books where I found particular solace at night, reading by flashlight under my covers. Reading seemed to soothe the fear and anxiety that frequently gripped me in the middle of the night. For the most part I was a healthy child but I was prone to stomachaches and rashes and in the spring of my senior year in high school I was diagnosed with a peptic ulcer. High expectations were the norm in my household and I was accepted to six of the seven colleges to which I applied. In the fall I left for college and thought that a new environment would be good for me. And for the most part that was true, but year after year spring was still a problem. I often thought that the rest of the year merely supplied me with the enormous strength I needed to get through the spring.

I made it through college successfully and got a music industry job in New York and years passed. I worked long hours because sometimes it took a very long time for me to accomplish even a simple task. My low periods began to increase and eventually it was not just the springtime that got me down. But I was determined to fight the depression on my own. I would go to work earlier or stay later. I would just apply myself harder. I finally found the courage to ask a friend at work for the name of a therapist and then carried the address in my pocketbook for a year. By the time I called to make an appointment I was desperate. When I arrived at the office several days later I cried what seemed like an ocean of tears and then did the same thing for my next two appointments. My therapist suggested an antidepressant to take the edge off and eventually I agreed. When the medication started to take effect I woke up one morning amazed. Never in my life had I felt so clear and calm, and I thought to myself, "Wow! This is what everyone else in the world must feel like." I started to feel better and about a year later I decided that I didn't need medication any longer. For several years I was fine but then one spring the depression reared its torturous head again.

The winter of 1998 had been an emotionally difficult one and things got worse as spring approached. My birthday is in April and because of the depression, celebrating sometimes was of little interest to me. That particular year I sidestepped conversations with friends about birthday plans, and the Saturday before my birthday I could not get out of bed. I simply didn't have any energy. My friend Lori called me and insisted that I get up and go out, and I did manage to do that, and I also went to work the following week and things got worse. I don't remember much from this period of my life except that when I went to my therapist the following Friday, I was the lowest I'd ever been, I was in more pain than I could imagine, and at the end of my session my therapist quietly said, "We've been talking about your getting a rest and I think you should be hospitalized for a few days. I don't think you should be alone." Even though we'd recently discussed this I still couldn't believe what I was hearing. I was tired, but with sleep I thought I could make it through. My therapist then asked if there was someone I could stay with. Since my family was 600 miles away, we called my best friend and my therapist explained my situation.

When I got to my friend's house I slept for sixteen straight hours. I went down to the kitchen to get something to eat and I was in such a bad place that even her cat knew that I wasn't well. I'm not a cat person and the cat always knew that, but today instead of being its usually pesky self, the cat simply curled up and lay at my feet. When I moved to a different seat the cat moved and curled up again.

I slept more that afternoon and into the next day. My therapist called to see how I was doing and quietly suggested that I needed a longer rest and medication. I decided that I needed to do what was necessary. Early Sunday evening my friend and her husband and two other friends took me to the hospital, where I stayed for several days, and then started to live the rest of my life.

That was almost ten years ago. I haven't had another major episode. I'm no longer in therapy or on medication, but if at such time that becomes necessary I will do what I have to do to not live in pain. It is important to know what triggers our depression, because if you look deeply into yourself you'll begin to recognize the patterns.

I had an extended bout of insomnia following 9/11 and immediately called a therapist for a tune-up, and there were also other issues that I wanted to address and during the next year and a half we worked on them.

Today my relationship with God is first and foremost in my life and my prayers and daily devotional with Him, the love of my family,

> Every year, without any treatment at all, thousands stop suffering from depression. Because it kills them.
>
> —DR. PAUL GREENGARD, 2000 NOBEL LAUREATE IN MEDICINE

friends, and wonderful Bible study family keep me lifted.

We don't have to live in pain.

The Silent Killer

Depression kills.

That's the bottom line. If I could communicate only one thing about what depression does, my message would be simple: It can kill you.

When I give talks, people often ask me, "What does depression look like?" I always give the same answer. Depression looks like your cousin who just got sentenced for dealing four grams of cocaine. It looks like your sister who works eighteen-hour days and hasn't made it to Sunday dinner in weeks. Depression looks like your sixteen-year-old neighbor who's having her second baby. Depression looks like the boy whose drive-by shot hit your niece instead of the rival gang member he was gunning for. Depression looks like the black-and-blue bruise on your troubled nephew's wife. Depression is the overweight mother of two who keeps forgetting to take her blood pressure medicine and has a heart attack in the supermarket where you shop every week. Depression looks like the corporate executive who wears an airtight game face all day and collapses at home every night, so tired of acting the part that he can't enjoy his own life. Depression looks like the twenty-eight-year-old Black woman who's starving herself to death to look like white models in her industry. Depression looks like the pastor who preaches like a man lit up with the holy

> When truth is replaced by silence, the silence is a lie.
>
> —YEVGENY YEVTUSHENKO, RUSSIAN POET AND FORMER SOVIET DISSIDENT

spirit on Sunday mornings and drinks himself to sleep every night. Depression looks like your best friend who's stopped cleaning her house or doing her hair or taking any interest in your friendship. Depression is your coworker who's chronically late and blames everyone else for her missed promotions. Depression is your uncle's suicide that no one wants to talk about. And, yes, depression is being *evil* and irritable every day for months on end.

Suicide is the most obvious way that depression kills, and according to current statistics five African Americans a day take their own lives. But as frightening as those numbers are, they represent only a fraction of the deaths that can be laid at depression's doorstep. We face so many tough challenges in a year, a month, a week, or even a day. Do we respond to those hard knocks by going to a therapist and, as the Reverend Calvin Butts says, "getting a checkup from the neck up?" Or do we try to soothe our pain by shopping on already stretched credit cards, secretly binge eating in front of the TV, drinking every day after work and all day on weekends, doing a little recreational cocaine, using sex to numb ourselves out, ignoring our kids because we just can't take one more demand, not taking our medication because "it doesn't really matter . . ."?

I want to go beyond what depression looks like to what it feels like, what it is. To look at the life-threatening effects and side effects of depression when it's not acknowledged: suicide, crime, addiction, overeating, high blood pressure, overwork, juvenile detention, prison relapse, sexually transmitted diseases, shattered relationships, job loss, hopelessness. Or the connection between depression and HIV/AIDS, rooted in the bigger problem of Black self-esteem. As HIV/AIDS activist Tony Wafford says, "Too many Black people don't value themselves or the lives of others. Having unprotected sex, not informing your partner of your condition, is reckless disregard of Black life." And depression is one of the main reasons for that disregard of Black life.

I also talk in these pages about overeating, my own biggest symptom. Just as drug use can be a response to low self-esteem that leads to depression, which in turn fuels lower self-esteem, compulsive overeating almost always starts as a "solution" that quickly becomes its own problem and makes other problems—like depression—even worse. And I look closely at how violence operates in many of our lives not only as crime, but also as domestic and child abuse. I explore violence as the way we express frustration and hopelessness—and homicide as the way we flip suicidal impulses. Take hip-hop mogul 50 Cent, whose gangsta game face almost cost him his life. In an interview in *America Magazine* he says, "I spent the majority of my life being angry. Anger is my most comfortable feeling. If I'm upset or my feelings are hurt, I become angry; if I'm confused, I become angry. Like if one of my homies got shot or stabbed at the club. You're upset because you feel for him, but instead of going somewhere and crying about it, you get angry. Then, after you respond, you change to having jitters about law enforcement finding out about what you just did."

> *You just don't know what I've been going through . . .*
>
> –FROM THE SONG "YOU JUST DON'T KNOW," BY THOM BELL, CYNTHIA BIGGS, AND KENNY GAMBLE, SUNG BY PHYLLIS HYMAN ON HER SOUL-STIRRING ALBUM *LIVING ALL ALONE*

Depression at Its Deadliest

Silky-voiced soul singer Phyllis Hyman was the kind of artist people call "a singer's singer"—among her legions of devoted fans were musicians much more famous than she, who would do anything to hear her sing—but even with all her gifts and all her devotees, she was unable to escape the demons of her manic depression. As she got older, her condition became more and more debilitating and she self-medicated with alcohol and food. Alcoholism aggravated her condition and contributed to her increasing despair about her weight gain in her late thirties. Blessed with the tall, stunning looks of a fashion model, she was racked with anxiety over what she thought was the loss of those looks. She was wrong—she was beautiful

Depression Statistics: Suicide Fact Information

- Two out of every three people who commit suicide visited their health care provider in the month prior.
- Two out of every three people who commit suicide have talked about suicide to friends or family.
- Suicide is the third leading cause of death for people between the ages of 15 and 24.
- Suicide is the sixth leading cause of death for children between the ages of 5 and 14.
- The risk of suicide increases, particularly in adolescent boys, if the person has a conduct disorder or substance abuse problem in addition to depression.

–PROVIDED BY DR. SAMPSON DAVIS, COAUTHOR OF
THE PACT: THREE YOUNG MEN MAKE A PROMISE AND FULFILL A DREAM

right up to the end.

In the 1980s and early 1990s she threw herself into fighting AIDS, not only by raising money through one benefit concert after another, but by visiting people dying of the disease in hospitals and hospices all over New York. Many patients asked specifically for her, and while she was gratified that her visits could bring pleasure, she despaired about not being able to "really" help, and the visits left her drained emotionally as well as physically. Her sense of helplessness was magnified in 1993 when both her mother and her grandmother died less than a month apart. She honored them in the beautiful song "This Too Shall Pass."

> If one were given five minutes' warning before sudden death, five minutes to say what it had all meant to us, every telephone booth would be occupied by people trying to call up other people to stammer that they loved them.
>
> —CHRISTOPHER MORLEY,

She kept recording, kept performing, kept doing benefits, kept paying visits, but her depression was closing in on her like a storm cloud, and she was acting out her anguish in ways that went way beyond "diva" behavior into downright self-destruction. Even as her work became more and more emotionally honest and open with every new album, she was unable to bring that open honesty to help herself, and her life became more and more unbearable. One bright June day in 1995 she ran into fellow diva Jennifer Holliday, who had lost 200 pounds in the previous year and a half (see chapter two for more on Jennifer's battle with depression). She was full of praise for what Jennifer had accomplished, but there was so much agony in

> We live in a jungle. I see pain and depression every day, everywhere. I see twelve- and thirteen-year-old kids popping E-pills, saying, "If you pop, you are the shit." They have nothing to lose; their parents don't give a damn. People are hurting for real—and using drugs to "clear" their minds.
>
> —FELICIA "SNOOP" PEARSON, COSTAR OF HBO'S THE WIRE

> The condition of being Black in America *is* depression.
>
> —TONY WAFFORD, COMMUNITY ACTIVIST AND DIRECTOR OF THE COUNTY-FUNDED
> PALMS RESIDENTIAL CARE FACILITY FOR MINORITIES LIVING WITH HIV/AIDS

her face that she seemed to be saying wordlessly, *You have done what I can never do. I'm beyond help.* Three weeks later, on June 30, hours before she was supposed to open for The Whispers at Harlem's famed Apollo Theater, she took a lethal mix of pills and liquor, and died in her apartment, alone.

What's Going On?
Too Many of Us Crying, Too Many of Us Dying

Over the last thirty years I've suffered from three serious bouts of depression and lived with dysthymia (a low-level and long-term form of depression), but it's only in the last two years that I've been able to face on a daily basis that I suffer from major depression—that I am a victim of a disease. Like most Black folks, my resistance to naming the life-threatening cluster of symptoms I suffer from ended up ruining years of my life and jeopardizing my health. Facing the fact that I am depressed was the greatest challenge of my life.

As a child of sharecroppers who moved north and fought hard for a better life for their children, I am part of a generation that lived the first reality of integration. My parents had come up the old-school way, with old-school beliefs: Black life is hard, you don't talk about your feelings, you have to work harder than those around you to achieve, and you should never forget to give back. All this made a lot of sense for the ugly centuries when our people's lives were not their own. After all, we could be raped and tortured without receiving any help, our children could be sold away from us, our loved ones murdered without repercussion—we had no choice but to play it close to the vest.

> Depression is at an epidemic rate in this country. Pain and sadness don't keep you from functioning. Depression does.
>
> —DR. JANET TAYLOR, PSYCHIATRIST

No one "owns" us anymore, but avoiding painful emotions has become a cultural habit, a habit that prevents so many Black peo-

A simple fact is that depression is occurring more often and at earlier ages than in decades past. Often I see the patients in my Emergency Department in the inner city of Newark, New Jersey. At times it is a failed suicide attempt by a teenage girl who broke up with her boyfriend or a successful suicide by a middle-age man who recently divorced and lost his job. What the great majority of these patients have in common is the medical illness, depression.

When it comes to depression, many individuals in our community do not understand the dynamics, the warning signs, and the available treatment. For decades, depression has been considered a stigma or a crippling label in our social circles. Many people jump to pin the label "crazy" on anyone who is suffering from depression. What many don't realize is that depression is a medical ailment that can be explained in terms similar to your achy joints or seasonal allergies. Whether it's genetic, situational, or spontaneous, depression is as common as a stuffy nose.

One must realize that a person doesn't choose to become depressed any more than a person chooses to catch a cold. It happens! What we have to do as a community is move past the prevailing ignorance that has held us back in understanding, treating, and preventing depression in our community. We have to encourage discussion in our circles as it relates to the topic. Become open-minded. It is the only way we can begin to address the issue.

Many of us feel uncomfortable admitting to depression simply because of the repercussions we may experience from our peers. Where do these people go? Well, oftentimes they end up in my emergency department as a failed or successful suicide. Many times they cry themselves to sleep at night haunted by the fact that they have no one to reach out to. No one is "crazy" because they are depressed, just as no one is crazy because they have a cold. Today or tomorrow, a great majority of us will experience depression. Now that you know the truth, become a part of the solution.

—DR. SAMPSON DAVIS, COAUTHOR OF
THE PACT: THREE YOUNG MEN MAKE A PROMISE AND FULFILL A DREAM

ple from openly acknowledging sadness and pain. We pay a high price for these habits of survival: The price is our well-being. To make matters worse, we're scared to death of being labeled mentally ill—in a society still struggling with racism, our fear is powerful and very understandable. Yet evidence of our pain is everywhere, even if we haven't named its source or acknowledged its effects and presence in our daily lives. The reality of depression can be seen in our long artistic legacy, from early slave narratives to novels such as *72 Hour Hold* by Bebe Moore Campbell and *Beloved* by Toni Morrison to popular films like *Menace II Society, Boyz N the Hood, South Central, Colors, Training Day, American Me,* and *Hustle & Flow* to the blues itself. I believe that depression has become an epidemic in the Black community, an epidemic that has been growing stronger with every generation. This is an obstacle we must overcome. We can no longer afford to be afraid to admit how depression is affecting us.

I can only imagine how many cases of unacknowledged depression have come out of Hurricane Katrina's destruction. I fear for the mental health of hundreds of thousands of African Americans as they try to put their lives back together. What will be the toll of Black *denial* of pain coupled with distrust of the mental health agencies set up to provide help? How much suffering will continue over the next few years as whole families remain psychologically untreated and their grief turns into full-blown depression?

But What *Is* Depression?

Let's start by talking a little about labels, especially those nasty ones that get stuck on people. The mother of all psychological/psychiatric reference books is the *Diagnostic and Statistical Manual of Mental Disorders,* 4th ed., more commonly known as the *DSM-IV,* a big fat volume of almost a thousand pages that's used by just about every mental health care professional: social workers, psychologists, psychiatrists, among others. (Stay with me—I'm going to say this in English in a minute.) First published over fifty years ago, it's now updated regularly to reflect new research and deeper understanding. But even this book does not encourage the use of labels. According to the very useful Web site allaboutdepression.com, "the *DSM-IV* is not used to categorize *people,* but to categorize conditions or *disorders* that people have. This may be a subtle distinction, but it is a very important one. We do not say that a person *is* cancer, or *is* heart disease, or *is* an illness. A person *has* an illness. Likewise, we should not say that a person *is* a depressive, but that a person *has* clinical depression."

Am I Depressed?

But how do you know if you're depressed?

According to the *DSM-IV* a person has major depression if:

A. The person experiences a single major depressive episode.

- For a major depressive episode a person must have experienced at least five of the nine symptoms below for the same two weeks or more, for most of the time almost every day, and this is a change from his/her prior level of functioning. One of the symptoms must be either (a) depressed mood, or (b) loss of interest.
  - ✦ Depressed mood. For children and adolescents, this may be irritable mood.
  - ✦ A significantly reduced level of interest or pleasure in most or all activities.
  - ✦ A considerable loss or gain of weight (e.g., 5 percent or more change of weight in a month when not dieting). This may also be an increase or decrease in appetite. For children, they may not gain an expected amount of weight.
  - ✦ Difficulty falling or staying asleep (insomnia), or sleeping more than usual (hypersomnia).
  - ✦ Behavior that is agitated or slowed down. Others should be able to observe this.
  - ✦ Feeling fatigued, or diminished energy.
  - ✦ Thoughts of worthlessness or extreme guilt (not about being ill).
  - ✦ Ability to think, concentrate, or make decisions is reduced.
  - ✦ Frequent thoughts of death or suicide (with or without a specific plan), or attempt of suicide.
- The person's symptoms do not indicate a mixed episode.
- The person's symptoms are a cause of great distress or difficulty in functioning at home, work, or other important areas.
- The person's symptoms are not caused by substance use (e.g., alcohol, drugs, medication) or a medical disorder.
- The person's symptoms are not due to normal grief or bereavement over the death of a loved one, they continue for more than

two months, or they include great difficulty in functioning, frequent thoughts of worthlessness, thoughts of suicide, symptoms that are psychotic, or behavior that is slowed down (psychomotor retardation).

B. Another disorder does not better explain the major depressive episode.

C. The person has never had a manic, mixed, or a hypomanic episode (unless an episode was due to a medical disorder or use of a substance).

I don't know about you, but I find the *DSM-IV* a little cold and hard to follow. I must have read that definition a hundred times without ever really seeing myself in it—and I should have! So let me break it down in a more human way. Here are a few things that should have tipped me off years ago if I hadn't been so busy denying my own feelings. I call it:

Twenty Signs That You Might Be Depressed

1. You are always too busy—never have or take the time to give yourself the care you need.
2. You are running from something; something is eating at you.
3. You keep things that bother you locked up inside, festering. You are afraid to speak about disappointment, hurts, fears; you are afraid to express anger. You hold on to grudges for way too long.
4. You can't ask people for what you need.
5. You lie about everything, even simple things.
6. You can't wait to get home to eat—something, anything—and lots of it. It's the only thing that soothes you.
7. You just don't have energy to do anything—you have to force yourself to do everything.
8. Everything is so hard that you're sleeping a lot. It's damn near impossible to get up. You are afraid to get up.
9. You can't seem to concentrate—on any one thing. You look at the same piece of paper five times.
10. You are steadily gaining weight. You *know* because everyone tells you in their demeanor, words, glances, and in advertising campaigns that you are not desirable, and definitely not some man's idea of eye candy. Oh, you might be very cool to hang out with; they love your energy,

your spirit and contacts, but you feel "less than" and your self-esteem plummets.

11. You are not doing work that brings you joy; you are just working a gig and holding out for the check.
12. You haven't been touched in months or years; you haven't gotten any (yeah, I said it!) in who knows how long; hell, you haven't even had a massage!
13. You have a persistent, gnawing feeling that something is wrong. And you're right!
14. People are talking—you know this because their lips are moving—but you have no idea what they are saying. You aren't even there.
15. You used to care a lot about what you wore; now you just wear anything that fits.
16. You stay home a little too often. You call in sick at least once a month.
17. You think this is the end of your rope—there's no way you can face another day.
18. You wonder if you're having a nervous breakdown.
19. You cry a lot and without warning.
20. Every morning you wake up with crippling anxiety, terrified to get out of bed and face the world.

And these are some common things you might hear a depressed person say. I'm guilty of saying at least five of these things in the last two weeks alone!

What Depression Sounds Like

I just don't feel like it.

Go without me.

I don't care.

I just want to die.

You want a piece of this, motherfucker?!

I'm 'a bust a cap in his ass.

Shut up, bitch.

Somebody's gonna pay.

I'll give you something to cry about.

Go away.

There's a big hole inside me.

I can't feel anything.

What's the point?

I don't drink too much!

I'll stop drinking next week.

Something inside me has died.

I don't feel right. I know something is wrong with me, but the doctor can't find it.

It's just nerves.

I can't stop crying.

I can't handle it.

I don't need anybody.

People just let you down.

I don't trust anyone.

Can you supersize that?

I'm fat and ugly; nobody would want me.

I can't breathe.

I think I'm having a heart attack.

Nothing good ever happens to me.

Life sucks.

I ain't shit.

That nigga ain't shit.

I feel like blowing my f***ing brains out.

Every day we bear witness to pain, yet most of us are so numbed out by the pain inside us and around us, and the constant media images of violence and despair, that we no longer register it. We may not be able to take in that pain, but we keep *being* it. I think the pain of depression is all over daily headlines like these:

5 ARE SHOT, 2 FATALLY ON DETROIT STREETS

DEPRESSED BROOKLYN MA'S HORRIFYING CONFESSION: DE-
MONS TOLD HER TO KILL HER BOY

RALLY OF RAGE: BACHELOR PARTYGOER KILLED IN HAIL
OF 50 POLICE BULLETS

OFFICIALS SAY SLAIN DETECTIVE AND MURDER SUSPECT
CROSSED PATHS BEFORE

Roots of Depression

WE BLAME THE SELF AND PERSONALIZE OUR LOSS:

- We feel powerless and helpless
- We feel a loss of control
- We feel a sense of distrust
- We feel there is something wrong with us because we cannot keep the pain away
- We feel vulnerable or sad: we cannot rest on our laurels
- We do not get total satisfaction from relationships, work, or material gains
- We sense the hollowness of our self-created identities
- We blame our inability to control reality

THE OUTCOME:

Our sorrow and helplessness make us turn away from our pain. The pain congeals and depression sets in.

—DR. DENESE SHERVINGTON, PROFESSOR OF CLINICAL PSYCHIATRY AT
COLUMBIA UNIVERSITY MEDICAL CENTER

DAD SLAY IS THIRD MURDER IN TURF WAR

COLD-BLOODED KILLER BLEW AWAY "BEGGING COP"

SUBWAY MURDER: FAST-FOOD DEATH FEUD

GRANDMA DIES AFTER GUN HORROR

14-YEAR-OLD THROWS OWN INFANT FROM WINDOW

HARLEM BOY KILLS FELLOW TEEN

MOTHER CHARGED WITH KILLING NEWBORN IN MICROWAVE

I Need to Tell You Something

Finally, I would like to provide you with an option. You may be in pain, reading this book and wishing you could somehow tell another person what it feels like for you. But, like me, although you want to "let it out"—to share your feelings, you find it hard to put them into words, and somehow the right moment never comes up. Because coming out about being in pain is so important, and because isolation can be so hard to break, I'm including the line below for you if you need a little extra help sharing your story. I wish someone had given me this option years ago. I wish I could have had someone explain to my therapist, my mother, my sister, and my best friends that I was suffering so deeply inside, but just didn't know how to reach out and tell them. This book could be your lifeline. Sign your name and give it to someone you love, and/or your therapist/doctor. Let them know you're suffering and begin the road to healing through truth. And if this book is for you, see my "Guide to Breaking Our Silence and Getting the Healing Started" at the end of the book.

Maybe you're reading this book because a loved one is in pain, or maybe you're reading it because you're in pain. Maybe you'd like to help a loved one share their pain with you, or you would like to let a loved one know that you're hurting. If that's the case, I urge you to give this book to someone you love as a gesture of setting yourself free. "Hey, Loved One, this is me. Maybe it's you, too." Even if for now you still can't talk about the pain, you don't have to be alone. Write your name in the sentence below and begin the process of setting yourself free.

I, _____, would like to tell

you that I'm in pain.

Chapter Two

I'M NOT YOUR SUPERWOMAN

Overworked, Undervalued, and Under Pressure

> Of all the things I've lost, I miss my mind the most.
>
> —TONI COX BURNS, COMMUNITY ORGANIZER

When I was finally diagnosed with depression, I wondered if my symptoms were unusual for Black women. Was I unique? If not, how many other Black women felt the way I did? Did they show their pain more visibly? Were they in a better position to receive help than I was? The sad truth is that the form my depression took is all too common. Black women's documented rate of depression is twice that of Black men. But what's more surprising is the way we show our symptoms. Overeating is a primary symptom, and it's exactly the mode of coping I used to numb my own pain. Overeating came from my inability to express my feelings, or even bear them. Two-thirds of adult Black women are overweight, and fully a third of us are obese, higher than any other ethnic group in the United States. In fact, overeating is twice as common among Black women as white women.

To be honest, I expected to be in pain every day—pain seemed normal. As I talk to hundreds of Black women across the country, I see myself reflected in them over and over again. I have come to believe that as Black women our threshold for pain is too high. We have embraced very destructive beliefs about our ability to "handle it all," our power to overcome in the face of trauma, our ability to put ourselves aside as we tend to the needs of our employers, partners, children, family—everyone but ourselves! So many of the Black women I meet live in terror of letting anyone down, but could care less about the number of promises they break to themselves every day.

Working 24/7 is a primary symptom of depression for Black women. That's a symptom I know so well I could have invented it. In my business, I was known for holding it together for everyone else. I was the one who was always worried about whether other people were over their limit, stressed, or overworked. But when it came to myself, I had no mercy. I would work until I dropped, meet unreasonable deadlines, sacrifice weekend days at the office, and generally push myself beyond normal endurance. And like many Black women, I felt the sacrifices I needed to make in the interest of my business, clients, family, and others were more important than my needs. For me it meant that I didn't marry because I didn't have time to be truly available to my man or kids—I didn't feel entitled to take the time, either. At one point in my life I thought briefly about having a child, but by the time I began to understand my destructive impulses, that window had closed. Depression took a lot from me when I was young, and the longer it remained untreated the more it became a way of life. Of course, I was unaware that depression had a hand in everything I gained and lost.

> I think many of us suffer from a low-grade depression that has to do with social issues.
>
> —MARY PENDER GREENE, PSYCHOTHERAPIST AND RELATIONSHIP EXPERT

At a book party hosted for me by Mayma Raphael, owner of Paper Passions in Westchester, Ilyasah Shabazz, the daughter of Malcolm X and Betty Shabazz, introduced me to a wonderful woman named Solliah Bryant. I thought her name was striking and asked her what it meant. She told me that she'd been sexually abused over the course of many years by her father, who also had molested other family members. She had spent the majority of her teen years and young adulthood living the aftereffects of trauma and depression. When she was finally in a position to begin working with a therapist and start healing, she legally renamed herself. Her father had chosen her name at birth, but she knew she would have to reclaim it if she wanted to move out from under his abusive shadow. Her new name, given to her by God, S.O.L.L.I.A.H., remarkably stands for "She Only Looks Like It Ain't Hurting." The moment she told me, I thought, *That could be the middle name of every Black woman I know,* and it inspired the title for this book.

Every time I give a talk or a workshop I am almost overwhelmed by the number of sistahs I meet who are in pain. Some days I can literally *feel* the desperation rushing out to me like a solid wave, because it's desperation I myself have lived. (You know this book is "by us for us," but these are experiences that can hit every woman.) These women are me—regular everyday women looking for a lifeline, a way to stop hurting, some way to understand the hurt they've already had. They seek me out, writing me heartfelt letters, sending me e-mails and coming to my talks, because when I name what ails me, it helps them begin the process of naming what ails them. For me, our stories have the power to break this emotionally crippling silence. Our stories empower us to seek outside help for our problems. Our stories show the myths for what they are, and educate the mental health community about who we are and what we need. It's our stories that let us know that it *is* the sharing—if you will step outside your safety net—that lets you know that there are millions just like you.

It's our stories that will save our lives. When women see that I'm living through my pain, talking about it openly and without shame, they believe that maybe, just maybe, it's possible for them to do the same. Talking about my pain isn't the hardest part anymore; it's trying to get the women I meet to understand that the beginning of a way to heal our pain lies in our willingness to look at the issues that make up pain's foundation.

In the following pages I'm going to share stories of a particular kind. These stories explore issues that bring many of us the kind of long-term pain that can lead to depression.

The Double Whammy:
Being a Woman and Being Black

I recently read a statistic on blackwomenshealth.com that depression among African-American women is almost 50 percent higher than it is among white women. Can anybody really be surprised at this? We *should* be twice as depressed as white women—we suffer double the discrimination.

What we believe about life and the world is shaped by our environment, both our home life and the larger society. This puts Black women smack between a rock and a hard place. While many of us feel the double bind, few of us understand it. So let me break it down for you. We all know too damn well that in this world "it's hard to be a Black woman," but what do we really mean when we say that?

Real simple, 1-2-3:

- Women are discriminated against as a group, regardless of race and ethnic roots.
- African Americans are also discriminated against as a group, regardless of gender.
- Since we're both Black *and* women, that's how we get "the double whammy."

And it's not just being beat up on 'cause you're black *plus* being beat up on 'cause you're a woman—it's bad *times* bad! Every single day, 24/7, we are on the receiving end of two distinct forms of oppression at the same time. But don't think it's just institutions in the broader culture that we have to worry about, like corporations and schools and the media. This double whammy is also alive and well in our family lives, our friendships, and our love relationships. And it's not just other people doing us wrong, either—we're doing it to ourselves! The craziness of it could make you laugh if it didn't make you cry, but there's no laughing at the secret shame that comes from being at the bottom of everyone's totem pole.

Yvonne is a young woman I met at one of my talks. She was the darkest member of her family, and the only girl. When her lighter-skinned brothers made fun of her dark skin throughout her childhood, Mom and Dad had nothing to say—didn't defend her, didn't console her. When she hit thirteen her little-girl prettiness took on a deeper womanly beauty, a fact that was not lost on the boys and men who she noticed staring at her with hungry eyes. But for all her new beauty, Yvonne believed that the darkness of her skin made her "ugly." Despite all the new male attention she received, she could not perceive herself as desirable. It was at this point that her mother, never an affectionate woman, began to seem even more distant and cold. Whenever people commented on Yvonne's beauty, her mother would respond by saying, "Yes, but too bad her hair isn't a better grade," or, "She has such an attitude, I don't know who'll want to marry her," or some other remark that Yvonne felt drew negative attention to her darkness. And as her mother withdrew from her even more emotionally, her father took a new and uncomfortable interest in her. At first she tried to resist when her father came into her room and molested her. Ultimately she gave up, feeling powerless to stop it. She wanted to go to her mother, but her mother's hostility made it seem pointless. In school Yvonne was at the top of her class, and she kept entirely to herself. By the time she graduated from high school, she had been continually raped by her father and had secretly aborted his child while in the eleventh grade. Her feelings of isolation and worthlessness were almost unbearable. The only thing keeping her together was her belief that, if she could just get away to college, everything would be okay.

Because of her outstanding grades and high test scores, Yvonne was given a full scholarship to one of the top universities in the country. She left home as soon as she could and swore that no matter what she had to do, she would not return. Her first semester passed in a fog of challenging academic work. She made no friends, but maintained her A grade point average. But in the second semester cracks were starting to form in her shield. She found it hard to get out of bed for her early-morning classes. She had trouble concentrating when she read, and she began to dread having to talk with her professors or peers. She resented the stares of her classmates, never realizing that they were often commenting on her beauty, but didn't dare come close because she seemed distant.

Feeling like every day was a nightmare, Yvonne finished the semester with two incompletes, which put her scholarship on hold. When she told the financial aid officer that she was having emotional difficulties, the woman suggested she talk about it with (check this out!) her social worker. Yvonne was stunned into silence by this woman's racist assumption that every Black woman in America, no matter what her circumstances, must be on welfare and have a social worker. She immediately got a summer job working for the town theater (refusing to go home despite her parents' threats and demands) and decided to take the next semester off while she finished her incompletes. In the middle of the summer, she met a young man who was deeply interested in her. She agreed to go out with him, but only after much patience and persistence on his part. Her reluctance had as much to do with her deep-seated fear of trusting anyone, especially men, as it had to do with his whiteness. After a few dates she was won over by his intelligence and gentleness and they became inseparable. It seemed like things were improving for Yvonne.

The beginning of her sophomore year found Yvonne living off campus with her new boyfriend. Whenever she wasn't working, she was with him. But after a few months the old feelings came crashing down on her again.

She was plagued by flashbacks, nightmares, and feelings of profound despair. Her boyfriend was deeply worried, unable to figure out what was wrong. Finally, unable to bear another hour of agony, she told him about the abuse. He listened silently and then told her he needed some time alone to process what she'd told him. When he left the apartment she became desperate and took an overdose of valium with alcohol. He came back to find her unconscious and rushed her to the emergency room.

In the following months of therapy, Yvonne confronted not only the childhood trauma of her incestuous relationship with her father, but the pain of feeling unloved and abandoned by her mother, and her relentless feelings of self-hate and guilt. Yvonne believed that these things had happened to her because she was a dark-skinned woman and didn't deserve any better. And despite her outstanding academic record, her elite, predominantly white university offered her no support when she went to them for help. She believed that, in their eyes, she was a Black welfare recipient unable to measure up to their rigorous standards.

The fact that she was a brilliant and beautiful Black woman meant nothing to her. All she could see was the inadequacy of her skin color; how her darkness had lost her both her mother's love and protection, and allowed her father to feel entitled to abuse her sexually.

Yvonne's story is a classic case of how both our home and our society can send us the message that being Black *and* female makes two strikes

---

I [work with] a sister who came in recently to see me with a catastrophic medical diagnosis. I told her, "There's still work you can do, and if you do it, you just might live," and we rolled up our sleeves. Initially her response to my helping her investigate was, "Oh, no, my life is fine." When we started to dig, out came major trauma she'd never looked at or realized she had. She'd reacted to it, though, by trying to be perfect. She looked perfect, had a perfect education, a perfect house. No matter how tired she was when she came home from work, she'd clean her house. Overcompensating and seeking perfection is what made her sick. Deep shame and the resulting sense of her unworthiness drove this behavior.

—DR. BRENDA WADE, PSYCHOLOGIST AND AUTHOR

against us before we even get up to bat. Yvonne could blame herself for abuse and neglect that was totally out of her control only because she grew up in a household that had bought into the worst of society's stereotypes about being Black and female. Because her mother, a medium-brown woman, saw darkness as a strike against her daughter, she did nothing to help Yvonne feel better about herself. By not teaching Yvonne's brothers not to make fun of her color, she cast her vote with theirs without saying a word; by refusing to protect her daughter from her husband, she made it clear that being a girl means being abused. And when Yvonne looked out past her family to the world outside, she didn't see anything much better: She was assaulted everywhere by images of white women as the feminine ideal versus stereotypes for darker Black women as the maid, the prostitute, and the hip-hop "ho." Her academic counselor also sent her the message that since she was a Black woman, none of her successes gave her any reason to be invested in her continued success. Yvonne felt she was always only a step away from failure, humiliation, or rejection.

Later, when Yvonne joined an incest survivors' group, she couldn't believe how open and angry the many white women in the group were when they shared their experiences—it took her weeks of listening before she could even tell the bare bones of her story. So many women I meet don't feel able to talk about their pain because they don't feel they're important enough to get help. Just like Yvonne wasn't entitled to see herself as attractive, to say no to abuse, to feel secure at her university, or to think that she had worth at all beyond the assignments she could finish, the deadlines she could meet, and the services she could render others.

> Occasionally I wished I could walk through a picture window and have the sharp, broken shards slash me to ribbons so I would finally look like I felt.
>
> —ELIZABETH WURTZEL,
> AUTHOR OF *PROZAC NATION*

When I look at Yvonne's worldview, I can't help but be struck by how much it overlaps with age-old racist ideas about the Black woman's role in society: A Black woman isn't worth anything; she's just a workhorse; her emotional needs don't matter; her body is there to be exploited. And it's not like you can only think this way if you're poor and not well educated—Yvonne went from a college-educated middle-class family to the upper reaches of higher education, and none of that kept her safe from the poisonous power of those ideas. That double whammy cuts across class lines, and none of us is protected from the violence of the racist images and expectations that surround us. And when we hold those ideas inside, we're at a double risk for deep depression. If you're still confused, let me break it down one more time:

- Being Black and being women make us more vulnerable to all negative aspects of our society—poverty, poor health, single parenting, HIV, and homelessness—which makes us even more vulnerable to things like abuse, workplace harassment, incarceration, and drugs. Did you know that according to the Bureau of Justice statistics, for every 100,000 Black women in the country, there are 359 in prison? That means Black women are four and a half times more likely than white women to wind up behind bars.
- Women are generally more victimized, and victimized more often, than men, so there's a greater likelihood that we'll be victims in general. We're especially more likely to be victims of domestic abuse and sexual abuse, and to be targeted as easy marks of crime.
- Because women are more likely to be poor, and more vulnerable to poverty if they're not yet officially poor, we are more vulnerable to other kinds of abuse as well.

Your Silence Won't Protect You

Not acknowledging trauma is one of the most common causes of depression, and Black women are no exception. So many of us have had a traumatic event or events in our lives, something terrible that we were powerless to prevent. Most of us have simply had to live through the agony and its aftermath without ever dealing with the helplessness, powerlessness, fear, and anger that it brought up. (Plus we're moving *so fast* a lot of stuff doesn't get dealt with!) Chances are when it happened we were too young to seek help, too ashamed to seek help, worried that we somehow made the terrible thing happen, caught up in the idea that we can handle anything no matter how bad, or pressured by other people to believe that "we should be over it by now," and that therefore, if we *should* be over it, we *must* be.

The truth is, we're not to blame, shame won't help us, and we're not all powerful. We can't always cope with bad things by ourselves, and often we really need some kind of professional help. When I hear the stories of women who've carried agonizing memories of trauma around for twenty years, unable to grow fully into their spiritual or creative selves because the part of them that is hurt is still stuck, it breaks my heart. What these women don't realize is that, by keeping the trauma a secret, they're not only sowing the seeds of depression but preventing themselves from growing emotionally. Trauma doesn't go away if you push it to the back of your mind. It comes back stronger through another door, asserting itself in the form of alcohol abuse, fear of relationships, panic attacks, hopelessness—and if it goes on for long enough, it will likely turn into depression.

As a people we already have to deal with trauma in the form of everyday racism. Let's not make it worse by not dealing with our *personal* trauma—that only sets us up for the devastating effects of long-term depression.

Tiffany Warner read my *Essence* magazine piece and wrote to share her story with me. It's a heartbreaking tale of unacknowledged trauma and ignored despair.

By the time Tiffany was thirteen, both her parents had had psychotic breaks with reality. Her father believed he was Jesus Christ, and her mother believed that she and her children were white. But instead of receiving treatment so they could deal with their parents' mental illnesses, Tiffany and her sister were repeatedly told to keep quiet. "We learned never to divulge what was going on in our family to others. You know, 'What happens in the family, stays in the family.' Looking back we should have had some form of therapy or counseling to realize that we were not alone and that we should not have felt ashamed of their mental illness, but therapy was never an option."

When they moved in with their grandmother, Tiffany recalls feeling intense fear and loneliness. The stress she was under was so severe that during her sophomore year in high school her hair fell out. It grew back eventually and she spent the remainder of her high school years clinging to her boyfriend and hoping that their marriage after graduation would make her life normal again.

She and her boyfriend married at twenty, but their relationship was far from ideal. He became drug addicted and began cheating on her. After a fight where he broke her nose and tooth, they divorced.

For a while, things were looking up. Tiffany went to secretarial school and got a BS in business administration. She also began dating again. Eventually she met a man she felt deeply for, and they were married. But six months later her sister, the one stable person of her childhood, died at age thirty-seven from cardiovascular disease and morbid obesity. Tiffany believes her sister may have been depressed, too, and she remembers a period when her sister hid the fact that she was taking antidepressants. At the same time, her father was having another mental breakdown, and two years later he died, too.

Shortly after this Tiffany started finding it difficult to walk. She was hospitalized and diagnosed with systemic lupus erthematosus (a disease that causes your body's immune system to attack internal organs), scleroderma (the formation of scar tissue on the skin and/or internal organs), and Raynaud's disease (a condition that limits blood flow to the body's extremities). With a three-year-old and a fifteen-year-old at home, she had to take early retirement and move to a rehabilitation clinic. By the time she was encouraged to see a therapist, Tiffany refused both talk therapy and antidepressants. It wasn't because she didn't want what therapy has to offer; as she says, "I refused because I had internalized the stigma attached to therapy."

Three long and painful years later she was home and regaining her independence when she developed gangrene in her fingers. In constant pain, and on high doses of pain medication, three of her fingers were amputated.

When we're little kids, we all have this idea that if we pretend something isn't happening, we can wish it away. We usually learn pretty fast that it doesn't work like that, but we hold on to the idea at a deeper level: If I just have this one drink/take this one pill/smoke this one joint/buy this one pair of shoes/eat this one pint of ice cream, I'll feel better. But pushing away feelings is like trying to catch mercury—the harder you try to box them up, the more they squeeze and go to a place where you don't want them to go. For many of us, that place is depression—the place where you can't even have your feelings if you want to. For Tiffany, looking back, many of the things that have happened to her are the result of not acknowledging trauma and depression. With the proper help in her youth, both she and her sister might have been spared the physical effects of depression. Her sister might still be alive, and Tiffany might be healthy and whole.

Yvette Hyater-Adams is a writer, consultant, and inspired practitioner of transformative language arts. She shared this story with me, and I thought it spoke deeply to the nature of trauma. It is, as you will see, addressed directly to depression:

I never really wanted to own you. Depression is what white folks do. Black people have had to persevere through all kinds of obstacles. We didn't have time to be depressed.

But you did sneak up on me. I didn't have a name for you because you were never acknowledged. You were invisible to our people. Yes, there was family history of addictions such as alcoholism, eating disorders, and emotional numbness. We never called it pain. We couldn't. There was no scar, no cut, and no blood. It wasn't something that Bayer could fix, or even one of Grandma's hot toddies. Therefore, it wasn't real. Didn't happen. Wasn't possible.

You first showed yourself to me at a retreat in Princeton, New Jersey in 1993 . . . I don't fully remember how you entered the room, but memories began to flood my mind. All of a sudden, I felt you stroke my hair. I flashed back to seventh grade, when a boy attacked me in the music room closet as I put away my guitar. We were alone when he overpowered me, ripped up my blouse, and fondled my breast. I was scared. I thought he was going to rape me. He just looked at me and smiled, like he was Caesar—he came, he saw, he conquered. That was the first time my nearly six-foot frame felt little and weak. This so-called brother hurt me and made me feel shame.

Another image came around, the pain of home life, the yelling, the cursing, the emotional ups and downs. Where was the line? When

---

Generations ago, somebody in your family was enslaved, and we have to understand that daily trauma of being degraded, humiliated, treated like an animal, treated as if you have no rights and no feelings. The luxury of being depressed or taking a day off didn't exist. So we've incorporated it in our own mentality today that, no matter how tired I am, no matter how bad I feel, no matter how much pain I'm in, I will keep moving, keep performing, keep working. But if you're in pain and you keep pushing, you're going to reach for anesthesia. It's going to be drugs, alcohol, food, sex, shopping, gambling. For us it's often eating [and working] and shopping and sex that hurt us.

—DR. BRENDA WADE, CLINICAL PSYCHOLOGIST AND AUTHOR OF *POWER CHOICES:*

does a parent cross the line from authority to abuse or violence? In black families, we were never taught "the line." Today, with my own teenagers' drama moments, I ask, "Where is the line?"

Examples filled my head like pouring water—like not being able to have our "all girl" rock band play at local nightclubs unless the women in the band agreed to have sex with the bar owners; throwing up in the bushes every day as I went to work, where the head of our division routinely made passes and once locked me in his office to make sexual advances. This same man came to my second job where I was teaching guitar, posing as a student to harass me further. Finally, on two different occasions, the men who hired me for work gleefully admitted that my legs were the deciding factor. As I reran years of harassment and psychological abuse, I couldn't help but think, *Is this what it means to be a woman?* Are my body, mind, and desires not my own, but things to be demanded, ripped from me, in order to acquiesce to the power of men?

I looked up to see my Black women colleagues staring at me. I was on the floor, curled up in a knot, weeping uncontrollably. I had been holding in all of this pain, all of this experience, and telling no one. Blame and humiliation stayed with me. For years, I tried to project the image of being sexually open and free, to avoid being thought of as uptight or prudish—"You're just like one of the guys" used to be the highest form of compliment. All the time, I was carrying the load, the fear DNA from our foremothers who had to fight off white and Black

Six Reasons Why I Run to the Fridge at Night

- I have finally wound up a very long and draining day and I need something to soothe me. I earned it.
- It fills an empty spot where "something is missing."
- I haven't spoken on something I need to talk about with someone close to me.
- I'm feeling anxious.
- Eating (very temporarily) puts off the pain and anger I'm feeling.
- It's been way too long since I got some.

men from taking their bodies and numbing their souls.

You were fully in me now. I wanted to do nothing but sleep, not get out of bed, just be in my quiet and still. There was a deep void inside me—an overwhelming sense of nothingness. I felt like a zombie. I was on autopilot.

Acting Out
What Is "Acting Out"?

All people on earth from the beginning of time until right now have had urges to do things they know aren't right because they think those things will feel good or make them feel better. When we take the energy of those impulses and channel them into something healthy or constructive, or even something that just isn't harmful, that's called *sublimating.* So if something in me says, "Girl, you had a rough day, so you deserve to order enough take-out Chinese food for a family of four and eat it all," I try to say, "Whoa, hold up—how about we do a couple of miles on the treadmill, take a hot shower, and eat a big salad instead?" A friend of mine who used to cheat on every woman he was with is now committed to a woman he loves; every time the urge to cheat comes up, he plans a beautiful, romantic getaway weekend—with his wife! Those are examples of subli-

> The real reasons we are eating are not related to our physiological needs or the original purpose of food. We are eating because we do not feel nourished. In the Holistic Health Counseling world we view foods in two categories: Primary Foods, which are relationships, physical activity, career, and spirituality, and Secondary Foods, which are the actual foods we eat. The lack of nourishment comes from eating to satisfy our hunger for these Primary Foods. Primary Foods nourish us in ways that Secondary Foods cannot, because it is impossible for Secondary Foods to fill us beyond the physiological level. That's why when we eat to fulfill primary needs we still feel empty. As a result we keep eating and overeating, creating a cycle that throws us completely off balance. We need help!
>
> —TONJA WARD, HOLISTIC HEALTH COUNSELOR AND FOUNDER, WITH HUSBAND CHARLIE WARD, OF WARD WELLNESS GROUP

mating.

Acting out is the exact opposite of sublimating. It means taking those hurtful or destructive urges, and giving right into them. Little kids act out their feelings all the time—think temper tantrum—because they haven't yet learned about consequences or their own ability to manage painful feelings in healthy ways. Acting out is the confirmed alcoholic telling himself "I just need one drink, and then that's it," even though he knows there's no such thing as "just one drink" for him. It's the guy who's promised his girlfriend and himself that he'll never hit her again, but when the rage comes over him—instead of taking a walk around the block, or pounding the bed, or screaming into a pillow, or even just taking a few deep breaths and trying to talk about his feelings—takes the impulse and runs with it, treating his girlfriend like a punching bag. It's the Terrie Williams who, on a bad day, *knows* there are better ways to go but still goes ahead and eats that pint of Godiva vanilla ice cream. There are all kinds of ways of acting out—overeating, undereating, overspending, lashing out, romantic obsessing, drinking, drugging, gambling . . . I want to share the stories of people who've been there and done that, and lived to tell the tale.

1. Eating to Beat the Blues: Body Image

All too often mainstream media talks about how Black women don't have the "body image issues" that white women do, because in our community it's acceptable for a woman to have a fuller body. In other words, according to the media, white women have to be sticks, but Black women are allowed to have curves. Yes, well, but . . .

Sure, to a degree Black men have appreciated the curvy proportions that many of us possess, and for centuries men of all races equated plump with healthy and thin with sickly. But for at least a generation we have *all* been pounded with so many images of women whose bodies are closer to Barbie's than to ours that our heads—male and female alike—are crammed with these pictures of what we *should* look like.

The result is that for every Janet, Halle, Angela, or Beyoncé, there's at least a couple million of us whose bodies don't match up to what we're told they should, and every ounce of us feels it. More often than not we show it in the results of overeating, but in the past few years the numbers of us who suffer from bulimia (binge eating followed by vomiting) and anorexia (a fear of getting fat that makes sufferers diet to the point of malnutrition and even death)—diseases that supposedly didn't exist in the Black community—are rising like the Mississippi at high tide.

Many of us have grown up with meals at the heart of our family life. The smell of good "down home" cooking serves to remind us of who we are and where we come from. It can take us back to our childhood and, if we've spent the day managing stressful jobs in predominantly white settings, it can reaffirm our identity. For some of us it also has other ripples from the past. If our parents were busy, or didn't show their feelings, food might also have been the place we felt most taken care of, an "eatable" sign of being loved and nurtured.

As we grow up and face the many stresses of the workplace, relationships, parenting, and resisting the daily barrage of racial stereotyping or feeling invisible, food may also offer us a measure of control. One woman said, "The whole world may be spinning around me, but when I sit down to eat, I feel calm." Cooking elaborate meals may be the way you show love to your family; eating may be the one thing you do that feels like it meets your needs.

The ACE (Adverse Childhood Experiences) study began in an obesity program where, in the mid-1980s, in spite of several internists' and researchers' demonstrated ability to reduce patients' weight by as much as 300 pounds per year, nonsurgically, there was a high dropout rate. These patients were educated and had access to health care.

Interestingly, this was almost exclusively limited to patients who were successfully losing weight. Exploring this vexing problem by obtaining detailed life histories, the ACE researchers learned from about 300 such obese individuals that childhood sexual abuse was remarkably common and, if present, always came before the onset of obesity. In addition, they found strong histories of major household dysfunction in childhood, also before the onset of obesity. Indeed, obesity was not the problem for many people; often it was their unconscious protective solution to earlier problems that had never been acknowledged.

−CARL BELL, MD, PRESIDENT AND CEO,
COMMUNITY MENTAL HEALTH COUNCIL, CHICAGO, IL
This study can be found at: www.cdc.gov/NCCDPHP/ACE

In a world that can feel hostile and out of control, food feels safe. If you feel empty, food fills you. Food is not unpredictable, it doesn't leave us if we're not perfect, and it never demands anything of us in return. If you wake up scared and alone at 3:00 A.M., food is there.

So, yes, big *can* be beautiful, but it's often not healthy. For me personally, weight gain was not something I celebrated. I didn't do it to be more "bootilicious." As I've said, overeating fed my depression, masked my depression, was all about my depression—as it was for Jennifer Holliday, who has become a dear friend as we fight the good fight together.

Jennifer Holliday had the kind of overnight success that most people dream of, and even most professional entertainers never come close to. Discovered at seventeen in her church's gospel choir, she landed a starring role on Broadway in *Your Arms Too Short to Box with God* at eighteen, and she became a full-fledged star at the age of twenty for her role in *Dreamgirls*. But after she brought the house down with *her* signature song, "And I'm Telling You I'm Not Going," she would go back to her hotel room, alone and lonely, and do her best to drown her unbearable feelings in food.

She put on over 100 pounds in 6 months. That was the beginning. As her star rose, so did her weight. Before long she was carrying 340 pounds on her five-foot-five-inch frame. "Food was my best friend," she says, and it felt to her like her only friend, but that friend couldn't insulate her from the ravages of depression. She came to feel that her incredible voice, the very thing that had won her so much acclaim, was practically her enemy. After all, as much of a gift as that voice was, people loved *it*, not her; if she didn't have her voice, if she stopped using it to please, if she stopped performing, then no one would love her. "No one would even pretend to love me." Things sank to an all-time low when, the day she turned thirty, she tried to kill herself with an overdose of sleeping pills.

Sometimes you hit a tree so you don't drive over the cliff. For Jennifer, that *attempted* suicide was the beginning of the positive turn in her life. The first major step was a six-week stay in a mental health care facility, where for the first time in her life she began to sit with her problems rather than run from them.

At first, like so many of us, she mistook the symptom for the illness. She knew she was depressed, but she thought it was her weight causing her depression, and not the other way around. She put extraordinary—and successful—effort into losing weight. With the help of her doctors, she reduced her food intake, made it healthier, had her stomach stapled, and worked with a personal trainer. She managed to lose an almost unimaginable 200 pounds in under two years.

But as she lost the weight, she discovered that the depression didn't leave with the unwanted pounds. She took on the even harder work of psychotherapy for three years, which was made more productive by taking antidepressant medication. Weight loss had let her outer beauty shine through; her work in therapy let her inner beauty shine just as brightly. This very funny and witty Tony and Grammy Award winner went on to play a recurring role in the TV series *Ally McBeal*. She earned a doctorate in music from the prestigious Berklee College of Music, and still makes beautiful music. Now she also gives talks around the country about her experiences with depression and tries to encourage others to get help for themselves. She has also found many ways to protect herself against the warning signs and helped to guide me in my healing.

2. Dying to Be Thin

You know how people like to talk about diseases like bulimia and anorexia like they're "white-girl problems"? Well, despite what people may want to think, the lack of research on Black women and eating disorders has led some researchers to believe that these diseases are "Black-girl problems," too. There may be fewer of us affected than white women, but the pain is no less real, and that pain can have depression at its core, as Kathryn Wilson-Duprey can tell you.

Kathy was a basketball player turned college basketball coach (seven years between University of Mississippi and George Washington University) who started her own coaching and personal empowerment company. She's the CEO of Life Leadership Unlimited, and spends her work time "empowering women to create and live their greatest lives"; the rest of her time she spends enjoying her husband, her daughter, her friends, and herself. But her life wasn't always this rich. In fact, for many years it was downright excruciating.

"I grew up in a predominantly white environment—no one else looked like me, or made me feel okay." She felt dark and ugly and, to make matters worse, when she was in eighth grade her mom made her put on a girdle because, according to her mom, that was the age girls were supposed to start wearing a girdle. "I was mortified, because I felt she was saying I was fat." In reality, she wasn't even close to fat. "I was tall, athletic, and rail thin with long skinny legs and a short waist." The only part of her that wasn't long or thin was her butt, and as she recognizes now, "it wasn't big, by any means—just cute and round."

But hindsight is always twenty-twenty. For several months Kathy tried to hide her "fat" in a girdle, being ashamed that she "needed" a girdle, coming late to gym and arriving late to her next class so no one would see her in the girdle. Then toward the end of high school she discovered "the answer"—she found out about bulimia and knew instantly that it was what she'd been looking for. "It was a release. It was cleansing. And nearly every day for the next eight years, I attempted to vomit my self-hatred away. I numbed my pain and hatred with food, and then I vomited it away."

> You cannot find peace by avoiding life.
>
> —VIRGINIA WOOLF, AUTHOR

Once in a rare while an alcoholic can quit drinking by sheer force of will; even more rarely, some of them don't go back to drinking (though most do). The problem is that even though they've quit their active addiction to the substance that was playing hell with their lives, they haven't worked through any of the self-destructive patterns of thinking and feeling that made drinking feel like such a good idea in the first place. People like that are called "dry drunks," because all their thinking about themselves and the world is still what it was when they were drinking, even though they're no longer consuming alcohol. That's what happened to Kathy with bulimia: One day she was actually able to make the conscious choice to stop bingeing and vomiting, and she stuck to her choice—but she didn't feel any better!

Even aside from her "fat," she had always felt she was ugly. People in her schools called her racist names, and Kathy says her mother—who Kathy always thought was beautiful—never said anything to affirm her looks. "I'd ask her if I was beautiful and she'd say, 'Pretty, ugly, pretty have to stay that way,' or 'All monkeys think their babies are cute.'" Years later she learned that her mother had always thought Kathy was beautiful and had only said those things because that was what her own mother had said to her. Kathy didn't date, because she couldn't believe anyone would want to go out with someone so ugly—even when they asked her out!

Finally, desperate to find a way out of her despair, she decided to see a therapist. It took her a while to find the right one. The first thing she learned was that underneath all the concerns about her looks and her general inadequacy lay depression, and she figured out where she had learned it—from her father.

> I'm very close to my dad. He's my best friend, but I think he's had low periods, too. He's not very affectionate, he never wants to go anywhere, he bowls occasionally, but mostly isolates and just sits on the couch. He seems happy at occasions, but he's not a happy person—I never remember my father being really happy. Once he wrote to me about experiencing things in World War II that left him feeling like he couldn't share them with anyone, and not being happy, but he refuses to acknowledge that he's in emotional pain.

Kathy realized that, even though her father had never come right out and told her she should be afraid and depressed, he passed on to her the "coping skill" of feeling down. "But he couldn't be an example of how to resist stress and racism in a productive way. So I feel there are things about my life, about what I'm doing that I can't speak to my father about if he can't be supportive. How can he teach me if he hasn't overcome his own fear?" The first place all of us learn coping from is home. Sometimes the coping skills are life-affirming, showing us effective ways to deal with the hard parts of our lives. Too often, though, those skills aren't really about

---

CHECK THIS OUT:
WE DON'T NEED WHITE FOLKS TO BE RACIST

We all remember the rhyme "If your white, you're all right. If you're brown, stick around. If you're Black, get back."

Cold, hard fact. We do judge each other by our skin color! And it is one of the deepest sources of pain in our community. So many of us are in agony because we judge ourselves and each other so quickly and harshly by how light or dark we are. Dark folks have complexes about being too dark and some light folks think light is better while others have complexes about not being Black enough. At some point we've got to let go of the shame about our bodies, about how we came out of the womb, and heal this stuff. Feeling shame about our color brings nothing but unbearable pain.

coping at all, but about escaping from what feels unbearable. When the "skills" we learned at home actually make us feel worse—like when Kathy reproduced her father's low periods—we have to be willing to see them for what they are, and to work at letting them go.

3. When What We *Put* On Covers Up What's *Going* On

Some forms of acting out our feelings don't have such obvious results as compulsive overeating, or do as much hidden physical damage as bulimia and anorexia. Because they're not as easily recognized and acknowledged, they can be harder to treat. For example, when you see a sistah all dressed up, made up, hair and nails done, your first thought probably *won't* be something like, "Poor thing—she must really be hurting . . ." And when *you* walk out the door in your Sunday (or Saturday night) best, that's certainly the last thing you want anyone thinking about you! But there are times when that's exactly what we should be thinking.

One of my closest friends, Susan Taylor, speaks powerfully to this issue in her inspiring book *Lessons in Living*.

> I was in over my head. I was overwhelmed by the responsibilities that were taking over my life, stressed out from parenting solo and from the effort of faking it much of the time. A host of fears haunted me. I was afraid that the smart, accomplished people in my world would discover that I wasn't up to par. Afraid that I'd never earn enough to stop worrying about money. Afraid that I'd blown my chance for a stable life by marrying young and becoming a mother before I was emotionally or financially ready. I was afraid that I'd never find a satisfying love relationship. With my many fears under cover, I greeted the world each day buffed and polished like the models I presented on the pages of *Essence*. My clothing, hair, nails, and makeup—all impeccably done, and no one seemed to notice the cracks lengthening beneath the façade of cheerfulness I wore like armor. I became so skilled at the masquerade that even I began to believe it was real.

Not many of us look as tight as Susan when we do ourselves up, but it won't surprise you to hear that a lot of us have *overspending* as our drug of choice. We might pat ourselves on the back for how clean we live—don't smoke, drink, drug, cuss, or cheat; hit the gym three times a week; go to church on Sunday—but we use shopping to "take the edge off" the same way other sisters gotta have that drink or light up that joint the second they walk in the door. Call us shopaholics, spendthrifts, compulsive shoppers . . . Whatever we're called, just like a compulsive eater, we can take something perfectly natural and even necessary (a girl's gotta wear clothes, right?) and use it to numb ourselves against feelings and pain we don't know how to handle.

Michelle Wolford used to be a poster girl for this kind of acting out. The loss of a baby through an ectopic pregnancy brought her to realize how depression had been on a low flame throughout much of her life. Before the pregnancy, she used to work around the clock, trying to ward off feelings that she was worthless. She knew she wanted love desperately but, like so many of us, felt she didn't deserve to be loved for who she was. She was a constant people-pleaser, always doing backflips to be liked. In relationships, she was always with men who didn't value her. In friendships, she never knew for sure whether her friends liked her for who she was (unlikely, in her mind) or for what she did for them and what she gave to them. "I felt like I had to buy friends; I felt like I couldn't say no." But the behavior wasn't limited to other people—she tried again and again to buy *herself* off, too: "I kept spending to make myself feel good." And yet, just like a good buzz, it never lasted long enough. When it was gone, what was left felt even worse than before.

I really worry about our attraction to the quick fix, the instant status boosters that make us seem momentarily more desirable on the outside, but change nothing about how we feel on the inside. I worry about them because so many of us are in real distress, and we end up confusing status—or the symbols of status—for wellness.

I grew up on a diet of Black Pride and Black Is Beautiful. For us back in the day, an Afro was not just a great style, but a sign of wellness with ourselves as Black people. And it meant that we had moved beyond a sense that light or white was better—that we felt comfortable in our dark skin and with our "nappy" hair. I've always expressed a unique sense of personal style and would never want to begrudge anyone else the opportunity to do the same. But there are times when I'm talking with a young sister who's wearing blue contacts and blond extensions and dreaming of diamond-studded necklaces, and I wonder if what she's calling "personal style" isn't really just plain old self-hatred.

Feeling good outside requires you to feel good inside, and feeling good inside will take you a lot further than a $700 weave ever could. So when I see young women with butt-length extensions and all the (sometimes fake) bling they can bling, I worry that all that stuff could be a way of medicating ourselves, of pushing away feelings of being less than, unwanted, unimportant, or uncomfortable with our bodies. That's why I wonder sometimes if what we *put* on is a cover-up for what's *going* on. Which reminds me of Maureen.

I met Maureen Jackson a few years ago when I was doing a workshop at a college. She was head of the African-American center that had coordinated my visit. An energetic woman in her early forties, the light-skinned child of successful and ambitious middle-class parents, she had gone to one of the top colleges in the country and from there to Harvard

> Your body will talk to you. Ask what feelings you have more often than others. Do you feel tired, sad, angry? A primary symptom of depression for Black women is not "I feel sad," it's "I feel mad." We tend to manifest depression by getting angry because our ancestors could not get depressed and stop. So when you see an angry Black woman, you're seeing a depressed woman.
>
> —DR. BRENDA WADE, PSYCHOLOGIST AND AUTHOR

Business School, but had dropped out when she realized that business was not really her passion, and she had only gone to please her parents.

She grew up in the Black middle-class section of Flatbush, Brooklyn, and remembers vividly the friendly but intense keep-up-with-the-Joneses game that went on between her parents and their friends. When Maureen got into college and her neighbor got into a less prestigious college, the girl's parents bought her a BMW to compensate for the blow to their collective ego.

In her early thirties she was single, well educated, and making her way up the administrative academic ladder. When I met her I thought she was a stylish, somewhat plump, well-off young woman. As the two days progressed and we got to know each other better, she revealed that she wasn't happy at the university, but felt trapped because she had $40,000 of credit card debt. I was surprised—this seemed so at odds with her image as the got-it-all-together gal in the prime of her life.

She explained laughingly that Filene's Basement was her best friend— that the stress of her parents' ever-looming disappointment, her own fear of failure, and working in a job that didn't make as much money as she had hoped to earn left her feeling empty. Her one comfort was shopping, and she did it every weekend.

When I asked her how many outfits she owned, she laughed harder and told me she had turned her small second bedroom into a closet. She even joked that she was the Black version of Carrie Bradshaw from *Sex and the City*.

Maureen's was hardly the first story I'd heard of Black women masking their despair and depression with shopping. Like food, it's one of the ways some of us feel we can give to ourselves when nothing else is feeding our souls. When I pressed her about her "habit," she confessed that her parents were often too busy with her father's career and their social calendar to spend much time with her as a child. Her fondest memories were of shopping with her mom.

I suggested that she ask her parents for help paying off her credit card bill and start from scratch. She shook her head and told me her parents had already paid off her credit card bill when she was in graduate school— and the tab had been even higher—and now they refused to bail her out again. When I gently suggested that she might be a compulsive shopper she seemed genuinely startled.

"You make it sound like I have a problem. It's not like I'm an alcoholic!" Sadly, unnecessary credit card debt that high does sound like an addiction. Maureen is addicted to shopping, like I'm addicted to food when things get stressful. Because women are expected to look good and shop—especially Black women!—we often don't realize that buying is a way of acting out every bit as toxic as drug addiction or gambling. When you destroy your credit rating, juggle multiple minimum credit card payments, take from the Verizon bill to pay the gas and electric bill, yet drive a Lexus and still feel you need that cute pair of $350 shoes, you have a problem. Debt is stressful. It prevents you from changing to a more fulfilling career, taking vacations, and having savings for a rainy day.

Debt is a kind of enslavement, and the sense of being enslaved so limits your options that, whether you explain it to yourself that way or not, it can easily lead to depression.

From Stressed to Depressed

When sisters tell me that they're evil, I often suggest that they read Brenda Lane Richardson and Dr. Brenda Wade's book, *What Mama Couldn't Tell Us About Love: Healing the Emotional Legacy of Slavery, Celebrating Our Light.* In the chapter called "You're Not Evil, But You Might Be Depressed," they do a wonderful job of showing us the connections between depression and mean-spirited, impatient, or overly critical behavior:

> Many of us mask our depression with this attitude of [got it all under control]. The deep feelings of grief continue [without stopping] because they don't fit into our schedule. So we get mad because we tell ourselves we can't feel sad. When people see that many of us are hyperirritable, which is a symptom of depression, they mistakenly call us evil. In fact, many of us are depressed and exhausted.

> We need to give up the closet regarding mental illness. There is help available, but only if we admit we need it.
>
> —BEBE MOORE CAMPBELL, AUTHOR

How sad but true. Many of us act out our pain, yet don't believe we're entitled to *feel* it, much less address it! Wouldn't it be better to know why we feel irritable and negative, why we may be hurting the feelings of those around us, than to continue to live with a feeling of low-grade misery? I think the answer is yes, but of course that's easier said than done. For generations, Black women's pain threshold has simply been too high. We have been taught to minimize our problems, take on more than we can handle, always put ourselves last, and never slow down, because maybe if we're running we won't fall. Although this strength has often been the backbone of the Black family, it has also meant that we are unable to recognize when we've reached our emotional breaking point—when we're just stressed the hell out!

Lately, I can tell that I'm feeling stressed when I start feeling irritated over little things, in other words, acting "evil." I don't intend to be rude, but sometimes when I'm overworked and can't handle another phone call or e-mail, I just snap! I'll cut people off on the phone, raise my voice, stop listening when someone is speaking, or let my impatience show. Nowadays I'm *trying* to get to a place where I can stop before the stress reaches that point. By the time I'm that stressed, there are already dozens of fires I'm trying to put out and it feels like I'm about to go up in flames myself. Instead of acting evil, I need to learn to set boundaries and ask for help *before* I feel completely and totally overwhelmed.

Karin Grant Hopkins, a longtime colleague, told me this story about being "evil":

> I remember my first awareness that something was wrong with me. I was in my early teens. Back then my family labeled me "evil" because I would retreat into my own world. As I grew older, I bought into it—I would warn friends and lovers so they would not be surprised when I became "evil." In truth, at those times, I was emotionally unavailable, and ignorant of the underlying medical condition; but to everyone around me, I was just a bitch. Insanely, this was a status booster. Unlike my bubbly cousins, I was tough and in control. If only they had known how fragile and out of control I really was.
>
> Through the years I felt like a war was raging inside me, compounding the pain. The "bitch" image had been around so long that even I believed it. So when soft, sad Karin would take over, all hell would break loose in my psyche. For many reasons, I could never verbalize this in detail to anyone. My friends were accustomed to leaning on me during hard times. I think I felt I owed it to them to always be their rock of strength. My family saw me as a symbol of success. I just couldn't burst their bubble. They loved to brag about my accomplishments, first as a television news anchor and later as a public relations executive. My depression would have stolen their pride.

> *Every woman in my fix is bound
> to feel blue too, 'cause
> I love my man better than I love
> myself*
>
> —"ANY WOMAN'S BLUES," BESSIE SMITH
> (LYRICS BY LOVIE AUSTIN)

Being evil and seeming bulletproof are the female versions of swagger and machismo in men: It's a painfully common cover-up for depression. What we call "evil" is really the inability to set bound-

> *I'm goin' down
> Cause you ain't around, baby*
>
> —"I'M GOING DOWN," MARY J. BLIGE
> (LYRICS BY ROSE ROYCE)

Yes, there *is* a gender crisis.

Let's say a Black woman wants to go on a date. Figure there are two women to every available man, and she's been disappointed so many times, but she still goes out with her girlfriends in search of a man. She goes to singles events with few men, and the few men there are feel like they have many choices and don't need to be stuck with just one.

If she does meet a man, he may well be less educated than she is. They have to struggle with what it's like to have her make more money. They have to struggle with how to deal with the ways society treats Black men. It's harder for men to move ahead—besides plain old racism, his colleagues are often frightened of him, and convinced that he's not as intelligent as he is. If you're sane, these things make you angry, and if you do show your emotions, especially your anger, then white people—who've been trained by a lifetime of consuming racist images of Black men—are afraid.

And all this cultural baggage comes with the relationship, like a fringe benefit you never wanted.

So when our Black woman's man comes home he's already mad, but can't express it openly to her. When that anger is turned inside, he feels depressed and needs to medicate it in some way, or blow off steam. Sometimes things happen that he's embarrassed by, and he expresses his embarrassment by being silent and distant. Each of these things complicates the relationships between them.

It's a lot to ask that men and women come emotionally and intellectually prepared to handle the larger culture's impact on their relationship. Most often we act it out on each other.

—MARY PENDER GREENE, PSYCHOTHERAPIST AND RELATIONSHIP EXPERT

aries for ourselves, to say, "Hey, this is more than I can handle right now. I need some help, or some downtime, and preferably both!"

Sister Drama

Another version of being evil is what I call "sister drama." When I see a woman creating drama with her boyfriend or child or turning a regular life event into a crisis, I immediately look for signs of depression.

Drama is the chaos we create on the outside to make sense of the fear, pain, and desperation we feel on the inside. Many of us don't even know when we're feeling scared, alone, angry, hurt, desperate, sad, or needy, and so when the feelings hit we need a release. And the easiest release is a crisis, a confrontation, or a big scene.

Some of us saw our parents and families at their most vibrant, engaged, and passionate during times of crisis. In fact, we often mistakenly celebrate drama as part of our cultural style. We may even believe that emotional blackmail, silence, screaming matches, or physical abuse is the way love is supposed to be. If your parents didn't provide you with healthy models for love and intimacy, then getting your emotional needs met can be really tough. Growing up with drama instead of healthy love produces a basic lack of trust in ourselves and others, and actually prevents us from believing that our needs will be met without the drama.

And here's the worst part of all: Instead of knowing how to admit to ourselves that we haven't gotten the love we need and deserve, we pick a person who can't love us. In trying to win their love we resort to emotional theatrics. We're miserable, but in a twisted way that misery makes sense to us. As much as we want to believe that we're lovable and worthy, it's more comfortable to reproduce the neglect and abandonment we *know*. If you are unable to achieve intimacy, you may use drama to hide from yourself. Drama is a big elaborate smokescreen that hides you from your own pain, from your fear of your own pain. Joy in friendship and love are the product of feeling like we can share all of ourselves. Where parts of the self are hidden, there is shame, and there is usually depression.

> I went from one relationship to the next, and all a man had to do was say he loved me and I would believe him. All I wanted was for someone to love me because I couldn't love myself.
>
> —ANONYMOUS

Relationship Blues

Because we are so often not valued and made to feel less than by the larger culture, many of us believe the only place left for us to receive validation, respect, acceptance, and care is in our intimate relationships. But if we're not secure in our sense of self, confident of our own worth, then relationships, instead of feeding our souls, can be emotionally devastating, because they shine a spotlight on all the places where we're most vulnerable. A relationship can certainly be a safe haven in what's often a hostile world, providing love and support and shelter from the storm. But that's a very different model from the one those of us who look to relationships to save our lives, or make up for the hurt we've endured, are used to. Looking for love in this way has a lot more in common with addiction than it does with committed partnership. It often leads us to choose partners who are untrustworthy, unloving, or both. Once we've had one or two or three hurtful relationships like this, we begin to feel like there is no place where we can be safe and loved and cared for. We are more than brokenhearted; we feel like our only shot at emotional happiness has been taken away from us. That despair can leave us feeling worthless, empty, and hopeless—a strong formula for depression.

You may be nodding your head about now, but I know so many women who don't recognize this dynamic, even though they live it again and again. We hear a lot on talk shows about women who love too much and women who are codependent, but movies and TV dramas and love songs still portray suffering for your man as something noble or honorable, the mark of a real woman. Lots of Black women point to these representations of suffering to say that what is happening to them inside their relationship is normal, especially on the romantic tip. This kind of programming has led many women I know to accept relationships that are just no good for them. So many of us believe that any man is better than no man, or that it's normal to be in a relationship where you don't feel fulfilled or happy. Or, worst of all, so many of us buy the lie that ongoing hurt is part of love.

And by the way, just to be up front for a moment, I spent most of my adult life as one of these "so many women"—I have a long and painful history of getting involved with men who would not commit (things were just fine for them, why change anything?) or could not commit (as in, for example, they were already committed). For many years I wondered why I had such "bad luck," why "it just so happened" that every man I was attracted to was somehow or another unavailable. I finally came to understand that my connecting with these men was no sad coincidence—it came directly out of my own sense that I wasn't worthy of a committed relationship, that I didn't deserve the love of a man who would want to commit himself to me. My own workaholism was my other favorite way of justifying that so-called bad luck ("I don't have time for that mess . . ."), but I no longer look for excuses, or point my finger to blame. Nowadays I actually believe I *am* worthy of that kind of committed love, and I'm not running away from the possibility of it.

Think of Madea's wise words in Tyler Perry's *Diary of a Mad Black Woman* when she tells her granddaughter Helen, "Love is stronger than any addiction, baby; hell, it *is* one."

Although Helen is an attractive, smart, educated woman in her late thirties, she's emotionally crippled by her desperation to hold on to a husband who no longer values her or their relationship. She's so blinded by her need to be in the relationship that she stays no matter how much he verbally and emotionally abuses her. Not until he physically throws her out on the street does she even begin to realize love doesn't have to hurt.

> There has been an 800 percent increase of Blacks in prison, and many of these inmates are incarcerated by virtue of their association with a felon. This is particularly true of Black women.
>
> —JULIANNE MALVEAUX, ECONOMIST, AUTHOR, AND PRESIDENT

Keisha Rollins is a thirty-year-old single mother of two, who has been "keeping up appearances" for over ten years, ever since the father of her first child raped her. The day the rape happened she went home, took a shower, and told a few friends what happened, but quickly dismissed their concerns and her feelings. She never spoke of it again until after her breakdown years later, though not a day passed that she didn't think about it, crying and cringing on the inside at the memory of it. Every time it came up, each and every day, she ordered herself to forget about it—not because it didn't hurt, but because it hurt so bad she was terrified of admitting it to herself. Still, she kept living her life, and trying to move on. A few years later she met and fell in love with Kenny, a man she

> We started looking at my mother as everything, the man and the woman. And looking at every woman that we came in contact with as our male figure, because we wasn't even searching for [male love] anymore.
>
> —MARY J. BLIGE, SINGER AND SONGWRITER

thought was the man of her dreams, a man who treated her with the love and care she thought love was all about.

Keisha was in a good place when she met Kenny. She had a great job and an active social life that included taking care of herself first. Allowing herself to fall in love again from this place of strength gave her a chance to experience the positive sides of love that she had never known before. However, problems soon began to surface. Kenny introduced her to Donna, a woman he described as his best friend, and she and Keisha soon became friends, too. Several months later, Keisha became pregnant with her second child. Content at the thought of making a new family with Kenny, she was blown apart when she discovered, two weeks before giving birth, that Donna, his "best friend," was also pregnant with his child.

Keisha's relationship had gone from fairy tale to nightmare. She was speechless. She couldn't say a word, even to Kenny. But the betrayal threw Keisha into an emotional tailspin. She felt like everything she valued, everything that meant anything to her, had been systematically destroyed before her eyes. And once again, like after the rape, she didn't feel her life would give her the space to have her true emotions about it. She has to show up at work every day, and do a good job if she doesn't want to be fired, but every moment she doesn't break down sobbing is another Oscar-worthy turn—and when the curtain comes down on the day's performance at work, it goes up on the evening's performance at home, where she can't let her kids see what terrible shape she's really in. "Because I have never truly dealt with my feelings, I'm dying inside."

> My mother died at the moment I was born, and so for my whole life there was nothing standing between myself and eternity; at my back was always a bleak, black wind.
>
> —JAMAICA KINCAID, AUTHOR

Instead of moving on, she feels hopeless and depressed. "I'm even ashamed to look to the Lord for help. I feel like this whole situation is my fault. I've never felt any pain like the pain I've felt every day for the past nine months. I've been crippled by the hurt and betrayal I feel. I don't know how to move on. Even after everything he's done to me, I still love him. I miss him incredibly, and still want to be with him. Even the pain of being raped when I was younger can't compare to the pain I feel in this situation. I don't know how to move on."

But not having the emotional tools to stand up for yourself in a relationship or recover from a failed relationship are not the only causes of relationship pain. An abusive history can also leave women terrified of the very
intimacy they so desperately seek. In an interview with the amazing Mary
J. Blige on MTV's *Growing Up Black in America*, the interviewer, Sway,
asked Mary how she saw Black men. Her response was heart-wrenching. "I
saw you as savages a long time ago because I've seen nothing but savages.
I've seen men slap women till their heads almost look like they're turned
around. I've seen my mother abused. I've seen my aunt punched so hard
it looked like her head went through the wall. I've seen nothing but abuse
from men." Nowadays Mary is happily married, but that doesn't make her
earlier experiences any less powerful.

Losing the Most Important Woman in Your Life

For many of us, the phrase "the most important woman in your life" instantly conjures up an image of our mother. Who else, right? Well, for lots
of us, those same words call up a picture of a grandmother, or a sister, or a
best girlfriend so close she might as well be family. Whether she was mama,
granny, sis, or girlfriend, she was the person who—in our lives and in our
minds—we could come home to; for so many of us, this woman *was* home.

Hold up, did I just say "was"? Yes, I did. A lot of sisters are lucky enough
to still have that special woman in their lives, and I hope you let her know
how much you cherish her. I am so blessed to have my vibrant, smart, and
courageous mom, Marie, in my life. Many of us, though, have lost that
special woman. How do we deal with that? How do we deal with the loss
of the person who may be the anchor in the stormy sea of our crazy life?

Grieving, for starters. Grief is one of the few positive expressions of emotion that Black women are encouraged in, and a good number of us get to work
through those powerful feelings of loss in ways that ultimately leave us sad but
whole, and even grateful for the memories of the one we lost. But not everyone
is so lucky. For some of us, that loss is so profound that it takes us years to
work through, if we can work through it at all; and depression rarely misses
a chance to jump in and hang on for the ride.

Ilyasah Shabazz, author of *Growing Up X*, is the third daughter of the
late Malcolm X and the late Dr. Betty Shabazz. Only two years old when
her father was assassinated, she may have been too young to feel the grief

at his loss that would only hit her years later. She was an adult when her mother died, in 1997, and fully present for the agonizing pain of that loss.

Her grief began before her mother died, after she was horribly burned and fighting for life, unable to see and with the skin of 80 percent of her body removed. She died soon afterward.

I think the loss of my mother is the most traumatizing experience I've ever had. The first stage of my grief was awful. Initially I felt like a motherless child; it was a very lonely, empty feeling. I had to go deep inside myself. I found myself asking questions like is there life after death? Is there God? Is there heaven? I began looking at life so differently; things took on more meaning, and my life became more purpose driven. I made sure the Betty Shabazz Center was completed. I tried to finish the things she wanted finished.

In retrospect she feels she did so much as a way of keeping herself busy. Ilyasah didn't want the image of her mother as she last saw her to be the one that stayed with her, so she got tons of pictures of her throughout her life and put them up all over. But even as she reminded herself of what her mother had looked like before the fire, her pain was still overwhelming. She reflected on her mother's whole life, not just her years as a mother, but as a human being, from childhood onward, and drew inspiration from her reflections.

And she thought a lot about what it means for a woman to lose her mother. "A lot of women are alone. They don't have their fathers, they may not have their husbands, but if they don't have their mothers . . . Well, your mother is your backbone. So when you lose your mother, you lose someone who truly loves you unconditionally, who has your back unconditionally, and it's not easy to find anything like that again. It's psychologically traumatizing—how do you cope with that loss so you are emotionally functional? I guess you never truly get over it—how can you grieve correctly? You learn to accept the feeling that the feeling will never leave. You begin to find the parent within you."

Amen to that!

Donna Solomon is a professor of education at a well-known university on the East Coast, and her most important woman loss was her sister. Anita was eight years older than Donna, but throughout her whole childhood, Anita was a second mom to her, and later, a best friend. "We became so close people couldn't tell us apart." Donna moved across the country and they lost some of that closeness, but whenever they spoke on the phone, "we reconnected spirit to spirit." After years and years, Anita came east with her grandson, staying with Donna and her husband until she got a job and found a place of her own. She soon did, and they began to rebuild the beautiful relationship they had once had.

"Every weekend we held a dinner where our friends would come with whatever food they had, and we would add ours in and cook. My sister would come, and when everyone was gone, we would sit at the kitchen table and talk and talk." Anita was so warm and charming that Donna's friends adored her. Life felt for Donna the way it had back when she and Anita were growing up—"It seemed the universe was in divine order." They began planning a trip to Africa, to visit Donna's husband's family. "It was going to be a wonderful adventure for her grandnephew, an escape and a dream come true for her, and a recharge of batteries for my husband and me. We showed her our slides, and talked endlessly about where we would go and what we would eat. It was an exciting time. All around us the intellectual and spiritual atmosphere grew—and only in a positive direction."

Then Anita developed a backache that just wouldn't go away. She tried different remedies, but nothing helped. Finally, Donna insisted she see a doctor, and two weeks before they were supposed to leave for Africa, Anita called to say she couldn't do the trip; she had a cancerous growth on her kidney. "That phone call marked the beginning of my downward spiral into depression."

Anita insisted that Donna and her husband still make the trip, and that they take her grandson with them because "he has to see where he came from." And every time Donna would start to cry, Anita would say, "Don't you dare fall apart. Don't you do that to me. I'll be okay." So they went to Africa, the three of them, calling Anita every other day and reporting on their adventures, until two weeks later, when Anita told Donna that cancer had been found on her lymph nodes, and she was going into the hospital for surgery. A week after that, when one of her kidneys was removed, she had a stroke and fell into a coma. Anita's daughter called to tell Donna. "Through my denial, she explained, 'Auntie, you don't understand. Mom is not going to come out of this. She's dying.' Thousands of miles away, I sobbed in my husband's arms and hit bottom."

Donna and her grandnephew came back a week early; her husband would follow in a couple of days. At the hospital, Anita "couldn't see, couldn't move, couldn't speak, but she could cry." And her condition was getting worse, fast. She had told her daughter and Donna that she didn't want to be kept alive by artificial means, and they had to make the horrible decision to take her off life support.

"My niece left and I sat next to her bed and watched her breathing become more shallow. I had been through many deaths, but I had never watched anyone go. I asked her to just wait one more day until my husband could come and say good-bye. Tears streamed down her cheeks and I knew she wanted to let go. I said to her, 'It's okay. I love you from the bottom of my soul. But if you have to, I understand. Let go.' And she did. And whatever spark I had left went out."

For Donna, it seemed like the spark left not only her, but her whole life.

Our home fell silent. Friends no longer came by, or if they did I didn't care. My husband was wrapped up in the struggle to finish writing the paper for his doctoral degree. I made myself walk the two miles to work every day through snow, rain, and heat. I walked past the hospital where she died, the building where she worked, the café where we used to eat. I did my job, stayed vertical, stayed strong—I thought. I cried whenever TV shows portrayed death. I stopped reading books. I drank a glass of wine every night to go to sleep. I had no feelings for the work I did; no sympathy for my husband's woes, but I could not just fade. I was told all my life that I had to be strong. Therapy? That was something white people did and what did white people know about my pain? What did anyone know?

When a good friend at work decided to go to graduate school, she looked at Donna and said, "You don't belong here either. Go back to school and follow your heart. Do what you love." But Donna just stared at her. She didn't know what she loved. "I didn't love anything. I didn't feel anything. I just was. Some people think that when you're depressed you sit in a corner looking sad. It wasn't like that for me."

She felt that, as a Black woman, she could never let white society know what was inside of her.

I could never let the white people I worked with know what I really felt, thought, wanted. I had forty years of keeping the inside of me at one level and the outside of me at another. The outside of me never changed, but inside I had hit bottom. It was an amazing charade. I looked inside and asked myself what did I love, and the first response was my sister and she was dead and so was I. For one whole year I had been running on nothing but air; the idea that I should "follow my heart" destroyed the charade.

It was raining when I left work. I walked home and cried all the way. I stopped in the middle of the bridge that led to my sister's workplace and cried some more. I always thought that if you kept moving, stayed engaged, stayed active that you could beat depression, but I had not. What released me was the admission that for one whole year, my spirit had withdrawn.

In that rain, looking at everything growing green, feeling the chill and the wet for the first time, really was my release. I could hear my sister laughing at me: "You silly goose! There's work to do. Get busy!"

I don't ever want to go there again. I know now what it feels like to be locked in the dark. I was fortunate having a support system, husband and friends who encouraged me to live again. I was fortunate in having a sister who believed in living and laughing—I still had those memories and something to work toward. Going back to school, challenging my mind, looking for what I really loved to do, allowed me to break through the dense, swirling, muddy world of depression.

You always hear that Black people don't do therapy, we're not crazy, it goes against how we're socialized, blah blah. I hope to God I never experience depression again, but if I ever do, I will definitely seek professional help.

Ellin LaVar is "the hairdresser to the stars"—luminaries like Whitney, Oprah, Venus and Serena, Iman, and many others have come to her for the magic her hands can do (and now her reality show, *Hair Trauma*, on the WE network is funny as hell). Her studio, LaVar Hair Designs on Manhattan's Upper West Side, is always packed. Her line of hair care products, Ellin LaVar Textures, has been embraced by women all over the country. She is in constant demand in Hollywood and on location, doing hair design for such movies as *The Bodyguard, Notting Hill, Waiting to Exhale,* and many more. She works seven days a week, and somehow still has time to be a passionate photographer. Talk about motivated: this is a woman who graduated from college, bought an apartment, and opened up her own salon—all in the same month! That's why it was a surprise to everyone when she became suicidal one New Year's Eve.

Actually, it was a surprise to everyone but Ellin. Abused throughout her childhood, she used work and success as "drugs" to take the edge off the pain of feelings she could barely look at, let alone dig into. The harder she tried to stuff her demons into a box and lock them away tight, the more powerful those demons became. Finally, one dark December 31, she decided to end it all.

Despite the depression that had its roots in her childhood traumas, the thing that sparked this "final decision" had happened only a year before. "A friend had died in my arms. Watching her die, I couldn't help thinking how peaceful she looked, and feeling guilty that she had died and I didn't. I started to dream that she was free, and think about how lucky she was. I imagined that dying would stop everything that made my life unbearable: how I felt, how others felt about me, how I'm perceived even by people who haven't met me . . ." After months of thinking along these lines, suicide started to look very good to Ellin.

Then the phone rang. It was Susan Taylor, both a friend and a client. Ellin was sixteen when she began braiding Susan's hair and Susan was well aware of Ellin's pain. Ellin told her what she planned to do, and when Susan, who was calling to check on Ellin from Bali, couldn't talk Ellin out of shooting herself, she called me and asked that I go to Ellin's home. A couple of minutes later *I* called—I said I needed her address. Ellin screamed through the phone, "Leave me alone! I just want to go to sleep!" I really hoped that was all she wanted to do, but since I couldn't be sure, I "invited" myself over and stayed with her. The next day she went to a therapist.

"That first session I had a flashback that lasted an hour. When I came out of it, and realized what had happened, I saw that the therapist—a Black woman—had tears streaming down her cheeks. I felt someone could feel the pain that I was in, so I went back." Her therapist saw that Ellin kept having flashbacks in the office, so she had them meet over breakfast, where Ellin could feel more in control.

She was adamant, though, that Ellin be on medication because of the flashbacks, which Ellin found hard. "There's a real stigma around taking medicine—that's the white man messing up your mind, you don't need medication—you need a man, God, better friends, vacation, to organize your life, et cetera, et cetera." But her therapist sent her to a psychiatrist to prescribe an appropriate medication, and he turned out to be someone who, like her therapist, was easygoing and natural, and could speak with Ellin on an intellectual and spiritual level. "They didn't treat me like something broken that needed to be fixed, they treated me like a whole person with complicated feelings."

Still, getting used to the medication wasn't easy physically. At first it made her groggy, and it was hard to get up in the morning. Her life was so busy in general that sometimes she would just forget to take it. Other times she wasn't sure she'd made the right decision—she went on and off the meds for the first six months before she decided to stick with them. And then, with the combination of medication, therapy, and girlfriends who watched over her like loving parents, things started to get better.

"Susan and Oprah kept talking to me and trying to get me through. Susan was out of the country but called every single day—she even had another friend stay on me so I would keep going to therapy." The loss of a friend had pushed Ellin over the edge, but it was the love of friends that brought her back.

> Sometimes I wish I could walk around with a HANDLE WITH CARE sign stuck to my forehead . . . Sometimes I think that I was forced to withdraw into depression because it was the only rightful protest I could throw in the face of a world that said it was all right for people to come and go as they please, that there were simply no real obligations left.
>
> —ELIZABETH WURTZEL, AUTHOR OF *PROZAC NATION*

* * *

Writer, producer, performer, and designer Deborah Gregory was already an award-winning journalist before she became the author of the hugely popular *Cheetah Girls* novel series, and coproducer of two *Cheetah Girls* movies for the Disney Channel. A contributing writer to *Essence* since 1992, she had a column in *Grace* magazine and often writes for major publications like *Vibe, Heart & Soul, Us Weekly,* and *Entertainment Weekly.* Her upcoming novel is called *Catwalk.*

What makes her success all the more remarkable is the fact that one day, around Deborah's third birthday, her mother became homeless and her three children—Janet, Deborah, and Robin—became wards of the state of New York. Janet was taken away from her two little sisters and labeled "emotionally imbalanced" because she fought physically not to be

CHECK THIS OUT

Think about the instructions you get before a plane takes off. "If you're traveling with a small child and the oxygen mask drops down, put the mask over your own mouth first. *Then* if you have a small child sitting next to you—or someone acting like one, place the mask on them." Think about how this applies to life outside the plane: No matter who depends on you, no matter who you're responsible for, you can't *really* take care of anyone else unless you are taking care of you first. (And, yes, I have to remind myself of this at least ten times a day.)

separated from them. Deborah and Robin were placed in different facilities. Deborah was traumatized. She refused to eat—for months. She lost her teeth and her hair. Her skin was covered with lesions caused by malnutrition. She was profoundly depressed; at the age of four, she was so keenly conscious of the loss of her mother that she had made the decision to die. Janet was brought back from the group home where she had been placed to try to get Deborah to eat; Deborah was overjoyed to see her older sister, but too weak even to move.

Once it seemed that she would probably not die, Deborah and Robin were put in foster homes: one home after another, with parents who abused them physically, emotionally, or both. Deborah aged out of the foster system as soon as she turned eighteen, but as a young adult searched to find her mother, or even traces of her. She would periodically hit a dead end and give up, try again, hit another dead end and give up again, until one day she called a number in North Carolina and found a relative of her mother—a first cousin.

The discovery didn't lead to a heartwarming reunion of mother and child, or even a warm reconnection with long-lost family. One sibling had seen Deborah's mother upon her release from a mental institution. To make matters worse, she learned that her mother's father was a vicious man, violently abusive to his wife and all thirteen of his children; of Deborah's mother's twelve siblings, eleven were

> I am so busy being a wife, mother, friend, employee, church usher, and worship leader I forget who I am.
>
> —ANONYMOUS

dead; the twelfth was in a home for the physically handicapped. Her cousins told her they'd heard that Deborah's mother had been imprisoned for killing "some white man that was messin' with her." As Deborah dug deeper, she found out there was no validity to that story, but upon obtaining a court order she was able to view the records at the mental institution where her mother had been for nine years. It was there that she saw the correspondence that her mother wrote to relatives and even to her, correspondence that had not been mailed due to its incoherent content. One such letter to a cousin claimed that she wasn't crazy but that she would be if she stayed there. The trail ended there. Her mother had been released into a women's shelter and then disappeared.

As much as Deborah has suffered because of her abandonment, she also has deep compassion for her mother—especially after learning about the horrible circumstances of her mother's life. But for all the understanding she has worked to have, all the success she has achieved, and even the personal peace she has strived so hard to get and maintain, the loss of her mother casts a long shadow on every day of Deborah's life.

Deborah's compassion creates more compassion. I used to see her all the time, and for some reason I just couldn't seem to "get" her—until I learned her history. Once she had the courage to share her story in *Essence* magazine, I immediately connected with her. Looking back, I see that I had the kind of feeling toward her that people showed toward me when I "came out" about my depression. The valuable lesson I learned from this was to resist the impulse to judge. We shouldn't make assumptions until we know someone's story. And we all have a story!

Last on Your List

Almost every depressed Black woman I know, including myself, suffers from the same condition. I call it "everything comes before me" syndrome, or Last on Your List. Throughout my childhood my parents told me and my sister, Lani, in word and showed us in deed how important it is to serve others—that a good woman does service to her family, her community, and her people.

Being the child of parents who worked hard to give us the things they didn't have as children, I felt it was my responsibility to excel at everything I did. I worked hard at school, I did my chores at home, and I volunteered at school in my spare time. Now, don't get me wrong. Serving others is God's work and there's nothing better for the soul. The problem comes when we never *stop* serving others and never *start* serving ourselves.

My work and service ethic became an all-consuming way of life. I worked all day every day, and when I wasn't working on my career, I was taking care of family matters, or volunteering with troubled teens. There was no such thing as Terrie Time. In fact, when I had down time I thought something was wrong and quickly searched for a way to fill it. In Cherise Jones and Kumea Shorter-Gooden's groundbreaking book, *Shifting: The Double Lives of Black Women in America*, they coin the phrase "Sisterella Complex" to explain how Black women become depressed.

"If you're trying to identify depression in Black women, one of the first things to look for is a woman who is working very hard and seems disconnected from her own needs. She may be busy around the clock, constantly on the go, unable to relax, and often not getting her sleep so household, child care, and job tasks get done. Not taking the time to tend to herself makes her more vulnerable to depression. Or her busyness may be a way to keep her mind off the feelings of sadness that have already arisen."

Nadine Thompson is a wonderful friend, and a kindred spirit. In 1999 she became the cofounder and president of Warm Spirit, Inc., a line of incredible natural botanical face and body products for women of color. Like me, Nadine began life as a social worker, and she brings that desire for wholeness and well-being into her company. In her words, she is committed to "social action, cultural change, and instilling a sense of well-being in others."

However, being the head of a new and thriving company has also taken its toll. For as much as she has infused thousands of women with the entrepreneurial entitlement that is the hallmark of her company, she herself often feels depleted and empty at the end of the day. Twelve-hour days leave her with little time for exercise, and by the time she gets home she's often not in the mood for much other than eating comfort food and going to sleep. After being there for women in her company all day, "There is no one here for me." In addition, Nadine is married with two young children, so she has the demands of parenting to contend with and a marriage to be present for.

Despite all the good she does, she often feels like everything rests on her shoulders, and there's very little give-and-take. She heads up a business that has 24,000 consultants. "I constantly feel underappreciated. People want more from me. I work all day with mostly Black women, some are broken and wounded, and they don't always have the experience or emotional resources to give back to me." She also tells me about the pressure of working with women who feel deeply deprived, and as a result can be very demanding and unforgiving.

That's one of the things that's become very evident in my work with many of these women. They can be very unforgiving with me, very unforgiving with themselves. They want me to be perfect because they want to believe that we can be lifted up, and that we're a great Black women's corporation. And I'm striving for that, too, but in the midst of that we've got to forgive each other if people are going to heal and mend. As a social worker I'm always trying to hear what's going on psychologically and emotionally. It's very draining. Every day I have to be full of wisdom, full of information, and putting it back out to them.

> Loneliness is a distinct condition— unfortunately, a condition that has been found to be a huge causal factor of depression. [John] Cacioppo's research has shown that a lonely woman has an eight times greater likelihood of becoming depressed than one who's not. For men, the incidence is even more striking: 13 to 1.
>
> —MAMIE HEALEY,

Nadine has often shared that she thought her challenges with weight gain and obesity are directly related to her challenges with depression. She feels like she goes into hibernation mode when she is overwhelmed or sad and her metabolism slows down completely due to a lack of physical activity. Nadine says that she can be highly productive during those times but gets very little exercise, and while people just believe that she is tired or overworked, which may be true, that is not all there is to what she is feeling. That's where the lie comes in, it is sharing half of the story and not the entire truth. Nadine recalls witnessing a phenomenon in her early adult years where her girlfriends who wanted to keep their weight down picked up cigarette smoking and alcohol, while others were doing other drugs and finding other ways to manage their weight and anxiety. For Nadine she had to maintain the façade of being a good girl for her very conservative parents. It was okay to have a chocolate bar but not okay to light up a cigarette; it was okay to cook a huge dinner and dessert for the family but not to pour a drink or get stoned. Later in her clinical practice with young women she saw the same pattern for young Black women, especially those involved in their church. If they were struggling with anxiety, emotional or sexual abuse, depression, or emotional stress, food became an acceptable addiction. No one judged your character based on your weight or the extra serving of fried chicken you ate. The problem was that the fat girls were the last to get a date or get married, so the irony was that you were being judged "as good enough or not" as opposed to whether you were a "bad or good girl." Talk therapy or counseling could make a world of difference for young women, since self-medicating, be it drugs or alcohol or food, are never long-term solutions.

Nadine really believes that her healing and the healing of her sisters will begin when we are willing to put down our pain—and for many of us, the years of intergenerational pain and abuse we have suffered—so we can recover our authentic selves. Nadine has found that antidepressant medication and weekly psychotherapy has been extremely helpful in her own journey toward well-being and wholeness.

The same pressures hold true for Ellin Lavar, whose drive for success coupled with her refusal to address her own emotional needs resulted in a suicidal depression. I told you earlier about how a girlfriend's death was the trigger for her own cry for help, but I want to share with you some of the background.

Ellin first realized she was depressed five years ago. "I didn't want to talk, eat, see people, it was difficult to fly, difficult to leave the house, the worse I felt inside the harder I tried to look right on the outside. Folks would say I had everything but it only looked that way on the outside. Looking back I realize I had been depressed for some time."

Ellin often feels very alone in her success. "My body can't shut down, my mind can't shut down. The business demands me twenty-four hours a day. I don't have the luxury of winding down. You lose friends and acquaintances because you're working all the time, you're shouldering all the responsibility. And being a Black woman, you have to fight four times harder to succeed. Being a woman alone, you're already called a bitch; if you're a Black woman alone, you're called a bitch with a capital B."

Like so many of us, Ellin's beliefs about being self-reliant, capable of handling anything, were hurting her the most. "If you're a Black woman with a problem, you're supposed to pray on it, and talk to your girlfriends, but you need more than that—you need support! For white women there's less stigma . . . it's okay to ask for help. But it's not okay for us to ask for help. We hold everything together, and if you say you need help, the people who rely on you begin to worry."

And, just like for me, that drive to meet everyone else's needs left Ellin little time for herself. "For a long time I didn't have a personal life because I didn't need another person needing me, and I didn't want to add another responsibility to my plate. I feel like I work so hard, I deal with business problems, I deal with everyone telling me how strong I am and then not really being there for me because they think I'm successful, so I guess I *must* be handling it . . ."

Alicia Evans, president of Total Image Communications, had this to say on the subject:

I find myself helping others so much, especially with securing jobs and offering advice, that I forget about myself. Then, with all the running and servicing of clients, you run into that wall where exhaustion becomes that unwelcome, long-staying roommate. Just who do you

---

It's really about the Black woman falling in love with her own image of beauty. I know that I've been in a fight to love myself and experience reciprocity in a relationship. I thought that a perfectly reciprocal relationship was an impossibility. That's that "Black woman is the mule of the world" thing. It says she can't get what she deserves, no matter how dope she is. And, you know, you have to go through the fear. You do have to do something with the insecurity, ghosts, and demons that have been programmed in us for centuries. You have to master the voices, all the insecure and inadequate men who put garbage in a woman's mind, soul, spirit, and psyche just so they can use her. You've got to break free of that crap. I didn't see many of the women who came before me fight that war successfully. And when you don't see it, you don't know if it can be done. But that's what faith is for.

—LAURYN HILL, SINGER AND SONGWRITER

In July 1980 Westina Matthews found herself on "the edge of depression and desperation" as her ten-year marriage faltered. As she held a loaded gun and waited for her husband to return home in the early-morning hours, she cried and prayed for God to intervene in her life and fell asleep with the gun in her hands. "I was awakened at sunrise by the sound of the front door opening," she writes. "I whispered to myself, 'Thank you, Jesus.' That day I got on the plane with $50, two suitcases and a draft of my dissertation. And I never looked back. Everything I own today, down to my panty hose, I have acquired over these past twenty-some years. A defining moment. A moment I survived only through the grace of God."

—FROM *HAVE A LITTLE FAITH: FOR WOMEN FULLY GROWN* BY WESTINA MATTHEWS, PRESIDENT OF THE NEW YORK CHAPTER OF THE PRESTIGIOUS WOMEN'S FORUM, A GROUP OF LEADERS FROM AROUND THE WORLD

turn to at those moments when all you really want is someone to listen to you, where you aren't being asked to give, but simply resting and receiving for a change?

Over the past two years I'd really been thinking about transitioning from public relations. I was weary, worn-out, worried, and exhausted all the time. This past year has been a whirlwind—traveling while maintaining my business at home. It was beyond intense. In August, I just took off because I couldn't function. Burnout is the best way to explain it. And I kept asking myself, "Where does the seasoned professional turn?" Luckily, I finally had several long talks with another senior-level associate, and I worked through the burnout.

Now I commit to taking more downtime to regroup mind, spirit, and body. I'm taking more time to do the things that really nourish my spirit, like my essay writing, which I absolutely love to do, but hadn't been doing for a while because of work. I am more conscious of actually closing shop (not answering that one last call after hours) and that really helps. I am more consciously taking time to stop during the day to go outside and soak in the sun because habit had me at my desk from 7:30 A.M. till dark . . . and there I was, wondering why I was so tired!

Throughout history, women have been valued for being selfless. And we, in particular, have felt that we need to make sacrifices to keep our families well, our communities whole, and our race alive. And we have taken this message in so deeply that we often don't recognize the "last on the list" symptoms in our friends. I actually heard one sister say to another, "Girl, you think that's rough? I had to put my mother in a home *and* plan my cousin's wedding last week!" What hit me hearing them was how incapable both women were of focusing on the other's needs. Each one was so needy and overburdened herself that, instead of each supporting the other and suggesting that the other had taken on too much, they tried to top the other's story of how much she had done and still had to do! Being last on the list became a badge of honor, not a misery to guard one another against.

Even when women do feel more connected to their exhaustion, they sometimes choose not to confide in a sister because they know how many burdens she also must carry, and they don't want to add weight to her load.

At one point, putting ourselves last was a strategy that made sense. Under slavery and segregation, Black women felt constant worry and anxiety about the well-being of their families, but the last thing in the world we could afford to do was show that worry to our children or the larger white world. Black women still need to worry about their families, but the old pattern of hiding our needs, masking our anxiety, and putting everything else in front of caring for ourselves is still with us. Living this way is not healthy. It leads to being emotionally exhausted, feeling resentful, and poor health. Is that the legacy we want to leave our daughters? If it isn't, we have to struggle to model a way to take care of ourselves while still taking care of our families. That's the most powerful way we can ensure that they grow up respecting their minds, bodies, and feelings.

> When I know me, I stop doing what's not good for me.
>
> —IYANLA VANZANT, AUTHOR AND
> SPIRITUAL LIFE COACH

Knowing Our Worth

We're so good at thinking about how racism impacts our men and their sense of manhood that we forget how racism impacts us and our sense of being a woman. We've all spoken these words at some point: "It's hard to be a Black man in America." We are painfully aware of how racism diminishes a Black man's sense of confidence in himself as a man—how being called "boy" at fifty is belittling, how the corridors of power admit more Black janitors than bankers, how Black men are more likely to go to prison than college, how Black men feel helpless to protect their families or themselves.

But for all we understand about the ways our men are put down and kept down in this country, we're often brought low by the ways in which racist American society denies us a sense of well-being in our femininity. In almost every sphere of life, Black women are either desexualized completely or represented as sex machines. This was once again painfully brought to light in 2007 when radio talk-show host Don Imus referred to the Rutgers women's basketball team as "nappy-headed hos." It's telling that Imus would pick on girls who were both gifted athletes and scholars, our best and our brightest. Sadly, this incident shows us that no matter what position we hold in American society, we're not safe from racist and sexist abuse.

My friend Stephanie Clark, founder and CEO of My Daughter's Keeper, Inc., told me about what happened the time she was speaking to a group of young women. She started by asking them, "Who is Don Imus and what did he do to stir up such anger and outrage throughout the nation?"

> *Everyone knows that a man*
> *ain't supposed to cry*
> *But listen, I got to cry, 'cause*
> *crying eases the pain*
>
> —THE TEMPTATIONS,
> "I WISH IT WOULD RAIN" (LYRICS
> BY NORMAN WHITFIELD, BARRETT
> STRONG, ROGER PENZABENE)

I was met with a roomful of blank faces. As I explained more about the controversy, I was anticipating that there would be some signs of anger or disappointment about the situation. There was none. Only looks of unconcern.

I went on to become more specific and asked, "Is anyone angry about what he said about the Scarlet Knights? As a young woman, did his demeaning words offend you?" Still nothing. By this time, I was the one feeling confused, wondering why I did not get the response from my girls that I anticipated. I had expected some expression of anger, disappointment, annoyance . . . I expected something, but I got nothing.

What I soon came to realize is that many of our daughters have become desensitized to the *b*, *n*, or *h* words. Some of them admitted that they use the *b* word frequently as a form of affection toward other young women. Why? "I like how it sounds when I say it, it's my favorite word and I use it a lot."

I took a deep breath after that one and thought to myself, I have a lot of work to do. Seeing that many of my desensitized daughters were not affected at all by the words of Don Imus, I put up a photo of rapper 50 Cent with the caption, "What's Up, My B****." "He's different than Imus," one girl said. "He is not talking about me in his music, he is talking to someone else." Then, I put up a photo of R & B singer R. Kelly. "I love his music" was the first comment made about him. "Oh, he likes young girls," someone else shouts. So I ask, "Why do you want to buy, listen to, sing, and dance to music by men who call you demeaning names and sing about abusing young girls?" No answer.

> In this society, the Black man feels he can never rest, he can never relax, or just be himself.
>
> —ANONYMOUS

That "desensitizing" Stephanie's talking about, becoming numb to the million tiny darts that get thrown at us every day—even by people close to us—is one of the many things that makes depression possible. Desensitized girls grow up to become even more desensitized women; desensitized women are very likely to become disconnected from their feelings, and depressed.

This fracturing of our womanhood is a secret pain way too many of us are holding.

We need to realize that acknowledging racist sexism, putting it on equal footing with that of the pain of our men, should not cancel out our men's pain or jeopardize our relationships to our men. We're not in a competition. We're all oppressed, and we need to use every tool we have if we want to understand that oppression and keep it from separating us from one another—by any means necessary.

Chapter Three

I WISH IT WOULD RAIN
Black Men and Depression

The numbers today tell us that at least 7 percent of Black men will experience severe depression during their lifetime. We have no numbers to tell us how many more will be plagued by low-level ongoing depression. We do know that their death rates are twice as high as those of Black women for suicide, cirrhosis of the liver, and homicide. More Black men abuse alcohol than white men, white women, or Black women. To make matters worse, the Black men who live the reality of these statistics have adopted a "who cares" vibe to guard against the disappointment of dashed hopes and lack of chances of being someone in a culture that at every turn says the color of your skin means you're inferior, not worthy, or just nothing. According to Erin Texeira of the Associated Press, "Every day, African-American men consciously work to offset stereotypes about them—that they are dangerous, aggressive, angry. Some smile a lot, dress conservatively, and speak with deference: 'Yes, sir,' or 'No, ma'am.' They are mindful of their bodies, careful not to dart into closing elevators or stand too close in grocery

In 2000, 65 percent of Black male high school dropouts in their twenties were jobless—that is, unable to find work, not seeking it or incarcerated. By 2004, the share had grown to 72 percent, compared with 34 percent of white and 19 percent of Hispanic dropouts. Even when high school graduates were included, half of Black men in their twenties were jobless in 2004, up from 46 percent in 2000 . . . In the inner cities, more than half of all Black men do not finish high school.

stores.

"It's all about surviving, and trying to thrive, in a nation where biased views of black men stubbornly hang on decades after segregation, and where statistics show a yawning gap between the lives of white men and black men. Black men's median wages are barely three-fourths those of whites; nearly one in three black men will spend time behind bars during his life; and, on average, black men die six years earlier than [white men]." Of course, rather than actually protecting them, this false front becomes a prison. They are locked inside and cannot ask for help.

> I can't fully be who I am supposed to be if you can't fully become who you are supposed to be.
>
> —ANONYMOUS

This chapter will look at the unique pressures our brothers face acknowledging depression and seeking treatment for it. Maybe because they've often been more blatantly abused by "the system," Black men are even more suspicious than Black women of the primarily white professionals who might help them. They see these experts as being in part responsible for the social problems that contribute to their feelings of depression. I will focus on the myth of strong Black manhood, trauma and its aftereffects, the heartache of addiction, and the toll of incarceration.

Everybody has to die, but Black men are dying faster than any other group. There are a lot of causes for this, but no justification—in other words, our brothers don't *have* to die like this. I believe that one of the biggest causes of this out-of-control death rate is what blue-eyed soul man Van Morrison called, in a song of the same name, "underlying depression."

Take for instance Vernon Slaughter, a topflight Atlanta-based entertainment attorney, former music industry executive, and dear friend, whose undermedicated chronic pain has doubled the impact of his depression. Recently he shared with me, "Depression was one of the causes of my marriage dissolving and certainly the cause of some of the mistakes I've made in my career. It was the real reason some people may have thought I behaved unusual for me at times. I am deathly afraid of becoming old and helpless because of my chronic pain. I fear that my chronic pain and the depression it has caused will leave me with no one to help take care of me and with very little savings. All my education and professional achievements couldn't save me from depression and the damage it does."

A depressed Black man doesn't necessarily look like he's "down in the dumps," "cryin' the blues," or any of the other clichés we use to describe what depression looks like. A depressed Black man might be the most energetic man you know, a ball of fire who never stops moving or doing, whether or not the moving gets him anywhere or the doing does anything. A depressed Black man might be accomplished in all kinds of socially acceptable areas (career, church, sports, school), or he might be the kind of man who can't stop making everything worse for himself and anyone who loves him. What most depressed men have in common, and depressed Black men in particular, is that *they will do anything not to wind up sitting with unbearable feelings.* That's why it's so often underlying depression: that unexplored and not talked about pain that underlies the destructive *and* self-destructive actions in the lives of way too many of our brothers.

How many? Well, according to statistics only 9 percent of men have suffered or will ever suffer from depression—but statistics are only just so accurate. They never tell more than a small part of the story. In Terrence Real's powerful book on men and depression, *I Don't Want to Talk About It: Overcoming the Secret Legacy of Male Depression,* he argues, as I do, that men are suffering from depression at rates far higher than statistics show. When I look at our community and I see our brothers dying every day from violence or heart attacks or drugs or disease, or wasting the best years of their lives in prison, I know these men are not well in their souls. These

> Black men have this warrior thing we do—we put on our armor like we're under siege all the time. But there are natural things that penetrate this world of hardness, like music and love. My nephew is three years old. He looks like I did when I was a kid. I haven't seen myself as a child in a long time. Our bond is completely pure. Kids don't have hate; it's learned. Although he doesn't form full sentences yet, he expresses himself in a way that's more eloquent than adults sometimes. Once I was heading out and he was coming in the door. He ran past everyone, straight to me, and wrapped himself around my legs. I'm known as a tough, resilient, run-me-over-with-a-tank-and-I'm-still-standing kind of brother. That moment shook me to my core—the pure energy of it. It was the first time I felt pure love.

men are not making suicidal choices because they've sat down and calmly reasoned it out; nobody has ever said, "I *could* go to school, have a career, make a decent living, marry a woman I love, and build a home and a family with her, but I've thought about it a lot and I know I'll be *happier* if I drop out, do drugs, sell drugs, gangbang, make babies I can't support, spend half my life in prison, or just get killed." But when society (in the form of poor housing, nonreal health care, unchecked crime, education barely worthy of the name, and welfare programs that are hard to get off) doesn't support those choices for those unlucky enough to be born into its urban poor—when it often works directly against the things we might think of as wise and humane choices—it shouldn't be a surprise that so many choose against their own best interests, against *themselves,* so many times a day, every day of the week. The truth is that these men are deeply depressed, so deeply they can't even name it. And the horror is that it's *so* secret they can't even tell themselves.

So much of my drive to write this book comes from the belief, grounded in faith, that if I am not well, you are not well, and if you are not well, I am not well. Our brothers are not well, and something has to be done. We must help them name their pain so that they stop visiting denial, abuse, and destructiveness on themselves and those around them.

What It Takes to Be a Man

James Baldwin, one of the finest writers God ever blessed us with, nailed it: "The great problem is how to be—in the best sense of that complicated word—a man." Manhood is, by definition, something you come into, not something you are born with; manhood is earned, not received. A boy is not born a man, but *grows into being* a man by the way he *learns* to respond to people and situations, to handle problems, to stand up for himself. Even at two or three years old boys are told that it's not okay to cry or run to Momma when you're hurt or scared—that being a man means standing on your own two feet, even if you just learned to stand on them the week before.

That's a lot of pressure to put on anyone, much less a little boy. You can't just be yourself, you have to be a man in your parents' eyes, and you have to be a man outside on the jungle gym with your boys. You can't let folks know that you love your teddy bear or that you're scared of the dark.

This pattern of hiding parts of yourself so you'll be considered one of the boys continues throughout a man's life. And in a Black man's life, it takes on the added dimension of race. For a white man, the rules are clear: being a man means physical power, ambition, aggression, the ability to protect the self and one's family, being a breadwinner, a provider, a faithful husband . . . For a Black man, there are all the same requirements—but they have to be met without the means of achieving them on a level playing field with white men.

All men are sent the message that being aggressive, assertive, and ambitious go hand in hand with achievement. But Black men are sent the additional message that an aggressive *Black* man is a social threat, an ambitious *Black* man is uppity. The opposing pulls of these messages can lead to severe psychic pain. On the one hand, the boy/man who exists inside of every Black man just wants to prove himself—first to his parents and then to the world—yet from a young age Black boys receive subtle warnings that the world will not reward *their* masculine power as it does the power of white boys and men. A friend told me, "I can remember hearing my father say no Black man will ever be president. I was nine years old and I wanted to be president more than anything. I remember feeling like he was saying it directly to me, telling *me* that I couldn't reach the top of the mountain."

For Black men the never-ending quest to be a man, and society's putting down of that manhood, is an open wound that never closes. Some men find ways to provide themselves with a sense of worth that does not come directly from the outside world; for many others this task is harder. Unable to shake the idea that they are less-than in the eyes of the culture, they begin to evolve defense mechanisms that sow the seeds of depression.

Take Michael. At thirty-five, he runs a successful consulting business. He works on average seventy-five to eighty hours a week. Two years ago his wife filed for divorce, taking their three-year-old son with her, saying that his long work hours and business trips left no time for his family. Michael knows now that these events have led him to be depressed. Unfortunately, what he can't see is that his depression started long before his wife left. When he talks about being a young man, the center of his world is success. "I knew I wanted to be successful more than I wanted anything else. My father worked as a janitor until he died and that wasn't going to happen to me. I'm going to be a Black-American success story." Although Michael loved his father, he saw him as a failure, a man who couldn't make it in America, a lesson of what he could not let himself become. In making that need a reality, he began closing down his emotions until all that was left was work. Clearly Michael felt he had something to prove—that to be a "real" man he had to be a success, even if that success cost him his family.

Then there's Bob, the son of an alcoholic father who drifted in and out of his and his mother's lives whenever he held down odd jobs. Bob dropped out of school in eleventh grade and ran with a group of boys who got into minor scrapes. He was arrested for car theft at seventeen and put on probation. Luckily, the experience actually made him realize he didn't want to lead a life of crime. He fell into a relationship with a girl from high school and got work doing different part-time jobs. When he was twenty, his son was born. Bob is a smart man, but his beliefs made him certain that life is unfair for a Black man. Instead of applying himself to any of his jobs or trying to find one stable full-time job, he complained about the system, drank with friends, and never really participated in his family life. After seven years of marriage his wife left him, moving out of the state with their eight-year-old son. He found himself repeating the same pattern he had had with his father: little communication, off-and-on child support payments, and distrust and distance between him and his son.

Both men are just heads and tails of the same coin. Racism played a large part in shaping both these men's expectations, as well as in their reactions to success and failure. For Michael, failure is the victory of a racist society trying to keep a Black man down. For Bob, failure is simply the

My Black pain comes from the scars of growing up in Gadsden, Alabama, and being one of the first Blacks in middle school, high school, and college. The scars of drinking from a water fountain that said "colored" or riding on a bus as a child, not understanding why I couldn't sit down when there was an empty seat. Seeing Black mothers, fathers, and children like me hit with electric prods and put in jail like cattle.

If our younger brothers and sisters understood the challenges we as Black people overcame, and the many lives given to ease our pain, our youth would embrace each other, stop the violence that destroys our communities, build economic opportunities together, and one day put an end to Black pain.

—MATHEW KNOWLES, PRESIDENT AND CEO, MUSIC WORLD ENTERTAINMENT confirmation that a Black man can't get ahead.

Many of our brothers feel like racism strips them of their power. They react either by overachieving at the expense of their emotional well-being, or underachieving at the expense of their material *and* emotional well-being. Both responses leave Black men open to self-doubt and low self-esteem, and fearful of their own potential weakness. Over time denying the self, and the shame that comes from having to constantly prove that the culture's racist attitudes are wrong, can lead a man to feel secretly like he's less than a man. Bob said, "Every time my wife looked at me, I knew she was thinking about the things I couldn't buy her." The shame produced by taking racism personally, letting it make you question your masculinity, is a big trigger of depression in Black men.

Two types of men seem to personalize the pain of racism: the man who holds himself back for fear of risking and failing, and the man who risks but finds that it wasn't enough. Neither is safe from feeling like a failure.

Racism has the added horror of making Black men feel like they have to mask their fear—not just fear of not being man enough, but fear of police brutality, fear of organized racist violence like the Klan's, fear of being falsely accused of a crime for being in the wrong place at the wrong time, fear of driving while Black . . . For a Black man to show fear in one of these situations makes him feel like the other team has scored a point against him, so the game face, the machismo, is a kind of self-defense. But as I said when I talked about acting out in the previous chapter, denying your feelings as self-protection has serious side effects.

When Black men disconnect from their fear by hiding it or denying it, they bring that "fearlessness" and the absence of feeling straight home—to their families, wives, and children. They don't do it on purpose. They do it because, at that point, anything that brings out their fear is an automatic enemy—a force that has to be fought and defeated by acting like you don't care, like it can't get to you. So what starts out as a real strategy of resistance becomes a personal loss because it cuts a man off from his feelings. Michael's wife used to say that he was not only physically unavailable, but emotionally unavailable as well; his typical response was something like, "Look at how we live. You have nothing to complain about." Did he really believe that the appearance of success—nice house, new cars, expensive clothes, lots of "things"—was the same as the reality of a warm and happy family life? Or did he just want them to be the same, because his fear of financial failure made it impossible for him to focus on anything else?

> There was a time when we were little that we could tell our mother about the pain, but then our mother, like lots of women raising boys, began to worry that we would be soft, that we wouldn't grow up to be men, that we had to toughen up. It was rough out there and she couldn't protect us. She knew one of the first things used to taunt boys is to say, "Oh, you're a mama's boy, go tell your mother." So after a while we begin to say, "Oh, I can't tell Mommy anything," and we stopped telling. Once we stopped telling her, it was easier not to tell anybody . . .
>
> —GEOFFREY CANADA, RENOWNED EDUCA-
> TOR AND AUTHOR OF
> *FIST, STICK, KNIFE, GUN: A PERSONAL
> HISTORY OF VIOLENCE IN AMERICA*

Depending on how old you are, actor John Amos is most famous for playing James, Sr., on the sitcom *Good Times*, Kunta Kinte in the miniseries *Roots*, or Admiral Percy "Fitz" Fitzwallace, the chairman of the Joint Chiefs of Staff on *The West Wing*. He shared with me his own experience of depression as a Black man in America. Different from Michael's and Bob's, it still has some tragic common points at its core.

As a veteran of over forty years in the entertainment industry as an actor, writer, producer, and most recently as a recording artist, I feel I have a very unique perspective on the issue of depression among African-American males. My childhood is typical of the average African-American male's childhood—single-parent household, extremely modest income, and very, *very* humble living conditions. Add to that the fact that I was called

Four Reasons Why It's Easier to Get Angry Than to Feel Sad

- I don't always know how to deal with my feelings, so when all else fails, anger works.
- I'm weak when I'm sad—and that hurts more.
- I'm more comfortable with anger as an emotion.
- Sadness is a form of weakness in my world; anger is more aggressive and masculine and makes me feel as though I am in control.

upon, with four other African-American students, to integrate two schools in the New Jersey elementary school system. Suffice it to say I was subjected to a great deal of insensitivity on the part of many of my white classmates, but, most important, I was constantly fed misinformation by my teachers, whose lessons were based on distorted concepts of my history as an African American.

Of course this would lead to depression. Time and time again the school system that had been entrusted with my education was the very instrument of my mental destruction and the deterioration of whatever self-esteem and ethnic pride my mother was able to instill in me. To be pointed out as "different" by your white classmates, to have the size of your nose, the kink of your hair, and your dark complexion perceived as something alien would be enough to depress Dale Carnegie (the famous author of *How to Win Friends and Influence People*). Then to embark upon a career in the entertainment industry that not only conceives racial stereotypes and misconceptions for mass disinformation, but perpetuates negative stereotypes to this day (think of *Survivor* dividing its contestants by race)—well, if you're not depressed by that, then something is very wrong.

Depression, bipolar disorder, antisocial, militant . . . these are all adjectives that have been used to describe my mental attitude for as long as I can remember. The state of New Jersey assigned a caseworker (psychiatrist) to monitor my behavior and counsel me during the years when I was only Black student in my class. Somehow I survived, but the scars of the unfair treatment I received as a child and as a grown man remain with me now and still cause me pain in my sixties.

Game Face: The Trap of Masculinity

We all wear a game face—the mask we put on when we have to take care of business and feel we can't afford to let ourselves be seen as weak. Sometimes it's very practical, like when we're actually competing in a game or negotiating a complicated deal. The problem is that many of us don't know how to take it off. What begins as a simple way to protect yourself becomes a way of life that traps you. We've got to learn to recognize that game face, and to see how hiding our pain disconnects us from ourselves and from each other. And I want our brothers to realize that one of the biggest game faces of all is the mask of masculinity—that they may be trapped inside a role that keeps them from knowing the vulnerability that makes love, joy, and intimacy possible. I want to talk about how our brothers' preoccupation with being men is killing them, and killing us.

Tom Lawson grew up in Harlem. He dropped out of school when he was fourteen after his mother became a crack addict. Left on his own, he started selling drugs, and in the mid-1990s he was convicted of manslaughter. The letters he sends me could make an informational pamphlet on depression. Without a father figure or any relative able to take him in, he felt under great pressure to become a man fast, and being a man in his neighborhood meant being up for anything. "I used to be scared, but I'd block out the feelings until I got back to my room, and then I would just start shaking. I would be going crazy. . . . You can't tell nobody shit like that because they'll think you're a bitch." Tom didn't start to deal with his "crazy" feelings until his cell mate was murdered. Feeling like he had nothing left to lose, he started reaching out.

Psychologist and author Derek Hopson puts it like this: "In my own experience working with Black men, we still have this wall we have to present so that we're considered strong and hard and not vulnerable, because we've felt under fire so long and had to protect ourselves and our families from attack and negative images. We're so busy fighting that war that we don't want to show that we're exhausted, that we don't want to fight. We will put on the game face to keep demons away. We don't look inside to see how we're dealing with things. We find it easier to be angry than to express hurt, disappointment, and the softer emotions." The fear of being vulnerable that creates this wall he's talking about separates us from our feelings and can lead to depression.

But we shouldn't let that game face keep us from demanding support structures for our men. Dr. Denese Shervington is a powerful and gifted psychiatrist whose holistic approach to psychotherapy includes yoga and exercise. A novelist, a teacher, and a women's advocate on top of everything else, she is someone I admire and learn from constantly. Recently, she blew me away at a panel when she talked about a study she had conducted between 1991 and 1993. I couldn't believe that her results hadn't been reported on the front page of *The New York Times,* the information was that significant!

She and the late Dr. Irma Bland had treated sixty men for sixteen sessions each, to see whether or not talk therapy would help a traditional drug treatment program for cocaine-addicted Black men. What they found was amazing. Not only did the Black men come to therapy, they came on time, looked forward to their sessions, and were eager to be heard. She told me, "For the three years that I participated in the study, I was unable to take advantage of my four-week winter break from the university. Given the huge commitment that it took on the part of the men to submit to the therapeutic process, I felt that it was my duty to be there consistently for them."

When they took the life histories of these men, they found that many of them had lost someone important to them when they were young. They had experienced trauma that made them feel helpless and powerless, and suffered from very low self-esteem. It was this powerlessness that led so many of them to turn to drugs, sex, and violence so they could feel more powerful and less worried.

Even more shocking were her statistics. She told us that almost half of the men had been victims of physical abuse, and a quarter of the men had been sexually abused! Many of them grew up in poor neighborhoods in homes where their parents abused them and/or couldn't provide them with a feeling of safety and where severe racism terrorized them every day. One of her clients who was able to pull his life as an engineer back together again summed up his experience of therapy by saying, "I am so glad to have been given the opportunity to look at myself and my past. I can now move forward with a brighter, more hopeful future!"

What shook me to my core about this study is that so often we hear folks say that Black men *don't* or *won't* do therapy. That's a lie and a stereotype, and one that we need to stop spreading immediately! Black folks would be much more receptive to therapy if we truly believed that we could see racially sensitive therapists at rates that were affordable to us.

Denese's study is deeply echoed by Glenn Townes's experience. He shared this powerful piece about the effects of therapy from his 1995 *Essence* article titled, "The Tale of a Wounded Warrior: One Man's Battle Against Depression."

I was The Man: single, 30-something and securely in my dream job as a journalist. But night after night, I would come back to my Kansas City apartment, sit in the middle of my living room and cry. If somebody stopped by, I pretended I wasn't home. If they called, the phone was off the hook. Later, when I would finally get to bed, I'd lie awake for hours and hours, then be too tired to get up the next morning. My fantasy: to get into my car, drive away and never return.

Depression had coldcocked me. But this dismal scene, which reached its peak about three years ago, wasn't my first bout. I can remember plenty of times over the years when I despaired for no particular reason. Back in high school, for instance, I'd written a paper for my English class called, "Is It Worth It?" Several teachers, friends and family members complimented me on the writing, but I don't think they picked up on the underlying pain.

In college, these periods of depression got longer. After college they got worse; and three years ago they became unbearable. That's when I found myself holed up in my apartment sobbing like there was no tomorrow. The dark cloud of gloom would lift for a week or two and then strike again. As I look back now, I remember feeling tremendous pressure. My work days often stretched to twelve hours. My answering machine was crammed with messages from people waiting for me to call them back. My family wanted me to come home for a visit; yet it was hard to get away, which made me feel like a bad son.

It got worse. My relationship hit the skids and my writing slipped. I began to hate my job. Over and over I asked myself, Is this all there is? Is this what I'm going to be doing the rest of my life? What contribution was I making by covering a city council meeting or writing about a woman who had opened a plant shop? It used to be wonderful seeing my name in print. Now I didn't care.

[Then came a] second job as a medical billing specialist for a group of Kansas City therapists and psychologists. . . . Patients would sometimes call, start talking about their bill and end up discussing their treatment. Or they would chat with me when their doctor was running behind. It was only through them that I learned that insomnia, irritability, crying spells and mood swings were symptoms of depression. It seemed odd, but in getting to know some of the patients, I began to understand myself. It was like looking into a mirror or listening to a tape recording of my own thoughts.

> Even when we do everything right and play by all of the rules, we still don't get the respect we deserve, and that is very, very stressful.
>
> —ANONYMOUS

Up to then, I'd written depression off to weakness, something people had to find a way to face and get on with their lives. Besides, I figured, my ancestors had it a lot worse than I did. But I had to reconsider, seeing all these people—men, women and children—flowing through the doors of the therapists' posh offices and freeing themselves of their deepest, darkest pain. If Black folks traditionally didn't undergo therapy, which is what I'd always heard, maybe it was time for me to break with tradition.

I finally went to one of the therapists at the office. I told her about the tension and the stress and she told me she understood. For about six months, I had regular sessions with her. They were informal. She would sit in a chair next to mine and ask me questions about my feelings; help me see where they came from and how to deal with them so they didn't cause me so much grief. . . . These days when I get blue, I still give my therapist a call.

I'm a Man Because I Handle My Business

Khalid Sumner is a young brother with a beautiful soul and a dear friend in his middle twenties. By all external measures he is a success. The problem is that his daily achievements hid his underlying depression.

In his job in the financial district Khalid works about sixty hours a week. In addition to the stress of his demanding job, he has many relationships resting on his shoulders. His parents, his twin daughters, their mother, his brother, his grandfather, and his tenants all depend on him. "I take my responsibilities seriously and I don't want to let down those who depend on me. There's a time for feeling down and a time to get the work done. I can't indulge feelings of depression. I don't have time to be depressed!"

> I tried to deal with it myself. But I found out that I couldn't do it.
>
> —CALVIN PEETE, PRO GOLFER, *CELEBRATING LIFE: A GUIDE TO DEPRESSION FOR AFRICAN AMERICANS*

When I ask him if he's ever thought about therapy, he laughs and says, "It sounds expensive. My mortgage is my therapy." When I press him, he tells me he thinks it would be hard for him to get good professional medical attention because he's not connected or rich.

Khalid's responsibilities began in his senior year of college, when his girlfriend got pregnant with twins. "I thought we were too young. Neither of us had a job. I told her that I didn't think it was a good idea." She understood, but wanted to have the babies anyway. At the time he felt like she was disregarding his feelings, but that at the end of the day it was her body. "But I also knew that, at the end of the day, having the kids would be on *both* our shoulders." Although the relationship didn't last, Khalid is a regular presence in his daughters' lives, both financially and physically. On top of that, he's a homeowner with tenants, the sole support of his grandfather, and the man other family members come to when things get tough. But there are also stresses that come from outside that small circle, stresses he didn't volunteer for.

"I got pulled over by a cop yesterday for talking on my cell phone, and I was really nervous. If the cop had been having a bad day and I said the wrong thing, something really bad could've happened. I feel like, if you're a Black man, it doesn't matter if you're guilty or innocent. And that's depressing. I really feel vulnerable to violence by the police because I'm Black, and that feeling is always there, and it's stressful."

Now that he had mentioned the *d* word on his own, he was willing to talk about depression, which he admitted was a regular issue in his emotional life. "I'm most likely to get depressed when I feel overwhelmed; then I just want to hit the pause button. When the stress is too much, I come home, sit, and watch TV like a lump. I'm not productive—I don't want to talk to anyone, I go to sleep early, I go off my healthy diet and just eat chocolate cookies. I don't care about anything. Nothing feels right, and it doesn't make sense to try things because I'll only mess up. It affects my work, too, because when I'm depressed I don't feel as smart as other people at work. Sometimes the feeling lasts three or four days. I'm so used to these feelings coming and going that I don't talk to anyone."

I ask him why not. "I don't have to tell my twin brother, Hanif, because he just knows, but I'll seldom mention it to a friend, because I feel like people have their own problems and issues, and they don't want to hear about yours, or engage your pain. The only thing that can really pull me out for a while is spending time with my daughters. When I'm with them I don't think about anything else—even depression."

His legacy of depression stems from childhood, where he grew up in a family that didn't talk about feelings. "We're not a real emotional family.

My mom and dad are not emotionally articulate, and 'feeling' talk is not encouraged. My mom and I don't really talk about things like this. My mom is from Jamaica, the oldest girl with three younger brothers, and she grew up raising boys. She's one of the strongest women I know, and I've only seen her cry twice in my life." When no one in our youth models a healthy way of dealing with emotions for us, we're unlikely to figure it out on our own, and all too likely to stomp on those feelings in ways that feed the depression monster.

The Peacock Feathers of Our Oppression

The real horror of depression in Black men is how well they cover it up. I'm constantly struck by the magnificence of Black male style: the swagger, the flair, the sheer originality. What other group of men could make prison style seem like the latest word in fashion? Yet I'm constantly struck by just how much sadness lies underneath those polished surfaces. That is why it's so important for us to be able to see beneath the shiny exterior to the vulnerability, shame, frustration, and pain. Take some of our biggest entertainers: Richard Pryor, Rick James, Marvin Gaye. I would wager that not a single one of these men was unfamiliar with depression, but instead of giving it a name or reaching out to others, they internalized their pain and shame, and ultimately self-destructed.

Think of Djay, Terrence Howard's character in the movie *Hustle & Flow*. A pimp in the middle of a midlife crisis, he realizes that there has to be more to life than running third-rate hos out the back of his Chevy. But even as he tries to realize his dream of hip-hop stardom, he's confronted with just how powerless he is. No matter how pressed his hair, how fly his clothes, or how smooth his game, the gates to the kingdom of success he imagines stay closed to him.

Two success stories come to mind that embody this model of how some of our best and brightest are secretly suffering on the inside.

Calvin Peete is a pro golfer whose passion for the sport pushed him to break racial barriers. He shares his moving story in *Celebrating Life: A Guide to Depression for African Americans*. When he stopped enjoying the game, he knew

> Show no love. Love will get you killed.
>
> —MARCUS FROM
> *GET RICH OR DIE TRYIN'*

something was wrong. His father left home when Calvin was just a boy, and the family was plunged into poverty. Calvin took on adult responsibilities and earned his keep. He started golfing at twenty-three, incredibly late for a serious player, but he was a natural, and began winning tournaments worldwide. But after ten years of high-profile professional play, the pressure of the tours began to get to him. More often than not he was the only Black man in the tour, but that wasn't the worst of it.

The better he did, the more people started expecting from him; the more people expected from him, the more he started expecting more from himself. Eventually the anxiety disturbed his sleep, so he started to drink. The more he drank, the more he had to drink. As the drinking got worse, he found himself hating practice, hating the tour, and hating travel—all the things he used to love. When it got to that point, he realized that he needed help because golf was his livelihood.

Eventually he was diagnosed with depression; with the help of medication, therapy, prayer, and his family's love, he restabilized his game and life. "I still take my medication, and I still have depressive episodes, but I'm able to come out of them—with the extra help of family, faith, and loved ones—better than I was before."

Matty Rich, born Matthew Richardson, the celebrated filmmaker from Brooklyn's Red Hook, shared some of his painful story with me.

Matty's father had been in Vietnam, and when he returned his personality was altered. "If you met my father during the day, he would be the most pleasant man you could meet—kind, giving, very intelligent. But Friday evenings, after he cashed his weekly check, he'd go straight to the liquor store and buy a pint of gin. Most Friday and Saturday nights he would get drunk and break everything we had, then physically abuse my mother."

These experiences went into his heartbreaking and critically acclaimed first film, *Straight Out of Brooklyn,* made when he was only nineteen years old, and financed by his mother's and sister's credit cards. Unfortunately, the success of his film didn't alleviate the pain of his childhood. "I was this young kid with a lot of responsibility on my shoulders that I never faced in my life. That's one thing I was not prepared for, 'success.' A lot of people say, 'I want success,' but they are missing what it truly means to have success. I was very scared of this new image and iconic film figure named Matty Rich. Being Matty Rich was the most frightening experience in my life. The media created this 'darling' young filmmaker born and raised in the Red Hook projects. The hard part of being Matty Rich was when I was alone. When there were no cameras and no news reporters, I had to deal with something I was running from—myself."

The more critical acclaim he received, the more pain he was in and the more he acted out in egotistical ways. "I had a sharp tongue, as lethal as a samurai sword. It didn't matter who it was, if I was rubbed the wrong way, I would just let my feelings out. I later learned that this was my way of masking the unresolved pain from my early childhood—and the fear of my new position in life."

It never occurred to him that his behavior was a product of depression until someone called him on it, and he listened, and started to get help. He has spent seven years in therapy and going to church, and even though he can't say he's seen depression's back for the last time, he's much better able to deal with it when it comes for an uninvited stay. He now has a very successful video game company and is back in the game.

Matty's story makes it very clear that success alone isn't the answer. Many of us fantasize that making it will take our pain and shame away, but ultimately Matty had to deal with himself, and each of us has to do the same. Much as we may imagine the glories of success, the stress of it actually compounds our emotional vulnerability. If there's one thing I've learned from working with celebrities, it's that living out the fantasy doesn't make the pain disappear, and that success and celebrity will bring on as many problems as you might imagine they'll solve. That's good news if you acknowledge the truth of it, but our brothers still seem to focus on looking like they have it all together while inside they may feel like dying. . . .

> When one of my brothers was killed and I learned who it was, it was a natural instinct to want to avenge my brother's death. But the deeper I looked into myself, I realized that's not who I was. All I kept thinking about was my mother's reaction and that young man's mother's reaction; and that there would be no difference in the level of pain that either would suffer. So I let it go. The guy went to prison. Although this young guy (fifteen years old) had the opportunity to change his life, almost ten years to the day of my brother's death the young man was killed.
>
> —HEAVY D., ACTOR AND HIP-HOP ARTIST

Both Calvin Peete and Matty Rich are warriors who engaged us with their seemingly boundless abilities to go from nothing to something big. But that jump can have a terrifying flip side—if I could make it this far this fast, I can also fall just as far, and just as fast—and that fear of falling is often what fuels the swagger and the mask that, as I've said again and again, becomes its own prison.

Get Rich or Die Tryin': Sorrow's Mask

> When men can no longer love women, they also cease to love or respect or trust each other, which makes their isolation complete. . . .
> Where it is impossible to have either a lover or a friend, the possibility of genuine human involvement has altogether ceased. When this possibility has ceased, so has the possibility of growth.
>
> —JAMES BALDWIN, AUTHOR

The fantasy of getting rich and powerful, and real-life attempts at realizing the fantasy, cripple men and women emotionally. This is very different from realistic ambition and definite plans for increasing success over the long-term. This is an elaborate cover-up for feeling powerless, hopeless, and the despair that masks depression.

Because Black men have no language to talk about painful emotions, they find themselves attracted to things that validate the hard "lesson" they keep learning from childhood, the lesson that says *Don't let anyone know you're hurting.* Football validates that lesson, boxing validates it, gangsta lyrics and movies validate it, but nothing glamorizes it more than the movie *Scarface,* starring Al Pacino as Antonio "Tony" Montana, aka Scarface.

Almost every Black man I know has a special place in his heart for this movie, and most own a copy of it. If you doubt me, just flip on *MTV Cribs* and try to find a hip-hop artist who doesn't spotlight *Scarface* while showing off his plasma screen and DVD collection. But why? Why does a 1983 movie starring an Italian-American man playing a Cuban criminal speak so loudly to so many Black men?

If you look closely, you'll see exactly why this is the number one players' movie of all time. Tony Montana begins his life in the movie as a man with nothing. A soldier turned criminal turned prisoner in Castro's Cuba, he washes up like garbage on America's shore. The only legit job he can find is washing dishes, so he pounces on the chance to make some "real" money running drugs. On his first job he is forced to watch his friend be hacked to pieces with a chain saw, but when his other friends come to rescue him, he doesn't miss a beat before chasing down his friend's killer, shooting him point-blank in broad daylight in front of a dozen witnesses. Then, with cop cars nearing, he calmly walks to his car and takes the coke and the money to his employers, like it was business as usual. Tony lives a life of horror, but never registers any emotion from it.

So many Black men can relate to him, because he starts from the bottom, with no hope of making it and no skills for making it besides a willingness to put his life on the line for the deal. To deal with the pain (and let's not pretend—nobody who traffics in violence goes unaffected by it), he turns it into a mask, the ultimate game face. But by the time we meet him it's no longer a mask; it's what he's actually become—an unfeeling, uncaring monster. The payoff for Tony, and for our men, is the fantasy that if you become a monster, you never have to feel powerless again. When the fantasy bubble bursts toward the end of the movie, when even Tony cannot tough his way out of what he has brought down upon himself, his reaction is to put his head in a mountain of cocaine for one last blast of high before what he must know is suicide.

Black men connect with Tony because he seems untamed. "The only thing in this world that gives orders is balls," he says. *He* has not been castrated even though he comes from nowhere and had nothing; even though, according to other people in his world, he is "an animal," "a peasant." The problem with this fantasy of being invincible is that it can't be lived, even by Tony Montana. So it's a fairy tale for those who have nothing and feel they can never achieve anything.

Tony is the kamikaze self that lives inside the addicted, the powerless, the despised. His denied pain and ruthless ambition create a man who is pure rage, and totally unable to love. No man has power over him because he doesn't care if he lives or dies. As a matter of fact, the prospect of dying before his time seems to rev him up—it heightens the feeling of being alive, and actually keeps the hounds of despair at bay. After all, if you can imagine no other way out of pain, then death *is* the ultimate solution.

I was talking with Dashaun "Jiwe" Morris, a reformed Blood and a young man I mentor who is like a son to me, about that death drive. He tried to explain what he called "the pressure of living, day in and day out, paranoid and suicidal."

"After a while," he said, "I wasn't paranoid on the streets anymore. I had lost a number of homies, and life was not meaningful to me anymore, so I didn't fear death. I walked in its company every day, and every day I put myself and family at risk." Somebody who lives like this, he said, is "a soulless soul."

"That's a person who appears to be functional, or even sane, but inside he's a ticking time bomb. He doesn't value his own life so why should yours matter?"

But of course death only ends things—it doesn't solve anything. And if we really look at Tony, we see that even at the height of his power he hasn't overcome anything: He's depressed! He has no feelings, no trust, he's addicted, all his relationships are dysfunctional, and he's always causing drama. In Tony's mind his options boil down to get rich or die. In the end, they amount to the same thing, whether it's the hollow victory that leaves him cut off from the few people he might care about, and who *did* care about him, or the death that just ends everything. The wife who he might have loved ("Can you see what we're becoming, Tony? We're losers. We're not winners. We're losers!") is his first major emotional casualty, and that loss is a snapshot of what fuels part of the crisis between men and women in our community. By not valuing ourselves we devalue each other, and in that way we perpetuate depression.

Snoop Dogg, in an interview for MTV, understood the truth of Baldwin's wisdom.

> The large number of trauma cases we see in urban areas involving Black males, in large part, stem from the hopelessness and helplessness that is depression. Treating these cases requires not just surgery on the body, but surgery on the soul.
>
> —ANGELA NEAL-BARNETT, PHD,

I was taught that a woman was a bitch, she was a ho, she wasn't nothing. My influence was the street. When I went on the streets and seen it going down like that, that's what I picked up. I seen the guys with the money could make the girls do what they wanted them to do. You understand what I'm saying? So it was a powerful position to have money to have a "bitch" to do what you want

> Black people don't need welfare; we need mental health care. What we need is to parachute psychiatrists into the ghetto like soldiers storming Normandy. As a people we can't keep getting beat in the head by poverty, racism, broken homes, drugs, police brutality, suspicion of character, unemployment, cheating husbands and wives, incest, homelessness and not freak the hell out sometimes!
>
> —JIM GLOVER, CREATIVE DIRECTOR, CAROL H. WILLIAMS ADVERTISING

her to do for you. And that's what it was. And it wasn't, "I'm 'a have a girl and my woman," it was, "I'm 'a make that bitch do what I tell her to do."

As psychologist Derek Hopson told me:

We still react to images of what we believe we are. In relationships we get caught up in presenting an image or a mask. Men want to come across as strong and confident and in control, and really tone down soft emotion.

We'd rather appear powerful and capable, but in doing so we don't acknowledge the common fears and hurts. And Black women, finding themselves having to appear as if they're not ho-ish or desperate to find a man, are sometimes seen as aggressive and hostile. As Black men and women, we have so many myths and stereotypes interfering with our ability to be two human beings trying to connect. Reacting to these images and stereotypes prevents real and honest connecting. We don't even talk about those misperceptions of each other, and they get in the way of our being open so that intimacy can evolve. We're not immune to believing these negative images—they are there in the back of our minds. And it's also why prejudice is hard to get rid of, because there is a part we buy into.

Some people might think that *Scarface* is only entertainment, but we know that nothing embraced this hard is "just a movie." In working-class Black life, the movie plays out in the ways the pimp mind-set is glorified and romanticized. We all know that a pimp is literally someone who trades in women's bodies. Like Tony, pimps are usually men who had no avenues for success open to them other than crime.

In the larger sense, a pimp is a man who can get the most for the least, a man in control of the playing field, a man who others serve, a man who allows no disobedience. A lot of Black men say, "Hey, if we can't play by the rules and win, then we won't play by the rules." For some, this is a spur to think creatively, to create a new rhyme—think about the way basketball has changed in the last twenty years. But for some men it's just an excuse to be unethical, to use people for personal gain, and ninety-nine times out of a hundred it's our *own* people who are getting used. That's a high price to pay to get over feeling powerless.

The truly tragic thing about the hustle is that it repeats the social relationship that created our current problems: plantation slavery. Plantation slavery was a hustle: White people made money off our bodies, off our sweat and blood, without even paying us for our labor—just like pimps get money without having to pay the women who earn it. We have to be careful about how we take in and repeat these dynamics. As *Washington Post* columnist Courtland Milloy wrote in a piece on pimp pop culture, "Celebrating that pathology—even when it's 'only a movie' or 'just a song'—is cultural suicide." I have to agree with the brother: Using our

> I can't see 'em comin' down
> my eyes
> So I gotta make the song cry
>
> —JAY-Z, "SONG CRY"

pain for gain isn't just selfish and self-destructive—it's plain dangerous to the race, and everyone's humanity is at stake and compromised in this process. This is recycling pain. Pimping in any form is about not caring about who gets hurt or how it feels, it's just caring about getting paid. That's slavery.

When we use the hustle to level the playing field, we hurt other people because we can't lay claim to our own pain; we exploit the minds and bodies of other people because we feel powerless to develop our own talents in productive and socially acceptable ways. Don't be fooled by the stone-cold pimp exterior: It is a mask for pain, and we have to start calling it what it is if we want to help the brothers who wear the mask, instead of judging them and feeling righteous.

If *Scarface* can really teach us anything valuable, it is the danger of living for a fantasy instead of in reality. The temptation to live in fantasy because reality (poverty, abuse, danger, helplessness) is so painful can sometimes feel irresistible. And if you're Black and poor and you look to your neighborhood and media for inspiration, for ideas about what might free you from the rat race, what you see is sports, music, gangs, hustling, and the lottery. But what happens as we get older and realize that only the smallest fraction of people can ever achieve these "hoop dreams"? I believe the reality is crushing; it makes the feelings of failure we were already running away from much stronger.

One of the things that makes us easy marks for the lure of the *Scarface* fantasy is the way so many of our messages tell us that wealth and power matter more than anything—certainly more than old-fashioned passions like fighting for social justice, and raising up the race, but also more than boring values like honor, compassion, friendship, education, and love. These messages, which we can find in every magazine, every newspaper, every commercial, and every billboard, make a regular man's perception of his "failure" even more excruciating. And an impossible fantasy, like a dream deferred, leads to pain, hopelessness, and depression.

It Never Happened

One of the hardest things any of us can ever deal with is emotional trauma—an intense negative experience that can leave you unable to function emotionally in the short run and mess with you in all kinds of ways in the long run. Trauma can range from molestation (a major hidden problem among men), to the disappearance of a parent, physical abuse, constant gunfire in your community, or knowing someone who was hurt or killed. As horrible as trauma is for women, I think it may even be harder for men. Many of the brothers I've met and spoken with share a deeply destructive belief in the deepest part of themselves: They think that if they were "real men," the traumatic incident wouldn't have happened; but even though it did happen, they think it shouldn't hurt them or affect them in any significant way. In other words, most men believe that just the very fact of their having been victims means they weren't "man enough." And that means that the energy that *might* have gone into healing gets channeled into denial instead.

The fact is, trauma does happen to Black men as much as anyone, and possibly more. Trauma happens, and its repercussions are real. But instead of dealing with it—getting help, talking about it, or joining a support group—men are more likely to experience shame. And that shame spirals, driving the trauma deeper into silence. Open discussion of male trauma is virtually taboo: How can a Black man reveal a horrible experience and his unbearable feelings about it to another man without reducing himself *as* a man? Better to swallow the pain, he thinks; better to keep it to myself.

The biggest obstacle to honesty about trauma is that so many men believe that what happened, happened *only* to them. Since there's no acceptable space for them to talk about their wounds, why would Black men think otherwise?

Here, ironically, is one of those rare areas where women have an advantage over men. We women don't always deal effectively with our emotional injuries, but in a twisted way, society expects us to be victims—of discrimination, abuse, physical violence, or sexual violence, among other things—and accepts our admitting it. But men who are hit by these things, instead of being seen as victims, are somehow made out to be cowards, sissies, or punks, or something less than men. If a woman is hurt, at least she doesn't have to question her essential womanhood.

From girlhood on, women develop a vocabulary of suffering that has no parallel in the world of men. Because there's no place in Black men's lives where they can feel safe not to front, they don't even have language to describe what has happened to them, or how they feel about it. How can you feel pain that you can't name? The only place where Black men are allowed to name their pain is in song. It's perfectly okay for a brother to pour his heart out in music—gospel, blues, soul, hip-hop—and he can even get props from other

> *Suicidal, I'm ready!*
> —NOTORIOUS B.I.G.,
> "READY TO DIE"

men for doing it ("Hey, man, that was beautiful . . .") but no way can he sit in front of you and tell you that his whole world has been torn to pieces, and that he needs help because life feels pointless.

The fact that there is no safe space for Black men to *have* their pain, much less talk about it, is fuel for the fire of depression. Depression in turn becomes fuel for the fire of the million ways Black men *act out* their emotions instead of having them. Denial—being unable to deal with the feelings that come out of pain and vulnerability—all but forces Black men to destroy themselves and take their loved ones down with them.

So much of Black inner-city life is traumatic in so many ways, big and small, that even if we somehow make our way out of it, we are still likely to experience its effects long after we've left the actual trauma behind. In fact, sometimes those effects don't even rear their ugly heads until many years afterward. If you are going through this, or someone you know is, what you're feeling is not weakness or oversensitivity or any other kind of "defect." This is a real psychiatric condition, and it's called posttraumatic stress disorder—PTSD for short.

If you saw a kid being brutalized, you know that he was experiencing trauma; it doesn't take a PhD to understand that. But what if you never saw that kid young, and now you see him twenty years later, a grown man, maybe holding down a job, paying the rent, raising a family—all the things that *look* right on the outside—but that young man is squirming in agony on the inside, still reeling from the aftereffects of that old trauma. Or maybe he doesn't have the outside looking so good—maybe he's dropped out of school and is not working but still somehow making money, maybe he's making babies and not supporting them, maybe he's in prison or just out, maybe he's peddling dope or women—and all you see is this angry young man, dangerous not only to those around him but to himself. Hold up a second. Remind yourself that nobody gets that way for no reason. Nobody is "born evil," no matter how many times we might have heard our mothers or grandmothers use the phrase. We are born whole and then life happens. If you see a man who spreads pain everywhere he turns, don't think for a second—no matter how he fronts—that he's not in agony himself. And that brand of ago-

> **FOR TERRIE AND MADELINE**
>
> *Land of dreams that are broken*
> *I live*
> *Lacking the option of hope*
> *Two girls who learned to dream*
> *   are now lights*
> *Dare me they did*
> *Dare me to dream*
> *Beauty I feared*
> *Skin of a kind I saw danger*
> *Sisters I never knew*
> *Knew my inner*
> *Soulless I was to be*
> *They love me*
> *Though I never love*
> *Sisters I never knew*
> *My sisters help a power I knew*
> *   didn't exist*
> *Showing me a light in my dark*
> *Their beauty is now I*
> *Shine on they shall through me*
> *Their light is my dreams*
>
> —A POEM BY JAY DAVIS
> AFTER A YEAR OF BEING MENTORED

ny, more times than not, is PTSD.

Technically speaking, PTSD is an ailment that can afflict anyone who has lived through or even just witnessed personal violence (like rape or murder) or violence on a bigger scale (like war—on the streets or abroad—a horrible accident, or terrorist attacks). Anyone who lives through something like this is going to experience painful aftereffects like horrific nightmares and feeling disconnected from everything, but for most people these symptoms pass after a while; the more support people have to get over trauma, the sooner they leave the worst of it behind them. About 8 percent of all Americans will experience PTSD at some point in their lives; for people who have lived in what could be called a war zone (even if it's not overseas, even if it's right here at home on our streets), that number jumps to 30 percent. They share the symptoms of those who have recently gone through trauma, and then some. Besides sleep problems and detachment, PTSD sufferers can experience problems with memory and thinking, severe flashbacks, physically lashing out in their sleep, and many of the things we connect with depression. They are likely to have trouble holding on to a job or staying in a relationship, to have regular or ongoing family conflict, to be awkward or even hostile in social situations, and to have trouble parenting.

PTSD is not a form of depression, but almost half of those who have it experience major depressive episodes; even more combine it with alcohol abuse or alcoholism, and about a third combine it with drug abuse or addiction. In fact, Black men are so much more likely to act out their pain than work on healing it that PTSD can be considered a warning sign for depression in our men. The good news is that, as with depression, there are ways of treating PTSD, often in conjunction with treatment for depression (see chapter nine for more information on treatment).

Jay Davis is like a son or younger brother to me, a beautiful soul I mentor with my friend Madeline McCray through the Stay Strong Foundation. He is an extremely passionate person with an easy, warm smile and hearty laugh, but he'll be the first to tell you that it's the mask he wears to hide the fact that "joy" is a foreign feeling to him. At twenty-six, he is a young man in years but a grizzled veteran of life's wars, particularly gang warfare. Harlem-born and -raised, he had both parents at home, but their relationship was troubled and turbulent. Jay spent as much time away from home as he could, which meant time in the street, and when he was sixteen he joined a local set of the Bloods, where for the first time in his life, he felt good—at first.

For one thing, he got to take all the hatred he felt toward himself and channel it toward others. "It made it easier to hate others; it was a relief, because the hate wasn't just on me anymore." For another, he didn't feel so isolated anymore, so totally alone in the world. "The unity the Bloods were giving to the people in the streets—I didn't have that in my life, and I wanted it so bad . . . If a friend is late on the rent, I will do what I can to make sure he's not evicted, and his kids are fed. We're willing to risk jail or a casket for a brother or a sister. Nothing gets between us, nothing gets in our way—the love is that strong."

> After a while, it's not acting when you have to suppress your feelings. Everybody has feelings, but there are some people who have trained themselves over time not to be out crying and doing all kinds of shit. Where someone else would cry, we replace those feelings of anxiety and get angry instead.
>
> —50 CENT, HIP-HOP ARTIST AND ENTRE-PRENEUR

But the positive feeling of that unity and that refocused hatred was short-lived. For all the violence Jay had seen and been a part of before, it was nothing compared to what became part of his daily life as a gang member. "The gang lifestyle is not easy. We watch our loved ones die. When you see the people you love and respect die senselessly, it makes you bitter and hate more." And the senseless violence doesn't just happen to other people. "One time someone pulled a gun on my friend. I jumped the guy with the gun, but when I did someone else stabbed me in the calf and in the eardrum; someone bit my lip off and knocked out three teeth."

Nobody can live in a world of horrific daily violence like that and not pay a price in psychic pain. Jay's first way of dealing with the pain was prescribed drugs: Prozac, OxyContin, Percocet, Zanaflex, and Promethazine, among others. "Drugs are the sedation we need to deal with trauma. They would put me in a dark place, and that's where I would feel most comfortable." But comfortable soon became miserable. Whenever Jay thought about the deaths of the people he cared about, he wondered why they had died and he hadn't; it was so bad that he envied them, feeling like they were lucky to escape the way they did. He started to burn himself to relieve the pain. When one of his close friends, who was deeply depressed, killed another close friend and then hanged himself, Jay became more overtly suicidal. He would pour bleach into his liquor and drink it, hoping to poison himself; he would cut himself, hoping to die, or at least deaden the impulse to hurt someone else. He didn't die, but soon cutting replaced burning as the activity that would distract him

> Many of us spend our whole lives running from feeling with the mistaken belief that you cannot bear the pain. But you have already borne the pain. What you have not done is feel all you are beyond that pain.

from wounds he couldn't see but could feel way too deep. His arms are a testimony to his suffering. They are covered in artistically designed keloid scars: long scratches, third-degree burns with words and symbols that he has branded in with quarters, cigars, cigarettes, and wire hangers. When I look at his arms, the scars take up half of them and look like an elaborate tic-tac-toe board. Given all he's been through, it makes me happy to know that he is now healing his wounds and working as a consultant with the Stay Strong Foundation to help other young men stop the cycle of gang violence. When Jay talks to anyone, particularly young people, about the value they should place on human life, he hides nothing. Most men won't let you see them cry—Jay is incapable of telling the truth without baring his soul. Even as he struggles every day to place value on his own life, he's made saving others from the same living torment his personal mission. This is part of the healing work. Talking with youth and showing them how to live their lives differently, that they *can* live their lives without violence.

Street life is a war, and many of our boys are drafted into it as child soldiers when they're too young to be able to make sane life choices, let alone wise ones. If they haven't fallen in senseless battle or been incarcerated by the time they reach young manhood and start to realize that there has to be something better, they are often like veterans who don't know any other trade. The problem is that there's no Veterans Administration to help them transition to civilian life, or to treat their trauma-induced wounds.

The Most Secret Trauma: Male Sexual Abuse

Most of the time when we hear about sexual abuse, whether it's rape or incest or molestation, we hear about it in relation to women and girls. The fact is, there is probably every bit as much sexual abuse of men and boys as there is of women and girls—for all we know, there's even more—but it's the most underreported crime there is, and the one that bears possibly the most shame for its victim: A boy who is sexually abused believes he can never really be a man, and a man who is sexually abused believes he is not a man anymore. Boys are often victims of coerced sex in juvenile detention centers, immigration detention centers, homeless shelters, and foster homes—and most often in places they consider sacred like home and church. A recent study found that in prisons, 20 percent of men behind bars reported being forced into sex. That's *reported*—since reporting is rare (and often retaliated against), unofficial estimates range from 50 to 80 percent. Laveranues Coles, a wide receiver for the New York Jets, bravely told the media about having been molested by his stepfather. "I haven't talked about it in . . . forever, but I know that holding something like that inside has been a burden for so long." And he's certainly not the first high-profile man I've encountered who's been sexually abused by a family member. He is, however, one of the few to break the deadly cycle of silence, and hopefully through his story some of the other thousands of men and boys who wrote him will have the courage to speak out.

> As a young African-American male, you have to have your war face on at all times. This was a challenge during my trial. Potentially facing up to fifteen years in prison humbled me. I was scared to death, but I wouldn't show it. I had to maintain my swagger. But, one of the ways I dealt with the pressure was to sleep excessively. Some people like to run away from the uncut truth, but I tend to go inside myself to deal with the pain.
>
> —SEAN "DIDDY" COMBS, ENTERTAINMENT AND FASHION MOGUL, RECORDING ARTIST

What happens to these boys and men who are abused? Physically, once the wounds are healed, they are *ten times* more likely to have syphilis, gonorrhea, hepatitis A and B, and HIV/AIDS, diseases that will probably not be found or treated where they are, and will almost definitely be spread once they are out. The mental costs are at least as high: Besides the obvious PTSD, they are prime candidates for flashbacks, nightmares, drug and alcohol abuse, depression, and suicide. But that's just the beginning, because everything they stuffed down is bound to explode in violence of one kind or another. It might be sexual or not, it might even be raping or sexually abusing someone else, or it might be the kind of purely self-destructive behavior they couldn't have engaged in when they were in more controlled environments. The one certain thing is this: People who are abused and not treated for it, not helped to deal with it in healthy ways, will without a doubt add more links to the long chain of abuse.

Acting Out:
My Pain Is Not in What I Say, but in What I Do

Psychologist Derek Hopson told me that he thinks of anger as "the most aggressive emotion. Whenever we're under fire, there's a fight-or-flight response. As men, we're more apt to fight and defend than run, because to flee has this negative connection—that you're weak, timid, cowardly. Taking the offensive is usually a position of anger and aggression, and it can give you a sense of empowerment, that you can handle the situation. That kind of behavior can keep you alive in a prison setting or a dangerous area, but on a daily basis you're constantly in alarm mode, and it wears our systems down. The reason we're so often angry, and so often perceived as angry, is that Black people don't feel safe in America; everywhere we turn, we are evaluated, criticized, unfairly treated, and unfairly perceived."

It is a well-established fact that men tend to act out their feelings more than women do, and this is especially true when it comes to depression. As I've pointed out over the last several pages, when men disconnect from feelings that they've failed to live up to an ideal of manhood, when they try to mask the effects of racism or hold in trauma, those feelings don't just go away; they have to come out somewhere, somehow. To put it bluntly, if you can't feel it out, you'll act it out. For Black men, the most common ways of acting out are addiction, promiscuous sex, violence, crime, and suicide.

Three Kinds of Self-Medication

The big reason we have to focus on addiction as a part of treating depression is that, for many men, addiction and compulsion are behaviors that mask the actual depression. According to psychologist Terrence Real,

People began to medicate themselves with whatever they could get their hands on; if the first thing you tried was heroin and it took the pain away, you're gone. I watched group after group of the guys just disappear looking for that. Drugs, alcohol . . . almost everybody had something that they ended up with, if you stayed there and never got out of that situation. I don't know anyone who got through it healthy.

No one ever talked about the pain. The equivalent of talking about the pain was that, if two guys got really really drunk, to the point that you weren't gonna remember what you were talking about, you might tear up and say to the guy, "Yo, I can't take it." But you'd be so drunk that the next day there was no way he was gonna look you in the eye and say, "Wow, you know what you said last night? I can't *believe* . . ."

We were conditioned from very early on to divorce ourselves from our feelings. The worst thing you could be was in touch with those feelings. People look at how bad off so many of our men are in relationships, and they don't understand that we were working on separating ourselves from our feelings starting at 8, 9, and 10 years old. You had to get away from the fear, you had to get away from the embarrassments and humiliation. You had to get away from all of that stress that was a constant part of growing up. And the way you did that was you denied that you felt anything. "You scared? Naw, I'm not scared. You care about her? Naw, I don't care about her, she ain't nothing to me."

There was a simple reason: The moment someone found something you cared about, they could hurt you with it. So your job was to make sure there was nothing anyone could use as a weapon. The problem was, after you spent years divorcing yourself from your feelings, if one day you want to share them with somebody . . . it's not realistic. Knowing your feelings, showing your feelings, having empathy for other people's feelings—those are learned things, not something you just do naturally. So many of us grew up without that. If you spend your whole life learning how *not* to feel, you have to turn around and put that same effort into learning *how* to feel.

—GEOFFREY CANADA, RENOWNED EDUCATOR AND AUTHOR OF

therapy begins in three phases. "First, the addictive defenses must stop. Then, the dysfunctional patterns in the man's relationship to himself must be attended to. Finally, buried early trauma must reemerge and, as much as possible, be released."

1. Killing the Pain: Acting Out with Drugs

Christopher Westlake is a forty-four-year-old native of Tennessee. Six years ago he entered a recovery program for substance addiction, but it was only after he had completed the treatment that he was diagnosed with depression. Nowadays he can see the connection between depression and addiction, and how it impacted his life. His drug abuse was a reaction to not only his fear of being depressed, but to his feelings of shame about being depressed.

For Christopher, depression first started in college. His parents had divorced the year before and as the youngest child of an established southern middle-class family, Christopher felt some serious pressure to make good. Instead of attending Morehouse, his family's first choice, he went to a small university in New York state. For the first time in his life outside of the society he had grown up in, he felt free of the kinds of social expectations that used to be part of the air he breathed, and got along easily with many different crowds. He also started drinking heavily, and in his freshman year he had his first blackout.

"In retrospect, a lot of things were happening together. I felt pressure to succeed academically, to keep it all together, and to play different roles for different groups. Then there was the pressure to satisfy my parents and

---

We all lie like hell. It wears us out. It is the major source of human stress. Lying kills people. The kind of lying that's most deadly is withholding, or keeping back information from someone we think would be affected by it. Psychological healing is possible only with the freedom that comes from not hiding anymore. Withholding from other people, not telling them about what we feel or think keeps us locked in the jail. The longer we remain in jail, the quicker we decline. The way out is to get good at telling the truth.

—BRAD BLANTON, PSYCHOTHERAPIST AND AUTHOR

my grandparents, to live up to their bougie values." Christopher discovered that he could fit in with many different circumstances, so he hung out with people who didn't hang out with each other: deadheads, jazz lovers, hip-hop people, etc. But all that fitting in got in the way of his finding his own center. "When you adapt bits and pieces from other cultures, you find yourself at two extremes in the same body. You're not there because you have a true sense of who you are. You're there because you're seeking acceptance, and your identity gets caught up in other people and outside things."

He was known around campus as a party animal and his grades were beginning to reflect his habits. Then one day when he *hadn't* been drinking the night before, he woke up with what felt like a severe hangover. He knew something wasn't right; he was frightened. Unfortunately, everyone around him just assumed his hangover symptoms meant he'd been partying again the night before. The first bout lasted only a day. "Then it would come back, and at its most severe it would last several days. I would just stay in bed, and not tell anyone that it *wasn't* a hangover."

In his second semester it started happening every few weeks. He kept up his attendance and was able to stay in school, but in his second year he had a lot of incompletes, and he finally dropped out. But this didn't motivate him to get help, or even to try to understand what was haunting him. "I moved to New York and found a new cast of characters, with lots in common in terms of not being able to deal with what was really troubling us. My addiction progressed."

For the next few years he was one of those people who seemed to "manage" his addiction. From the outside he looked like a guy with lots of promise, a guy who could make good, if only he could get it together a little more. He held on to jobs and supported himself, but in reality his whole social, spiritual, and relational growth had stopped in college. "I was completely focused on controlling my internal feelings and keeping them at bay." And that meant more drugs.

"By that point there were a million emotional distractions. I hung out with people who used, partied, and did extreme things. I medicated myself in a more socially accepting environment. Party all night, pass out all day." When he first started using cocaine it made him feel normal. "My response to it wasn't one of anxiety, fear, and speediness. I felt more *relaxed* on coke. Maybe because I was depressed the coke brought me back up." But of course that up was only temporary.

Drugs took him further away from the darkness that kept coming around to swallow him up, but over time even the drugs didn't work, and the old feelings would still kick up. "In the addiction state you're trying to feel the way you felt to mask the pain, but then there comes a point where you just keep feeling the same. So you're depressed *and* high." When the old drugs don't work, the addict looks for new ones, and what Christopher found was crack.

The first time he smoked it he had no reaction. "Of course, by that time I couldn't see my own role in anything that had happened to me. But I felt lots of shame and humiliation." So he tried crack again, and this time it fulfilled its promise: He became addicted. "It took me so far away so fast. That first high you end up chasing the rest of your time using, and you can never get it again, and while you're chasing, you become an addict."

Crack addiction led to homelessness. "I started staying at the houses where I was using." He supported his habit by participating in drug studies. "They paid you to take crack and cocaine and do this study for the government. It's mostly African-American addicts. In one study, they blindfolded me, put a pipe in my mouth, and told me to take a hit. Every hour they would ask me if I wanted more money or another hit. I would think about all the things I could do with the money, but every time I asked for another hit.

"I took crack for two years. Using is a hard life. You're totally out there, and the things that you see . . . like the time I sat at a table and smoked crack with a girl who was eight months pregnant. My response was to take a bigger hit to try and numb this, too. It was all about the drugs."

At some point he began to think about getting clean, about returning to New York because he'd heard that there were walk-in programs there. After two years he got money from participating in a study and came to New York, but it was another year before he finally made it to a treatment center. "I walked in off the street at 6:00 A.M. I had just been in a crack house with a fellow addict who was beating his girlfriend. I was so desensitized, yet I couldn't block that out; I tried to help and told the man to get out. Outside I started walking and found myself, crusty and tore up from the floor, up at a substance abuse treatment center in Midtown. I just asked for a brochure, but they kept me there for hours—the whole time I kept telling them I was just there for a brochure! When I finally saw the intake nurse, she looked at me and said I was going to die sooner rather than later, and she asked me if I wanted to die or if I wanted help. I stayed and did the paperwork, and was transferred to a detox facility in New Rochelle."

The rehab worked and Christopher went from there to a one-year residential program. After he began dealing with his depression, he felt more able to handle life. "Now when feelings hit, I'm able to smile and laugh and not cringe with fear. Now I'm able to have a relationship, spirituality, to go back to school. I didn't always get what I wanted, but what I wanted changed in recovery. I'm now able to be human, to have and understand the human connection. I now realize that dealing with depression is just one part of who I am, like addiction is just one part of who I am. I still have pain, but I also have tools. Some days life stinks, but it's just a feeling and it passes, and you open yourself to other things that can happen."

Today Christopher is taking life one day at a time and blossoming in his life and career as a senior coordinator for a mental health facility.

2. Sex Addiction: Acting Out with Sex

Erich Williams is a friend from my hometown in Mount Vernon. He read the *Essence* article I wrote about my own depression, and willingly shared his story because he wants to help others recognize what he went through, and maybe spare themselves some pain.

Erich is one of five children, born and raised in the projects, abandoned by their father and therefore forced to live on public assistance. His mother was abandoned by her husband of eleven years and, having very little worldly experience, she suffered from poor self-esteem and struggled with obesity. She was a very affectionate, deeply religious woman who made sure the kids said "I love you" daily to one another, accompanied by a regular dosage of hugs and kisses; but she also had to be hard as "the man" of the house because there was no man. This being the case, she could not be as nurturing as she might have been, having been forced into being both mother and father.

Erich was very quiet and shy as a child, so he didn't get a lot of positive reinforcement. Innocent chiding from siblings telling him he had a big head while always commenting on how good-looking friends of his were did little to help his self-esteem. To make matters worse, he stuttered terribly and people often mistook his stuttering to mean that he was stupid. While in the sixth grade he was denied entry into the most advanced class of his grade despite having very good grades that would have merited his placement there. Because of his mother's overwhelming responsibilities and own struggles with self-esteem, she did not recognize the need to come and fight for him. He was ashamed of his poverty, his stutter, of not being recognized for his academic achievement—of himself in general.

He would ask teachers to not call on him to read aloud, and offer to do any other kind of work in exchange. Most were happy to spare him the humiliation of stuttering in the spotlight of his classmates' attention, but one called on him anyway. Of course he stuttered and was ashamed, but worked out his rage with his fists on some poor kid whose crime was laughter—but who didn't really deserve it. That's when he discovered that he had a temper, and that unleashing it could make him forget how bad he felt—at least temporarily.

Then when he was in high school, people started to respond to him as if he were handsome. He'd spent his whole life thinking he was somewhere between funny-looking and downright ugly, and now he was suddenly desirable—even sexually! Sex was a much better escape from himself than fighting, though it never occurred to him that he was going from one physical form of acting out to another.

Practically overnight people's perception of him flew from one extreme to another: He started to work as a model, and kept doing it through high school and college. If you watch any of the makeover shows on TV, you might think that going from ugly duckling to model is about as close to having a fairy godmother grant your wildest wish as anyone can get, but the reality is a lot less wonderful than the dream. As Erich put it, "When other folks grade you exclusively on your looks, your gift can become your curse real fast. When people only look at you physically, it is easy to start to see yourself only in a physical sense. Once you do that, it's a short step to internalizing the gratification that comes with that; you can come to believe that the only real pleasure, the only real happiness, the only real fulfillment, is physical."

> Eddie went into show business headfirst. I went to the streets. But all my friends from back then are either dead or doing life, which is another form of death.
>
> —CHARLIE MURPHY,
> COMEDIAN AND ACTOR

For Erich, things only went right when people looked at him physically, which became the measure of his worth as a human being. Physical affirmation became his drug of choice, and he would do whatever it took to get his fix. He learned that control over his image meant control over

There's a big blank space in the Mike Tyson story. Mike has been depressed many times, and for long periods of time; he's a very lonely guy. When he was growing up there was no background of love, or teaching, or support. His life kept going but no nurturing was there. Then, when people realized he could fight, everyone was greedy for millions, for money—when they see Mike, all they see is dollar signs. From the very beginning people wanted him to fight, but they had no interest in creating a foundation for his emotional life and development.

Mike and I are from the same neighborhood; we've had the same kind of losses and the same kind of pain, so I could always talk to him. He's a man who needs a lot of love, just like any of us, but I think he gets less love than almost anyone. When things go wrong, he needs to be heard—it helps him deal with his manic depression.

I hate that when people look at Mike, all they see is the fighter, or the guy in the headlines; I hate that they don't see the human being—not just the man in pain, but the man who tries to help other people. He turned *my* life around. I'm a businesswoman, head of Jacqueline Rowe Public Relations, because of him.

—JACKIE ROWE

the terms of the relationship, and that could provide him with constant validation. Everything came to be about appearances. His life was full of putting on the good face. Underneath, though, he lived in fear of rejection, of not being enough, of not being validated. And any rejection was all he needed to act out.

At first he didn't see how sex could be a problem, because young and old men alike applaud sexual conquest, and our society actively promotes it. A man who can have sex with almost any woman he wants is cast in a positive light, even if his behavior can be reckless to the lives of the people around him—especially his partners. Sex in and of itself is not a bad thing, but when we become dishonest with our partners, or lose our sense of its natural place in our lives, it becomes a compulsion, an addiction.

And that is what happened to Erich. When things went wrong he turned to sex. He medicated pain with sex. It could be physical sex, cybersex, phone sex, or "merely" inappropriate talk with people. Married twice, he cheated on both wives. But just like with a drug, what used to get you high won't do the trick after a while, and you need to escalate. He did things—accepted as "male sexual behavior"—that he would have never done if he were not compulsive. "If you continually give in to your bad habits, you will go further than you ever thought possible, and suffer more than you deserve."

If he hated himself before, his sex addiction began to make him feel even worse. He went from feeling good about himself only when other people liked him to feeling worse when that happened, because now he knew he wasn't the person they liked. When the mother of his son would offer heartfelt expressions of love, he squirmed inside because he knew he wasn't the person she was talking about. When his son talked about wanting to be like him he would cry inside; it was all he could do not to scream "No!"

Even with all that, it took time for him to accept the possibility of his sexual addiction. At the end of his first marriage he actually went to a 12-step meeting for sex addicts, but he could not identify with the group he met with and thought it wasn't about him. He didn't understand the complexities of addiction as it related to sex. He didn't know he was an addict until his second marriage ended. His wake-up call came when he realized that his actions were painting a picture of him as a vile and disgusting person—that people saw him as hateful—and he lost the only woman he was ever in love with and the ability to have his son, whom he adores, in his life on a day-to-day basis. That's when he began to connect the dots and see the pattern of the addiction. He could not change how his now-estranged wife would see him, but he did not want his son to perceive him as others perceived him at the time, and he realized he would need help.

Suffering from deep depression, he started seeing a very good therapist, joined a 12-step program, and "prayed for help like nobody's business." He also sought medication to "detangle the wires," because he couldn't think straight. Once he stopped acting out sexually, he no longer felt out of control the way he used to, sex was no longer "the compass" by which he navigated his life. While the medication provided him with the clarity to see that sex had

> Self-acceptance is my refusal to be in an adversarial relationship to myself.
>
> —NATHANIEL BRAND,
> AUTHOR OF *THE SIX PILLARS*

been his previous drug of choice, used to ward off the intense depression that was at the root of his sense of self, it also made him lethargic and miserable at times.

Erich has been in recovery for two years now. He has stopped taking antidepressants, under the supervision of his doctor. He perseveres in the outpouring of his innermost thoughts in regular prayer for a "pure heart." He feels that he is less compulsive, but knows if he does not keep an eye on clear, honest communication with his partner, or persevere in prayer, his deception and/or not accepting the need for "strength beyond" his own ability will invariably lead to compulsive behavior again. One thing's for sure: he no longer sees sexual compulsions as an escape hatch out of depression. And he can now feel good when his son says "I want to be just like you when I grow up."

> The streets don't love no one, except those that devote all their time to it. And when the streets are finished with you, they dispose of you. Death or jail . . . your choice . . .
>
> —DASHAUN "JIWE" MORRIS,
> AUTHOR OF THE MEMOIR
> *WAR OF THE BLOODS IN MY VEINS*

Nathan Hughes, another good friend of mine who has also used sex as a way of numbing his feelings, summed the situation up theoretically. A professor of religion, he shared his story in the open forum at a conference in Atlanta. Like many men, he had always felt an intense craving for intimacy without being able to ask for it. What he could ask for, because the culture praises men for asking for it, was sex. Instead of intimacy, Nathan used sex as a way to feel close to people. Not only did sex provide a way of relating to women, but it also worked like a drug to keep him from having feelings of low self-esteem and loneliness. Too often men use sex instead of intimacy to meet their emotional needs. Unfortunately, it's like using gasoline to put out a fire. Instead of reducing the need, it only fuels the hunger. When Nathan became aware of the vicious cycle his impulses kept him running in, he decided to go into therapy. He knew there had to be a better way.

3. Acting Out with Violence

Mike Tyson was a smart and creative little boy, forced by his circumstances to hide his sensitivity, and turned as a young man into a raging, fighting animal. As an adult he continues to pay the price for years of not allowing himself to experience his true feelings.

When I spoke to Mike about his depression for this book, he had the

The prison-industrial complex is not only a set of interest groups and institutions. It is also a state of mind. The lure of big money is corrupting the nation's criminal-justice system, replacing notions of safety and public service with a drive for higher profits. The eagerness of elected officials to pass tough-on-crime legislation—combined with their unwillingness to disclose the external and social costs of these laws—has encouraged all sorts of financial improprieties.

—ERIC SCHLOSSER, *THE ATLANTIC MONTHLY*

courage to show a side of himself that the world never sees—a man who was broken by a brutal childhood; a man who, despite his physical strength, is still in pain; a man who has never truly healed. He told me about how his mom suffered from depression and how she made bad choices when it came to men. She died when he was fifteen, but before she did he saw her become an alcoholic who had sex in front of him and was beaten in front of him. She also took him for psychiatric evaluations before he was ten years old—maybe at some level she knew how much her actions were hurting him, even though she couldn't stop them. He has since been diagnosed as bipolar or manic-depressive, but his depression first started manifesting itself as sexual addiction. It started when he was eighteen and it's gotten bad enough that he's been treated for it in rehab.

"We get contaminated by our family members," Mike said. "I come from a sewage pipe. And because of my upbringing, I'm morbid with depression. I just want to die, or get high. I get high so much. I don't want to do nothing. I don't care about nothing. I've lost everything I've ever loved or cared about—me, my character, my wife, my kids. Every day I want to die." In fact, he told me, if it weren't for his kids, he would have killed himself by now. Luckily, as he put it, "If you really care about somebody, you want to live. I hold on for tomorrow."

In 1995, 16 percent of Black men in their twenties who did not attend college were in jail or prison; by 2004, 21 percent were incarcerated. By their mid-thirties, six in ten Black men who had dropped out of school had spent time in prison.

—ERIK ECKHOLM, *THE NEW YORK TIMES*

Dashaun "Jiwe" Morris, who I mentioned earlier, came into my life a couple of years ago. A Blood member since he was nine, he has a tender spirit, but he hasn't found a way to expose that side of himself to very many people. He has a beautiful smile that he rarely uses because in his own words he doesn't think he deserves to be alive most times. He is angry and disappointed with himself and constantly trying to find his place in a world he never knew existed outside of the one he grew up in. This is a young man who needs and wants to give love and he does this through mentoring. He is a born leader.

After reading a column I wrote in *F.E.D.S.* magazine called "The Human Side of Crime," he sent me a powerful e-mail about the work he and his friends have been doing to help end gang violence.

> You don't have to control your thoughts; you just have to stop letting them control you.

Most of America never see Bloods doing anything good, so they believe all the negative hype, but there are some of us out here who are making change, not only for ourselves, but [for] all those that we influence.

These days I sit in the mayor's office in Newark, New Jersey, discussing how to clean up the Blood problem in the streets of Newark. Since I am one of the most respected Bloods on the east coast, my word speaks volumes. People are so quick to judge me based on how I dress or speak, but what they don' know is that this past Valentine's day I used my own money to arrange a Feed the Homeless drive in Newark. About fifteen of my most decorated homies and I served spaghetti and handed out roses to the women. I also hosted a street cleanup a few months back where about fifty Bloods cleaned up one of the baddest blocks in Newark. I do my best to try and help my homies see that murder and drugs leads to death and the cell.

I lost my innocence at the age of nine and didn't find myself until the age of twenty-five. I was very suicidal in the past. I have suffered from depression for fifteen years and I have expressed it through violence.

Believe it or not, I wasn't born like this. I was born to be a loving creature, but my surroundings didn't encourage that lifestyle. Instead, they encouraged me to steal, rob, and kill. I put my life on the line for individuals I called my brothers, but truth be told, they are not brothers—not to me, not to each other, not to anyone else. They don't really love you. They love the service you provide.

Jiwe understands that we don't use violence; violence uses us. Acting out with violence can never leave us feeling better. The best it can do is distract us for a moment from the psychic wounds that are still bleeding in us, untreated.

Prison: Depression's Dead End . . .

I had a heartbreaking encounter with the penal system some time ago. Jiwe was on his way to meet me and have a therapy session with my friend David Grand. We were going to talk about how he wanted to get his life straight and help other gangbangers stop the vicious cycle of killing. He never made it to the meeting. That day he was wearing an RIP shirt in honor of a recently murdered homie, and he was carrying a gun, both violations of his parole. He was picked up by the police for parole violation and saw his whole life—all the positive things he had struggled for—go straight off the tracks.

There was a reason he was packing that day—not a great reason, but a reason all the same. One of his old crew found out who had killed their mutual friend and was going to murder the murderer. Jiwe went to talk him out of it, taking a piece with him *just in case.* He was successful—he convinced his homie not to keep the spiral of violence going—but that didn't carry any weight with the cops who picked him up.

A lot of people would say, "Well, he knew the rules and he decided to break them, so he had it coming to him." But those people assume that Jiwe is the picture of mental health, able to see the world in terms of pure reason and act on it accordingly. I don't know *anybody* who's that healthy, much less a young man struggling to claw his way out of hell. The reality is that, like his close friend Jay, he suffers every day from posttraumatic stress disorder, and even though he no longer uses or resorts to violence, the streets of Newark still have the power to invoke paranoia in him. As Jay said when he heard what happened, "I didn't even realize he was catching these phobias as bad as he was."

In the days after his arrest, I found myself grappling with what it meant. I thought about Neina, his fiancée, and his daughter, and the ways imprisonment destroys family life—how it challenges emotional bonds, creating a big divide between those of us who are truly alive in the culture and those who are almost the living dead. Even as I was using all my resources to fight for him, I was stunned by the feelings of despair and depression the situation aroused in *me*. The system is so much bigger than us as individuals, and it's so easy to feel helpless and hopeless as time goes on without anything getting better.

This particular incarceration hit me hard, but so many of the young men I meet and have mentored either have been through the criminal justice system, or see their future as eventually leading to its doors. Can you imagine the sense of hopelessness that this kind of thinking breeds? Now take that hopelessness and multiply it by the despair that is so often the revolving door of prison after you've been in once.

I receive so many letters from brothers in prison that all I have time to do is send a prayer or book and encourage them to believe and stay strong. These men tell me again and again that they feel abandoned, worthless, like slaves. Most of them know that the actions that put them behind bars were wrong, but felt like they had no choice. Once they're in prison, they see that no one is interested in their rehabilitation, so they fold more layers of pain over the pain that was already there; they become that much more hardened to their own humanity in an effort just to survive. If you think about it, how could anyone *not* be depressed in those circumstances?

I read a frightening statistic that said in the United States there are more mentally ill people in prison than in hospitals. According to Jamie Fellner, U.S. program director of Human Rights Watch, "Prisons have become the nation's primary mental health facilities." One in six U.S. prisoners is mentally ill; many of them suffer from bipolar disorder and major depression. The tragedy is not just that there are three times as many mentally ill people in prison as there are in the population, but that there are three times as many people with mental illness in prisons than there are in mental health facilities!

> Give of yourself only to those who deserve your help—not to everyone who needs it. You must preserve your spirit.
>
> —DR. HANAN ISLAM,
> DOCTOR OF NATURAL MEDICINE

So many young men are picked up for gun possession, but if we look at what happened with Jiwe, we can see that they are not always with an intent to commit violence. Sometimes—maybe often—carrying a gun is a response to the *fear* of violence. Don't get me wrong, guns are not the answer to anything! But, too often men are punished for responding to their emotional fears without being able to express those fears in any language except violence.

Tony Rose, publisher of Amber Communications Group, Inc., and executive producer of the TV show *Literary Living* on the Black Family Channel, shows us the horror of how several generations of one family can get sucked into the nightmare of the criminal justice system.

I am a product of the criminal justice system. Two of my four sons are caught up in the criminal justice system.

One son worked himself from doing one month, to three months, to six months, to one year, to three and a half years, to eight and a half years to life under New York State's three strikes law, which gives three-time felony offenders life imprisonment. He has been incarcerated in New York state now for fifteen years straight (except for when he escaped in 1995 for five days and went on a crime spree), all his young life wasted. On January 26, 2004, his parole was rejected. He was up again for parole on January 26, 2006, and was rejected. He will be eligible for parole again January 26, 2008.

> Befriending myself seems to be about opening my heart as a homeless shelter for all the destituted and prostituted aspects of my being that I have been running from for years without even knowing that's what I have been doing.
>
> —DAWNA MARKOVA,
> *I WILL NOT DIE AN UNLIVED LIFE*

The other son, through being in the wrong place at the wrong time and using bad judgment, lost a promising football scholarship. He was captain of his team and missed graduating from a prestigious school he'd been attending since first grade. We were able to save him from a three-and-a-half- to five-year sentence, but with probation and a lifetime stipulation. His life has changed forever.

I was born and raised in the criminal justice system. My father was a heroin drug user who spent thirty years of his adult life in and out of the criminal justice system. He was a gangster, a pimp, a hustler . . . an out-and-out criminal. He finally straightened up in his last twenty years. I loved him very much and buried him, as he wanted, strapped and ready.

My stepfather spent fifteen years in the criminal justice system for killing a man when he was nineteen. When I was twelve, he was released from prison, called my grandmother (my mother was his last girlfriend before prison), came over, and moved into our little project apartment. He was, in some ways, a good man; but, with incarceration, institutionalization, drugs, and medications, he was a ruined man. I was finally able to get him out of my mother's life fifteen years later.

My uncle was involved in a massive manhunt and shootout with the Boston police. After shooting and wounding a policeman, he tried to take his own life, and served fifteen years in prison, blind. My mother's family never recovered from that trauma in their lives. He ruined himself and ruined them forever.

I was raised in prison. The Whittier Street housing projects in Boston were run by former, or soon to be, inmates of the Massachusetts state prison and criminal justice systems. Everybody I knew had been in prison or was going to prison, men and women, boys and girls. Rape, robbery, insanity, death, drugs, and murder were a normal part of life. I have no childhood friends from that project, from that time, because they either died in prison, still are in prison, were killed committing a felony, died as victims, or are outside still living in prison in their minds.

I, myself, have been jailed. I was in gangs as a teenager, lived in the ghetto and did stupid things, little things that would get me jailed here and there. My father was actually proud of me and began grooming and instructing me for The Life. Of course, I was jailed, it was all I knew and somehow it seemed right. My longest stretch was a week in the Los Angeles County Jail and criminal justice system, when I was in my early twenties, for a DWI, traffic infractions. I pled hard before the judge, explained where I had come from, what had brought me to Los Angeles, and where I was going. I pled hard, but I never pled guilty, my father had taught me that. I was released, went to my apartment, moved, leaving no forwarding addresses, and never went back to jail again.

Out of My Mind and Mad at the World

This story of Larry Stonehurst, born in a Louisiana ghetto, is painfully typical of the prison letters I receive every week.

By the age of ten Larry was regularly getting into fights. "I was sad and always in tears, very brokenhearted and depressed, even though I didn't have a clue as to what I was going through." By fourteen he was involved in petty crimes and abusing alcohol and marijuana. He was suspended from school and ultimately kicked out of the house by his mother (also a depression sufferer).

By sixteen Larry was a crack addict; that same year he tried to commit suicide. His mother had him committed to a psychiatric ward, but he was there only six days before being released. The experience was crushing: Not only did he feel separated as one of the few Black people in the ward, but he also felt rejected and outcast by the staff.

Back on the street, he turned to crack once again, and before long he was arrested for armed robbery. "I was out of my mind on crack and mad at the world, and I almost killed a guy I was getting a ride from." The man ran from his car, understandably, but then claimed that Larry had stolen his car. Who would believe the truth from a crack addict fresh out of the psych ward?

Prison life was as hard and horrifying as life on the streets. Larry served two and a half years and was released, but five months later was arrested again, for gun possession. A gun he had purchased because life in the streets left him fearing for his life every day. This time the prison he was sent to was rougher than the first. The violence was so extreme that he ended up stabbing another prisoner in self-defense and being rebooked for aggravated battery. He was then transferred to the notorious Angola State Prison.

By the time of his second release, his mother's ongoing depression had escalated to cocaine and alcohol abuse, and a suicide attempt of her own. With his mother hospitalized, Larry found himself homeless. For a time he found employment and things were looking up, but then trouble struck again and he found himself under house arrest. It became almost impossible for him to support himself and the stress led him right back to crack. This time the addiction was more ferocious than ever, and he says he felt more and more paranoid. In one paranoid episode he shot at police while on his bike, and finally found himself in a six-hour standoff with the police in his girlfriend's apartment.

Once Larry was back in prison, his girlfriend, who works in a brain injury unit at a hospital, asked one of the physicians to review his file. He determined that Larry suffers from bipolar manic depressive disorder (a kind of depression where you swing from intense highs to intense lows), a condition that does much to explain his drive to self-medicate and his continual cycle in and out of prison. But the condition is not acknowledged in prison, much less addressed, and if it continues to go untreated, it will only get worse and worse. This is truly the dead end of depression. Without treatment, without hope of treatment, the depressed in prison seem to have only two possibilities, each as bad as the other: explosion or implosion. In other words, they will either take out their anguish against others or against themselves.

Life After Life

Evans Derrell Hopkins was born into a middle-class family in Danville, Virginia, a model of segregation in the twilight years of Jim Crow. At sixteen he joined the Black Panther Party and upon graduation from high school moved to Oakland, California, where the party was headquartered. He wrote for the newspaper, was party historian, and participated in numerous activities (including party founder Bobby Seale's campaign for mayor of Oakland). He left the party in 1974, when COINTELPRO (the FBI-sponsored "vigilante operation" against groups the Bureau believed posed a violent threat to the country) had fostered dissension and helped cause the Panthers to collapse from within.

"Depression and mental illness helped destroy the party. Huey Newton suffered from depression and paranoia. I guess after you've been shot three times and sent to prison and all the spy agencies of the Western world are spying on you and either trying to kill you or have others among you try to kill you, it could lead to paranoia and self-medication. It tore Huey apart, and many of those around him."

Having left Danville with the fiery zeal of the righteous, he came back disillusioned, with his dreams and values in ashes. A young father, broke, with poor prospects made poorer in his own mind by stress and depression, his hopelessness let him gamble everything: He tried to rob a bank. "I may have acted when I was young because of the pressures of becoming

125

a father, and felt like robbing a bank instead of seeking help. At the time I thought that was an acceptable way of getting out of that situation. Part of the culture of rage. Young people see the world as hard and harsh against them—gangsta rap plays right into that." Given life for armed robbery, he spent the next two decades behind bars.

In prison he saw depression all around him, and as much emotional implosion as explosion. "I had a very good friend, my best friend in prison. He was a fairly dangerous guy, two life sentences when he was sixteen. He said he didn't get depressed, but when his girl broke up with him they found him with a plastic bag over his head and a cord around his neck. Some of the men believed he was killed because he was larger than life, but those of us who knew him best believed it was just what it looked like, that he committed suicide. Maybe he just gave up on it, or maybe the rage made him figure he would end it all as a revenge against the world that had rejected him."

But prison suicide was so common that it hardly got noticed, and that was only the most obvious kind. "There are all sorts of suicides. I was told after my first crime that many bank robberies are committed by middle-class men as a form of social suicide to escape the lives that they live. Our youth are being bombarded with messages like 'get rich or die trying.' Very few of them are going to get rich, so what happens after that? They commit crimes and know they are going to prison; they're committing social suicide the same way I did. It's hard with men, because we don't think about that as a reaction to depression."

I see a lot of our young people who are depressed. They don't know they're depressed. They've basically thrown in the towel. They just don't have the energy. If you looked at them you'd say, "Well, you don't care." You know that's what people say to kids all the time, "You don't care about anything." Why don't they care about anything? Well, what are the signs that someone is depressed? For one, this sense of giving up, this sense of a lack of energy. Part of the challenge in reaching young people is understanding the degree to which they feel totally disconnected.

—GEOFFREY CANADA, RENOWNED EDUCATOR AND AUTHOR OF
FIST, STICK, KNIFE, GUN: A PERSONAL HISTORY OF VIOLENCE IN AMERICA

Out of prison for a decade now, Evans became a writer while still behind bars and has kept writing ever since, as a journalist and as the author of a powerful memoir, *Life After Life: A Story of Rage and Redemption*. He has also returned to his activist roots, but with emphasis on mental health, in Richmond, Virginia, where he now lives with his wife.

"A lot of middle-class Black parents wonder why their kids are doing a lot less well than they were able to do. I'm trying to work against it with the Reclamation Movement I've founded, a national effort to reclaim our young people from the culture of the streets, and to also reclaim former prisoners from the revolving door of incarceration. In both groups we're addressing mental health and depression. Just being able to acknowledge our mental health problems is the first step toward dealing with it."

Four million children and adolescents in this country suffer from a serious mental disorder that causes significant functional impairments at home, at school, and with peers. It is estimated that one in 10 children and adolescents suffers from mental illness severe enough to cause some level of impairment. However, in any given year, it is estimated that fewer than one in five of such children receives needed treatment.

An alarming 65 percent of boys and 75 percent of girls in juvenile detention have at least one mental disorder. We are incarcerating youth with mental disorders, some as young as eight years old, rather than identifying their disorders early and intervening with appropriate treatment. Mental health is an essential component of young peoples' overall health and well-being. It affects how young people think, feel, and act; their ability to learn and engage in relationships; their self-esteem and ability to evaluate situations [and] options and make choices. People's mental health influences their ability to handle stress, relate to other people, and make decisions.

—GLENN ELLIS, HEALTH EDUCATOR, COLUMNIST, AUTHOR OF
WHICH DOCTOR? WHAT YOU NEED TO KNOW TO BE HEALTHY, EXECUTIVE EDITOR OF
BLACKDOCTOR.ORG, AND PRESIDENT OF STRATEGIES FOR WELL-BEING

Chapter Four

IT'S A HARD KNOCK LIFE

The Young and the Depressed

I have always believed strongly in the rights of young people. In fact, there has never been a time in my adult life that I haven't had regular—often weekly—contact with kids through a youth group or organization; for the past five years it's been through my Stay Strong Foundation. I've always been able to sense when children are in pain, even when I was a child my-

Five Reasons I Give Back or "Recycle the Inspiration"

• I believe in Karma; what goes around comes around.
• It makes me feel good about myself.
• People give to me so I understand what a blessing it is to receive.
• Working with young people is an investment in our future as a people.

self. For as long as I can remember I have felt for the teenagers I knew in foster care who couldn't communicate their suffering. Maybe this was because I understood from the inside what it's like not to give voice to one's emotions. I didn't know it then, but their inability to say what they felt was mine, and so was their pain. I was able to reach out to them and offer help. But I wasn't able to reach out to others who might help me.

Since I've recognized my own depression, my feeling for these kids has grown tenfold, and so have my efforts to speak to young adults about mental health and my journey. They are often amazed to hear a grown-up talk about pain, suffering, and being vulnerable. We tend

> People can be slave-ships in shoes.

to act like we have it all together, but even though their instincts tell them we're fronting, children learn and grow from hearing an adult admit to having troubles. They learn that speaking your truth, tears, and asking for help is really a sign of strength. That's real and genuine role modeling. For me, there is nothing more gratifying than reaching a child in trouble. My hope is that this chapter will help professionals and parents do just that.

The biggest stumbling block to treating youth depression is that we ignore the signs of pain until the symptoms become public problems—instead we use catchall terms like "at risk" that mask how many teens are actively suffering the effects of depression. Depression in young people is *ten times* more common than it was two generations ago. Since 1980 the rate of suicide for Black boys from ages fifteen to nineteen has skyrocketed. A study reported in *The New York Times* showed that in 342 detention centers around the country there were 15,000 emotionally disturbed teens with no mental health care resources to address their psychological issues. What happens to them? They're warehoused in juvenile centers and prisons. Untreated depression is increasing in children and showing up at younger and younger ages. I shudder to think about how many *more* depressed adults there will be in ten years.

> If we don't give our kids time, the system will.
>
> —STAY STRONG FOUNDATION MOTTO

Wake-up Call

Stop. Hold that thought, whatever it is. Whatever you were thinking the moment before you turned to this page, put it on hold and try to take this one in: Young people are challenged and suffer from depression. That's right, even little kids. If you're with me already, then you know where I'm going with this; if not, if this sounds kind of funny to you ("Little kids depressed? Come on, now, Terrie, that's pushin' it . . ."), then think about this:

According to David G. Fassler and Lynne Dumas's thoughtful book *Help Me, I'm Sad: Recognizing, Treating, and Preventing Childhood and Adolescent Depression,* "children, who are just learning how to express the many emotions they feel, may communicate their distress very differently from adults. Very young children who don't yet have the verbal skills to put their feelings into words may never say, 'I'm feeling down' or 'I feel like there's no hope left.' Instead, they often act out their upset by behaving in ways that look very unlike what we think of as 'depression.' But a child who bullies his baby sister, picks fights at school, or suddenly suffers frequent and unexplained aches and pains may be expressing his pain just as surely as the child who becomes tearful and withdrawn."

That's why I say that if we want to deal effectively with depression, with this affliction that plagues us as a people, we have to go right to where it starts: we have to go right to childhood. We never get tired of talking about how children are our future, and we shouldn't ever stop, because those aren't empty words. But unless we take children more seriously as fully human beings (that means having them at the table with us!)—and take the issues that trouble them just as seriously—we are dooming them to repeat the worst pains of our own lives.

If you didn't think depression hit children and teenagers, or it never even occurred to you before you started reading this chapter, you had plenty of company. Before 1980, there was no official diagnosis of childhood depression—mental health professionals didn't even have a category for it, and with the society so blind to depression overall, we regular folks sure weren't seeing it in our kids. The basic reason for that particular blindness goes way beyond our ideas about mental health; it starts in the ways we, as a society, devalue children—we don't take them seriously as thinking, feeling human beings; we do not honor how complicated their lives are and how they view the world. To put it bluntly, by the time we've been adults for a while we develop ideas about kids and teenagers that are seriously prejudiced—if you took our unexamined thoughts about young people and labeled them "what adults think about kids," then kept the same thoughts but changed the label to "what white people think about Black people," you would say our ideas were racist!

Many years ago there was a TV show called *Kids Are People, Too*. The title may sound a little hokey at first, but if you think about it, the idea is actually revolutionary. The fact is, for thousands of years and right up to the present, adults have not believed that kids are as human as adults are. They don't have the same human rights, they don't have the same civil rights, they don't have the same legal rights—after all, if you haul off and smack an adult,

> Nothing has a stronger influence psychologically on their environment, and especially on their children, than the unlived lives of the parents.
>
> –CARL JUNG,
> PSYCHIATRIST AND AUTHOR

you can wind up in court, but if you give your child the same treatment, the abuse has to be significant before the law will step in.

The bottom line is that kids *are* people. They have the same range of feelings that we have, the same capacity for joy, the same capacity for hurt; I would even argue that, since they haven't had nearly enough practice at numbing themselves out, they have the ability to feel even *more* deeply than adults do. We may like to think of them as shielded from many of the concerns we have to deal with, and they probably should be, but many of our young people have to deal with questions of survival every day (too many are soldiers fighting a war on the streets), and none of them is protected from feelings of fear, sadness, confusion, and desperation. Basically, kids have *all* the same problems we have, but fewer resources—internal or external—to fall back on. Is it any wonder that depression is growing faster among young people than in any other age group?

If you have to reckon with depression, there's a good chance you had to deal with it before, even if you didn't know it by name, because depression in childhood increases the likelihood of depression in adulthood. Even though nobody means for it to happen this way, the army of wounded adults starts recruiting very early. If we don't see it, it's in part because of the reasons I've been talking about here, but also because depression in young people can look different from how it looks in us.

The Sins of the Parents Are Visited on the Children

Our children grow up looking at everything we do, and learning from it, too—whether we want them to or not. No matter how many times we say those famous words, "Do as I say, not as I do," we shouldn't kid ourselves—we should *expect* our young people to watch and learn from our dysfunction. No matter how much you may want to protect your child from life's difficulties, if you are depressed, addicted, not around a lot, or violent, you are creating a direct legacy of pain, addiction, absence, and violence in your child's life. Now wait—don't get defensive. I am not out here to blame or condemn anybody, least of all parents.

Life is damn hard, and parenting is even harder. It's tough enough for a single person with no dependents to lead a life that's healthy, mindful, and spiritually strong (I should know—I'm working my tail off at it, and I've still got a long way to go!). If you try to lead that kind of life when you've got people who depend on you for their lives—their food and shelter and clothing, but also their basic daily lessons about *how* to live—you must feel sometimes like you're climbing Mount Everest on roller skates. I'm willing to bet that some of the most successful people in our world today may be the worst freakin' parents on earth—or they may have avoided parenting altogether because they knew they couldn't do a good job!

Let me give you a horrific example of what happens when we're not up to the task of parenting. I was taking the subway one day when I saw a young Black woman with her son. The boy was about five years old. The young woman looked tired, and I could tell she was stressed. Her son had a lively personality and was still in a boundary-testing phase, because each time she told him to sit down he giggled and jumped farther away. Exasper-

Within dysfunctional families the tendency is to have subtle rules regarding secrecy which ensures that family members continue to have their emotional needs not met. For example, the message is given that you do not go outside of the family to ask for help and expose the family's deficiencies. Another unspoken rule is that it is not safe to express feelings openly or honestly; therefore, pain can go unnoticed and unattended by school, church, or social services. Generally as a means of survival these family members adopt and conform to unhealthy roles within the family system as a way of coping. Some of these roles include the child as "caretaker" (the selfless one), or the family hero, protector, or martyr, or peacemaker and pleaser (constant approval seeking). A common element in abusive families is that these parents with unmet needs in childhood try to meet those needs through their children; generally this is unsuccessful, which further perpetuates the vicious cycle.

—DR. CLAUDETTE RODNEY, PSYCHOLOGIST

ated, she snatched him by the arm and pulled him into the seat next to her. The boy was startled and looked around. I could tell he felt embarrassed to be treated this way in front of strangers. Trying to salvage his five-year-old manhood, he defiantly stood up again. The mother reached the end of her rope and yelled at him to sit down. When he angrily refused she slapped him upside his head, saying, "Nigga, you ain't shit, now sit your behind down." The interaction took my breath away and everyone in the subway car shifted uncomfortably. But the real casualty was the boy. I could feel a little part of him dying inside. The public humiliation coupled with his mother's brutal words left him crying in his seat. I was crying in my own. I understand how exhausting parenting is and how hard it is to manage a child who's willful and bright and willing to talk back, but nothing can ever jus-

Please be advised that the N-word is profanity. Listen to someone's conversation who uses the N-word and see how profanity soon follows. Words are very POWERFUL! Become conscious of what you say, and see how your environment improves. Help our children by thinking before you speak. Most of all RESPECT YOURSELF!

—TONYA ELLINGTON, PROMOTER, AND

tify lashing out verbally or hitting a child! I shudder to think what else this little boy had to endure.

At the youth homes, juvenile detention centers, and prisons where I speak, I see the end result of what happens to the children of parents who are in pain. I see boys and girls who look up to gang members, who feel worthless and suicidal, who don't think they deserve love or kindness or consideration, boys and girls who grow up without the love they need to become good parents themselves, who think violence is the price of love.

> Use the gifts and resources that are uniquely yours to recycle inspiration . . . because no dream should be thrown away.

I am trying to make us aware of how our actions play out in the lives of our kids. I want us to have choices for ourselves so we *can* have choices for our kids. I love to quote those airline safety instructions: "Put on your own oxygen mask before placing the mask on your child—or somebody acting like a small child." In other words, you ain't helpin' *no*body else breathe if you yourself cain't breathe! Make sure *you* can breathe if you want to help

From the ages of five to eighteen, I grew up in orphanages and foster homes. The emotional scars are deep and lifelong. I got no nurturing, no sense of confidence, no self-esteem, and no real sense of identity. I never felt good enough, smart enough or able enough. I went to a vocational school and got a degree in woodworking because no one believed in me or encouraged me.

When I witness the gangbanging, pimping and hoe-ing, I know it is because our kids don't know who they are. And they don't know because we parents never told them. Once our kids figure it out, their lives will change.

—GEORGE C. FRASER, AUTHOR OF
SUCCESS RUNS IN OUR RACE: THE COMPLETE GUIDE TO EFFECTIVE NETWORKING IN THE BLACK COMMUNITY

someone else with *their* breathing.

The first step we can take is to not lie to them. That may sound easy or hard, depending on how you think about talking with kids. If you believe you are always honest with them, then great. If you believe kids can only handle so much information, or only certain kinds—that you have to "manage" what truths they get and how often—you may want to rethink your strategy. If, for example, there are

> Erik Erikson said that one of the most deadly sins of all is the mutilation of a child's spirit. Take a child under your wing, it will be a gift to both of you.
>
> —MARIE K. WILLIAMS,
> COMMUNITY AND YOUTH/PARENT ADVOCATE,
> MOUNT VERNON, NY

things you hold back because you're not exactly proud of them (an extramarital affair, gambling losses, drug use, etc.), and you're telling yourself "They wouldn't understand," the real reason you're holding back might be that you have some negative feelings about those things yourself—it could be a signal to think about whether or not you want to keep doing something you feel uncomfortable discussing with the young people in your life. If there are things you hold back because you want to spare your kid the sadness or suffering of knowing about hard things (money worries, health concerns, grief, problems between you and your partner), you might want to look at how that holding back affects you, the child, and your relationship. Trust me, they know *something* is going on.

Sylvia Milom, a dynamic young woman who for years was the personal assistant of a good friend of mine, is a whip-smart sister and later became an executive at a branding company. But before she took control of her life, there were many years when she was a social cocaine user and sometime pill popper.

Sylvia was twenty-three when her son Curtis was born, and the pressure of being a single mother with no real social support felt overwhelming. "I was an only child. My mother had passed from breast cancer when I was twenty-one. My father remarried three years later and moved to Texas, so I rarely saw him. One of the reasons I didn't want to have an abortion was because I felt that, with no real family in my life, a child would be a blessing."

Curtis *was* a blessing, but raising him was also a lot of stress for a young

Too often our Black sons and daughters are being treated differently from their non-Black peers in school. Parents must recognize the signs of discrimination and be able to step in on their child's behalf to make sure that he or she is treated fairly and afforded the same opportunities as fellow students. Three important but subtle forms of discrimination to look for in the educational system are: (1) discouraging class participation or not allowing black children to express themselves (a teacher ignoring an eager, enthusiastic, intelligent Black child's attempt to answer a question or characterizing the child's consistent eagerness to answer questions as "selfish and inconsiderate" to the other students); (2) insensitivity to and perpetuation of negative stereotypes (assigning the "bad guy" role of thief or prisoner in the school play to the only Black student in the classroom); and (3) failure to inform Black parents about special opportunities for children who are excelling academically, such as early exposure to college admission tests, educational internships, and scholarship opportunities.

—DARA P. RICHARDSON-HERON, MD, CHIEF MEDICAL OFFICER,

woman without a career. "I took a job as a hostess at a fancy restaurant in the city so I'd only have to work nights and I could be with Curtis during the day. The pay was good, but often after shifts, late at night, the crew would ask me out for a few hours to play, and you could be sure there was always lots of good cocaine. I didn't mean to start using, but I was so tired that it helped me feel up, like I was on top of things."

Unfortunately, after a year she started taking a little bit before work so she'd be "up," and sometimes in the middle of the day, so she could keep up with Curtis, by then a very active toddler.

When I look back on it, Curtis was only a baby, but I swear he knew when I was using. He used to ignore me a lot more when I was high, like he knew I wasn't really there. It hurt me to realize that, but I was in the throes of addiction and couldn't stop.

Then, when Curtis was almost four, I met Ira. I liked him so much—I liked *myself* so much when I was with him—that the fear of losing him finally made me stop. I've been clean for over five years now, one day at a time, and I'm not clean for Ira—I'm clean for me.

Life has been very good to me since then, and I'm very grateful.

My only regret is that I didn't stop sooner, for Curtis. He's seven. A few months ago we were talking about people doing drugs and he said, "Like when you used to get high." That blew me away. I asked him how he knew, and he just kind of shrugged. Then I asked him how he felt about it. He didn't answer me but he hugged me tight and said, "I love you, Mommy." When I think about him knowing that I was using, I feel so ashamed of myself. Kids know everything. If you think otherwise, you're only fooling yourself—'cause you can't fool your own child.

Kids are smarter than we think—always. If we're keeping something secret from them, they know about it. They may or may not know all the details of the secret, but they know there *is* a secret, and they usually think it's for one of two reasons, if not both: Either it's because we don't trust them, or it's because we're concealing something shameful. Either way, kids see secrets as lies; believing that they're being lied to—no matter how good the reason—makes something curdle in their hearts and spirits. What doesn't do that, what makes them grow, is the truth.

Despite what we tell ourselves, kids can handle pain, sorrow, grief, disappointment, and all kinds of unhappy feelings; they don't enjoy the feelings any more than we do, but they can deal with them—especially if what we do and show them are healthy ways of dealing with what's hard in life. What makes them suffer is having pain denied, whether it's theirs or ours; what makes them suffer is being lied to. Showing yourself as an adult who has *real* problems but deals with them is a far greater gift to your child than pretending life is just great but acting like you're carrying an unbearable burden.

I said before that the kids of depressed parents are ten times likelier to suffer from depression than kids who don't have a parent who's depressed. Ten times! How's that for a reason to put on your own oxygen mask and take care of yourself? It's sad enough if for whatever reasons we don't try to deal in a healthy way with this disease in ourselves, but *damning* our kids with it? I don't know a parent alive who would do that to a child—that is, I don't know a parent alive who would do that *on purpose*. But how many of us are doing it without even knowing it?

Like it or not, everything we do (like smoking or lying) is an example to the young people in our care (children, grandchildren, stepchildren, foster children—the label doesn't matter). Depression is a dangerous example to give them. Kids watch us *so* closely, and if they see nothing but our hopelessness, our sadness, our inability to motivate ourselves or connect to other people, we are basically telling them, "Look—see what I'm doing? This is how you deal with life's stresses." The same thing goes for domestic violence, whether we're doing it or receiving it; the same thing goes for drug and alcohol abuse, whether or not we think we're addicted; the same thing goes for child abuse, whether we're abusing or letting it happen. And when we behave this way for them day after day, month after month, year in and year out, a million orders to "Do as I say, not as I do" will not be enough to undo the training they've been given to become the depressed adults, the alcoholic or addicted adults, the abusive or abused adults of tomorrow. The children *are* our future.

* * *

Parents who are drug users and addicts are usually self-involved and unreliable at best; at worst, they can be flat-out guilty of neglect. Whether heavy or light users, they teach us addictive behavior as a way of coping with life's ups and downs.

> If you deliberately plan to be less than you are capable of being, then I warn you that you will be deeply unhappy for the rest of your life.
>
> —ABRAHAM MASLOW, PSYCHOLOGIST AND AUTHOR

Reggie Hatchett is a gifted young man I mentor who became a close friend. Now a teacher and a community activist in Hartford, he spoke with me about the depression that affected his teenage years.

Reggie's mother has been a drug addict all his life; he also has never lived with his mom, though he was taken in by his *great*-grandparents. He never spent more than a couple of weeks at a time with his mother—she could never stay clean that long and was in and out of jail throughout his whole childhood. When he was in tenth grade, she tested HIV positive; in the years since then she hasn't given herself the care she needed, and she now lives in a shelter for people with HIV.

Soon after Reggie heard about his mother's HIV status, his great-grandfather, whom he loved dearly, had a stroke. He lived for several years more, but he was only a shell of the man he had once been—as Reggie says, "It was like seeing Superman die." The home that had once been his shelter now became a space of fear and uncertainty, sickness and looming death. Aside from the fact that it was often in a chaotic state, he came home each day wondering if his great-grandfather would still be alive.

Reggie started to have trouble sleeping—serious trouble. No matter how busy he had been during the stay with schoolwork and basketball, no matter how exhausted physically and emotionally, he couldn't get to sleep. "I'd think about stuff going wrong, stuff I didn't have, stuff I needed and how I would get them. I would lie down at 2:00 A.M. and not fall asleep till 7:00 A.M. Then I'd oversleep and miss classes. The lack of sleep made me feel sluggish and affected my energy level. I was mentally tired." It got so bad that he had to repeat his senior year because he'd been marked absent for all the days when he'd missed the morning attendance, and failed the classes he never made it to.

In the middle of this nightmare, he got lucky. People at his school didn't just assume that he was another Black boy on his way to being a statistic; they noticed that this bright young man who had always been an all-around achiever was starting to fall apart, and they sent him to counseling. Once his counselor diagnosed him as depressed, Reggie was able to begin the work of bringing himself back from the abyss.

Here is a poem Reggie ("Water" when he writes) wrote in response to seeing a Stay Strong Foundation screening of the movie *Antwone Fisher*—the story of so many young people. Fox Searchlight execs were so touched by the poem that they featured it in full-page ads they placed in *The New York Times* and the *Los Angeles Times* to promote the film.

SOMEBODY PLEASE . . . LISTEN!
BY WATER

*When I was younger my teachers would always tell me I made too
     much noise,*
But I was only considered a minor nuisance because "boys will be boys."
*I always wanted to be the class clown or the kid with the quickest tem-
     per,*
*Yeah, I guess you can say I craved attention for as long as I can remem-
     ber.*
*You may have seen me in the principal's office or even had me in your
     class,*
*You may have whispered under your breath, "Somebody needs to
     whoop his ass."*
I may have made you clinch your fists or even grit your teeth,

I think sometimes we overlook all the images and messages that are sent to the youth at such an early and impressionable stage. Such messages, especially those that are negative or stereotypical, can greatly impact the self-esteem and self-worth of young people of color.

In the 1940s Dr. Kenneth and Mamie Clark conducted a "doll test" in which Black children were given both a Black and white doll and asked about their preference. The majority of the children preferred the white doll. This was said to demonstrate the effects of racism and segregation. In 2005 I decided to reconduct this test for my film entitled *A Girl Like Me*. The film focused on the standards of beauty imposed on today's Black girls and how certain standards affect our self-esteem and self-image. Sadly the test results for the new "doll test" were very similar to the original. The results did, however, help the film to illustrate how Black children as young as four and five already know what society values . . . and they know it's not them. Through the journey of making the film I realized how damaging certain messages are to both our physical and mental health. I've also discovered the importance of not allowing others to define you. Instead we must define and celebrate ourselves even when we aren't celebrated by mainstream society. It is also important to acknowledge that these types of issues still exist today and therefore they can't just be pushed under the table. We have to realize that we can never fully heal these scars if we continue to hide them.

—KIRI DAVIS, EIGHTEEN-YEAR-OLD AWARD-WINNING FILMMAKER OF *A GIRL LIKE ME*

But did you ever stop to think to yourself "What really lies beneath?"
I tried to get your attention with anger, and you had security beat me
　　down,
I tried to get your attention with laughter, and you labeled me a clown.
I tried to get your attention with crazy hairstyles; you told me I looked
　　absurd,
I tried to get your attention with grades, and my peers called me a nerd.
I tried to shut down and appear uninterested; you told me I had ADD,
So I tried to be hyper and energetic, you had the guards come and
　　medicate me.
I tried to start conversations; you told me you didn't have the time,

I made myself good in sports and all you saw were dollar signs.
I tried becoming a slouch, that made me unhealthy and heavy,
I tried promiscuity that made me a father before I was ready.
I tried drugs and alcohol, that made me even more sad,
I tried hanging with the wrong crowd and you told me I'd be just like
    my dad.
The few times you offered your help, it was only for a minute,
Because loving me wasn't convenient, your heart truly wasn't in it.
I guess you wanted me to jump for joy, be happy and accept it,
Well excuse me for being a skeptic but I'm used to being neglected.
I'm not so easy with my trust, which is sad for a child to say,
But I've reached for too many extended hands that were only snatched
    away.
So finally I tried running away hoping someone would find,
And since you never seemed to have enough, the system gave me time.
Now, this was just an illustration of the pain that people don't see,
No child is gonna come up to you with a sign that reads, "Help me!"
But they're out there in your path and you see them every day,
Most of them slip through the cracks and slowly drift away.
Our children are being ignored, neglected from the day they are born,
They may be screaming out for help, but in a non-verbal form.
So extend your hands and open your heart and give redemption a try,
You have no idea what that child could be, or who you let pass you by.
The next Malcolm X, the next Tupac Shakur or the next Muhammad
    Ali,
Or think about if it had happened to you, I wrote this because it hap-
    pened to me.

"Harmless" Neglect

So far I've been focusing on things parents *do* that can sow the seeds for future depression in their children, but there are other, less obvious ways we may steer our young toward painful lives. We can also sow seeds by the things we *don't* do.

It isn't only absent parents who are uninvolved in their children's lives. Sometimes parents who live with their children check out from them without even knowing it. They might see themselves as very focused on their children, but be obsessed with markers of success, like sports or academics,

Depression is a silent killer in the youth community. It kills esteem, it kills motivation, and it kills dreams. But it is only able to destroy these things because it kills hope. And in a world where so many young people already exist in environments where they are not expected to make it, we now have hopelessness on top of hopelessness.

These conditions turn our community's best into candidates for suicide—for no other reason than because we fail to accept and address depression in young people as real. If we can spiritually, emotionally, and psychologically address and treat depression, we will witness a resurrection of hope in our children that will not only save their lives, but also change the future for the better.

and ignore the emotional realities of their children's lives.

Sometimes we're so aware of the ugliest forms of racism that we forget how subtle it can be, and we don't think about the ways "undercover" racism can affect young people. Goals, ambitions, and dreams deferred because kids believe the negative messages they are sent, or because someone discriminates against them, can lead to depression in kids. And it doesn't matter if these messages are more "subtle" than the classic lynching/beating/terrorizing variety of race hatred—in fact, the less obvious it is, the more powerful the negative effects can be. This is why it's so important that we be watchful about what's going on with and around our kids. Not paying sharp and daily attention to what's important to your child, how he or she is doing in school, or what his or her ambitions are, can be experienced by the child as a form of abandonment—and that abandonment can lead to depression. We as Black parents *must* always be on the lookout for these subtle forms of racism that undermine our kids' self-esteem. We often forget that kids are every bit as complicated as we are, because they're little and they use smaller words—and because it's all too easy to ignore their complexity when we're busy or overtaxed. As busy as we are, we need

It was books that taught me that the things that tormented me most were the very things that connected me with all the people who were alive, or who had ever been alive.

—JAMES BALDWIN, AUTHOR

to be careful each day not to let that happen—that accidental dismissal can reinforce the way American culture already devalues Black kids, and feed into a sense of themselves as less worthy.

Take Janelle Robins, the only child of an insurance executive and a corporate lawyer. Her parents were the first in their families to attend college, and their career success is the pride of both families. Driven and motivated people who expect the same drive in their daughter, they both work seventy-hour weeks. Janelle attends an elite, predominantly white school in New York City where she is one of only a handful of Black students. The racism there is subtle, but very present: Two teachers assumed she was a scholarship kid, a classmate told her that she got into the school because she was Black, and a guidance counselor suggested that Janelle's being Black would give her an advantage over her "highly" qualified peers getting into a good college. Her senior year she developed an ulcer. The stress of staying on the honor roll, applying to Ivy League colleges, and continually meeting her parents' expectations, in addition to the stress of being "the only one" at school, left her feeling tired, socially uninterested, and withdrawn.

This is one of the high costs of integration. Parents like Janelle's are rightly proud of their children's achievements, but because they are cut off from their own pain and stress at being "the only ones," they often fail to see the pain and stress that their children experience.

And this brings me to a related point. College students are an important group to watch for the symptoms of depression. I read a University of Michigan Health Minute Update and learned that as many as 15 percent of college students may have symptoms of depression, and about 10 percent (like Janelle) come to college already having experienced depression. John Greden, MD, executive director of the University of Michigan Depression Center, says, "[It's] a huge problem in the college student population. The age of onset for depressive illnesses tends to peak during the ages of fifteen to nineteen." An American College Health Association study found that 93.8 percent of college students feel "psychologically overwhelmed"—ripe ground for depression to start. So college is an important time to identify depression and get treatment because untreated depression will most likely lead to future episodes.

In the generation since white folks adopting Black kids went from being acceptable to being almost the norm, many white couples have believed that they were striking a blow against racism by adopting a child who didn't

"I grew up in a foster home because my father molested my oldest sister when I was six years old," Game recalls. "We got split up, and that was ultimately why I am as fucked up as I am today. I stayed there until I was in high school. That shit was like a kiddie prison. Ceramic floors. White sheets on the bed. Fucking oatmeal for breakfast for ten years. My mom tried to visit me every chance she got, but when you are a ward of the court, you are dealing with a lot of sanctions and welfare workers. It's a lot of drama." Twenty years later, you can still hear the pain of his childhood in The Game's voice. "That fucked my relationship up with my parents, especially my mom. Everything is still fucked up. I don't talk to my mom or dad right now. Sometimes that's how things roll. Family can be your worst enemy. It's fucked up because when you've made it to where I am, it would be great to have them in my life. But when you grow up in a broken home separated from your sister, mom in the courts and dad out in the streets, that's not no family, man. That's why my son is growing up with me and will know the deal."

—*THE SOURCE*, DECEMBER 2006, NO. 205

look like them racially. While their intentions were good, few of them understood the confused identities they were creating in the souls of their adopted children. Take Julie, for instance.

I had a lunch scheduled with a fellow publicist, a white woman I had recently met at an event. Karen and I were meeting to talk about possibly doing some work together. When I got to the restaurant she asked if her niece could join us for dessert. I said, "Sure," and thought no more about it. As dessert arrived, a young Black woman approached the table and hugged my companion. This, it turns out, was Karen's niece, Julie.

Karen had wanted Julie to meet me and talk about the possibility of a summer internship with my firm, because she wanted to be supportive of her niece's efforts to discover her Black heritage. Karen's sister and brother-in-law, committed political activists in Vermont, had adopted Julie when she was six months old. They had also adopted a little girl from Guatemala four years later. Although Julie had grown up securely middle class and in a warm and loving home, she had always felt like an outsider. While her sister wasn't technically white, as a Latina with straight hair she had a much easier time fitting in in Vermont than Julie did.

"I always felt like the outsider," she told me. "I wanted to be like my family, but if we went to a new restaurant or on a family vacation, strangers wouldn't realize that we were together. I know it seems like a small thing, but to have outsiders make me feel like I didn't belong, on top of being adopted, well, it hurt. Even when I didn't have words for it."

When I asked Julie how her parents responded to this, she smiled tightly and said, "Oh, they would just ignore it. And if I brought it up, they'd tell *me* to ignore it."

I asked her if they tried to talk about race with her.

"No, race was a big taboo in our house. My parents grew up in Vermont in the sixties, and they aspired to have a race-blind society. But the problem is that being 'race blind' made them blind to me!"

Julie was majoring in Africana studies at college and was really trying to find out what it meant to see race in herself and the world around her. Her parents had good intentions, but by avoiding the issue of race altogether, they neglected a whole part of Julie's identity—a part society was telling her mattered every time she walked out the door.

Then there are parents who are too caught up in their own drama with each other to have a clue about how that drama impacts their kids. Carrie Emmet can tell you about the effects a dysfunctional relationship between parents can have on a child.

I've struggled with depression and, thank God, have come through to see the light on the other side. Fighting my demons and winning has made me a better man and a better father. In fact, it led me to found the *Proud Poppa* newspaper, whose mission it is to celebrate, elevate, and replicate fatherhood success principles in the Black community. *Proud Poppa* is helping many Black fathers along the paths of their own personal healing with depression and life's challenges. I believe that the cavalry is not coming to save the day in our communities and that Black men and mentors must creatively lead and leverage their social capital and personal assets to create community collaborations for healing, empowerment, and social entrepreneurship. We must become masters of our own media and contribute to positive change in our own lives, our families, and our communities.

—SHAWN DOVE, PUBLISHER, YOUTH DEVELOPMENT PROFESSIONAL,

Until I went into therapy I did not realize that I had been fighting depressive episodes on and off since I was sixteen years old. Depression runs in my family, on my mother's side. When I was growing up my father always told me it was a sign of weakness and that I should be able to overcome anything by learning to be strong. During my teenage years there was a lot of tension in my home. My parents were involved in a very nasty divorce. After the divorce was finalized we all still lived under the same roof because they were waiting for the house to be sold. My mother had a heavy wooden door constructed in the foyer to separate both levels of the house. My father lived downstairs. She lived upstairs. My bedroom was upstairs, but I was in his custody, so I always had to pull back this door to go downstairs.

During that time I used to cry and sleep a lot. I would come in from school, go to his area downstairs, fall asleep on the couch, wake up for dinner, then go upstairs to my room and sleep more. When I would have my little breakdowns, my dad would always tell me, "Mind over matter, Carrie. You have to be stronger." That living arrangement continued for me until I left for college.

> There's nobody out there teaching a man how to be a real man. There's nobody out there teaching a father how to be a real father, nobody teaching a husband how to be a husband.
>
> —SNOOP DOGG,
> RECORDING ARTIST

No relationship comes with a guaranteed lifetime warranty, and we may realize after our best efforts that our relationship is not healthy and needs to be ended. That is one of the most painful things any adult can go through, but no matter how painful it is, it is never fair to act out our feelings—and ignore the impact of what we do to each other—on a child. It's never okay to sacrifice your kid or put anyone before your child!

Finally, Joi Sears, an up-and-coming young model and actress, shared this heart-wrenching description from a child's perspective of what it feels like when your parents literally aren't there to answer your call for help.

It was my senior year of high school. I lay in the middle of the floor, screaming at the top of my lungs—screams that came from the core of my being, screams that shot from my heart and soul. I was screaming and crying, begging for someone to help, needing someone to hear me, only to hear my own voice echoing through the halls back at me.

I picked up a bottle of aspirin. I needed to be heard. I needed to be seen. I needed for someone to know that there was something wrong with me and I needed help. I needed attention. I needed to be acknowledged. I needed someone to hold me. I needed so much and I was given nothing. I looked at the pills. I thought about taking them, the whole bottle, and then calling 911 to tell them what I had done. I thought about taking them, and going to sleep, and how my parents would react when they came in and saw my lifeless body lying on the floor.

I called them. No answer. No boyfriend, no sister, no brother, no friend, no one . . . but me. I cried out to God. I told Him that I needed Him—I needed Him to give me strength, I needed Him to give me life, I needed Him to give me peace . . . and He did. There in the middle of the floor, I fell asleep.

Daddy Blues

LaTonya Jefferson is the daughter of a single mother and the oldest of four children. At seventeen she went to high school during the day and worked part-time at night to help with the bills at home. When I spoke to her she had just delivered her first child, but instead of joy she felt only sorrow. Her baby's father had sworn that she was the love of his life and that they'd move in together after the baby was born. During her seventh month of pregnancy she found out from a mutual acquaintance that he had a one-year-old child with a former classmate. LaTonya's feelings of betrayal spiraled her into a deep postpartum depression (see chapter five, page 180). Now she feels like her child won't have a father, and she will still have to struggle financially, just like her mother.

LaTonya is not alone. In 1999 a Morehouse College study estimated that 80 percent of all African-American children will live apart from their biological fathers for some period of their childhood, and that 70 percent of Black children are born to unmarried mothers, compared to a total of 40 percent of American children of all races. According to the National Center for Health Statistics, at least 80 percent of African-American children were born to married parents in the 1940s; that number dropped to around 32 percent at the beginning of this decade.

Those numbers have a profound meaning. Children growing up in single-parent homes are five times more likely to be poor, three times more likely to commit crimes that could lead to prison, and twice as likely to drop out of school. Households where the father is absent are almost always poor, which adds stress to every part of family life. According to Dr. Alvin Poussaint, consultant to *The Cosby Show* and widely considered the best-known Black psychiatrist in America, a big part of the gender crisis is due to boys and girls being raised without both a mother and a father in the house, and if there's resentment toward the father, they see that, too.

Here are some more chilling facts:

- The latest census tells us that 23 percent of children in America are being raised in single-mother homes. For us that figure is at 50 percent.
- Single-mother households with only one breadwinner, who is a woman, can plunge a family into poverty.
- Single mothers often have to have more than one job, which means less time with their children. This often leads kids to the streets, gangs, or lower grades.
- A third of all Black men will go to prison in their lifetime. This is a major reason why fathers are absent and why boys without fathers are at greater risk of going to jail.
- Ninety percent of homeless and runaway children are from fatherless homes.
- Seventy-one percent of pregnant teens are from fatherless homes.
- Sixty-three percent of teen suicides are from fatherless homes.
- Seventy-one percent of high school dropouts are from fatherless homes.

CHECK THIS OUT

Always give yourself permission to say "no." It's not personal—it's just a resounding "yes" vote for you.

- Seventy-five percent of patients in drug abuse centers are from fatherless homes.
- Seventy percent of teens in state-operated institutions have no father.
- Eighty-five percent of youths in prison are from fatherless homes.
- Fatherless boys and girls are twice as likely to drop out of high school, twice as likely to end up in jail, and four times as likely to need help for emotional and behavioral problems.

Where Is the Love?

The numbers are very telling, but what they don't tell about is the pain of children who don't get the support and love they need. The problem of absent fathers goes way beyond being physically present in the house and earning money, which is already important; the biggest problem with absent fathers is the missed love. Fathers are important because they are the primary models—for boys *and* girls—of what men can and should be. When a father is absent, it affects boys and girls very differently. Boys and girls may think they don't know an absent father, but they do. They know he wasn't there and that's an absence they *know* every day of their lives.

While there's a joy particular to growing up in a secure two-parent home, a present father is no guarantee that a boy will grow up to be a whole and healthy man. Single mothers can be perfectly good parents to boys—millions of them have been and have raised sons who, in time, became loving and responsible fathers and contributing members to society. I'll say it again: What a fatherless boy misses out on most is a father's love. (We've all heard brothas say that their moms were both mother and father to them, so they didn't miss their pops, but we know it's not true.) If we focused more on that missed love, and less on ideas about how the physical presence of a father instills masculinity or turns out "real men," more young men without fathers might be able to grow up and become present fathers themselves.

Many studies say that the absence of a father at home leads girls to sexual activity at a younger age and higher rates of teen pregnancy. These girls also grow up looking, as Mary J. Blige did, for male figures who will make up for the love they lost. As Mary J. herself says, "When it was time to start dating, that's when we were looking for . . . that fatherly 'I need you, don't hurt me' kind of love."

Shanene Pinder, a talented writer who I've mentored for twenty years, grew up without a father. Throughout our friendship Shanene has shared her family's history of intergenerational fatherlessness with me. Shanene once told me, "I know how bad it hurts to grow up without the consistent, reliable, unconditional love of a father. It is a painful void that affects how you see yourself in the world—like you're missing something and somehow not part of 'the norm.' I talk about this a lot with my daughter (I probably sound like a broken record to her), because I don't want the experience she and I had to be the one her children have."

> Adversity is the breakfast of champions. You want to learn how to eat this stuff. We must learn to get nutrition from each attack or setback.
>
> —PASTOR RICK GODWIN, FOUNDER AND SENIOR PASTOR OF EAGLE'S NEST CHRISTIAN FELLOWSHIP CHURCH, SAN ANTONIO, TX

Jade Pinder, another member of Shanene's family, shared her father loss with me and touched on these very points. Throughout her early childhood she had blamed her mother for her father's absence. But as she grew older and met her father she realized that the blame had been misplaced. Her father had simply chosen not to be there. She sums up the pain of that loss by saying, "Growing up without a dad is a hard thing to do, especially when you know he's not dead and has no excuse or reason for why he isn't there. When I finally met him, all I wanted was for him to love me and want me as much as I wanted him. And I thought that would happen. Sadly, I was wrong.

"For as long as I live, I will always have a big empty hole inside of me, in my heart, because of him. I hate my father for this. He has put me through more pain than anyone else could ever imagine. I am grateful for the family that has been there, but sadly this doesn't change how I feel inside. Whenever I talk about him, I can't help but cry. A part of me will always want my dad. And a part of me also knows that I will never have him."

Many girls who don't have fathers find themselves repeating the pattern of single motherhood. Lucille O'Neal is one of the founders of the Odessa Chambliss Quality of Life Fund, a charity foundation established in honor of her mother, and president of My Sister, My Friend, a mentoring organization—as well as the proud mom of Shaquille O'Neal. She shared this poignant story of her struggle to be a single teen mom in the seventies. It could have been written by any young woman today.

In 1972, a few months after I got out of high school, I gave birth to my oldest son. Being a teenager with a young child was a sin in my mother's house. She was very disappointed in me at first, but vowed to help me raise this child in any way she could. My grandmother felt burdened, but she also stood by me and helped me to nurture this young man-child. Despite the support they promised, I felt that my life was over and I had no direction, so I felt even more alone, ashamed, and mentally depressed. I was in a deep valley with no idea how I would get out of it. With no money, my health in question, no help from the baby's daddy, no nothing . . . I just felt empty and cried most of the time.

I didn't know what I was doing or what I was going to do, and I didn't see any way out of the mess I was in. It took so much for me to even get up out of the bed and care for this baby night and day. I did not want to be a mother yet, I didn't care about being a mother, and I didn't even know what "being a mother" meant—but I did know that I *was* a mother, and the responsibility was mine, and mine alone.

It did not help that people reminded me every day about the mistake I had made in my life. I learned then how much words could cut me, how they could mess with my mind and my self-esteem to the point that I went from feeling terrible to feeling worthless. I withdrew from family and the rest of the world. For a long time I couldn't talk to anybody about how I felt inside.

Being a single mom isn't as stigmatized now as it was a generation ago—after all, it's much more common—but it isn't any easier now than it was then, and in some ways it may actually be harder. "Daddy blues" stresses more than just the mom who's left to raise a child by herself; it stresses the whole family.

I don't know how many letters I've gotten from women who were molested by men other than their fathers. Our girls are at constant risk for sexual abuse, even by their own boyfriends, as well as physical abuse, both of which destroy young women's self-esteem and in turn lead to dropping out of school, teen pregnancy, drug use . . . and the whole vicious cycle continues.

My younger brother came to visit me after I had been in Maine for two years. It was my sophomore year. We were talking, and then he looked at me and said, "They got you."

I said, "What are you talking about?"

He said, "They got you. You done became one of them."

I realized that he was still in warrior mode, still in the mode where you had to be prepared to fight for every scrap of your dignity and self-worth. You had to be prepared to lose your life over it, otherwise people would try and take it from you, and that's how we were raised. And I tried to explain to him, "No, no, no! That's not the way the rest of the world acts—that's just this crazy place where we grew up. And it *is* crazy, but we're not crazy."

But that was not his experience, or my experience, and it wasn't the experience of lots of folks growing up in poverty.

—GEOFFREY CANADA, RENOWNED EDUCATOR AND AUTHOR OF *FIST, STICK, KNIFE, GUN: A PERSONAL HISTORY OF VIOLENCE IN AMERICA*

When Verna Jacob sent me this account of growing up without her biological father, I knew she could understand the pain it creates from the inside.

Her mother, desperate to have a man in her life, sacrificed her children's safety and well-being to preserve her first marriage.

I grew up in a small southern community, a place where everybody knew each other; so we thought. No one in the neighborhood was aware of what was really happening in my house. There were five children, a mother, and my stepfather. The last two children were my stepfather's biological children. We didn't know he wasn't our father until we were teenagers. We were all ten months apart, and my mother registered us in school under the same last name as our stepfather. My oldest brother was three, my sister one, and I was two when he and my mother met.

My stepfather used to make us do things like stretch our legs across his back, or scratch his butt; he would make me sit on his lap as he rubbed my chest. My sister would be in the room with him for hours. I never knew what was going on, but by the time she was thirteen my mother would sit outside the room. And when he let my sister out of the room, my mother would start fighting her as if she were a stranger from the street. Once my sister ran outside, trying to get away from my mother, but my mother chased her and beat her until she was almost unconscious.

On top of the sexual abuse, we were beaten every day, and the emotional abuse was just as bad. He would tell my mother not to speak to me and she wouldn't! This would go on for two weeks at a time. There was hardly ever enough food to eat, no running water, lights, or gas . . . Our stepfather would have pancakes, eggs, and sausages, while we had oatmeal, or pork chops while we ate beans. There were many days when there wasn't any food, and my brother and I ate Purina dog food. I was a teenager and I needed my mother, but she chose her husband over her children.

Unfortunately, stories like this are an "everyday occurrence," says Dr. Angela Moses, a youth pastor and choir president at the New Life Tabernacle Church in Brooklyn, NY. She is also the cofounder and CEO of the

---

Most men are not open to books about masculinity. So we get [a lot] of this stuff that becomes what I call the mythology of maleness. People have these myths about manhood that have been repeated so many times that you think this is what you have to live up to, and this is what you have to be.

One thing that I felt growing up [that] was a difference between boys and girls was that men were convinced their manhood could be lost—that it was something someone could take from you. If you allowed yourself to be messed with, people actually took your manhood away, and you could not get it back.

So one of the things we were taught was not to let anyone take our manhood, even if it meant dying. Now maybe when you hear about kids who kill or die over a pair of sneakers, you're thinking, "What the hell? Who would die over a pair of sneakers?" But those kids are convinced, like I was, that it's not the sneakers being taken, it's your manhood—and if they take it, you can't get it back. You can't even look at yourself anymore.

—GEOFFREY CANADA, RENOWNED EDUCATOR, AUTHOR OF
FIST, STICK, KNIFE, GUN: A PERSONAL HISTORY OF VIOLENCE IN AMERICA

Family Life Development Center, Inc., and executive director of Uth Turn. Uth Turn is an organization that provides intervention and prevention to high-risk youth, many of whom are court adjudicated. She started the organization out of the desire to help rebuild families and communities by teaching social responsibility and self-sufficiency.

Sometimes fathers don't consciously choose to abandon their children, but their actions cause them to abandon them just the same.

Roland Jenkins is a bright young boy with dark soulful eyes and curly hair. When he was six, he saw his father stab his mother in the leg during one of their more heated arguments. By the time he was seven, his father was in prison for armed robbery. His home, already unstable because of domestic violence, was plunged into poverty when his father, the primary breadwinner, began serving his sentence.

Roland had always had behavioral issues in school, but with his father's imprisonment, things got worse. His mother no longer knew how to handle him and withdrew from Roland and her small circle of family and friends. Most evenings she was passed out drunk by 7:00 P.M. Roland, feeling abandoned by his father and now his mother, spent more and more time out in the streets. When he went to see his father every two months, he would sit motionless and expressionless as his father lectured him about staying on the straight and narrow. As far as Roland was concerned, nothing his father said counted, since he wasn't there to be counted on.

By the time Roland was thirteen, he was being initiated into one of the toughest gangs in his neighborhood. He found in the older boys of the gang the father figure he so desperately craved. And winning their approval meant following the same path that had landed his father in jail and made him unavailable to parent.

Boys at Risk: Depression and Suicide

Black young men used to be among the least likely groups to attempt or commit suicide, but as I said at the beginning of the chapter, they are heading fast toward first place in this terrible race. The suicide rate of African Americans between the ages of 10 and 19 has increased by 114 percent since the 1980s! Khalid Sumner, who you met in the chapter on men, was particularly eloquent about being young, depressed, and suicidal.

Khalid's parents are first-generation immigrants, his father from Guyana, his mother from Jamaica. They did not express emotion, and they did not encourage talk about feelings, though they were very clear about the value they placed on his success—in school, in sports, in anything he did. When Khalid was nine years old, he tried to commit suicide.

I did it because I thought it wouldn't matter if I was here or not. But I didn't know how. I thought that if I cut my wrist and went to sleep, that would be it. I woke up with a scab, and covered the cut with my watch, but I also wanted people to see it. This girl in my class, Alicia, we didn't like each other much—we fought all the time—but that day she told the teacher what she saw, and she cried. From that point on, Alicia and I were friends. I had to go to the principal's office and have special time with him. The whole thing felt like I was in a movie. My dad was very worried and took me to see a psychiatrist, and I remember the psychiatrist asking me if I thought I would hurt myself.

THERE *IS* HOPE: PAYING IT FORWARD

Well, I'm still a homie, meaning I'm still a Blood. Nothing can change that. But I'm conscious, I make better decisions, I don't let blue and red dictate who is enemy or friend. My red flag represents strength now—it's the bond of unity among brothers who come from the same struggle I'm going through.

Now, I can't control how society views us, or me, but the only person's approval I *need* is my own, and I know how I live today. My role is counseling the homies, mentoring them, helping them make better life decisions. They look up to me, and I try to give them hope so they know their life purpose isn't just to die—that they can live out their dreams.

I can't say all Bloods live this way now, but I do. There are too many dead homies in the ground to turn my back on the nation now. When I decided to grow up and become a man and a father, the honorable Prince T. Rodgers told me I shouldn't abandon the hood; he said I should stay and give back, pass down the things I've learned that help me live better. In other words, the only way to be down is to stay down.

—DASHAUN "JIWE" MORRIS, AUTHOR OF *WAR OF THE BLOODS IN MY VEINS*

Of course I said no so I could go back home and watch cartoons, and I only saw him a handful of times after that.

Khalid thought that seeing the psychiatrist was pointless, and that he only needed to see him because that was what was expected.

As baffling as the whole thing seemed to him at the time, he now knows that he was depressed, and that the feelings that motivated him to try to end his life never fully left him—they were always there, sometimes rising to the surface, sometimes sinking down deep and lying in wait. In high school he found himself again doing what was expected of him—studying, working out, going to football practice, studying—but wondering what the point was, why he was even there.

Khalid's parents, like so many, didn't know how to address his problems, much less how to follow up on them. This is very common in the families of suicidal children because adults often don't understand what's happening, or on the brink of happening—they just can't believe that children could be suicidal. The terrible truth is that they can, and they are, and we must become more aware and watchful if we hope to save them.

Youth at Risk: When Violence Masks Pain

Depression can mask itself as anger, the anger covering the helplessness and frustration of sadness, and the anger can too easily play itself out in violence, especially among young men. Dr. Joy DeGruy Leary, author of the groundbreaking book *Post Traumatic Slavery Syndrome: America's Legacy of Enduring Injury and Healing* and creator of the African-American Adolescent Respect Scale (a way of measuring how many socially positive attitudes Black male teenagers have), has done important research on young Black men and violence. She talks about the fast trigger point in young Black men, and links it to their sensitivity to anything that seems like disrespect. Racism has created a sense of powerlessness in us that makes it possible for one Black man to kill another Black man over an issue that most people would consider trivial (like sneakers or saving face). In Leary's considered judgment, a crisis in *self*-respect has turned *dis*respect into a life-and-death issue.

Reggie Hatchett talked with me about this in one of our conversations: "Today's Black youth live in a state of depression. That these young men are content with dying is a depressive state. They have become comfortable in their misery; they enjoy the block that houses drug dealers, and they glorify 'mama drama.' They want that. I've heard a teenage boy say he can't wait to be shot because it will solidify him with his peers. He's not as tough as them till he gets shot. Living in a world where a fifteen-year-old boy can utter those words is to live in a state of depression." I hear what Reggie is saying, and I want to take it a step further. I would say that what looks to Reggie like comfort and enjoyment is another kind of masking, a version of the bravado that so many young men feel is their only option in the face of the unbearable.

In the previous chapter I talked about posttraumatic stress disorder and the ways many brothers act out the anguish they feel from never getting to process the feelings that come from trauma (see "It Never Happened," pages 98–104). I mentioned there that women also suffer from this disorder, but it is not only men and women who experience symptoms such as a hair-trigger temper, horrific nightmares, and the inability to concentrate. Very often the adults who experience PTSD have been suffering from it since childhood or youth. Kids traumatized by violence—as victims or as witnesses—are likely to be labeled as having ADHD (attention deficit hyperactivity disorder) or a learning disability, be placed in special education classes, and be stigmatized as different or "defective." Too many of these kids are actually gifted and bright, and labeling them this way without ever treating the root causes of their unhappiness puts them on the path toward failure in school, dropping out, drugs, gangs, the streets, and prison. This is why community violence, which for decades has been considered solely a criminal-justice problem, is now a major public *health* issue as well.

Dashaun "Jiwe" Morris, whose story I told part of in the last chapter, lived the reality of this. He joined the Bloods when he was nine; now he works with the city of Newark for gang peace, leads a park cleanup incentive in his own and other communities with Jay Davis, and tries to guide other young men toward healthier ways to handle life. He went to Delaware State University on a football scholarship. He became a star—the best kick returner in the country in 2002, and an all-star—but his skills did not keep him from being expelled twice. The first time was for having a handgun in his dorm room; he was later readmitted, but in 2004 he was expelled again when he stabbed another student. A month later he was charged with attempted murder, assault, conspiracy, and possession of a firearm.

Jiwe could not wrap his mind around the idea that disputes were not handled at college the same way they were handled when he was growing up. His "reward" back on the block was hurting someone who he thought had disrespected him. "We handled the possibility of death by knowing someone had to pay no matter what." He finally had to readjust his thinking from, "If you have a disagreement with somebody, you get on the phone and call up your boys," to finding nonviolent ways to resolve conflicts.

Avenging wrongdoing is a way to feel less powerless. Says Jiwe, "People can't be allowed to get away with hurting people that I care about. There have been times when girls from my neighborhood were raped or beaten up, and we didn't have a chance to retaliate against the individual directly responsible. But we would avenge those situations at the first opportunity, and it didn't matter that it was a different person . . . somebody had to pay." The problem is that vengeance can never address the root causes of the acts that made it seem necessary, and it virtually always escalates.

I talked with Carl Bell, a highly respected African-American psychiatrist and president/CEO of the Community Mental Health Council, about Jiwe and the young men like him that I know. He had this to say:

> Had there been social fabric around the young brother while he was growing up, he would not have needed gang fabric around him. Had he been connected to someone or some activity that could have improved his self-esteem and given him a sense of power, he would not have needed to carry a gun. If he had a sense of models, he would have understood not to love what won't love you back. If he had had something to minimize the trauma he talks about, his path would have been different. If he had an adult protective shield around him, he would have been able to stay out of prison until he had the time

> Appreciate your learning process, for it is of equal value to have realized there is a need for change as for the change itself.
>
> — BETH JOHNSON, AUTHOR

to grow up and learn what he *has* learned the easy way instead of the hard way he is still having to learn it.

His bottom line, though, was that for all the obstacles Jiwe has encountered, and for all the obstacles yet to come, he is still *able* to learn. As long as he keeps trying, there is hope.

Then there's Jerome Everson, the youngest in a family of four headed by his single mother in Chicago. His depression started after his first run-in with the police. He was carelessly rounded up after school one day with two other boys who already had police records. The cops let him go after a couple of hours, but not before they treated him like he was a criminal—or if he wasn't one, he would be soon. At home his overworked mother lectured him about staying out of trouble. She had three kids to feed, and getting him out of jail had cost her an afternoon's pay. Without anyone to stand up for him or even tell him that he didn't deserve to be treated that way, much less help him sort through his feelings of anger and powerlessness, he started skipping school—choosing instead to hide out at home and watch TV all day. His solid B average slipped to a D, and the modest goals he used to have now seemed pointless. In addition, his feelings of powerlessness led him to begin running with a more dangerous group of boys. Many of the boys were gang members and their status had a new appeal for him. By joining their ranks he could win back some of the power he felt was taken away from him during the arrest.

I'm frightened by how little value is placed on Black boys' lives and horrified at how often they're the victims of racial profiling. In this society, just *being* a young dark-skinned Black boy is often equated with being a criminal. What's worse is that people don't realize the impact a clash with police, school administrators, or welfare officials has on young minds and how much it increases the likelihood of teen depression and violence. So many kids feel abused by authority figures, the people they otherwise would look up to as models and protectors, that it makes perfect sense that they would choose to reclaim some form of power through gang membership.

Many of our young men have turned to gangs to give them a sense of belonging that their families don't give them, and boys from fatherless homes can be especially vulnerable to a gang's appeal. Dr. Leary, the author of *Post Traumatic Slavery Syndrome*, has this to say

> Be who you are and say what you feel because those who mind don't matter and those who matter don't mind.
>
> —THEODORE GEISEL,
> BEST KNOWN AS CHILDREN'S BOOK
> AUTHOR DR. SEUSS

about gangs:

> In communities and neighborhoods which their friends and peers
> frequent, youth . . . will often get their advice and support from mem-
> bers of an underworld they respect and understand. This illicit culture
> provides the youth with exposure to new opportunities by belonging
> to a street or community-based reconstituted family. The members of
> this group provide each other support and encouragement as well as
> security and respect.

She gives the example of Jamal, who grew up on Chicago's South Side.
His mother used to beat him and verbally abuse him on a regular basis; he
didn't have to do anything to bring on the abuse, and nothing he could
do would prevent it—it was his mother's way of letting him know that
she was in charge. As bad as the blows were, the words were worse ("I felt
worthless, like I wanted to roll up in a ball and die"), and yet he knew that
after each beating his mother would be nice to him—briefly. One thing
her vicious treatment taught Jamal was that he could use violence to "demand" respect from other people, and he confirmed this theory when he
got involved with a gang, where his rage quickly brought him to leadership.
It was also, he says, his way of trying to kill the part of himself that was not
loved. According to Dr. Leary the formula for teen violence is adding disrespect to damaging conditions in the family and the larger society.

The dangers of the streets don't just impact boys. In 1997, Ashley Hutchins
and the father of her children were sentenced to twenty to sixty years in
prison for a drug-related crime. She wrote me this letter from prison,
showing how quickly the streets can change a life:

> I can't exactly say when I started feeling depressed, because I blocked
> out my feelings for so long. As a very young girl, no older than 7 or 8, I
> used to pretend nothing hurt me. I thought to myself, 'If my own mother
> doesn't care about me, then surely nobody else does.' My mother always
> put her drugs or men before me. I'm the oldest of my other three siblings.
> I was the first great-grandchild and niece so I received love from everyone
> but her. I was always trying to do something to receive love from her.
> At the age of 11, I was raped by someone I knew. My mother didn't
> press charges because one of the men that raped me was a brother of a

big drug dealer in the neighborhood. She was paid two or three hundred dollars, and bought me a pair of Nike Air Jordans. The only father figure I had was my uncle, and I assumed he would do something—after all, he was the man in my life and it was his job to protect me—but he didn't. After that I felt like it was me against the world, and I cut off anything I ever felt for anyone except my little brother. And I hated my mother, who by then had graduated from taking pills to smoking crack.

I turned to the streets. I lived with my great-grandmother, but she didn't have a clue as to what I was doing. Most of the other children's mothers smoked crack also, and there were no fathers around, so we embraced each other. I started skipping school and hanging in all the wrong places.

My uncle introduced me to selling crack when I was 13. I started getting paid to open bags, and I was a driver sometimes. I was already smoking weed and drinking beer. I got turned on to fifty-ones—a marijuana joint laced with crack—by older teenagers. When I started selling drugs myself, there was no turning back.

I had dropped out of school without my family's knowledge, except my uncle, who let me sell with him. My mother moved in with us because her crack addiction had left her homeless. One day she stole a sack of rocks from me. It was bad enough that I felt like she had sold me, but I could've been killed if I didn't pay those guys their money.

I didn't know what to do, so I went to the guy, told the truth, and said I would work for free until I paid him back. After that I got a reputation in the street as a good businessperson, and I went to a different level in the drug game. I had so much money I didn't know what to do with it. Eventually, I got a boyfriend. Reg lived next door and his mother smoked crack, too, so we had a common bond. Even though he was young, he had a reputation as a fighter and he wasn't afraid of anyone. With him I knew no one would mess with me.

I became pregnant at the age of 15 and got my first drug arrest. When I received two years probation, I decided to cool it with the drugs, but then I had two more daughters and started back selling. Reg and I were two lost kids trying to figure out who we were, and we abused each other in the process. I abused him mentally and he abused me physically. Both of us sold drugs and to everyone on the outside it looked like we had it going on—the cars, the house, the clothes, etc.—but no one realized how much pain both of us were in.

There is another side to violence in our communities. It's the trauma experienced by those of us who live with the aftereffects of witnessing violence. Sandra Goodridge, whose childhood exposure to violence left her scarred for life, says, "I suffered my first bout of depression at the age of twelve when my best friend Jackie was shot in the face by a boyfriend after she ended the relationship."

Sandra and Jackie were the only children of very strict parents, and became like sisters. They met two boys and began dating them secretly. When Jackie's father discovered his daughter's relationship, he demanded that she stop seeing the boy. The next time Sandra saw her friend she was being hurried across the courtyard by her mother, with bandages covering her face. "I later learned that her boyfriend broke into their apartment a few nights before, confronted Jackie, and shot her in the face. She spent a few days in the hospital and was released with the bullet fragments permanently lodged in a bony part of her cheek."

Jackie was lucky to be alive, but she became a recluse. "She refused to answer my calls, and I never saw her again. The rest of the summer I spent my nights sleepless, afraid that someone could just as easily enter our apartment and shoot me." The insomnia was the first step toward depression, and both plagued her for years, but her fears were not groundless:

"During my late teens the crack epidemic engulfed New York and the echo of rapid gunfire would keep me awake at night. Our neighbors were shot in their apartments by stray bullets. Whole families slept on their floors instead of their beds, hoping to avoid a bullet entering through the window. Despite the mice, I often chose to sleep on the floor instead of my own bed. During this time I experienced the same prolonged, hollow sadness I first felt when Jackie was shot."

Foster Care Nightmare

The foster care system is in crisis. The idea of foster care is great: Kids whose birth families temporarily can't take care of them—whether for medical reasons or because of homelessness, drug addiction, mental illness, parental neglect, or incarceration—are temporarily placed in homes with families who will take care of them until their own families stabilize. To cover the expense of adding another family member, the state gives foster families money each month.

That's the good part. The bad part is that there are over half a million kids in the system right now, enough to fill a good-size city, and the numbers are growing steadily—yet the only time you're likely to hear about foster care is when yet another child has died from horrible abuse or neglect by the foster parents who were supposed to save the child. At the same time that the number of foster children is growing, the number of people willing and able to care for them is shrinking, which means that more and more kids end up in institutions.

Kids in foster care have deep feelings of abandonment, betrayal, and loneliness, and they feel disconnected from "regular" kids. They rarely stay in one "home" for their whole time in foster care, they are often abused, and too often they have no models for future family. What makes the issue even more compelling is that two-thirds of the kids in foster care are African American, and they stay in the system longer than any other racial or ethnic population—meaning they're hardly ever returned to their real families. As my young friend Kristal Hansley says, "It's like another world in there that no one knows about, or they know but just ignore it."

Foster care is hard on everybody involved, even under the best of circumstances: Parents rarely think they're unable to adequately care for their own children (even if everyone else in the world disagrees with them), kids—even abused kids—are terrified about being taken from their homes to live with strangers, and even foster parents with the best intentions are often seriously challenged by the needs and/or problems of the kids who have been placed with them. And that's the best of circumstances, something most kids in the system never experience. Like my friend Gloria Arnau.

I met Gloria over thirty years ago, when I was still a clinical social-work student and she was twelve years old and living in a residential treatment center just north of New York City. At age seven she had been taken from her mother and placed in the care of her mother's parents. A male relative molested her for the next five years, until she ran away. She never told her grandparents because she saw them as so old and frail that it would "destroy" them to hear what the relative was doing to her. She wanted to tell the police but was afraid that if she did they would come to the house and it would kill her grandparents. At eleven she tried to kill herself with pills, but her brother discovered her and called 911. She starting acting out—being "disobedient" and running away—but still kept her vow not to tell her grandparents. The last time Gloria ran away she was placed in foster care, and her grandparents died while she was there, "protected" from the terrible truth of their granddaughter's living hell under their own roof.

Gloria's first foster situation was a group home. "Group home was hard because I wanted to be home with my grandparents, but better because I wasn't being abused physically and sexually. I didn't get close to people because I didn't trust anyone. I was so angry. I got into drinking and smoking pot, because it let me forget for a minute why I felt the way I did. Inside I wanted to tell someone that I was not a bad kid, and that I ran away because this stuff happened to me, but I always wanted to protect my grandparents." It's no surprise that she had a lot of anger toward adults.

Once, when she was fourteen, she went back to visit her grandparents, only to find out that they had moved. They had moved without telling her and, what's more, her grandmother had told the neighbors not to tell Gloria where they were living. She desperately searched the whole neighborhood for them, but couldn't find them or anyone who would tell her where they were. She tried to kill herself again, and this time she came closer to "success"—she threw herself out a second-story window and wound up paralyzed for six months.

Gloria lived in foster care for four years. In most foster homes a girl has to share a room with one or two or, in some cases, up to a dozen other girls. A girl who obeyed the rules could sometimes earn her own room, but Gloria never wanted her own room. "Me and the girls would stay up and talk. I liked that I was able to talk, but when it got personal we would shut down. You would hear that quiet, the girl would turn around, and that was the end of the conversation—or it would turn to jeans, or something like that. I can't say what was going on for the other girls, but for me, I didn't want them to know I had been molested. I always feared I wouldn't look the same to them if they knew, so I used to make up things . . ."

That element of make-believe is at the core of many young people's foster-care experiences. The reality—that their own mother or grandmother or other family members couldn't take care of them or *wouldn't* take care of them—is so painful that many of them fabricate a tale of a better life, a more loving family. Some will spin a narrative that's just the opposite, telling about how "bad" they were, because it's so much less painful to imagine oneself as the villain than as the victim. Sometimes foster kids will poke fun at one another's stories if the details get too exaggerated ("Oh, yeah? Well, I got *two* mansions—one in Beverly Hills, *and* one in Miami!").

Mostly, though, there's a kind of unspoken rule that "I'll pretend I believe your fantasy if you'll pretend you believe mine"—a rule that's almost made to be broken the minute somebody gets angry.

Gloria puts it well. "When you're in the foster system, you live two lives: the life in the system and the life you make up. The system is your real life now, but when other kids ask you about your real life *before*, you make up stuff. You pretend everything was fine in the other life. Then you have to keep pretending because you have to keep up the lies. You're not going to say, 'I'm here because I was sexually abused.' It's much more cool to say you're in here because you didn't respect authority, when really none of that went on. It's like role-playing—you don't need acting class for that. I got good at wearing a mask—even today you could walk in my house and have no idea that I'm depressed, and I feel like dying."

> No one can make you feel inferior without your consent.
>
> —ELEANOR ROOSEVELT, FORMER FIRST LADY, ACTIVIST, AND AUTHOR

Once again, secret shame is at the root of depression. It started hitting Gloria before her first suicide attempt, and it had her in its grips for decades before she even knew what it was. "When I was depressed I felt empty, hollow, like when you're missing someone real close to you, but you can't find them. Almost like I was homesick. I tried going to counseling, but I shut down when the deep questions started coming. I don't want to go back to that time and the things I went through, but it's always there. I dream it. I live it every day. Right now I just try to avoid it, but I know I need the help." Gloria has told me that I am the person she trusts most in the world, a trust I cherish. But even with me she needed to have this conversation over the phone. "I can share this with you because I don't see you. If this had been in person, I would have shut down. I wouldn't have been able to tell you all this."

But Gloria is not just a "victim of the system." For one thing, she has some deep thoughts about what is wrong with foster care. "Communication is the biggest key with young people, and even more with young people in the foster system. When we tell you everything is okay at home, it's really not. We need to be heard more deeply than our words—don't just stop listening once we give the first 'right' answer. Don't stop asking questions. Be persistent. You have to reach out to young kids. It might take

> Hip-hop is a means of improvising when the traditional means of learning don't work.
>
> —ANONYMOUS

a while to reach a kid who's used to keeping everything inside. It may take asking me three times before I break down and tell you everything. I believe that most kids who are put in foster care are depressed even before they get put in. And even if foster kids do get attention, it may not be as much as they need. But don't give up on them. Somebody has to take time out and listen to these kids, or they are lost—to themselves, and to society."

Beyond her own sharp take on what foster care needs the most, Gloria herself walks the walk. Her own three kids are in their twenties, and she is now a foster mom, doing her best to make a difference, despite her bouts of depression, one kid at a time.

Kay is about to graduate from high school, but no one who saw her early years would have predicted that she would make it this far. Her drug-addict mother abandoned her in the hospital, something she had done to two other children before. Kay was taken in by relatives who beat her regularly, blatantly favored a grandson over her, and said that Kay was ruining their marriage. By the seventh grade she was suicidal. "I needed attention and my behavior was crazy." A year later they put her in foster care.

Kay's first foster home, in a housing project, was full of roaches, but that was the least of her problems. Her foster mother was an alcoholic, and the foster mother's boyfriend was a drug dealer who used to come into Kay's room at night and stare at her. I met her at a talk; when this bright young girl told me she wanted to be a lawyer, I had no idea what her life was like, but I liked her immediately and sent her a signed copy of my dear friend and client Johnnie Cochran's last book. Another dear friend, Tracey Mitchell, a high-powered attorney who was a life force in the universe during her brief time here, was hosting a book signing for me. Renee Brown from the WNBA was there, too. When I introduced them to Kay, they immediately took her under their wing.

When they found out about her living circumstances, they got her out of there—but the next foster home wasn't a whole lot better. Kay could hear mice and rats in the walls, the foster mother was never there, there were six girls, and there was virtually no food—Kay had $30 a month to cover all her expenses, which meant all her meals plus clothing, transportation, etc. Tracey took her in as a younger sister. She bought her clothes, spent time with her, and, more important, she and Renee helped her back out of the dead end of dropping out of school—in eleventh grade her average went from a sixty-four to a ninety-four! Sadly, Tracey died of an aneurism in 2005. Now that she's gone, Kay is back in my life and sustained by Tracey's parents, Bert and Carole, her sister Robbin, her brother Ron, and her cousin Vanessa.

She's now living with her stepgrandmother. "I pray to God and feel better, and I know I'll be off to college soon—it won't be long till I'm on my own. In the meantime my grandmother gives me my space, but she's also pushing for me now."

A lot of girls in foster care have been raped, and it's one of the reasons pimps see foster girls as easy marks. "Two out of five girls ended up going with pimps while I was there. I would say that about half the girls in foster care get caught up this way if they don't have anyone who loves them, because it's so easy to get caught up in that horrible game. A girl in my home was doing pretty well, but she started messing around with a guy who turned out to be a pimp; she became a stripper, then a drug addict, and now she has HIV. I was one of the lucky ones; I had mentors to help me stay in school and keep away from guys like that. I also read the Bible and knew that God had a plan for me. But even girls who don't fall into that trap have it hard. When a girl I knew aged out of the foster care system at twenty-one, she was messed up because she didn't have anywhere to go. Maybe twenty-one sounds old enough to be independent, but when you've had a dysfunctional foster care experience, and you *don't* have the support of family or people who feel like family, you're totally lost." In one of those moments that make life worth living, Kay tells me, "If I hadn't met you when I was in eighth grade, and then Tracey and Renee, I would probably be one of those girls right now." Kay's amazing light after everything she's been through is an inspiration to me. Often I feel like I should be the last person to complain about anything when I hear her bright and cheerful voice say, "Hey, T.W."

As bad as it is for girls, it may be even worse for boys, because the peer pressure to "be a man" is so intense, no matter how self-destructive it can be. In virtually every home with more than one foster son, the question is not will there be a fight, but when, and the problem is magnified in group homes. Boys fight over insults—real or imagined, joking or serious—they fight over clothes, over theft of the few belongings they have to their names. If they drop out of school—and odds are they will—they become prime targets for gang recruitment. In a gang or not, once they start stealing or selling drugs, their estimated time of arrival in prison or at the morgue starts moving closer and closer, faster and faster.

I know that there are many solid and strong foster parents out there, like Gloria. I know she's not the only one, but it pains my heart to know that pretty much every young person I've ever known in foster care has told me that they never felt cared for by the people who were supposedly giving them a better alternative to their real homes. Time and time again these people have felt that the foster mothers or parents were mainly in it for the money, and that they as dependents were to make as little trouble as possible. Small wonder that so many people who come out of the foster care system have to grapple with depression, and pass it on to the next generation.

Young, Gifted, and Black

In the past quarter century hip-hop has been the center of some of the greatest artistic creativity in the Black community. And it is no exaggeration to say that it has had a profound influence on the popular music, style, and culture of this country and beyond—and it speaks to our young people like nothing else in our culture today. I have a hard time when I hear people disrespect hip-hop by talking about it as if it were only one thing and as if that one thing were only bad. In my opinion, hip-hop is right up there with jazz as an art form that has all kinds of variations and possibilities, and never comes close to exhausting them.

Some folks don't like hip-hop because of what they believe it is doing to our young people. Other folks say that hip-hop is just a reflection of what's out there, and the music and videos and magazines it generates don't have any effect on the thinking of our young men and women at all. I think the reality is a lot more complicated than either of those positions. For one thing, I think our young people are using hip-hop to talk to each other—and to us—and what we need to do is learn how to listen better, instead of condemn. For another thing, I think there *are* aspects of hip-hop culture that are really troubling, like when it glorifies so many of the things we've been talking about—gangbanging, violence, disrespect of women, obsession with bling . . . But telling the people who create this work to "Stop glorifying violence!" would be as pointless as telling a wounded man to "Stop screaming!" As a matter of fact, I am convinced that some of what

> Even in the tightest of families with the most vibrant of family rela-
> tionships, we have depression, we have people committing suicide.
> Now, people shouldn't blame themselves when that happens, but
> they should understand there are some people who are going to
> have depression because of chemical abnormalities, and hopefully
> the family becomes a place where it can be identified early and
> people can be supported in getting treatment.
>
> –DAVID SATCHER, MD, PHD, FORMER SURGEON GENERAL, DIRECTOR, NATIONAL CEN-
> TER FOR PRIMARY CARE, MOREHOUSE SCHOOL OF MEDICINE

people talk about as "the worst" of hip-hop is actually the cries of people
in pain. And I see a direct connection between this pain and depression.
As adults we need to start answering that cry by teaching them the funda-
mentals they lack and in doing so, truth be told, there's a whole lot we can
learn from them.

So much of hip-hop projects fantasies of wealth and power. As far as
I can tell, these fantasies are direct reactions to the real powerlessness and
helplessness that so many of us feel all day, every day. (Take a second—do
you think the people in this country who really are wealthy and powerful
take time out of their lives, let alone pay money, to watch actors put on a
show of what wealth and power look like? Of course not—they own stock
in all the record labels and TV networks, and they get richer every time
we pay to watch or hear the fantasy.) These fantasies of wealth and power don't offer any realistic examples of how the vast majority of people
might find a way out of unhappiness, let alone get wealth and/or power,

Five Reasons Friends Matter

- They tell me how I'm doing when I'm out in public.
- They give me advice about things I don't know or can't do myself.
- They have my back and support me when I'm down.
- They tell me the honest but loving truth about everything, whether I
  like it or not.
- Sharing my life with them makes everything I do more meaningful.

and that's fine. Or, rather, it would be fine if 99 percent of the images our kids consume of Black people in the media weren't only of professional sports, music videos, and crime on the evening news.

It troubles me that this is what any young African American looking for a "reflection" of himself or herself on TV sees. It especially troubles me that the only examples of how Black people rise above hardship come from highly paid performers—athletes, singers, and rappers. And it pains me that so many of these images rest on violence, the putting down of women, and the promotion of expensive things as sexy.

But as much as all this troubles and pains me, I still don't blame the people who make and buy hip-hop, because so many criticisms of hip-hop ignore the realities of the market. We buy and watch on TV things that degrade us; if we didn't, no one would make money producing these things, and they would have to make something else. But we don't consume things that degrade us because we're stupid or we don't know better, we do it because we ourselves feel degraded. Like the boy who told Reggie he couldn't wait to get shot, we live lives so stripped of hope at so many levels that we believe degradation entertains us, and that to be entertained is to be happy. This may sound pie-in-the-sky, but my heartfelt hope is that as there is more healing in our community, how we represent ourselves and what we consume will reflect our healing more than our pain.

> Suffering can be our greatest asset. If we have the capacity to learn from our suffering we have the capacity to improve our lives, improve our families, and improve our communities.
>
> —ALEXANDER MCKINNON, INVENTOR OF THE JIRO GOLF PUTTER

Chapter Five

THAT'S WHAT FRIENDS ARE FOR
How Loved Ones Can Help

When my symptoms of depression went from very bad to even worse, I didn't tell a soul—not even my family. It wasn't until after the article on my depression was published in *Essence* (when I was fifty-one years old) that my own sister confessed that she had suffered from periods of heaviness, difficulty, and pain, too! It turned out that my sister Lani *and* my mother had been going through pain, and each of us had been alone. My mom's depression has its roots in her sexual abuse by an older brother.

It must have started when I was somewhere around seven. My brother and his wife were living in the house with us. There are so many opportunities for people to isolate kids on a farm; I know now that other kids I played with were having similar experiences.

In the beginning, I didn't know how it felt—I just lay there. There was never any penetration, but I still felt a lot of shame, and I didn't tell anyone. It was a secret. He never said to me, 'This is our secret'; it was just something I didn't talk about because of the shame—What would my siblings think? What would my mother think if she knew? And that went on until I was about eleven or twelve, when I got my period, and I knew I could become pregnant; that's when I fought back, and that's when it stopped.

I didn't tell anyone because I felt so much shame. How could I face my mother, how could I face my siblings had I told them about what was going on? My way of dealing with the abuse was to achieve, bury myself in books, read, do what I had to do, go to school as much as I could to avoid thinking about it.

When my niece, my brother's daughter, was about twelve or thirteen, she shared with me that he had sexually abused her. I believed her, but when I told my sisters, they didn't believe it, and I couldn't tell them *why* I believed she was telling the truth. At that time, even as an adult with children of my own, I couldn't tell them about what he had done to me, because I was still carrying the shame and the guilt. And I was not able to tell my niece that her father had sexually abused me.

Going to college gave me a broader knowledge that it was okay to talk about it, and that knowledge has enabled me to get rid of my shame. I had never heard of the word depression when I was a child. I grew up in an environment where people didn't really talk about things, in a society where we just didn't talk about our feelings.

Just like my mom, my depression fueled my shame, and vice versa. But acknowledging my depression, just admitting to it, gave me a new lease on life. It not only brought me closer to my mother and my sister, it gave me permission to stop pretending that things were okay when they weren't and freed me to begin my life. Finally I could actually talk to people. I could tell them that I wasn't up to doing something on a given day, and they would understand that—despite how "together" I may look (and Lord knows I work at it!)—I'm very fragile.

I still can't get over how much the three of us lost by not knowing how to be there for one another—by not knowing how to recognize the symptoms of depression in one another and find a meaningful way to deal with them or even just talk about them. How many families are in pain right now because they don't know how to say, "Hey, I think you're depressed!" let alone "Let's talk about how we're gonna take care of you"?

I bumped into Karin and Noah Hopkins at the *Essence* Music Festival in 2005, and as we talked about my article and this book, Karin told me that she, too, suffered from depression. Before she could continue, Noah took her hand and said, "No, *we* suffer from depression." It was a very moving and telling moment. He understood how profoundly depression affects those around the sufferer. This chapter is especially for the friends and loved ones of a depressed person. If you're the one who's depressed, don't go anywhere—you're about to find out ways to help *other* people help *you*. You're going to read the stories of people who've lived with a depressed family member and had the disease affect them. But these pages don't just talk about the toll depression can take on a family system; they have a lot to say about specific ways to help the depressed person—*and* those who love him or her.

Hidden Casualties

The obvious victim of depression is the person suffering from it, but as Karin and Noah understood, anyone who loves a depressed person is also afflicted by this illness. If depression were a smart bomb aimed straight at me, all the people who care about me would also be hurt. And the closer you are to someone who's depressed—parent, child, husband, wife, boyfriend, girlfriend, brother, sister—the harder you're likely to be hit.

If you are deeply involved in the life of someone suffering from depression, it can really take its toll on *you,* too. As you see what this person you love is going through, you may feel all kinds of things: confused, angry, frustrated, responsible, betrayed, lonely, sad, inadequate, helpless . . . even depressed yourself. Even if you don't know what depression is exactly, you can tell after a while that something is very wrong—that what you are seeing is way more than a bad mood or "the blues." Maybe you try to make things easier on a loved one, try to ease their burden, to cheer them up, only to have your efforts be barely noticed. Then maybe you feel you need to "try harder," but that doesn't help at all. The most common feeling people have in these situations—and the most common *mistake* we make—is to assume that we are somehow responsible for the suffering of the person we love ("Oh, if only I had (not) done this or that . . ." "If only I were a better mom/dad/daughter/son," etc.). We often imagine that if we could only do the right thing, our loved one would magically get better.

"If only . . ." is right—if only it were that easy! The fact is, nobody can "cure" anyone of depression, but there are things we can do to help the depressed person in our lives work his or her way toward feeling better. And the first thing we can do is *name* what ails them.

All in the Name . . .

When you think about how reluctant we Black folks have been to identify depression in ourselves, you won't be surprised to know that we have a hard time seeing it in those around us, even the people closest to us. As a people, we have to get over the fear, shame, and denial of mental illness. When we do (and I mean when, not if!), we will be able to help not only ourselves, but our loved ones, too. Nine times out of ten, somebody who is in the middle of depression is not in the best position to evaluate his or her own condition; that's where *we* come in.

We need to be informed, unafraid, and forward-thinking in getting the people we love to understand what's going on and in providing them with the resources to help themselves. That's right—I said *help themselves*. Being a supportive friend, partner, or parent does *not* mean that you do all the work. It means that you let the person know you're there for them, and that you're ready and willing to help in the healing process. In this chapter I talk a lot about just what healthy helping looks like.

The first step in addressing depression—what it looks like, how it feels, and how it affects us—is learning about it and naming it. The second step is learning how to be supportive and self-nurturing while the depressed person begins the slow and difficult task of healing.

What's Wrong with M'dear?

One of the hardest parts of being an adult with a parent who is depressed can be just getting your mom or dad to listen to you! (And, yes, now we finally know how *they* felt trying to communicate with *us* for all those years.) For as much as our own generation feels like there is a stigma attached to asking for help from anyone but God, our parents' generation is even more resistant. If trying to get your sixty-plus mother or father to see a therapist or life coach feels about as effective as talking to a brick wall, you know exactly what I'm talking about. Or maybe you have the opposite problem— you still feel like the child when dealing with your parent, or regardless of what *you* think, *they* still think of you as a kid, and so you can't influence them because, in their minds, you have no more authority than you did when you were in diapers.

Sometimes you run into family obstacles before you even get a chance to have that hard conversation. Maybe your sister is saying things like, "Dad is not 'depressed,' he's just angry about blah-blah-blah . . ." Or your father is saying things like, "There's nothing wrong with your mother, she's just going through one of her things—she'll be fine in a couple of months . . ." Or you try to tell your brother about what you see Momma going through, and he says, "Ever since you read that Terrie Williams book, you think *everybody* is depressed!" And then there are different degrees of disagreement. Maybe your family member is willing to "respectfully disagree" and won't stop you from convincing Mom or Dad to go to a therapist but simply refuses to help. Maybe, though, they feel so strongly opposed to seeking help outside of church or a *medical* doctor that they see what you want to do as not just useless but downright bad. If you go ahead and do what you have to do, they'll be ticked off—or worse.

Now take all that and add to it the problem of time. You've got your own life at home and at work, your own family, your own obligations, and now you're driving over to see your mother every day because you're worried that she's not eating, that she's not taking care of herself in some of the most basic ways. Those visits are taking time away from the people who already depend on you and adding all kinds of stress to your life—which wasn't exactly a piece of cake before this!

Gifted actor and humanitarian Blair Underwood went through this with his mom, Marilyn Underwood, a woman he describes as "the glue of the family," the one who held everyone and everything together. Before her depression started, she was already going through life-changing experiences, and none of them were good: She was diagnosed with multiple sclerosis, had an emergency hysterectomy, had her gallbladder, part of the small intestine, and part of her pancreas removed because of a cancer scare, and *then* started menopause . . . It was only after she had survived and more or less recovered from the surgeries that she started becoming depressed.

At first Blair's mom's depression showed itself in her being obsessed—"She started worrying about finances, numbers, math," convinced that "something" was wrong, and she had to find out what it was and fix it. Blair didn't understand it then, but he later learned from a therapist that obsession is one of the ways depression begins, especially for go-getter, type A personalities, because they "feel as though they're drowning and can't catch their breath." After a while, though, Marilyn started showing some of the more common signs—she didn't want to eat (partly related to the MS), she didn't want to engage other people, she didn't want to get out of bed . . . and, eventually, she didn't want to live—she tried to kill herself on three separate occasions. "I watched my mother become someone I didn't know. She became almost a stranger. Although she had been a devout Christian her entire life—this was the woman who had taken us to church every Sunday—she was angry at God."

Blair felt helpless and bewildered in the face of his mother's condition. Then when he, his dad, his brother, and his sisters teamed up and started trying to get help for her, he began to feel more hopeful. A psychiatrist told them that most people dealing with depression like his mother's could be treated, and "the sooner you can administer medicine, see a therapist, and have the support and love of family, the better." As it turned out, his mother ultimately did respond, but it wasn't quick or easy—the ordeal lasted nearly seven years—and sometimes she would slide back into depression. Still, with the support and help and love of her family, she has been able to come out on the other side and wants to help others.

Experiencing his mom's depression, recovery, and relapses showed Blair "how fragile human nature and sanity can be. It allowed me to understand the pressures of everyday life, to understand—besides how fragile our bodies are—how fragile our minds can be; there truly is a thin line between sanity and insanity. It also helped me pay much more attention to my wife and family, to see when my wife is overwhelmed and to help her. Now I'm very sensitive to when my wife needs a break, and I try to give it to her, to let her have some alone time when she feels overwhelmed, to make sure our lives are balanced. I've also learned that depression is nothing to be ashamed of! If you catch a cold, get a flu, or get depressed, these are *all* conditions that can be treated."

Getting Older and Depressed

Although Blair Underwood's mother is unique, her experience of depression is not. In fact, depression is all too often a fixture of the lives of older folks. According to the National Institute of Mental Health, "Of the nearly 35 million Americans age 65 and older, an estimated 2 million have a depressive illness." And in the year 2000, people aged 65 and older accounted for roughly 18 percent of all suicide deaths!

These numbers are shocking, but it's easy to imagine why older folks might feel depressed. We live in a culture that tells us aging makes you worthless. Good health insurance is expensive, and most people who live on fixed incomes can't afford "quality" care. Brenda Hendy, a geriatric social worker in Mount Vernon, New York, says, "Men and women who grew up in the first half of the last century often find it even harder than their children do to ask for help or admit they can't handle their lives in the same way anymore." And if getting laid up with a flu makes you cranky, think what medical conditions like high blood pressure, diabetes, Parkinson's disease, cancer, and strokes do to a person's sense of self-esteem. It's hard to wake up one morning and realize that just walking up and down the stairs is a painful challenge. None of us wants to feel like a burden on our family or like we're alone and helpless in the world! Just look at how many men and women sink into depression when they move into nursing homes.

Take Alex McNair. At eighty-five he has led a long and full life. And up until two years ago you could find him playing eighteen holes of golf on any sunny Saturday. But two years ago his high blood pressure and ulcers started giving him trouble. He went from a still-active and youthful eighty-three-year-old to a frail eighty-five-year-old. The change was so sudden that Alex sank into a depression.

A son of sharecroppers, he had been taught to keep his feelings inside, so months went by without him talking about how he felt. His wife worried terribly about his loss of weight (forty pounds in a year and a half), and his children made sure he went to the doctor, but everyone was so worried about his physical health that no one thought about his mental health. It wasn't until his temper started to flare (something that was unusual for him) that his youngest daughter, Sonja, began to wonder if he might be depressed. She looked up symptoms of depression in the elderly on the NIMH Web site and found the following: "Feelings of nervousness or 'emptiness,' feeling guilty or worthless, feeling very tired and slowed down, not enjoying things the way you used to, feeling restless and irritable, feeling like no one loves you, or like life is not worth living." Also included in the definition were "sleeping more or less than usual, eating more or less than usual, and/or having persistent headaches, stomachaches, or chronic pain."

Alex *had* been irritable, sleeping more than usual, not eating, complaining of pains, and questioning Sonja and her sister Natasha's love. A trip to the therapist proved her right. Alex's sudden physical decline had left him feeling worthless and dependent, and those feelings had, over several months, turned into depression. After he saw a psychopharmacologist (a psychiatrist who prescribes medication—see chapter nine for a more detailed explanation) and started taking Lexapro, his mood improved and his appetite returned. And while he wasn't 100 percent his old self, eighty-five suddenly didn't feel so horribly old anymore.

It's important for those of us who are older not to give up on life. Just because you're older doesn't mean you're not entitled to live life feeling good. Hell, you've earned the right to feel good! So don't be afraid to admit that you need a little help if you're feeling low. And let's all think twice before we buy into this society's exaggerated focus on youth. Our elders are a national treasure and we need to make sure they feel that way, too!

What Have You Done with My Man?
Where Has My Woman Gone?

Toni was thirty-six when she met Daryl. He was a cable technician and she was an accounts manager at a large advertising agency. Both came from solid working-class families in Detroit and had relocated to New York to pursue greater career possibilities. They found kindred spirits in each other, and their relationship progressed quickly to marriage. Toni had never been married, but Daryl had a fourteen-year-old son with his high school sweetheart in Detroit. Life was good for the newlyweds, until around the time of their first anniversary, when Daryl started noticing changes in Toni.

She was coming home from work tired and cranky—not just some days, but every day, and there was never a particular reason. If Daryl pressed her too hard on a subject she didn't want to talk about, she'd snap at him. A passionate volleyball player, she stopped going to practices and games, and eventually quit the team. When Daryl played basketball on Thursdays, she used to go out for a drink with her work friends and then meet him afterward at their favorite restaurant; before long, it was no drink, no meeting, no restaurant. Soon she was spending most evenings and weekends in bed. Daryl got more and more worried, but his worry turned to anger when she refused to acknowledge that anything was wrong.

"Here I thought I'd found the woman of my dreams," he told me. "Athletic, good-looking, fun-loving . . . but instead it seemed like I wound up with a welfare mother in disguise!" Daryl's growing frustration didn't help things. It wasn't until he heard a therapist talking about depression on a call-in radio show that he began to realize that Toni's problem was not "laziness." Toni, who had kept depression away for years with long work hours and frequent dating, found her new life of stable and devoted marriage cracking open her defenses. Daryl knew he had to get outside help when he scheduled a surprise four-day trip to Miami, and she stood in their bedroom crying and unable to pack. "The only thing the old Toni loved more than travel was surprises. I knew the woman I married wasn't there anymore when a surprise trip made her break down."

Through a lot of encouragement, Daryl got Toni to see a therapist recommended by a friend of hers. Still, she was so reluctant to go that Daryl had to take her to the first four appointments just to make sure she went. The therapist sent her to a psychopharmacologist who prescribed an antidepressant in addition to talk therapy. Six months later Toni was still depressed, but much more able to connect with her former self. Daryl is still hanging in there, although there is no denying that the last two years have left him with scars. "I love her, but it's been hard to see the woman I love become a stranger. It's like we have to get to know each other all over again."

Depression can be hell for an intimate relationship. It can throw any couple, even a strong one, into a tailspin. If your partner is having the blues as a direct result of some event you know about (such as dealing with the death of a parent, losing a job, or being passed over for a promotion), you know these things happen, and that, as hard as they are, unhappy feelings pass and life moves on, however slowly; you certainly don't tell yourself it's *your* fault.

But when you see that those low feelings don't have an obvious cause or that even if they once did have a cause, the feelings are not getting better with time, your mind often takes a different approach. You look at the man or woman you love, you see the distress, you don't see the cause . . . and you blame yourself! You don't *know* that you're really the problem (Hint: You're not), and your partner might even tell you straight out, "It's not you," but you don't buy it. After all, if you're not the problem, why is your husband/wife rejecting you? Why do you feel (s)he doesn't love you anymore? You don't want to be "the problem," really, but maybe if you are, you can at least try to fix it . . . (Hint: You can't. Because you're *still* not the problem!)

Another common reaction, especially when you don't have a clear understanding of depression, is to blame the one who's depressed! I have a lot to say about this in chapter seven, "*Don't* Snap Out of It!" but for now let's assume that you know depression doesn't work that way, so you don't think your partner brought it on himself or herself. Even so, without pointing a finger at either one of you, you may feel like the relationship itself is a failure simply because you don't have the tools to fix a problem as serious as this one. And knowing it's nobody's fault doesn't do anything to relieve you of the very real burden of picking up the slack that your man or woman is leaving, depending on how much the depression has left them unable to function. That "slack" might be just their share of household chores, or it might be the bigger responsibility of taking care of kids or even something as big as paying the rent or the mortgage. In a situation like that, resentment would be the least productive reaction you could have, but it would certainly be the most understandable.

When Your Child Is Hurting

Just as heart-wrenching as a parent's depression is that of a child. Kids go through many phases in their growing-up years, so it's easy to see why many people don't take childhood depression seriously. "He'll grow out of it," "She's going through that phase," "He's mad at the world lately" . . . As I said in chapter four, it can be hard to recognize this illness in kids because they may act out their unbearable feelings rather than hang around and look sad. But once we can look beyond those actions and stop thinking things like, "That boy is nothing but trouble . . ." or "That girl just lives to do the opposite of what I tell her . . ."—once we can see that "bad behavior" is often a kid's way of trying to drive out feelings they can't stand or understand, we often go from feeling angry at them to feeling guilty toward them. Maybe we are the cause of their problems. Maybe we've been bad parents . . .

None of us is perfect, and I'm sure that if we take a long, slow look at how we parent, we'll all find that we have room for improvement. However—and I cannot stress this point enough—nobody *causes* depression in anybody else! And while it's true that a child who grows up with a depressed parent is much more at risk for depression than one who doesn't, it doesn't mean that those children absolutely will have to deal with depression. And even if they do, it is not the depressed parent's "fault"! I mean, let's get serious—depressed people have enough weight on their shoulders without having to carry the extra burden of other people's depression.

If you have a child who seems to be depressed, try to remember that feeling guilty about their suffering won't help them at all. On the other hand, there are a lot of things you can do to help, as you'll see below. The first thing you can do, though, is listen.

I Miss My Best Friend

Tanya McKinnon is a publishing professional in her late thirties and a brilliant writer who was an invaluable help to me on this book. Years ago she moved to New York City to pursue a master's degree and went straight from grad school into publishing. Three months after coming to the city, her seven-year relationship ended. Feeling lonely and friendless in the Big Apple, she turned to Karen, a close friend of a decade. Unfortunately, her needs coincided with her friend's first bout of major depression. Also in graduate school, though down south, Karen had recently suffered the loss of her father, to whom she was very close. This loss, coupled with a difficult relationship with her mother, turned her grieving process into full-blown depression.

I had gone to her father's funeral the year before, and I knew how hard his death had hit her, but I really noticed that she wasn't moving forward with her grief after I moved to New York. Before, we had always talked on the phone at least three or four hours a week. In the weeks after I moved, that number dropped to one. In the months that followed, it dropped to fifteen-minute callbacks—and even then her voice sounded flat and obligatory. I was going through my own hard time and needed all the support I could get, so it felt like a double loss to discover that my best friend was clinically depressed.

At first Tanya was sympathetic but, "After six months of feeling like I was carrying the relationship—and I'm ashamed to admit it now—I became angry. She had always had it all together, so it didn't even occur to me at first that she could be depressed!" It wasn't until a mutual friend, who had suffered from depression herself, told Tanya that Karen sounded "depressed" that she started being more sympathetic. For weeks Tanya encouraged Karen to see a therapist, but her pleas fell on deaf ears. "I felt helpless, angry, shut out, and uncertain where the boundaries of our friendship were anymore. If she didn't want help, was it really my place to insist?"

This is the dilemma friends of depressed people often face. When is intervention too much? Is it their role to take a stronger stand, or the family's? What if the friend's family is doing nothing or, even worse, *wants* nothing done? Tanya was lucky to find a family member who was willing to join the team.

I'd met her brother Alan a few times at family gatherings, and even though I didn't know him well, in the end I decided to call him. I couldn't think of anything else! He listened patiently, and agreed that something had to be done. Karen was going to work, coming home, and seeing no one—not even talking on the phone. She used to call her niece, who she adores, almost every day, but at this point she hadn't called her in six weeks!

After months of pushing from Tanya and Alan, Karen finally made an appointment with a therapist. Within four sessions, the therapist had diagnosed her with clinical depression and prescribed Celexa. Four months after, Karen was behaving more like her old self—and she was *dealing* with her issues, instead of trying to bury them and herself.

Not everyone is as fortunate as Tanya in being able to enlist a willing family member to get help for a friend. Sometimes family members, driven by religious beliefs or their own issues or shame, refuse to listen when a friend points out the obvious. In some ways, it can even be harder to deal with a friend's depression than a family member's. After all, you may have been best friends for the past twenty years, but that doesn't make you blood, so in a lot of people's eyes you don't have the "rights" that kin have—even the right to try to help. You see that something's very wrong with her, but if her family doesn't see it, you may be forced to watch from the sidelines as things get worse and worse.

Tough as it can be to get past the roadblocks that your friend's family or her man may put up, it can be just as tough or tougher to get through when your friend is unpartnered. A lot of times a single mom is the only grown-up in her household, so it's very possible that the people in the best position to see what's happening and to understand *are* her friends, not family members who may see her rarely.

Then there's the issue of overstepping the boundaries of your friendship. Even if what you're actually saying is, "Hey, I see you're hurting, and I want to help," what she may be hearing is something like, "Girl, you're a mental case!" Instead of giving you a fair hearing, much less being grateful that you care about her, your friend might feel like you're insulting her. Even if she talks to you, it can still take a long time and a lot of work to get past angry defenses and old ideas. (Shortcut: Give her a copy of this book!)

And what about your own anger? It's starting to feel like forever that it's been all about her, with you trying not to burden her and trying to cheer her up, and maybe you're realizing that lately you feel resentful toward her. Maybe you feel like if the friendship were really a two-way street, she would at least break through some of her misery, just every once in a while, to find out what's going on with you! This can lead you to start avoiding her out of frustration or, in a worst-case scenario, call it quits. That's a terrible pass to come to: You end the friendship as it is now because you desperately miss the friendship it used to be. She's depressed, and you're mourning your running partner, gossip girl, or all around go-to gal—the first one you would turn to in a bad situation (like this one), but she's just not there!

When Depression Wears a Different Face

Up to this point, most of the depression I've been talking about is within the range of your regular mainstream depression (see pages 24–28 if you need a quick reminder of the most common symptoms). I want to take a moment here, though, to tell you about four types of depression that you may see in someone you love. They are not as common as general depression, but if you're not familiar with them you might not recognize them as depression. The four are postpartum depression (sometimes mistakenly called "baby blues"), seasonal affective disorder (also known as SAD—it occurs in midwinter when there is only a short period of sunlight, but it's a real condition), manic depression (aka, bipolar disorder), which, because of the "manic" part doesn't always have the symptoms we associate with depression, and premenstrual dysphoric disorder, or PMDD.

Postpartum Depression

When Beverly Morgan was in college, she was known as easygoing and lively and was at the top of her class. Her parents, very middle class, were adamant that their children succeed. Beverly graduated as one of only a few Black women engineers in her class and went on to get her master's in business administration. Before she had her first child, she worked for a well-known environmental engineering firm as a team leader. "I'm one of the lucky few—stress doesn't faze me. All the people around me could be losing their heads, but I would just stay focused until we worked out the problem and met the deadline." This kind of dedication brought her workplace success and a fat salary to match.

When she and her husband, Ben, were ready to have their first child, she decided to take a year off from work, because she felt that her hectic schedule would mean too much time apart from her newborn daughter. Things that first year with her baby girl were tough—so different from the workplace stress that she handled so well—but rewarding. Then, eleven months after her daughter's birth, she got pregnant again.

> Listed as a manic depressive with extreme paranoia and, dog, I got something for ya. Hear my name, feel my pain . . .
>
> –DMX, RECORDING ARTIST WHO LIVES WITH MANIC DEPRESSION, FROM "F**KIN' WIT D"

Unlike her first pregnancy, this one was *not* planned. Beverly had always been pro-choice, but after the birth of her daughter she couldn't bear the idea of an abortion, and they had the baby. Two months after the birth of her son her husband became concerned. While their daughter's first year had been stressful for Beverly, she had managed it, and Ben assumed that the second child would just be more of the same. But it wasn't—dealing with two babies threw Beverly completely off.

"My workload wasn't doubled," she told me. "It was squared! My daughter regressed and wanted to be breast-fed; neither baby slept; Ben was working extra hours to make up for the loss of my income; and I felt like a single mother who happened to be married." The stress of raising two infants and being across the ocean from her family and friends was too much, and Beverly slipped into depression. For months she spoke mainly to the children, refused to let Ben touch her intimately, and wouldn't respond to phone calls or e-mails from friends. When her best friend, at Ben's urging, finally flew out to spend a week with them, she was shocked to find Beverly overweight, pale, and emotionally "flat."

This was much more than "baby blues." Beverly was clinically depressed. She said that as a devout Baptist she didn't "believe in" therapy; as a result, she spent much of the next two years emotionally and socially paralyzed. She lost touch with almost all her friends from high school, college, and grad school. Her former colleagues no longer called, and even the mothers of other kids knew not to try to include her in their mom activities. By now Beverly's postpartum depression was taking a toll on her marriage. Ben felt angry, frustrated, and betrayed. At first sympathetic, he now began to blame Beverly for how she felt. His anger often took the form of criticizing her parent-

> I was drunk. Stoned, too, and feeling sorry for myself. I wanted to die. So I set my Black ass on fire.
>
> —RICHARD PRYOR, COMEDIAN

ing, her housekeeping, and even her appearance. His constant criticism only served to make her feel worse, and she spiraled further down. It wasn't until they saw her daughter, then five years old, start to show signs of depression herself (bullying other kids at school and disrupted sleep) that Beverly finally acknowledged needing professional help and started getting the help she needed.

Despite popular images of pregnancy as a special, happy time for all moms-to-be, up to 20 percent go through depression; of those, between 10 and 15 percent are so depressed that they actually try to take their own lives. Depression during pregnancy is hard to diagnose because some of the symptoms, like disrupted sleep, fatigue, and changes in appetite are normal for pregnancy.

The less serious "baby blues," occurring in about 80 percent of mothers, usually start within the first week after birth and last for up to three weeks. Typical symptoms are mood swings, weepiness, sadness, anxiety, lack of concentration, and feelings of neediness.

Postpartum depression is much more serious. It starts more gradually (though it can begin any time in the first year and pick up speed once it starts) and symptoms include excessive worry or anxiety, irritability or a short temper, feeling overwhelmed, trouble making decisions, sadness, feeling guilty, phobias, hopelessness, sleep problems (too little sleep or too much), fatigue, stomach trouble, aches and pains without a clear physical cause, discomfort around the baby or a lack of feeling toward the baby, loss of focus, loss of interest or pleasure, and little interest in sex. Women who suffer from it also

> Daddy did not ask God to make him crazy so he could torment his wife and kids, just as other folks don't request cancer so they can die slowly in front of the people they love.
>
> —JUDGE LYNN TOLER, AUTHOR AND *DIVORCE COURT* STAR

experience changes in appetite with significant weight loss or gain. And, by the way, it's not only "natural" mothers who go through postpartum depression—adoptive mothers are susceptible to it, too.

The Department of Health Services calls maternal depression *the* most significant mental health issue interfering with children's readiness for school. Study after study has shown how hard a mother's depression can impact children from infancy through teen years if it remains untreated. On the other hand, when mothers *are* treated for depression, the whole family benefits.

Seasonal Affective Disorder

Jeff Anderson is a successful theater producer; he has also battled sex addiction for most of his adult life. For the last few years he has had the help of therapy and, more recently, a 12-step program. He has battled low self-esteem along with many personal issues caused by his sex addiction. The end of his most recent relationship came when his man, an interesting and attractive musician, found an e-mail trail for a male hustler that Jeff had hired right before Christmas.

His inability to stop acting out and the loss of this latest relationship threw Jeff in a tailspin, and he took a four-week "vacation" to attend a clinic that specializes in sex addiction. While there, he seemed to make no progress. One day a particularly sensitive counselor asked him to write down all the times he's fallen off the wagon. When Jeff brought the details back, the counselor asked him why all his slips occurred in winter. Jeff told the counselor he didn't see a connection, but, as it happens, he hates the cold and dreads winter. That was when the counselor suggested that seasonal affective disorder might be fueling Jeff's addiction.

It turned out that every year, like clockwork, Jeff would begin to feel increasingly worthless as November approached, and by January or February he would bottom out and undermine whatever good relationship was in his life. Generally his moods would become increasingly miserable in December. He had trouble getting out of bed, often getting to the office late. He craved sweets and would have to do double time at the gym just to keep the pounds off. Summers, on the other hand, made him feel alive—he would lose weight, exercise outside, and feel much more confident to meet other men.

The counselor explained that fewer daylight hours has a severe effect on some people. Some researchers think that melatonin, the brain hormone that regulates our cycles of being awake and asleep and has been linked to depression, is produced at higher levels in the dark. That would mean that the shorter the days, the greater the risk of your melatonin increasing and, along with it, a greater risk of seasonal depression.

Jeff was unsure at first, but armed with a new antidepressant medication and a journal in which he noted his changing moods, he approached February, his least favorite month, with curiosity. His journal proved that as the weather got better so did his mood. The change was so dramatic that Jeff felt a deep sense of relief. For the first time in ten years he could see that part of his addiction was linked to forces outside of his own willpower. The following winter he invested in a state-of-the-art phototherapy lamp (it's a lamp that imitates the sun's full spectrum rays) and instead of going to the gym spent as much time as possible hiking in the winter sunlight. His sexual compulsion is still an issue, but this past winter he managed not to fall off the wagon.

SAD is seasonal depression. Each year from fall to spring it hits about half a million people. The wintertime lack of sun creates a chemical imbalance in the brain. It usually happens every winter and can be mild or severe. The most common symptoms are sleep problems, lack of energy, overeating, feelings of low self-esteem, hopelessness and misery, social problems, anxiety, loss of sex drive, and mood changes. People who suffer from SAD often have a weakened immune system during the winter, which makes them likely to get infections and other illnesses.

Manic Depression (Bipolar Disorder)

One of my former interns told me the following story of her younger brother's battle with manic depression.

Janice was in graduate school when her younger brother, Sean, was a junior at the local college. He was living at home, working days, and going to school in the evening.

"He always liked to look nice, so even though my parents could pay the tuition, he worked the job to buy clothes and make his car payment. We noticed that he seemed a little wired and distant lately, but we supposed it was the normal stresses of junior year. Then one night I came home to a message from my parents begging me to come home. When I got there an hour later I found Sean locked in his room, making strange singing sounds.

My parents told me he had been that way for the last seven hours."
Janice and her parents finally broke into Sean's room and found him
sitting in his underwear, chanting religious scripture. Passages from the
Bible and other religious books were taped to his walls.

My mother ran over and hugged him to her, but he just pushed her
away and told her not to worry because he had been "chosen." We
called the family doctor because we didn't know who else to call. He
recommended that we take Sean to the emergency room for a psychiatric evaluation.

My mother cried all the way to the hospital, my father drove in
stony silence, and Sean kept chanting next to me in the backseat.
When we got to the hospital the psychiatrist on duty took Sean away
for about two or three hours. When he came to speak with us I felt
like the world was suddenly in slow motion. He told us that in all
likelihood Sean had bipolar disorder—that he would need immediate
psychiatric care and then ongoing therapy and medication.

The next day we moved him to a mental health facility and he
stayed there for a week. The medication slowly brought him down
from the weird behavior, and we could talk to him. We found out
he had secretly bought a second car and that he was $43,000 in debt.
Ten thousand of it he had given to a fringe religious organization that
promised to ordain him.

My parents were devastated. I went numb for a few days. A couple
of weeks later I was in class and
feeling so low that I confided in
a classmate about what was going on. She told me about Patty
Duke's book, *A Brilliant Madness: Living with Manic-Depressive Illness.* I walked straight to
the library, got the book, and
started reading. It was the first
moment of hope I'd had since

> Very few suicidal people want
> to die; they just don't want to
> live the way they're living.
>
> —ALTHEA HANKINS, MD, FACP DIREC-
> TOR, GERMANTOWN MEDICAL CENTER,
> PHILADELPHIA

we found Sean in his room. When I realized that bipolar disorder
could be treated, some of the shame I'd been feeling started to sub-
side, and I felt empowered to help my little brother.

That was only a year and a half ago, though sometimes it seems like twenty years have passed since then, and sometimes it seems like it was yesterday. Sean is set to graduate this spring with a degree in computer science and information systems, and I'm even more proud of him now because I know what he's up against. He still lives with my parents and takes his medication regularly—for the most part. The way his manic depression shows itself is that he starts getting over-involved with religious writing and groups and then starts spending money he doesn't have. But we've all learned to look for the signs that he may be having an episode. If he starts seeming secretive, look-ing like he's not been sleeping, walking around with a lot of different books, we immediately call a family meeting and talk to him about what's going on. The one time we realized he'd gone off his meds, we were able to get him back on after only a single conversation. But every day a little part of me worries if we'll catch it the next time.

You've probably heard of bipolar disorder under the name "manic depression." The "bipolar" part refers to the ways one's mood can alter-nate between the "poles" of mania (highs) and depression (lows). As if bouncing between these extremes weren't bad enough, there's no way of knowing how long a "swing" will last—anywhere from hours to months. Some symptoms on the manic side are high physical energy, super upbeat mood to the point of arrogance and even aggression, grandiosity, and even delusions. People in manic episodes are prone to going on shopping sprees they can't afford, going into debt they have no way out of, and believing that they are famous people or are in touch with famous people (whether dead or alive). Symptoms on the depression side are all the standard ones for depression (see pages 24–28 for a reminder).

To make things more confusing, the disorder is divided into two types. Bipolar I is considered the worse of the two because the manic episodes are extreme, and there are mixed episodes (mania and depression on the same day for a week or more) as well as episodes of major depression. Bipolar II is often mistaken for depression because the episodes of depression far outweigh those of mania, and the few manic episodes that do occur are much less extreme than those in Bipolar I—as a matter of fact, they are often comparatively mild enough to be considered just a little "kooky" by those who don't understand the disorder.

PMDD

Sean Longmire is a vibrant and expressive professional woman in her forties. I was blessed to meet the beloved aunt of Malaak Compton-Rock, philanthropist and wife of comedian Chris Rock. She has suffered from depression her whole life, but it wasn't until a few years ago that she discovered she suffers from a particular form of depression called premenstrual dysphoric disorder, or PMDD. PMDD might best be described as a severe form of PMS (premenstrual syndrome). For most of her life, Sean's depression would last for a month or a few weeks and then pass. "I couldn't put my finger on anything specific, but now I realize I also have severe PMS."

Although she does suffer from depression, her feelings of despair are doubled by the PMDD. At times things got so bad that she didn't know if she could hold on. She told me, "It angers me that no one would listen about the PMS. I finally met a therapist who has me on a schedule that tracks how severe my daily problems are. As you look at the chart it goes up and down and it relates to my menstrual cycle. It is affecting me as much as the depression because it takes over ten days of my life—for five to ten days a month I'll have severe depression. It is called PMDD, and when it connects to my natural depression, it's really, really bad. When I was planning to conceive I tracked my period and noticed that I had mood swings. That was the PMDD."

For years Sean didn't associate her mood swings with PMS because she had had a hysterectomy to remove fibroids. The surgery was a failure on two counts. "It left my ovaries, so I still have PMS. On top of that, the intense pain we had hoped the surgery would address turned out to be due not to the fibroids but to ovulation. (Some women feel physical pain when they ovulate each month.)"

Sean is far from alone. PMS hits up to 75 percent of menstruating women, and it's estimated that 5 percent of us suffer from PMDD. In fact, women with severe premenstrual symptoms are five times more likely than those with moderate symptoms to experience symptoms of PMDD every month.

The emotional symptoms of PMDD are like those of depression, or make existing depression worse, and women who are depressed are more at risk. PMDD's symptoms differ in that they come in cycles and last less time than an episode of clinical depression might be likely to last.

Sean experienced firsthand how severe the feelings of depression and hopelessness were. Some women even become suicidal. Jean Endicott,

PhD, director of the Premenstrual Evaluation Unit at Columbia Presbyterian Medical Center, says, "I frequently work with patients who have waited years to ask a doctor about premenstrual problems or have been turned away by their health care provider when they tried to discuss symptoms." A big obstacle is that many women "fear becoming the target of jokes, or [believe] that seeking help is a sign of weakness."

While it's less common than clinical depression, it's important for women (and their partners) to realize that PMDD is a real condition, and that depressed women can be triggered into severe depression by their menstrual cycles.

The Worst Thing in the World— When a Loved One Tries to Commit Suicide

Rasheed Williams is a Baltimore schoolteacher whose brother Mykel tried to kill himself the summer after he graduated from college. While Mykel got immediate help at the hospital and started recovering from alcoholism in Alcoholics Anonymous, his suicide attempt left deep scars in Rasheed and their father. They felt for the next twenty years that they had to cushion Mykel, let him have his way, make things easier on him whenever they could—even when he was acting out—so that he wouldn't have "cause" to try again to take his life.

On the surface they were successful: Mykel has been sober for over two decades and has never so much as mentioned wanting to kill himself. But Rasheed and their father have walked on eggshells all that time—always trying to soothe Mykel, always letting him have his way, always explaining away the temper tantrums and childish demands. But in "making things easier" for Mykel, they effectively agreed that he could never handle "the truth." As a result, while they may be trying to protect him, they can never *respect* him.

Suicide often seems horribly sudden, but whenever we learn the details of it, it turns out that suicide never comes out of nowhere. Ninety-nine percent of the time suicide is an act of total last-ditch desperation. And desperation, a word that comes from "no hope," is more often than not the farthest extreme of depression. For the record, 15 percent of people who suffer from extreme depression have a lifetime risk of suicide.

Even when we understand this, if someone we love is suffering, we may not see the signs that they are seriously considering killing themselves. Sometimes we just don't know what to look for, but sometimes we may see or hear things that could be signs but feel too overwhelmed by our own responses to take action—and sometimes we just can't imagine that someone would try to take his or her own life! When a person tries and succeeds in this terrible act, there is nothing we can do but grieve. The good news is that of the people who *attempt* to kill themselves, many "fail"—their plan isn't foolproof, or they have second thoughts, or they call somebody before the damage is too far gone . . . Whatever the reason, these "failures" can be blessings.

That's right. A suicide attempt that isn't "succeessful" can be a wake-up call for everyone who cares about the person.

Believe it or not, the first unexpected blessing is actually mandated by law. As Mykel experienced, in almost every state, when someone tries to commit suicide and is brought to the emergency room, that person must be kept for four to six weeks of intensive psychiatric care and observation. For most, this stay is the first time they will ever have tried to understand their demons with the help of trained mental health professionals. If they didn't want to accept help before, now they have no choice—and very often, to their surprise, they discover that help can help!

Hospitals cannot release someone who has attempted suicide if they have reason to believe that the person will try again. Many states require that the person have outpatient care (that is, therapy) for a certain period after their release. This is a time when the person may need our help most. So what can we do?

Rita Ewing, author, attorney, mother, partner in Harlem's Hue-Man Bookstore & Cafe, and ex-wife of Patrick Ewing, lived the worst-case scenario when her sister Karin Carr took her own life at age thirty-four. As bad as that is, it was worse than it sounds: Her sister knew she was suicidal and didn't want to give in to her own worst impulses, so she had actually checked herself into an acute care facility to be on suicide watch, and she still managed to hang herself—right in the hallway of the facility. How could something this horrible come to pass, and how could Rita ever get over it?

It started in childhood, when Karin would act out in various ways, only some of which looked like depression. "As a child," says Rita, "I didn't pay a whole lot of attention to it, or I learned to ignore it. I had a somewhat

dysfunctional upbringing, and we all saw her behavior as cries for attention and nothing more. The truth was that they *were* cries for attention,
but there was a reason for them, and they needed to be addressed." The
problem is that people who don't know about or suffer from depression
themselves can't always recognize it in others.

Rita's parents were convinced that they were doing everything possible for Karin. They first checked her into a psychiatric institution when
she was a teenager, where she was diagnosed as having bipolar disorder.
She also suffered from anxiety disorders and she self-mutilated. She
spent her life in and out of treatment centers and on medication. And
yet, as Rita told me, "If you ever met her or went out socializing with
her, you would never have known that she suffered."

That ability to bounce between the poles of mania and depression—
from superhigh, positive energy to lower-than-low I-wish-I-were-dead
feelings—often misleads friends and family into believing that bipolar
people have more control over their actions (and the moods that motivate
them) than they actually do. That's exactly how Rita was fooled. "I felt so
frustrated with her most of the time. Over the years I'd hear about some
crazy thing Karin had done, or see it firsthand, and time and time again I'd
ask her, 'Why are you doing this?! Why can't you do what every normal
person does?' Since I couldn't *see* the disorder, I used to think I just needed
to talk to her and set her straight—I really believed that communication
could shake her out of the 'crazy frame of mind.'" But nothing could be
further from the truth, which is why it's so important for us to be able to
recognize the signs and respond to them, not just react.

The baffling and painful reality was that Karin could hear Rita and take
in what she was saying—she was not irrational—but she was simply unable to carry out what to Rita seemed like a clear and obvious instruction.
"If you tell bipolar people how to get themselves together, they may know
you're right, they may really *want* to straighten out, but without medical
help they cannot stop what they're thinking or what they're doing!"

In other words, somebody suffering from manic depression is no more
able to "snap out of it" than somebody suffering from more conventional depression—or from leukemia or cancer or kidney disease—would be.
"If I had known then what I know now, I would have forgotten all the
talk, because there's no talk in the world that can alleviate that much pain.
What she needed was medical intervention, medication, and behavioral
reinforcement."

Rita was asked to speak at Karin's funeral. She spent days going through her Bible looking for the right thing to say, but the night before the service she still hadn't come up with anything. When she fell asleep she dreamt she was in her sister's body right before she died, hanging from the doorway and feeling exactly what she felt. "What I felt was so unbearable that I *did* understand why she felt like she needed to end it once and for all. It was like she needed me to feel her pain and explain it so people would understand why she needed to end it." When she spoke at the funeral, Rita tried to explain the dream so other people would understand it, too. And while no one believed that the suicide was justifiable, let alone necessary, many people there felt that they actually understood Karin's pain for the first time.

I asked Rita what she would tell other people who have a loved one suffering from depression, and here are her words of wisdom:

First and foremost, educate yourself about the illness. Once you're knowledgeable, you can become part of the person's care plan. Try to put yourself in a position where you're getting as much information from their caregivers as possible, so you can be that person's best advocate. And be committed to that role—it can be a long and frustrating road, so you *need* to be committed.

And she had one last bit of advice, especially for people who might still be on the fence about whether or not they should help or who still wonder if their loved one's actions aren't at least in part the result of weak character or bad judgment: "When people say they want to kill themselves, listen! I'm here to tell you that they may not have control over their actions; if they don't get help for themselves, and you don't help them get it, you may end up living with the sadness and the loss and the regret for the rest of your life." And while we must do everything we can, if a person we love commits suicide anyway, it is not our fault.

Some heal from the suicide of a loved one by reaching out and helping others, like Rita Ewing did, some need to ask for a hand, and some need to look inward to make sense of what often feels like the ultimate in senseless acts. Malaika Adero is an accomplished editor, a dancer, a poet, and an essayist. This is an excerpt from the powerful poem she wrote to deal with the suicide of her forty-two-year-old father, whom she describes as "a gifted and loving person."

**WILL & TESTA-
MENT**

*My father's ashes land-
    ed on our doorstep
Vacuum-sealed in clear
    plastic
in a plain brown box
This was new to us. We
    buried our dead
before.
The family. We drove
    to the old home
    place
with the box between us
high up in the moun-
    tains
where Grandma and
    Granddad were
    born.
We didn't have a map. We followed
the legends on the soles of our feet.
We are native to all manner of death, we think.
But only Daddy could imagine turning
the key in a vacuum-sealed car
running idle until his last breath.
We are destined from now on for great ironies.
Brightest son the star of the darkest day
A rainbow appears on our decline
against a sky of hammered steel; it mirrors
the hue of winding asphalt way down.
Mother walked a trail of tears
like a warrior mud striped
across the sacred terrain of her face.
The force of her grief deflects the devil's
aim. I am in awe of her power.
We kin and kind of find a common ground this day.
An open high place for a man's flesh and bones to feed
the earth.*

When my brother was diagnosed with bipolar disorder I was devastated and felt the stigma. I learned to "keep my business to myself," harboring my secret shame in silence. Then one day I told a friend. I realized that talking about it freed me to reclaim my joy. Once my tongue was untied, I was able to speak not only for myself, but on behalf of others to help them find their voices. Loving someone who has a mental illness isn't easy. I still fight my own personal battle against stigma, but I do it with the knowledge that I'm not alone and that my bad day will pass.

Where the music of water and wind is heard through
the trees.
Where the music of water and wind is heard through
the trees.
Where Daddy can be at peace.

So many accounts of suicide or attempted suicide talk about "the signs"—the behaviors that "should have" tipped us off if only we had known what they were and how to look for them. Sometimes, though, there are no signs to see, not even in retrospect, and the mystery of "Why?!" makes the pain of loss even harder to bear. Victoria Christopher Murray, bestselling Christian novelist and a dynamic sister, shared this story of her own loss, a loss that she felt was "without signs." I am deeply appreciative of her sharing her story because I know just how hard it is for her to talk about this and how much courage it took her to write this to me.

Tuesday, September 11, meant absolutely nothing to me. Because on the day before, a missile exploded inside my heart, tearing apart my life. On September 10, I was told that the man I'd loved for more than twenty years, the man who declared that we would live a long life together, the man who promised never to leave me, was dead. But the news of his passing [was] diminished next to the news of how he died. You see, the man who was my best friend and told me everything put a gun to his head and took his own life ten minutes after sending me flowers.

Stunned does not even begin to describe how I felt. Or how our family and friends felt. We were all in shock. Ray Allen Murray committed suicide? No way. Impossible. Not Ray: the straight-A high school student, Yale graduate, MBA-degreed comptroller for a major oil company. Not Ray: loving husband to Victoria, adoring father to Monique. Not Ray: who was respected by all who knew him and even the ones who just happened to cross his path. Not Ray Allen Murray.

What made this devastation more shocking was that there were no signs. Of course, no one expects someone who is suicidal to stand on a rooftop and shout his intentions. But surely, there had to be some signs. Surely, Ray should have mentioned something to me. Or his mother. Definitely his best friend. Surely, he would have given us some signs because that's the kind of man he was—analytical, straightforward, honest. He was a scientist, a mathematician. He lived in light that was only black or white. There was no gray. Only logic. So, how could he harbor such dark feelings that led him to drive five hours away from home, go inside a hotel room, and put a gun (that I later found out he'd owned for nine years without my knowing) to his head? How could he do all of that without anyone seeing the signs?

More than five years have passed, yet Ray's death is still haunting. Not so much because he's gone—God has helped me to accept that and has even given me the grace to move on. But what I still cannot reconcile, nor find peace with, is how Ray died. My heart still cries when I think about him alone in that hotel. I cry because I cannot imagine the lonely space he must have occupied to take him to the room. I cry because I suspect the darkness that claimed him that day was a part of him for years—way before I ever met him.

From Ray's early years, he was told he was an overachiever. Ray was the middle child. He excelled and was "the pride and hope" of his family. The day I met Ray in graduate school, he spent seven hours telling me how his life was planned. I was impressed—I didn't even know what I was going to watch on television that night, yet this young, very attractive man knew what his life would look like ten years from that day. And on the outside, Ray never wavered. He accomplished most of his goals, marching down a very straight and narrow path of perfection. But what I've come to realize was that Ray never moved to his own beat. He was marching to the standards and goals that his family—in their pride of who he was—had set for him. He lived how others expected him to live, and the weight of his achievements, the burden of his accomplishments, was too much. Year by year, his load became heavier. And that was the sign.

> It's not about you.
>
> —RICK WARREN, AUTHOR OF
> *THE PURPOSE DRIVEN LIFE*

It may sound ridiculous—how could someone who had everything want to die? But that may have been the problem. It was the price Ray paid for success as a Black man in America. On the outside, he was living right. No addictions: he didn't drink, smoke, gamble, or run with women. He had a six-figure income, a home inside a gated community, played golf weekly, and traveled the world with his family and friends. But on the inside, he was dying from the pain of his secrets—his fears that he wasn't living well enough, that he wasn't keeping up, that he

could one day lose all of it. Soon, there was no place left for Ray to go—
at least there was no place left for him
here on Earth. Because outside, he was
living. But inside, he wanted to die.

> God wastes no wounds.
>
> —ANONYMOUS

One day, I hope to forgive Ray for
taking his life that way. For tossing a
torpedo into the middle of our world.
For never sharing with me what scared
him most. For never letting me help save him. And then, one day, I also
pray that I'll be able to forgive myself for never, ever seeing the signs.

How Can I Help?

For starters, we can help by not rushing to do something. The first rule of being a doctor is *not* to do anything that will make the patient worse. Two responses that don't help, and might actually make things worse, are what I call the Avoider and the Savior.

The Avoider is what we become to the depressed person in our lives if we do not deal with the feelings of confusion, helplessness, and fear that our loved one's depression kicks up for us. We become a kind of emotional runaway by denying the problem or distancing ourselves from the person altogether. Even though we might think we're sparing ourselves some kind of pain in the short run, in the long run this kind of behavior only serves to make the depressed person feel more isolated, more alone, and perhaps even more ashamed of the feelings behind the depression. By avoiding, we actually do real damage, because we allow the situation to go on for

Five Reasons I Pray

- I am giving thanks and honoring God.
- I can tell God what I can't tell anyone else.
- I know He's listening.
- I will be blessed.
- Praying lets me feel connected to my higher self.

months or even years before a meaningful intervention occurs.

The Savior goes to the opposite extreme, feeling responsible for the loved one's depression and taking on the impossible task of "curing." Unfortunately, depressed people can't be fixed by good intentions, material goods, money, vacations, or charm; they need professional assessment and treatment! No matter how close you are to the depressed person, you are not a trained therapist, professional cheerleader, or certified miracle worker. Although it's tempting to want to "fix" someone you love, to stop their pain, the most loving thing you can do to see their suffering end is to help them get help.

The key to helping a depressed person is communication. When we share our time, when we listen actively, when we ask questions that go beyond the surface—and don't look for answers we want to hear—we show love and caring more powerfully than a million I love you's could ever do. The best way to create intimacy and keep it strong is to communicate! It helps us share our emotions and be better at noticing what's changing, for bad or for good. But real communication cannot happen every once in a blue moon. For it to work, for it to break the isolation and establish healthier ways of interacting, it has to be practiced as often as possible.

We're All in It Together: How Family Therapy Can Help the Depressed—and the Rest!

I think the most powerful first step we can take in helping someone we love get through depression is family therapy. While depression may technically hit only one person in the family, it's obvious that it is not just that one person's problem.

> When I started seminary back in the early '70s, a mentor of mine named Lawrence Jones said that in order to address the larger community concerns of the twenty-first century, ministers [are] going to have to be "dually competent." He explained that the Black minister has always had to do a number of things, but now the Black minister [is] going to have to do more: he's going to have to be a minister and a lawyer, a minister and an accountant, a minister and a physician, a minister and a social worker.
>
> —CALVIN BUTTS, SENIOR PASTOR
> AT THE ABYSSINIAN BAPTIST CHURCH
> IN NEW YORK

Family therapy creates tools to reduce the family distress that may contribute to or come from the ill person's symptoms. When we go to family therapy with our depressed loved one, we are sending a message that we're all in it together and waving a big sign of acceptance, of willingness to change and love. We are saying, in effect, that we want to put an end to all the deadly secrets—that we want to correct, not just to protect.

And if you're reading this and thinking, "Hey, therapy *sounds* great, but I don't have that kind of money," I have good news. Almost every city or town has a program through its local hospitals that offers therapy on a sliding scale to people who couldn't afford it otherwise. So get on the phone, make some calls, and get the services you have a right to!

When Linda Freedman's brother was diagnosed with Bipolar I disorder and put on lithium, he didn't get better. "Every day was a crisis for him," she told me. Alarmed that her brother's mania wasn't improving, she and her mother worked together to get him the help he needed by searching the Web for treatment options and getting third and fourth opinions when needed. Linda and her mother's hard work to find the right treatment for her brother is the kind of family coming-together that makes a difference. Her brother is now stable and has two sets of watchful eyes helping him manage his condition. Having people who love him step in, encourage him to take his meds, and help him keep his therapy appointments was what made it possible for Linda's brother to deal with his condition and begin healing.

It's not news to say that suffering from depression is painful, but few people think of how hard it is to have someone you love be afflicted by this illness. While we cannot cure another person's depression, and we are not responsible for that person's pain, there are many steps we can take to (one more time) help our loved ones help themselves. What matters most, for our own mental health as well as theirs, is not that we "succeed"—it's that we start *now*.

Chapter Six

A SPIRITUAL HOSPITAL

The Black Church and Depression

I grew up in the Baptist church, but when I was out of the house and on my own, like so many people, I got "too busy" for church. At first it was just temporary—I'd go to sleep Saturday night eager to go to church

> God is turning my mess into a masterpiece one day at a time.
>
> —VERONICA JONES,
> HOLISTIC COUNSELOR

the next day, but come Sunday morning I'd suddenly "realize" how much I needed to make up sleep and promise myself that next week I was definitely going. Now, you know how those "next weeks" can pile up after a while, and before I knew it I was one of those people I used to shake my head at— too *busy,* too *responsible,* too *important* to spare those precious hours from my busy, responsible, important life. Mm-hmm—I was too important to spare time for my heavenly Father.

Lucky for me, I didn't stay so important. A few years ago I crossed paths with the Reverend Lester Taylor, a powerful minister at the Community Baptist Church in Englewood, New Jersey, and I began to go to church more regularly. Not *too* regularly, mind you—at first I paid as little attention to my spiritual health as I paid to my physical and emotional health. Just as my body felt hungry when I didn't eat right, my soul felt very empty when I allowed work and fatigue to keep me from church. And, as I'm sure you know, a starving soul is the perfect ground for emotional despair. After my last bout of crippling depression led me to take medication and throw myself into the hard but rewarding work of therapy, I discovered that I "suddenly" had time for church every week. Imagine that! I wasn't any less busy than I used to be, but somehow there was time, week after week, for me to connect with God through my community of faith.

My relationship with God has kept me from harm's way and, in the deepest moments of my despair, has brought me closer to my calling. I know that God is working through me as I write this book, that through Him my pain is turning into something greater than my own private dark moments. The intense pain in

> I have discovered that the best way to work with fear is to get a better understanding of God, a better understanding of who we are in relation to God, and to work with the divine plan for our betterment.
>
> —REV. DR. BARBARA KING,
> HILLSIDE CHAPEL AND TRUTH CENTER,
> ATLANTA, GEORGIA

my life is what it took to bring me to the point where I could put this into words and hopefully reach out to others who are still in the darkness of their pain. The clarity of the mission I have nowadays is part and parcel of the pain I've been through, and its transformation is a gift from God.

In this chapter I want to affirm how important spiritual life is for healing. At the same time I want to talk about some of the ways that our practice of religion as Black folks can get in the way of true spirituality and healing.

Healing Faith: What Church Has Been for Us

> Keeping your faith strong during a challenge is always a struggle. But challenges are the training ground that pushes you deeper into your relationship with the Divine and the inner power you didn't know you had. Walk-on-water faith and working a plan will solve every problem, heal every circumstance, and open wide the way to God's promised peace and transformation.
>
> —SUSAN L. TAYLOR, AUTHOR AND FOUNDER OF
> *ESSENCE* CARES MENTORING PROGRAM

Black folk are a people of faith. About 85 percent of us identify ourselves as either fairly religious or very religious. We may be Christian, Muslim, Buddhist, or anything else, but regardless of our particular persuasion, what the vast majority of us have in common is a soul connection that goes beyond ourselves and other human beings; we believe in something bigger than us. Of the religious among us, most call themselves Christian; of those, a great many are churchgoers, and many of those who aren't churchgoers now have been before (and may be again—'cause I believe!). That's why the church can play a big role in our thinking and in our lives, and not only on Sundays—just think about that portable church known as "prayer"!

The Black church has historically been a rock for our people, from the earliest slavery times through freedom, Reconstruction, Jim Crow, civil rights, and straight up to today. It has often been the one place where we could find ourselves praised for who we were when everything around us said we were not even human, let alone precious. For many of our men, the calling to be a preacher has been the first step up from generations of backbreaking labor.

Under slavery, church was by law the only place we could gather in groups, and those precious Sunday mornings were the only times we could see one another outside of enforced work and could even come close to socializing. For generations the preachers' words and our songs might have been the only thing confirming our humanity in a world filled with people who constantly tried to convince themselves—and us—that we were not human.

After slavery, the church became the center of the communities we built from scratch. While we were all now *technically* free, too many of us have lived and died in conditions not much better than the slavery we left behind. Church kept us believing in the *possibility* of being equal—if not in this world, then in the next—and in our *being entitled* to equality, whether we got it or not. Our preachers were our leaders not only because they could reach the most people, but because their soul-saving

> **Your heart is your two-way with God.**
>
> —ANONYMOUS

message kept church at the center of our lives. With its focus on our souls, the church has always spoken to us, side by side—sometimes more subtly than other times—about social justice.

So many of us have grown up in the church that the language of the Good Book, the language of prayer, and the language of gospel music are second nature to us. We know the spiritual language of conversion and transformation, whether or not we actually practice what we speak. For most folks, that language is a lot more familiar to us than even the down-

to-earth language of psychology that we are likely to hear from, say, Dr.
Robin Smith on *Oprah* or Dr. Phil: We can often talk the talk of religious
healing but not of healing therapies.
This is especially true for those of us
who are hard up financially—if you're
working two jobs just to make ends
meet, church may be all you have time
for. Unlike a therapist, who you have
to get to know and trust, your pastor is
usually someone you already know and
trust; like a visit to a therapist, church meets once a week, but it is free . . .

> God has said, "I will nev-
> er leave you or forsake
> you."

Many Black folks believe in a direct connection between spiritual practice and belief on the one hand, and physical and emotional well-being on
the other. We're not wrong—what you believe can affect you on the level
of your body's cells, so believing in your spiritual well-being *is* an important part of boosting your overall well-being. Your spiritual practice can
be a way of making the difficult work of personal change (in your habits,
in your thinking . . .) more doable. Being part of a community makes you
feel less alone; God—often in the form of your church, your spiritual community—lets you know you're not doing it alone, lets you feel connected
to something while you try to kick an addiction or stick to an exercise and
therapy practice, etc.

For many of us church is the longtime heart of our community, but it
is also where we go to find and make community where we didn't have one
before—you could move to a new town for a new job, not know a soul, go
to church on Sunday, and find you're already part of something.

A few months ago I was at the nail salon when I ran into Tina, a friend
of a friend. Tina's a lively and attractive woman who works in advertising.
After exchanging news about our mutual friend's new promotion, we got
to talking about ourselves. I was startled to learn that Tina, too, suffered
from depression. I don't know why it surprises me! There is no one on the
planet not dealing with something.

She had spent three years in a dead-end relationship and found out
after she broke off with him that her man had been cheating on her for the
last six months they were together. Then there was the credit card debt,
close to $50,000 over seven cards. As she put it, "My relationship was in a
shambles, my finances were in a shambles. Quite frankly, my life was in a
shambles." And soon after her man moved out, Tina hit bottom.

"I was on the brink of losing my job for lateness and absenteeism." The only things that gave her pleasure were shopping and watching the shows she had recorded on TiVo. She would have stayed in her funk if a former college roommate hadn't come over one morning and dragged her to church. Tina was reluctant to go because it had been many years since she'd last seen the inside of a church, but her friend wouldn't back down until she agreed.

"That Sunday changed my life," she told me. "Everything the preacher said was aimed right at my heart. I was the sinner, the spiritual wanderer lost on the road. I realized right there and then that I had spent the last six years living only for myself and that, in doing so, I hadn't been living at all."

Six months later Tina was saved, accepting Jesus as her personal Lord and savior. But far from being a phase, her conversion, her return to the religion of her childhood, really did turn her life around. "I began going to Bible study classes at the church. I got my finances in order." A year and a half later, someone at the church introduced her to a male friend. "We've been going out for over seven months now. I didn't go to church looking for a relationship, but by reconnecting with my faith, by believing in God, I was able to let go of a lot of toxic habits. Reconnecting with my faith was like reconnecting with the best of myself and my community. Somehow I had lost myself in the quest to find a man, make more money, look sexy 24/7. I didn't know who Tina was anymore. But now when I'm praying, or tithing, or reading the Bible I feel like I have a purpose. I know God expects a lot from me, that he put me here for a reason, and I don't want to disappoint Him."

Tina's faith was not a crutch or a weak substitute for something she really needed. It allowed her to find her self-esteem, brought her back into a blessed community, and lifted the feelings of selfishness and loneliness that were making her so miserable.

In a basic way, the Black church is founded on the principles of self-help. We had to educate ourselves, inform ourselves and one another, and build forms of social change and fighting back—all from inside the church. This is why when we feel oppressed, even when that oppressed feeling is coming from within and not directly from without, we often turn to the place we know best—the church. After all, if the church could make slavery and segregation bearable, if it can be a remedy to the racism, discrimination, and other trials and tribulations that the world visits on us, maybe it can save us from our pain. In so many areas of our life the healing that happens through and within the church is 100 percent what our souls are craving.

Spirituality's Healing Power

Nonbelievers, take note: In the past few years, study after study after study has shown that religious belief, belonging to a community of faith, praying, *and* being prayed for can have powerful positive effects on physical illness. Over 100 studies have demonstrated that these things can be mighty weapons, specifically against depression! Most of those studies showed that religious people are less likely to be depressed than nonreligious people, though of course we're not completely protected, and that when we do get depressed, we are often able to work through it faster—at least by comparison. In fact, a survey on the importance of different aspects of depression care showed that Black folks value pretty much the same things as white folks (how the people treating us relate to us, the recognition of our depression by those people, and how effective the treatment we receive is),

One of the problems with the disease of depression is that it makes you think you are the only one going through it, which kills your support system(s) and can subsequently kill you. I suffered from depression since I was a little child but didn't know it. Unfortunately, like so many in the Black community, my family was in denial, and I wasn't diagnosed until I was an adult. I was working as a journalist and happened to interview a psychiatrist who authored a book on depression. It was then I realized I had all the symptoms of mild to severe depression depending upon my environmental stressors.

The positive side of my depression is that it's the reason I went into the personal/spiritual growth industry—to truly find ways to feel better about myself by helping others. Now, as a minister, I am dedicated to helping adults and kids suffering from depression and the many ways it manifests in our lives.

—REV. PHILIPPE "SHOCK" MATTHEWS, FOUNDING MINISTER OF
THE SHOCKPHILOSOPHY™ VIRTUAL MINISTRY OF SPIRITUAL
LITERACY & RELIGIOUS TOLERANCE

with one major exception: we are three times as likely to value spirituality in treating our depression. And yet, as Rev. John Parker Manwell of Baltimore's First Unitarian Church said recently, it is not that "spirituality can cure depression, but [that it] may provide a grounding in the midst of despair, may even help us find added dimensions of compassion and self-understanding from our suffering."

Look Out, Depression—
Prayer Power's Gonna Get Your Momma!

Prayer in particular has a power that would really surprise the skeptics. Numerous studies have shown that depressed people who pray seem to have an edge on those who don't. Again, it isn't as simple as "prayer makes depression go away"—if it were, we would all be praying our heads off. Nobody can say for sure what happens in prayer or exactly what it does for us, but I want to take a guess based on my experience. One of the biggest roadblocks in recovery from depression is our feeling that we are defective, our condition is shameful, we'd be better if we weren't so weak, blah blah blah. When you feel *that* bad about yourself, when you feel *that* low, probably the last thing in the world you want to do is tell somebody else about it— that would just make you feel *more* shameful, right? (Actually, it's wrong, but try telling that to someone in the middle of depression.) On the other hand, you never ever have to worry about God shaming you, much less about God not keeping your secret. God will go to the deepest, darkest, most shameful place with you. When you have feelings so unbearable that you cannot even imagine yourself sharing them with another person without cringing, you can lean up against the knowledge that God knows the "worst" about you and still accepts you, because you are worthy.

As powerful as prayer is on an individual level, the power of people praying as a group can be downright amazing and life altering. Douglas Bloch, in *Psychology Today*, told about how he was suffering from a form of depression that was characterized as "treatment resistant." That meant that nothing worked to relieve it. All the antidepressant drugs we know about had no effect, made him agitated, or even made him more depressed! He was suffering from anxiety attacks, so he could not be given the electroshock therapy he hoped might literally jolt him out of his private hell. The only option that seemed to offer him any hope at all was suicide—until the pastoral counselor of his church suggested a prayer meeting for him.

Douglas was suspicious until the counselor said that they had done the
same thing for a member of the congregation who was terminally ill with
cancer, and she had lived way past the time anyone expected her to live.

Twelve people made up Douglas's team: the senior minister, the pastoral counselor, parishioners who belonged to the prayer ministry, physicians, friends, and family. First he told them what he was going through.
Then they had him describe what being well would look like to him—how
he would feel and what he would do if somehow his depression lifted. His
team told him that what he desired was already true and that they would vi-
sualize his description for the next month, until their next prayer meeting.
The group met six times in total. Within three days after the first meeting,
Douglas started to experience more positive feelings; within three months
his symptoms of depression began to lift. *That* is the power of prayer, love,
and community.

> Thus says the Lord, he who created you, O Jacob, he who formed
> you, O Israel: Do not fear, for I have redeemed you; I have called you
> by name, you are mine. When you pass through the waters, I will
> be with you; and through the rivers, they shall not overwhelm you;
> when you walk through fire you shall not be burned, and the flame
> shall not consume you.
>
> —ISAIAH 43:1–2

My good friend Shellie Anderson-Tazi suffered a miscarriage, then was
diagnosed with breast cancer, and then saw her marriage dissolve. She is
now a three-time breast cancer survivor, having survived one bout while
she was pregnant! Yet in the face of this much adversity, she did not perish;
she persevered.

My life as a woman of twenty-nine came to a crashing halt when my
first husband left me the same day I received my first diagnosis. I
learned through surviving that life is about learning to live one day at a
time. How does a woman survive cancer three times, once while pregnant? Pray. Through each diagnosis I learned to peel away depression,
pain, fear, and anger. I forgave my first husband, because I realized
that prior to the diagnosis we didn't truly love each other from the

beginning, and I learned that I never really knew how to love. After all, he literally hated his mom, and I had major issues with my parents. I never learned to forgive my parents, which allowed me to hold on to a lot of pent-up, repressed emotions. Even though I smiled (with a game face) and still accomplished a lot, I was living with pain—the kind of pain that stopped me from truly taking good care of myself; it let me marry someone I knew didn't love me, and it pushed me to constant overeating out of fear. After I learned to forgive my family and my first husband, my life got sweet. I learned to stop blaming my parents for things that they don't know how to do. I learned to forgive so that I could heal. After I learned that powerful lesson, I was blessed with my fantastic husband, Tony, who loves me unconditionally. God is Good.

> We founded the congress to work in our communities, joining faith and good health. We are committed to the well-being of the people, but to be spiritually strong we must tend to our physical selves. Modern science has shown that depression is a physical illness. It is an illness that can be treated. If you recognize it, ask for help. By caring for ourselves, we can better care for each other. That's how we celebrate life.
>
> —BISHOP JOHN HURST ADAMS, FOUNDER AND CHAIRMAN EMERITUS, CONGRESS OF NATIONAL

Then when I got pregnant while I had breast cancer for the second time, I truly thought my life was over. This was my second child, and I was so excited, but the diagnosis had me wondering, 'Why, God? Why?' What more did I need to learn? Wasn't I living a joyous life? My current husband and my first son, Amir, were such blessings to my soul. How could I get cancer again? So, after three doctors advised me to terminate the pregnancy and save the little bit of life I had left, I felt depressed and very lonely. How could I terminate the life in my womb and take a chance on living for myself? Maybe the doctors knew what they were talking about—what sense would it make to spare the life of a child that may never live?

Two days prior to going to be examined for my termination, I was notified of a prayer group up the street from my house that would be praying for me. I joined twenty-eight people who prayed for me from

8:30 to 11:30 P.M. I couldn't believe it. I didn't know anyone in the prayer room. I was receiving unconditional love and care from people I had never met. Two days later a new oncologist told me that I didn't have to terminate my pregnancy. My son, Sherif, is now two years old and telling me what to do. He is amazing—he gives affection to everyone he meets! He was meant to be here on Earth. He fought his way in. God saw fit that I learn that he is the source of my strength, that there are people on Earth who are truly working on his behalf, and that in order for me to continue to live I must live my life through his guidance. I am now set free!

> You can safely assume that you've created God in your own image when it turns out that God hates all the same people you do.

I was diagnosed with cancer for the third time while I was pregnant. I now know that, no matter what, we must live day by day. NO FEAR! I really love everyone unconditionally, and I love my God every day. I mean, I *really* love God. I can't see him with my physical eye, but He has displayed His love for me daily, and I see His love and light inside of people and the world we live in. I am proud to say God is love and even prouder to say that when it's my time to leave this Earth it will never be because of cancer, but because it will be time for me to be with my Lord and savior Jesus Christ.

Instead of giving up and dying, Shellie's hard times led to blessings by using the power of prayer. In her book, *Soul Beginnings: Eight Strategies for Overcoming Life's Challenges,* she says, "Like me, you may not think that prayer is necessary, believing that whatever will be, will be. . . . Prior to my getting breast cancer, I'd spent seven or eight years believing that prayer wasn't something I needed, only to find out that at times, prayer was the only thing that would truly sustain me." She used the acronym PUSH (Pray Until Something Happens) to describe her newfound faith. "Humble yourself and realize that the Creator is in control of the outcome, and be open to guidance from a source that is outside yourself." For Shellie, prayer led to a better relationship with God *and* with herself. By admitting that she needed prayer, she was able to ask God to help her make the changes she needed to make to live.

There is this sense that enough prayer or fasting will get you through it. All those things are fine, everything in moderation. But we're trying to get across that mental illness is a disease. We'd like to train members of the clergy, so they realize a person can get treatment and also be a faithful follower of God.

—LAVERNE WILLIAMS, COMMUNITY OUTREACH COORDINATOR FOR THE MENTAL HEALTH ASSOCIATION IN NEW JERSEY AND DEACONESS OF THE UNION BAPTIST CHURCH, RECEIVED THE BETTY HUMPHREY CULTURAL COMPETENCY AWARD FROM THE NATIONAL MENTAL HEALTH ASSOCIATION

I never cease to be blown away by what prayer can achieve inside us. Prayer makes us feel stronger as individuals, more able to impact the world around us in a positive way. It lets us channel our goodness privately and powerfully, and in so doing affirms our humanity and desire for a greater common good. I do it every day—several times a day. Just thanking God for every little thing.

Popular novelist Bernice McFadden shared this wonderful testimony with me of the power of prayer in her life.

I'd always considered myself a strong, emotionally grounded woman. I was the one people came to when they had a problem. I knew all of the right things to say. I was the caregiver, the steel magnolia, steadily ignoring my soft pink middle—the part of me that needed nurturing.

April 1999 should have been the happiest time in my life. In a matter of two weeks, I'd secured a literary agent and a two-book deal with a major publishing house. Everything I dreamed of was coming true. I was finally going to be a published author, a full-time writer. I should have been jumping for joy, but I wasn't.

Before the ink was dry on my contract I began to worry—worry that I would not be able to write another book or that the book I did write would be a piece of garbage. I was plagued with feelings of inferiority; I began to wonder if I really deserved the blessing that had been bestowed upon me.

My appetite was replaced by insomnia. I began to believe that I would die a horrible death before I saw my novel hit the bookshelves. I started to shut myself away. I became afraid of everything. I had heart palpitations, facial ticks, cold sweats, and dizzy spells.

In February 2000, while at a book signing in Saint Louis, I can

> If only we could realize that our purpose is to be caretakers. We are responsible for leading our flock to the place where the grass is green, but it is up to them to eat! We cannot be responsible for how much they digest. We cannot make people mature. Yet many ministers are exhausted from playing God. We have worn ourselves out trying to be spiritual policemen. Sometimes we've done it through ignorance; other times, for fear of being ridiculed by our peers for having problems in the sheepfold. It is enough to be responsible for ensuring that our people have the opportunity to graze in the rich grass of God's nutritious word. Beyond that, we must trust the word to take its effect. It will work faster in some people than in others. The spiritual body grows and metabolizes food at different rates, much like the natural body does.
>
> —T. D. JAKES, AUTHOR AND SPIRITUAL LEADER, THE POTTER'S HOUSE, DALLAS, TEXAS

remember gripping the edge of the podium, willing myself not to pass out as I smiled my way through question after question, even though I was screaming on the inside. That night, back in my hotel room, I cried myself to sleep.

That would become a common occurrence.

I stopped accepting phone calls. It didn't make sense; I couldn't be engaged. I felt like I was living inside of a storm cloud. My temperament became erratic. My brother called up to ask to borrow money, and I broke out in tears. I felt like everybody wanted something from me. I felt bad about saying no, but I felt even worse after saying yes.

The low point came when a friend of mine, not one to hold her tongue, saw me and told me that I

> The guiding principle for God's vision is, where there is no vision, the people perish; where there is vision, the people will prosper. Jacob's son Joseph was given a vision early in his life, but it took thirteen years of betrayal, slavery, success, another betrayal, imprisonment, and, finally, because he persevered, endured, refused to give up, the vision released victory. Joseph did not perish because he held on to the principle of God's vision.
>
> —THE REVEREND DR. FRANK REID, BETHEL

looked sick.

I took my daughter to Jamaica for a vacation, hoping that the tropical weather could fix me, but my condition seemed to escalate. I checked and rechecked the lock on the hotel room door and drilled the combination to the safe into my then twelve-year-old daughter's head—along with instructions on what to do "should Mommy not wake up in the morning."

Yes, I truly believed I was dying.

Finally, when I returned, I went to visit my doctor. He diagnosed me with anxiety disorder and prescribed Buspar. Well, Buspar turned me into a zombie. I was fatigued, I couldn't write, all I did was sleep. After a month, I tossed the pills and turned to prayer.

Every time I felt panic beginning to rise inside of me, I prayed. Whenever my thoughts turned dark, I prayed. Slowly but surely, my panic attacks decreased and my depression began to lift.

Looking back now, I see that period of my life as being held captive by my mind. My liberator turned out not to be a tiny pill, but my faith.

I'm not sorry that I went through what I did. I've taken away some very valuable lessons and the experience has refortified my belief in my Creator and the power of prayer.

My friend Pam Perry, the head of Ministry Marketing Solutions, shared this moving story with me.

After my business closed in 2000, I went into a deep depression. I thought I would snap out of it. I kept myself busy and tried to act like things were normal. Though the bankruptcy was humiliating, what

---

People fear that treatment or counseling may need to go on forever, but that isn't necessarily the case, and people should just get help. I hope churches will recognize there is a difference between spiritual and emotional wellness. You can be spiritually well and yet need help for a chemical imbalance.

—LAVERNE WILLIAMS, DIRECTOR OF INTERNAL OPERATIONS,
MENTAL HEALTH ASSOCIATION IN NEW JERSEY

was worse was the denial to my spiritual self.

I didn't give myself time to grieve and express the anger, regret, and disappointment I felt.

Consequently, I spiraled into despair. I could not wake up before noon and kept the blinds closed all day. I overate. I avoided friends.

But I did go to church. I put on my "church face" and went. No one knew the depth of my despair—until one day a guest minister preached and asked if anyone in the audience felt like they were at the end of their rope and on the verge of suicide. If anyone was, she asked them to come forward so she could pray for them.

I was in such a state of denial that I thought to myself, "Surely I can't embarrass myself and go down there. What would people think?" The Holy Spirit then spoke to my heart and reminded me how much He loved me, and it didn't matter what other people thought. This minister was sent to get me out of myself and come to Jesus for real.

I quit the internal debate and ran to the altar. I cried and the minister prayed for me. When I went back to my seat, instead of peculiar stares, I got nothing but hugs and love. That was my breakthrough day. I just needed enough light to see my way at the end of my tunnel, and that day God sent a flashlight looking for me. I'm so glad He did.

When Church Takes Us Away from Spirituality's Healing Power

Five Things Good Christians Say That Shouldn't Keep You from Giving Yourself the Gift of Therapy

- You need to be delivered.
- Pray it away.
- We gotta get the devil out of you.
- God can heal you from anything.
- Church is all you need.

For all the love and beauty and power and glory that God can bring into our lives, the church is not always only an agent of God's glory and goodness.

Not long ago I was talking about religion and depression with Obery Hendricks. Obery is a professor at New York Theological Seminary and the immediate past president of Payne Theological Seminary, the oldest African-American seminary—as well as the author of a beautiful Biblical novel called *Living Water,* which I encourage you to run out and read right away! In his view, "Many of our churches are not really equipped to make a difference [for depressed people in the congregation] because there's no real tradition of looking deep inside yourself, of meditation, contemplation, and introspection. They confuse emotionality with spirituality."

Emotionality masquerading as spirituality—I immediately thought of people I used to know at church in my growing-up days who were what you could almost call the "stars" of each week's service, because they sometimes seemed like they were *acting* more than they were *feeling.* Obery distinguishes *emotionality* from *emotion*: "Emotionality means emotional release—crying and shouting out, getting out the burdens of the week. That's important, but it doesn't equal meditation, really contemplating and sitting in communion with God. 'Emotionality' may help you tune in with the worship service but not necessarily with God. Too many churches these days seem to worship worship."

To worship worship. I had to chew on that for a minute. I had an idea of what he meant, but I had to ask him to see if I was on the right track. "When that happens," he told me, "the worship experience becomes a performance, and the church becomes more audience than congregation." That was exactly what I had experienced as a child when I had the sneaking suspicion that some of those church "stars" were *per*forming instead of *trans*forming. But then what about depression, how can our religious life help us with that?

For Obery, "deeper spirituality can be a balm for depression because it helps you get more deeply in touch with yourself, and that helps us sort out the things in our lives that are good, bad, or hurting us. Meditation and contemplation slow us down so we can take notice. Church worship *alone* doesn't slow us down; it doesn't offer us that space for meaningful reflection."

I believe that the majority of our churches are truly focused on the spiritual health and well-being of their members, even if too few are really equipped to take depression seriously, let alone deal with it effectively. I am troubled, though, by churches that seem to focus more on external things—donations, clothing, style, "performance," congregation size, church size—than on the development of more thoughtful aspects of religious life. I worry about how attracted we are to mega-churches and wealth ministries whose members seem to draw a sense of personal power from being part of a wealthy congregation with a wealthy minister. A pastor whose personal wealth is more impressive than the example of his faith, who asks you to tithe your $40,000-a-year income while he drives a Bentley and flies first class, may not be the reflection of God's love we want to copy.

We often see our pain in terms of the "things" we lack—"If only I had _____(you fill in the blank), I'd be all right." We see wealth and status and thing ownership as ways to feel less powerless. In reality, faith in our God and His teachings, self-esteem, and wellness are the only true answers to feeling powerless. That is why when it comes to our spiritual shepherds, I'm most moved by those men and women who have sacrificed for their faith, who are more interested in saving souls than in savings accounts. You don't have to look hard to find pastors (like my brother-in-law Tom) whose calling has taken them away from high-paying jobs and from all the status and perks that go along with those jobs. We need to not be afraid to seek pastors and preachers who talk the talk *and* walk the walk. We need spiritual leaders who are able and willing to give us, and to model for us, their *presence*.

Listen to what Rev. Tom Ledbetter, a pastoral psychotherapist at Brandywine Pastoral Institute in Wilmington, Delaware, has to say on being present:

> For a spirituality to be life-affirming, not death-dealing, it must also place a premium upon presence . . .—the ability to be with another, for another, to give of self to another . . . who hurts and who needs, this is a spirituality that knows the value of presence of persons with persons, that knows the crucial importance of one human being being present with another human being.

He points out the difference between presence and what he calls "Christmas-basket" caring—"one that is only full of rules about this and about that . . . not a spirituality that will sit through the dark with another soul. Presence is necessary, for it signals care for persons, not just talk about caring. Presence is necessary, for it gives the lie to religions and religious people who are so focused upon correct theology that they are not present. They are more interested in control than in being with, more interested in right beliefs and correct practices than in serving, more interested in appearance than in substance."

We should always make the most of the gifts our religious practice has to offer, but we should never just sit around "waiting for the miracle," as if going to church were the only thing we had to do, and then God would step in and take care of everything else. That kind of thinking can function as avoidance of the role *you* have to play in your salvation, especially when it comes to depression. Faith is not a passive practice, but an active one, and you have to take responsibility for it—24/7!

Think of the story of Job—in my mind, a story about the true nature of faith. Once Job realizes that he cannot bargain with God, that even his faith is not a bargaining chip, when he rejects his wife's angry counsel to turn his back on God, when he allows his faith to transcend his circumstances, only then does he truly know God, only then is he truly faithful.

Why the Church Is Not All You Need

A DIRTY LITTLE SECRET IN OUR SPIRITUAL COMMUNITY

I can't tell you how many "first ladies" (accomplished in their own right) of the church have shared with me how stressful their position is. Their husbands are treated as "kings" while they are often ignored, blatantly disrespected, and talked about behind their backs. So many of them are the confidantes to their husbands (because often the preacher's wife is the only one he will turn to when he needs help). Meanwhile, the "first lady" often finds herself isolated in her own problems because of a self-imposed gag order. Unfortunately the sanctuary that is solace to so many is sometimes the place of alienation for a preacher's wife. Any personal turmoil in the life of a first lady is often perceived as a mark of imperfection by a blemished congregation.

—MARCIA DYSON, AUTHOR AND PRESIDENT OF THE FIELDS FOUNDATION

Unfortunately for so many of us this example of the church and mental health care professionals working together, or of the ability of clergy to not only listen to a member in pain but recommend further care when necessary, is not the norm. The Black church has made tremendous contributions to the community; however, there remains an "unenlightened side" when it comes to addressing mental health issues. Rev. Dr. Cheryl Anthony Mobley coined the phrase "spiritual hospital" in our conversations, and it seems to summarize both the potential strengths and challenges of the Black church. She thinks that when the church is seen as a place of "emotionalism," acting out difficult feelings in front of an audience rather than experiencing the personal transformative power of Christ through faith, it can mask or even allow symptoms of mental illness.

Cherise was considered a devout member of her church because when she received the Holy Spirit, she would scream and cry. A friend of mine (and a fellow social worker) suspected that Cherise was using the Holy Spirit to cover manic episodes of her bipolar disorder. The pastor of their church did not agree, although he had no training in mental health counseling. What was worse was that he flat-out refused even to speak to Cherise, let alone ask her in for counseling. Too many ministers are totally opposed to nonreligious intervention in anything other than clear-cut physical illness. Their belief that "church is all you need" keeps a lot of people from getting the help they *truly* need.

And they keep that belief alive in the minds of their parishioners. Dr. Gloria Morrow is a clinical psychologist, a pastor of the Victory Community Church in Pomona, California, and author of *Too Broken to Be Fixed? A Spiritual Guide to Inner Healing*. One of her specialties is depression, and she says:

> Those among the faith community may avoid seeking professional help because mental illness may not be correctly understood. Thus, our people may feel uncomfortable about seeking help outside their churches, especially if they have been taught that mental illness is a sign that their faith is weak, or a reflection of sin in their lives.

Too many of us believe that our pain is a kind of punishment for our flaws, that maybe if we were better people or better Christians we would not be suffering; we're punishing ourselves for our pain! This idea is reinforced by attitudes like those of churches that refuse to hold funeral services for people who commit suicide—a practice that hurts me to my Christian core!

Some members of the clergy "demonize" our afflictions. They literally call upon the devil and the devil's work when they talk about our problems with drugs, sex, and gambling, instead of educating people about how those activities are so often symptoms of even deeper problems—like depression—that need specific attention. Praying harder won't make an alcoholic sober, but a pastor who encourages those in his congregation who drink too much to find God in AA may be saving a life and a family—not to mention educating the rest of the congregation.

> My child, whenever you encounter an obstacle, remember, I have already provided a way around it or through it. The next time you see a cloud on the horizon, don't fear the storm. Look closely, and you will see and feel My presence.
>
> —FROM *DAILY PRAYERS AND PROMISES*, BARBOUR PUBLISHING

It is also possible that, although reverends are generally experienced in counseling, when we present them with just how deep our pain runs we may be expecting more of our pastors than they are qualified to give. They are human just like us—not God. That unfair expectation may put pressure on those pastors, who sometimes feel they should be offering more comfort than they can. Their own insecurities as human beings may make them hesitate to steer us to mental health professionals even though that's what we really need.

> Eternal God, Your ways are not our ways and Your thoughts are not our thoughts. We often forget this when we find ourselves caught between the rocks and hard places of life. Thank you for showing me that there are no tight spaces where Your spirit cannot enter and no sore spots that your love cannot soothe. In those times when what we face seems too difficult, assure us once again that you have a ram in the bush for every situation.
>
> —FROM *DAILY PRAYERS AND PROMISES*

Therapist Mary Pender Greene has some real insight into this issue:

> Ministers are invited into people's lives at the times they are most vul-
> nerable, when they are experiencing grief, sadness, anger, and pain.
> They help their congregation members deal with life's big questions
> and get to know their hearts, minds, and souls. People often feel that
> ministers know it all, and that God is working through the minister.
> As a result, the minister, if he isn't careful, can lose sight of what he's
> actually bringing and what is God's intervention—he can really start
> to feel as though he *is* God, or something very close.

Mary says that most ministers actually feel pressured to "know it all,"
unlike therapists, who have a keen sense of their human limitations and
aren't shy about saying so during therapy. Over time, ministers become
vulnerable to what is called "compassion fatigue," what happens when one
works with hurt and suffering and traumatized people all the time. (As
a social worker I know this one from the inside! And I have learned to
monitor carefully how much I take in.) "Because folks go to their ministers
mainly when they're in crisis or grief, ministers are handling lots of stress
without help. I definitely believe in prayer, but a combination of prayer
and psychotherapy."

And let's remember that pastors themselves are not immune to depression. A pastor colleague of mine suffers from "pastor blues"—the high a
preacher gets on Sunday mornings, which, like a performer onstage, he or
she has to come down from when the service is over. As he told me, "That's
my time up there. I've got God and the congregation all at once. It's hard
to drop back down into the daily routine. You have to understand, being
responsible for that many souls and their pain can be overwhelming."

My child, never fear when you walk through fiery circumstances. A
wretched failure, a business loss, an unexplained illness—they will
come like unwelcome flames in the night. Don't be terrified but look
closely. In the middle of that fiery furnace, you'll see a familiar face.
I'll walk through the flames with you.

—FROM *DAILY PRAYERS AND PROMISES*

The noted Bishop George Brooks of Mt. Zion Baptist Church in Greensboro, North Carolina, told me that he believes 90 percent of ministers are in pain. He shared this with me while speaking about his own emotional challenges, like his delayed reaction to his father's death. We have to remember that ministers are human and vulnerable just like us, and that their faith is tested by life's challenges just like ours.

And being a woman pastor carries with it additional challenges. I spoke to a dear friend and minister I admire greatly, the Reverend Barbara King. Reverend Barbara, as she's called, found her calling thirty-five years ago, at the age of forty. Since she was thirteen she dreamed of being in the ministry, but as a woman didn't believe she could do it. Then she met a bold and dynamic woman minister in Illinois who challenged her to live her dream.

She asked me one simple question, "What's stopping you?" and it turned my life around, because nobody was stopping me, but me. Her teaching reached out to my soul. It was practical and, as a follower of Jesus Christ, it spoke to me. She represented what I wanted to be: orderly, beautiful, with a congregation of over a thousand members. She became my minister, and I was on her staff as an administrator for several years. Later, when I had my own ministry, I was able to handle some difficult situations because I had seen her go through them.

Having been in ministry for thirty-five years, I've experienced many ups and downs—emotionally, mentally, and spiritually. For many folks, my being a woman in ministry is contrary to the will of God. I have been insulted, criticized, and told to my face that nothing I say has any meaning. During a low point, when I was going through a crisis with a relative who had chosen the drug culture, I was asked to come to the treatment center where he was staying. When I got there, being a minister, of course I felt I should be ministering to the people there. But instead, just being there for myself and my relative I learned something very important.

I learned that I was codependent—with my relative *and* my church. I would rush home after a trip and change my clothes to be in the pulpit in the morning. People called me day and night, and I felt I had to be available to each one of them. It had become an emotional crisis. Now I am blessed to have a few close friends around me, so when *I* want to cry, someone is there to help and support me. Sometimes I reach a point when I want to shout, "Will somebody pray for

No one is perfect, we are all broken somewhere.

That is not all bad. A key is broken in all the right places to fit a certain lock. When that key is placed in that lock, there is a quiet click. When we meet a person who is broken in the right places to accommodate our brokenness, there is a click.

It can happen in other ways: An introverted person hears that click when he finds a job that can only be done by a person who works well alone; or when we face a life-altering decision.

Whether it is a job, or a relationship, or even faith, something clicks when we find the place that accommodates our uniqueness, or brokenness.

Some religions teach prayer—some call it meditation—but there is within each of us some mysterious, inner thing that tells us when something clicks—we don't know how or why, we just know.

We are all broken. But listening for that click can help us to unlock many doors. The voice is always there, we have only to listen.

—BISHOP T. D. JAKES, AUTHOR AND FOUNDER OF THE POTTER'S HOUSE, DALLAS, TEXAS

me?" Whenever I get to that point, I always think of Psalm 27, "Wait on the Lord and be of good courage."

My friend the Reverend Sheila Evans-Tranum is pastor of the Bridge Street AWME Church, the oldest African-American church in Brooklyn. She is a counseling minister, and has wisdom on the subject. She describes the church as a healing station—not the be-all and end-all of healing, but the place you go either for the help church really can give or to get directed to someplace more appropriate. "People can come for counseling, and for a referral to do the deeper cleansing. It's like a wash cycle—some things need a light rinse and delicate drying that your pastor can and should offer. But some stains are so deep that you need an additional wash cycle, a kind of help that churches can't offer. Church should create a bridge to that more intensive counseling; as a pastor, I have to be able to direct a parishioner to someone who is more skilled and has better credentials than I have."

> Create a clean heart within me, O God: and renew a right spirit within me.
>
> —PSALM 51:10

Sheila says that mental health care workers are not our enemy, and that the church has to help us see that. (On the other hand, we cannot just assume that every mental health care professional we encounter will be sensitive to us as a people or be able to meet our specific personal needs; that's why we have to advocate for ourselves.) She also points out that pastors are human, just as human as their parishioners and just as likely to be troubled by the same kinds of issues. Try as they may to conquer their own demons and help us conquer ours, they don't come down from heaven with blank slates for pasts. "Pastors have also been raped, abused, and sent to foster care. Every day they're hearing about issues similar to their own. Very often they do not seek counseling for the deep-rooted issues in their lives." There is no one among us who should ever be put on a pedestal. It's not right and it's not fair.

And as much as *we* feel pressured to put a good face on our pain, our religious leaders feel that pressure tenfold. Says Sheila, "For your public persona you have to look like everything is all right, and Sunday most of all, but that's why Sunday night is so often the loneliest night for a minister. You've given everything that you have to help other people, a whole congregation, your community, but when the glorious preaching moment is over, you are left with yourself. Pastors don't have their own pastors; they have no one

> It's like a dark cloud moving in, and it's *not* something you can say "Snap out of it!" to.
>
> —BEVERLY JOHNSON,
> MODEL AND ACTRESS

to encourage them, no one to give *them* words of counseling. The healing message they've given to others they cannot give to themselves. And yet so often they don't seek the counseling they themselves need."

This is the most troubling legacy of pastor blues: Hurt people will hurt other people if they don't get themselves guidance and help. If they have unresolved issues because they don't believe in counseling, they cannot truly give counseling that will help those who need them most. If, as Sheila puts it, a pastor is "giving the word on Sunday and then coming home and falling into depression," what positive example can he or she possibly give to the people who look up to them?

When we need something the church can't offer, we have to recognize that. The church cannot be everything to everyone, and it would be unfair and unreasonable for us to think otherwise. After all, when we need our oil

> Many of us look up to celebrities and think they must have it all
> together. In my experience representing models and actors I've no-
> ticed that when those of us in the public eye are put under the
> unique pressures of superstardom (the rumors and the competi-
> tion), the combination of living our lives in a fishbowl but not nec-
> essarily having the right coping skills to handle stressful situations
> can be very painful. It's important to remember that celebrities are
> just as human as everybody else.
>
> —BETHANN HARDISON, TALENT MANAGER AND DOCUMENTARY FILMMAKER

changed, we don't drive the car into church; when we need serious help for
our emotional well-being beyond what the church and prayer can give us,
we must take that step.

Finding Our Way Back to God, Church, and Wellness

Even when we face a harsh world well armed with the weapons of faith,
community, and prayer, we need to remember that depression is a devi-
ous demon. Telling a truly depressed person to "Have faith!" or "Keep
prayin'!" isn't likely to do any more good than saying "Snap out of it!" A
number of our churches have been in the forefront of religious organizations offering mental health counseling that's more than encouragement
to pray. But those churches are still too few and far between, and it is up
to us to demand of our own churches that they be better informed and
more prepared to deal with the mental health issues of their members. And
when our churches, as much as we love them, can't offer what we or our
loved ones or our friends need, we must be able to look beyond them in
the search for help.

Cheryl Anthony Mobley is a wonderful model of the church at its best.
Founder and CEO of Judah International Christian Center in Brooklyn,
she sees the role of the Black church today as twofold: to minister to the
souls of its members *and* to their psyches. A former welfare mother herself,
she knows that the church is often the first line of defense, especially for less
wealthy African Americans. That's why she uses her ministry to put into
practice the care and concern that give dignity and responsibility to her
congregation. She feels it's not enough for ministers to know the Bible—

they also have to put science and psychology together with faith. What's more, they have to do it in ways that let the church work hand in hand with hospitals, health care facilities, and social service agencies.

Sometimes the church can present us with models that help us deal with depression, reminding us of religious figures who have overcome adversity and emotional suffering. King David, Elijah, and Jeremiah, just to name a few, were extremely depressed, yet found the strength to proceed with their lives. Sometimes, as Rev. Tom Ledbetter says, our pastors can tell us that depression is exactly the right response to a given situation:

> To say yes, you have to sweat and roll up your sleeves and plunge both hands into life up to the elbows. It's easy to say no, even if it means dying.
>
> —JEAN ANOUILH, FRENCH PLAYWRIGHT

> When a young gay man is tied to a fence in Wyoming and killed because he is gay, we will experience some appropriate anger, some appropriate depression, some appropriate pain. When an airliner crashes, when we see starving people on our TV screens, when unspeakable horrors happen to people we love and even to people we don't know, we should feel some depression, but we, as spiritual beings, cannot be the containers of all this pain or situational depression. We have to feel it, and we may need to take some action, but then let the feelings pass through us into the center of spiritual reality that we call the heart of God. We cannot bear all this alone.

So for all the times that depression is *not* helping us, every once in a while there are occasions when we *should* feel sad and despairing—not as individuals about our own lives, but as humans about everyone on the planet. The ironic thing is that we find it easier to fall back, regroup, and press on when we experience depression about terrible things on a global scale than we do when our depression is just about our own selves. Seems backward, doesn't it?

Madeline McCray, a good friend and a deeply spiritual sister, sent me a heartfelt letter about the time in her life when she was "mad at God." This excerpt speaks powerfully to what I believe faith can be for those of us leading imperfect lives in an imperfect world.

The moment the capacity to "love" enters your being, you know God. Just as the moment we send love away from us is the moment we step onto a path of misery and despair. A cold, empty heart can never receive or give love to anyone, especially to oneself. I was fourteen when I sat across from my mother's bed staring at her lifeless body. I remember the sounds of the policeman's walkie-talkies. I remember holding my breath and not moving when my brother walked in, drunk and lying about what had happened to our mother. He was ten years older and towered over me, and yet my silent rage caused him to back away as I stared him down with eyes that were filled with hate. It was during this time that I sent love *and* God packing. Didn't need either one, and vowed I never would again.

> *Ring the bells that can still ring.*
> *Forget your perfect offering.*
>
> —LEONARD COHEN,
> SINGER, SONGWRITER, AND POET

When they lowered my mother's coffin into the grave I didn't cry. When my brother went missing shortly after and weeks later I learned he was dead, too—still I didn't cry. When the man I married repeatedly beat me and called me names, I didn't cry. It was the birth of my first son that opened my heart to love again, and the birth of my second that completely sealed the deal, bringing love and God back to my heart. I know that God was with me during those dark hours. I also know God didn't want me to suffer; I chose to suffer inside myself. But, then again, I was a teenager who didn't know about therapy or healing. Today, if I thought I was slipping back into a dark place, I wouldn't hesitate to "pray and see a therapist," knowing that those sessions could help me be a better mother, grandmother, friend, sister, and child of God.

As much as I love the idea of being "too blessed to be stressed," I've never actually experienced it myself—even as I have experienced being blessed—and I don't know too many people who have found that being blessed makes stress up and leave town. But I have a suggestion for those of us who are trying to be good, active, devout, happy, "blessed of the Lord" women

Five Reasons You Shouldn't Snap Out of It

- There's no such thing as "snapping out of it."
- It's okay to feel bad—you're entitled to your feelings.
- There is no such thing as a magic bullet; healing takes time.
- Therapy and meds take months and sometimes years to work.
- Healing means having compassion for yourself, and having compassion for yourself means being patient.

when we're living with pain that kicks our butt every day.

Remember that we are the ultimate self-help people. I talked before about how the Black church is rooted in self-help. For the longest time, due to the devastation of slavery and segregation, *self*-help was almost the only kind of help we could get, and the only place we could get it was church. Church still has so much to offer us if we accept its generous gifts, in life in general and with depression in particular, but certain kinds of self-help thinking actually hurt us. After all, if someone we love has a terrible illness, we don't just sit back and say, "God will provide"—we get our loved one the best professional care we can find, *and* we pray. Why would we deny ourselves the same care when we are depressed? Depression may not show up on an X-ray, and you can't cut it out with surgery, burn it out with radiation, heal it with a plaster cast, or end it with a vaccine, but it *is* a disease, and it *can* be treated. As I work through my own depression, I want all the help I can get: the good Lord, therapy, medication, herbs, exercise, the loving support of my family and friends, prayer, and anything else I can think of! I refuse to let shame or guilt or any of my old ideas stand in the way of my getting better. How about you?

I have learned the futility of expecting anyone, including myself, to be perfect. People who go about seeking to change the world, to diminish suffering, to demonstrate any kind of enlightenment, are often as flawed as anybody else. Sometimes more so. But it is the awareness of having faults, I think, and the knowledge that this links us to everyone on Earth, that opens us to courage and compassion.

—ALICE WALKER, AUTHOR AND POET

Chapter Seven

DON'T SNAP OUT OF IT!

Healing in Your Own Time

For years I was afraid to show my pain because I believed what so many of us believe: that I am the only one feeling such deep pain, the only one who has secrets and shame and insecurities, that people who show their pain can't handle their business, and that it's okay to feel low for a day or two, but after that you should just "snap out of it." Because I believed these things, I lived my emotional life afraid, never certain if it was safe to let my feelings out of the box I kept them in.

These beliefs were my reality, and the folks around me reinforced them every day. One of my biggest reinforcers was Xavier, one of my best friends. We've worked together for years. In the sad old days, any time I let down my guard enough to show that I felt gloomy, uncertain, or even worn out, he was sure to say something like, "You gotta hold it together." Each time it would happen I reminded myself to be more guarded, more careful about keeping signs of anxiety and sadness to myself.

After my breakdown, things between us changed—for the better. It turned out that he had his own challenges he was trying hard to keep at bay and seeing my pain was threatening to him because it triggered his own. Now we can smile about how much time we wasted *not* talking about the things that brought us down. It's not like we pour out our souls all the time, but both of us are on roads to healing that don't make us monitor our own painful feelings or avoid each other's low moods. It's only made our work together more productive and made our friendship even stronger.

This chapter is about the pain that comes when people in your life make you feel like your pain is not okay or like your healing is too slow; it's also about how people usually do this because they feel that their own pain is not okay. Nothing around us says it's okay to feel bad. We all want to believe we're making it, we're on top of our game, a success story—or at least on the way there. We all buy into the old idea that the better you do, the better you are. And, of course, that doing well means looking like you've got it all together.

> Many of us harbor hidden low self-esteem. We deem everything and everyone more important than ourselves and think that meeting their needs is more important than meeting our own. But if you run out of gas, everyone riding with you will be left stranded.
>
> —BISHOP T. D. JAKES, AUTHOR AND FOUNDER OF THE POTTER'S HOUSE, DALLAS, TEXAS

The reality is that we can't all feel on top of the world all the time, and we shouldn't. Sometimes we feel low, sad, even hopeless—and that actually *is* okay in situations that *should* produce those feelings. With depression, though, these normal feelings last longer, sometimes months or years. The longer they last, the more sensitive we are to the fact that we can't pull it together, get back in the saddle, hold it all down, or "snap out of it." But every single day society sends us messages that people who can't snap out of it are losers.

In Atlanta I met Susan, whose mother had died of a sudden aneurysm while Susan was in law school. She returned to campus two weeks after the funeral, and after a few weeks she noticed that not only were friends and acquaintances avoiding her, but they seemed annoyed, disturbed, and plain uncomfortable when she brought up her mother's death, her own sadness, or how much she missed her. One day a friend asked her, "Shouldn't you be over it by now?"

Susan had already been grieving, but people's reaction to her grief

threw her into a deep depression. Without people to support her she spiraled into a deeper and longer depression. It took seven long years until she
was finally diagnosed and could begin dealing with the dark cloud that had
hung over her life for so long.

My friend Kevin Marshall is a public relations executive who had been
married for less than a year when his wife and baby died in childbirth. It
is impossible for anyone who has not experienced the devastation of this
kind of loss even to imagine what it feels like; after seventeen years, Kevin
still has trouble talking about it. He tells me there are days when he can't
concentrate, when he sleeps too much, when he can't even get out of bed.
Sometimes he has to close his office door and have a "get-the-mask" moment. The depth of his grief is baffling to his family members, who tell him
he should be "past it" by now, that he should "move on" with his life. "I
know they love me and don't want to see me in pain, but they don't know
how hurtful their words are for me."

Too Blessed to Stress, or Too Scared to Care?

We're often short with other people, sometimes totally unsympathetic, because we can't *see* their pain—sometimes because we can't see *their* pain
past our own. I hate to say it, but every once in a while I find myself "hatin'"
on someone . . . and then I hear that person's story. Nine times out of ten,
once I know the story of somebody's suffering, no matter how petty they
are or how much they might bug me, I just can't be mad at them anymore.
I have come to realize that this person is actually scared to death, or stuck
in life, or somehow or another emotionally wounded or incapacitated. So
often we *react* to people's stuff instead of *responding* to them as someone
who is a thinking, feeling human being, because we feel there's just no time
to get to the person behind the annoyance. But do we really not have time?
Can we *afford* not to have the time? I think this is what Buddhists probably
mean when they say that every waking moment is worthy of the awareness
that we bring to meditation.

Pain comes between us. It even keeps us from surface kinds of nurturing, from the daily kindnesses that make life quietly joyous. Instead of
admitting that we're too busy or too hurt or too scared to get to someone
else's pain, we make excuses, to them *and* to ourselves: We need to meet
a deadline, to make the next appointment, to catch the next train, etc. We

blame things outside us for keeping us from the emotional work we should be prepared to do in every encounter, and then we wonder why our encounters are frustrating and don't satisfy us—dull at best, hostile at worst. Why don't we feel uplifted by community spirit? Community requires caring; caring requires time; time lets us hear and understand where others are at, not to mention where we ourselves are, so we can respond to them with our whole and best self. Being present to ourselves lets us be present for others, and that presence gives us the space to acknowledge our own feelings and pain, as well as to sympathize and to really feel for others. It's been said that the only gift we can give another person is the gift of our time. Maybe this is why the idea of a "New York minute" is so brutal and, when you think about it, antihuman.

That's a lesson that depression can be brilliant at teaching us. But what do we do when we're dealing with people who haven't learned this lesson for themselves?

I'm Not Crazy—I'm in Pain!

If you asked Mariah Carey what her best year was, she would definitely not tell you 2001. In that one year the most successful singer of the 1990s was hospitalized with exhaustion, her semiautobiographical movie *Glitter* didn't fare well, nor did the soundtrack album, she was dropped by the record label that had signed her only months before, and her father was diagnosed with inoperable can-cer. Any one of these things would be hard, but let's back up a second to the hospitalization. How did that come about? Mariah explained it herself on national television.

> I never play what I can play. I'm always playing way over and above what I can play.
>
> —MILES DAVIS, JAZZ LEGEND

"I know I don't say this that much, but guess what—I don't take care of myself. I needed some time off, but nobody was really giving it to me.... My managers were a little upset [that I needed a break], and they were trying to press on and get through it, but that didn't work." This is precisely the problem we find when other people don't have time to let us take care of ourselves.

"I was with people who didn't really know me, and I had no personal assistant. I'd be doing interviews all day long, getting two hours of sleep a night, if that. I was burning the candle at both ends and in the middle, and it caught up with me."

Despite years of pushing herself to be superhuman, Mariah had the good sense to get help. "I began seeing a therapist, and he told me, 'Look, you didn't have a nervous breakdown. It's a form of torture not to be allowed to sleep.' He said I had to start setting boundaries in life, to learn how to say no. It's taken some people a while to understand that, but now they do. I've actually made up contracts that people who work with me have to sign, so they know I must have lunch breaks and dinner breaks, and five or six hours of sleep a night! For so long, I had been so busy taking care of everyone and everything else, including my career, that I forgot about me. But I've learned that there are certain lines that have to be drawn."

Wow. If Mariah Carey, with all the fame and clout that she has, couldn't get the people around her to see that she was in pain and cut her some slack, think how challenging it is for those of us who aren't "stars" to hit the brakes. And think how challenging it is for us to get the people around us to keep from rear-ending us or driving right over us!

Emotional healing is not quick and dirty, any more than physical healing is. If someone broke an arm, you wouldn't be nice for two weeks and then say, "Hey, isn't it time you took off that cast and got back to work?!" Recovery from depression involves thinking, feeling, and relearning the ways we used to think and feel; it involves seeking treatment, committing to treatment, and being patient with ourselves—these are the only ways to make healing meaningful and lasting. If you caught a bad cold in the middle of winter, you wouldn't take care of yourself for twenty-four hours and then walk outside in shorts and a T-shirt—you would know that your immune system was weak and needed time to recover before you could stress it again and hope for it to protect you. In depression, your emotional immune system is compromised, and it needs to be built back up again, slowly and with psychological vitamins, exercise, and good people. The last thing in the world you want to do is try to "snap out of it!"

What Do We Do When Our People Don't Get It?

We typically have one of two reactions when somebody close to us, maybe with the best intentions, tells us to snap out of it. The most common reaction is to feel even worse about ourselves than we already do, to take the cake of our pain and ice it with shame. The next most common reaction is to lash out in hurt and anger—"Go to hell! You have no idea what it's like! You think I *wouldn't* 'snap out of it' if I could? I'd like to see *you* snap out of this, dumb ass . . . !" and so on, and so on. And then of course there're those of us who do both—lash out *and* feel worse about ourselves. I've done all of the above. If you have, too, then you probably know that none of them makes us feel any better or brings the people in our lives any closer to understanding us.

So how do we make a meaningful connection with someone who wants to "cure" our depression by telling us to stop being so depressed? How can we push other people toward being comfortable with our pain when we may not be too far down the same road ourselves?

As always, everything good starts with communication. *Try* to explain to people what you're going through and what you know about depression. Use images of what it feels like. I often describe it as walking around in the summer wearing a 100-pound winter coat. Ask them to imagine themselves in your place. Even a half-successful try will take you to a slightly better place and take a little stress off. It also opens the door to better communication, with more openness, in the future.

> If you can't envision what it's like to be depressed, think of being at the bottom of a bowl whose sides are very slippery and how futile and frustrating it must be to climb out of this terrible trap. Each time you muster up the energy to climb halfway out, you slide back to the bottom. That's the experience of being clinically depressed. Over time, you run out of energy and motivation and are called lazy or weak minded. So you keep silent or pretend that all is well. Now you are doubly trapped. Without help that goes beyond saying, "Come on, you can do it," you remain stuck and defeated.
>
> —DEREK H. SUITE, MD, MS,

And by making the time to try to take someone who's close to you even closer, you're sending a message that you care about them. On top of that, I can't help noticing that every time I open up about my pain, there's just that much less of it that I have to carry on my own. Sometimes it helps just to have them really *hear* you.

Another good thing to do is to think about *their* pain. That might sound funny at a time like this, when you're the one in agony and someone in your world (mother, father, husband, wife, boyfriend, girlfriend, son, daughter, boss, coworker) is being thoughtless and hurtful to you, but there's a good reason. Chances are that if somebody is acting annoyed or even angry about how long your depression is lasting, it is probably because they are very frustrated about being confused and unable to help, which could in turn make them feel guilty, which could then make them feel angry about feeling guilty. They might even, like my partner in crime, Xavier, be going through something themselves that they can't articulate, that they're working hard at hiding.

Sometimes we have to set firm boundaries. In my experience, most people in the snap-out-of-it camp change their tunes—some quicker than others—once they have a better understanding of depression in general, and yours in particular. Sometimes, though, people are too defensive, too caught up in their own stuff, to be able to take in what you're putting out. They probably have good intentions. They may really *want* to get it, but something in them throws up a roadblock to understanding ("Maybe if you just prayed a little harder . . ." "If you would go to the gym and have a regular workout routine . . ." "You need to move—this apartment is depressing . . ."). With people like that we may need to establish some firm boundaries to protect ourselves. We may have to say things like, "Listen, I know you want me to feel better, and I appreciate that, but right now I don't think you're feeling me or what I'm going through. If you really just don't get it, then I'm gonna have to ask you to . . ."

Lastly, there are people we may have to push away for a time, if possible. If somebody in your life not only doesn't get it, but keeps hammering at you to get better *their* way, on *their* schedule, you may have to let that relationship go while you're healing. Depression is a heavy enough burden on its own. If there's anything we *can* do to keep others from making it heavier, we owe it to ourselves to do it.

Buying into Someone Else's Schedule for Our Healing

Janice Clarke was a twenty-five-year-old college graduate and political activist when she took a job as an abortion counselor in a Boston-area clinic.

The work was demanding but very much in line with her womanist beliefs and her dedication to activist causes. Several weeks after starting she began to experience anxiety attacks. Every day she counseled twelve to fifteen women who came to the clinic seeking abortions. Many of the women had sad stories, some of rape or incest or partners who were unwilling to help them raise the child.

Before working at the clinic, Janice had had "low months" as she called them, but never thought of herself as depressed. Within three months she was having trouble getting out of bed in the morning or calming the panic attacks that would overtake her while she was with a client in the counseling room. After three weeks of calling in sick on Mondays and faking it through the day, she scheduled an appointment with a friend's therapist. Within the first session, the therapist told Janice she felt that her work with the women at the clinic had tapped into her own pain in a powerful way. By her fifth session, Janice began recounting the beatings she and her mother had suffered at the hands of her father and how difficult her childhood had been. Her work at the clinic, which she needed to pay her rent, caused her to have flashbacks almost daily.

Unable to take it anymore, Janice went in to see her boss, a likable white woman who had been very keen to hire her as a woman of color. Her boss made sympathetic noises as Janice explained her situation—that she was experiencing a severe depression and that seeing upwards of twelve clients a day was adding to her misery. Her boss agreed to transfer her to the intake desk for a week and grant her a week's vacation early. Janice was grateful and relieved. However, when the two weeks were over and she returned to counseling, the panic attacks returned, too. Once again she went to discuss the situation with her boss, hoping there might be some middle ground for the next few months while she worked on herself in therapy.

This meeting with the boss felt entirely different from the first one. Her boss was colder and much less sympathetic. She told Janice that everyone had problems to sort out, and that she expected hers to be resolved by now. Janice was taken aback. The woman had a degree in counseling and considered herself a women's health advocate! When Janice explained that she didn't want to work less, just in a less stressful capacity at the clinic, the woman threatened her job. "I had exactly two weeks to get my life in order or I was fired," she explained, choking up at the memory. "I had to pay my rent, and finding committed and activist work that pays a living wage isn't exactly easy. I felt like she had me over a barrel."

Previously unwilling to take antidepressants, Janice felt compelled to start on Zoloft just to keep her job. The next six months were hell. Janice continued counseling during the day, and in therapy she continued digging and finding and reliving her childhood trauma. "It was all I could do not to have a complete breakdown," she says. "I'm a loyal and hardworking employee! What I needed was breathing room, not an ultimatum." Janice's need to mask her pain and suffer through a debilitating depression is lived daily by thousands of Americans who feel forced to choose keeping their heads above water financially over healing their wounded souls.

You've heard of get-rich-quick schemes. Well, how about get-well-quick? It's one thing to have individuals in our lives pressure us to get better faster—at least we know it's generally because they want what's good for us, even if they don't understand how things work. It's another thing to have not a person pushing you to get better, but something faceless and almost anonymous, like a company, a corporation, or an institution. We're talking about employers and insurance companies and HMOs that want to limit mental health care benefits like therapy and push you to rely purely on drugs instead. Don't let them bully you! Your therapist will usually do his or her best to make the strongest case possible to have your needs appropriately met. On top of that, many companies let you put money into a supplemental health fund, so you're not taxed on that money. If money is really tight, check into what's available through your town, city, county, or state—many of them have high-quality care services where you pay what you can afford. And if you're a veteran, don't forget the VA (now the Department of Veteran Affairs)! To twist the lyrics of the old Beastie Boys song, "You got to fight . . . for your right . . ." to mental health!

And for those of you who are uninsured (and in America today there are too many of you at 44 milion!) you may need to take mental health into your own hands. You can do this by finding a volunteer therapist-in-training at a school or someone who does volunteer work for under- or uninsured people. Looking takes a little work, but these folks are out there, and your mental health is worth the effort. You can also start a healing circle with folks that you know. A healing circle is a safe place to talk about your feelings and get advice and support from folks who've been there, too. Check out the back of the book for my "Guide to Breaking Our Silence and Getting the Healing Started."

Taking Your Own Pain Seriously

Beverly Johnson, the first Black woman to grace the cover of *Vogue*, is a businesswoman, a supermodel, and an actress, and recently she publicly came out about her depression in *Celebrating Life: A Guide to Depression for African Americans.* "Being a supermodel is stressful at times—the routine, the dieting, being recognized." Those are the prices we assume models and actors pay, annoyances that are part of the job. But Beverly had to deal with worse than that. She had to deal with depression.

"I remember being out sometimes, and it would be some of the most beautiful, glorious days, and I would *know* it was beautiful, but I'm like, 'Why don't I *feel* that?'" Or she would get a call from an agent telling her that she'd just gotten a great gig for some ungodly amount of money, and she would act as if she were happy and excited ("I would be performing for the agent"), but she didn't feel that way—she didn't feel anything at all. All she wanted to do was sleep. "I couldn't get enough sleep. As soon as I finished work, I'd go to sleep." And this was not just a sometime thing. This went on for years—until she was finally diagnosed with depression.

"Being diagnosed gave me a lot of understanding of my life. I look back on my childhood and I was very quiet. I think the reason I finally decided to find out what this was is because I had everything. I had the illustrious career, I had the beautiful home, wonderful daughter, my health and strength, my family was great . . . and I couldn't tell anyone that I felt awful because people were going, 'Yeah, right, what do *you* have to feel awful about?' My life totally changed once I was treated—I mean totally. I really began to find out who I really was." Beverly's story makes me think about the guilt people can feel about being depressed when they think they don't have any reason to feel depressed or (especially) when *other* people tell them they have no right to be unhappy. I know so many wealthy and successful people who are dying inside. Pain and suffering knows no boundaries; it doesn't pick and choose folks, it can happen to anyone.

Up to now I've been talking in this chapter about *other* people who want to deny how real our suffering is and our need to work on finding a healing pace that will really work, not for other people, but for us. It can happen, as you probably know, that the person who takes our suffering *least* seriously is us—the people doing the suffering! Americans in general are bad about acknowledging their pain, especially when it comes to mental anguish, and among Americans, Black people are the worst at it because the stakes of showing how sensitive you are are so high. So many depressed people already believe everything that is negative, harmful, and self-abusive. If we want to recover, and not just mask our symptoms as they get worse, we need to dispense once and for all with the idea that we can "get well quick." One of the best ways to do that is to practice sitting with our pain.

The first time I heard someone say, "You have to sit with your pain," I didn't even know what they meant, never mind how I was supposed to do it. Nowadays I think of it as being a lot like meditation. In meditation, the hardest part is often sitting still—physically *and* mentally. We're supposed to find a more or less comfortable sitting position and, while staying awake, let our minds and bodies settle—think of a leaf whirling and whirling in the wind until it slowly, slowly, slowly settles to rest on the ground. Think that's easy? Well, easier said than done! If you've never meditated before, you'd be amazed at how hard it can be just to sit still, let the thoughts and feelings come crawling out of the woodwork and then let them keep right on going without engaging them—especially when everything in you wants to jump up and run away screaming. No one who meditates achieves calm quickly or with ease, and the real growth comes with not running away, with sitting with the pain. (For the record, I've tried to sit with my pain, and I'm still trying, though it can be really hard since I have the attention span of a fly and I sometimes . . . I'm sorry, what was I just saying?) As my Buddhist friend Tanya loves to say, "Don't just do something—sit there!"

Sitting with our pain, or even just being willing to try, is the key to healing. We want other people to understand our suffering; when they do, it's great, and it can really contribute to our healing process. But if we don't honor that suffering ourselves, if we do not acknowledge what is wrong and how wrong it is, no amount of sympathy or empathy from others will be enough to heal us. We must believe that we deserve the space to understand and address this pain if we want to heal from it; and if we don't fully believe it *yet*, we should take a page from the folks in Alcoholics Anonymous and "act as if" we deserve it until we finally embrace it in our hearts.

Acknowledging our pain and staking a claim in an emotional world while not hidden behind the game face is one of the most important steps to recovery. We must learn, as individuals and as a people, to feel for ourselves and for others. We have to work every day at carving out, for ourselves and for others, a space in the world for healing. That space is as threatened by those who deny our ongoing pain, and their own, as it is by

238

us when we do the same; when we listen to the punishing voices of shame and self-hatred.

> When we speak, we are afraid our words will not be heard or welcomed. But when we are silent, we are still afraid. So it is better to speak, remembering we were never meant to survive.

Why Society Distances Itself from Pain

I keep saying that the culture of this country leads people to fear pain of any kind, and I won't stop saying it until it stops being true, but I want to talk a little bit about why. A few years ago *The New York Times* had an article about a survey that evaluated the happiness of people in sixty-five countries. Americans were fifteenth. Nigerians were first. Allowing for the fact that there will always be some happy people and some unhappy people everywhere, how is it possible that the people of Nigeria—a country traumatized by civil war and ethnic violence, poor despite all its natural resources, and devastated by corruption at all levels of government—could be happier *overall* than the citizens of the richest country in the world?

One simple reason: expectations. Nigerians understand that life, by nature, is difficult. They don't feel entitled to happiness, and they don't feel that they've somehow been gypped if things aren't going well for them. Actually, they tend to feel just the opposite—because they *know* that life offers no guarantees, least of all guarantees of smooth sailing, they have a keen appreciation of the moments in life that do go well, the moments when there *isn't* conflict. Nigerians don't welcome death, disease, failure, or loss more than anybody else, but they don't run screaming from these facts of life, either. Despite the many cultures that make up the country, Nigerians as a people are very good at finding and making happiness, for themselves and for others, even in the midst of misery.

Not so for Americans. For most of the twentieth century, there was a rise in wealth, not to mention the ability of many more people to make money after World War II, and mainstream white America started to promote idealized images of itself: "We" owned our own homes; "we" had two cars; "our" family consisted of Mom, Pop, Junior, and Sis, with pets Rover and Kitty to round things out; "we" had clean, straight teeth; "we" were vaccinated against all the bad diseases; "we" ate food with eight important

> Our community really needs to deal with the stigma of mental illness. I look at my uncle who is now seventy-four and who was diagnosed with schizophrenia years ago, and he is an example of someone who has fallen through the cracks. He would not follow up with a psychiatrist or take his medications. People in the community always called him "Crazy Sonny" from the time he was a teenager. Now he is wasting away in a nursing home and it's sad to see someone whose life could have been better.
>
> —GAIL HOLLIDAY, BOSTON, MASSACHUSETTS

vitamins plus iron that built strong bodies in twelve ways; "we" went for regular checkups; "we" worked hard and got promoted and made more money and moved to a bigger, better house in a nicer neighborhood . . . and, above all, "we" smiled. A lot. Because "we" were so gosh-darned happy!

Even white Americans were regularly driven crazy by the major gaps between their own lives and the lives they were "supposed" to be having. You can imagine how crazy it felt to us brown folks! People say that even though we had occasional riots before the 1960s, Black neighborhoods in the cities exploded in that decade because it wasn't until then that we all had television. Every single day, for hours and hours a day, we were hit with images of how we were "supposed" to be living and how "real" people did live. The wonder is not that we rioted but that we didn't tear down the whole country!

But let's not jump to assume that things are so very different now. I would even argue that things are worse; we are being hit by more images in all forms of media showing us what the good life is supposed to look like, and it takes a very, very strong person not to give in, at least now and then, to the temptation to compare your own life to the lives of the rich and the beautiful and the young and the powerful and the famous. Success and victory are held up to us as ideals so many times a day, every single day of the week, that there's no space or time to understand failure, frustration, disappointment, fear, or even just bad luck. These ideals make us feel freakish, like we don't fit into what "American" is supposed to look like—unless we fit into a handful of very narrow categories. American culture asks us as Black people to stereotype ourselves—as actors, athletes, singers, dancers, or prostitutes—and then rewards us for performances that are at the expense of who we really are. This equation of Black success with perform-ing for white people reminds me of when we used to perform in old-time blackface, and it doubles our discomfort.

Saying No to the Culture That Denies Our Right to Feel

Lack of health care in general and mental health care in particular sends the message that "wellness" is a low priority. American culture is built on a fantasy of do-it-yourself success with a pulled-up-by-your-bootstraps mentality, which makes us feel personally responsible for everything. And if we are personally responsible for everything, then pain is an individual problem, not a collective responsibility.

We fear death, and we fear feelings, and when those things come up, people become uncomfortable. Feelings in general and depression in par-ticular interfere with business and upset the work ethic—or so people think, because they can't even pro-cess how much is actually *lost* due to depression. Acknowledged pain brings people in very close proxim-ity to one another, something we're not comfortable with in this culture.

We avoid people in pain as a form of social pressure to make them *act* normal and try to *seem* normal, even if they don't feel anything re-motely like normal. Our lack of so-cial support structures makes peo-ple feel vulnerable. We're a society of image—buying things drives the

> You are responsible for the world that you live in. It is not the government's re-sponsibility. It is not your school's or your social club's or your church's or your neighbor's or your fellow cit-izen's. It is yours, utterly and singularly yours.
>
> —AUGUST WILSON, PLAYWRIGHT

fantasy that we're all middle class, that we're all making it, that we're doing well even when we're not. Black people in particular have been brought up to project that things are okay and going well, so it's a double whammy to see ourselves or others falling apart.

One of the things that troubles me lately is the talk show model of ex-pressing pain but not healing pain. People now feel that if they've expressed the pain, they've conquered it. It's very easy to find dysfunction around us and so hard to find a clear example of somebody moving through the steps of getting better.

The bottom line is that buying into "Snap out of it!" is like defending someone whose joy in life is hurting you. Buying into "Snap out of it!" is like having your own private emotional bully—the part of us that denies our own feelings, our right to healing. To *resist* this denial we have to acknowledge our own pain. Each one of us who does it allows another of us to do the same, strengthening our right to feel and breaking the cycle of pain that denying the feeling creates. It also makes us more sensitive, because when you acknowledge your own pain, you can see it so clearly in others. Living fully means feeling fully, and every last one of us deserves that.

Healing Takes Time— Give It to Yourself. You Are Worthy!

When you feel genuinely entitled to your feelings and entitled to your right to heal, on *your* timetable, it's like you're buying a kind of anti-depression insurance. When you feel that way, things are a whole lot less likely to reach the point of depression, or to stay there long if they do run that way. When you feel that way, you will have learned one of life's most important lessons about taking care of yourself: Time truly is the greatest gift we can give ourselves.

> Injustice anywhere is a threat to justice everywhere.
>
> –DR. MARTIN LUTHER KING, JR.

Chapter Eight

OH, LORD, PLEASE DON'T LET ME BE MISUNDERSTOOD

Can I Get a Diagnosis?

This is the part of the book that gets a whole lot more technical. My bad. I know it's heavy going; if I didn't believe so much in the importance of it, there'd be times when I would straight up bore myself. But don't space out—there's lots of good information in this chapter and the next one about why we're rightfully suspicious of doctors, and what treatments are out there for us. And don't let the technical stuff keep you from checking it out—just stay strong and keep reading. After all, reading is how we liberated our minds from slavery!

Black folks are proud of where they come from, and with good reason: We've come a long way! I cannot tell you how many times I have heard brothers and sisters, in public and in intimate settings, start off their stories of pain and grief by saying with respect and reverence that in our veins runs the blood of survivors. Survivors of the slave trade. Survivors of Jim Crow. Survivors of the struggle for civil rights (and it ain't over yet!).

Leaning on the strength of our ancestors to get us through difficult and dark times remains one of the many things about Black life that I thank God for. But sometimes our talk about pride is a cover-up for our deep fear of admitting we are vulnerable, let alone being mentally unstable or depressed. The French psychiatrist Julia Kristeva wrote, "The sadness that overwhelms us . . . is also a shield—sometimes the last one—against madness." When we compare our struggles with those of our ancestors, we unintentionally minimize our own suffering as a way of trying to stay sane.

Take Janet Scott, a recently retired corrections officer from Newark, New Jersey, who says, "My great-great-grandmother survived the back-breaking work of the cotton field and the master's whip. I handled working at a men's jail five days a week for twenty-five years. What was the difference?" I'm the first one to say that we are socially and economically haunted by the horrors of slavery, but my response to Janet and others who share her feelings is a simple one: Your great-great-grandmother was a slave; you're not. But this still leaves two very important questions: Why do so many of us feel like slaves? And who—or what—are we slaves *to*?

> That's why so much of that medicine they always after us 'bout takin' is agains' us. These doctors ain' nothin' but white folks, too.
>
> —VELMA CUNNINGHAM, *DRYLONGSO*

In her book *Positive Illusions* social psychologist Shelley E. Taylor says that most people have "positive self-enhancing illusions"—we think we're doing much better than we are. For Janet, who is also an alcoholic, her "self-enhancing illusion"—the line she fed herself to get through unimaginably hard days at work, where she experienced abuse at the hands of both inmates and her mostly male colleagues—was that her ability to endure, her strength as a Black woman, was more valuable than being a fully functioning emotional being. In her emotional life, Janet thought of herself in the way slave masters did of our ancestors: as subhuman. "Enslaved" by this negative image of herself, Janet allowed her depression to buy and sell her.

The most tragic thing about this is that our ability to *look* like we've got it all together fools even profes-

> The money ain't in the cure. The money is in the medicine.

sionals who might otherwise be able to help us. So many of us have grown up feeling like we can't let it all hang out around white folks, and white folks still make up the majority of mental health professionals. Our sound, historically based reasons for distrusting white institutions can lead us to hurt ourselves emotionally in the present. For most of us, placing impossible pressures on ourselves is more comfortable than being vulnerable in front of a white person.

On top of that whole mess, we put up a front to our own community, so that our friends, our churches, our employers don't recognize the signs or step in or offer support. We've been taught that problems are supposed

> **Maybe not. But the Lord willing, I'll keep you scratching.**
>
> —SOJOURNER TRUTH, A FORMER SLAVE WHO
> WALKED TO FREEDOM, TO A HECKLER WHO YELLED AT HER IN 1845 THAT HER
> ANTISLAVERY TALK DIDN'T MEAN ANYTHING MORE TO HIM THAN AN OLD FLEABITE

to be kept inside the family (and sometimes not even there), that complaining or feeling overwhelmed is a luxury we can't afford, and that we have to work twice as hard as anyone else but never let the stress show. This may help us *look* strong most of the time and *feel* strong sometimes, but when it comes to seeking help for something as serious as depression, this cover can be deadly.

The amazing thing is that even when we bring ourselves to ask medical professionals for help, there's a risk that we won't get it. Maybe it's their bias, or maybe it's poor research (which has been done almost exclusively on whites), maybe it's human error, or maybe it's some combination of all of the above; whatever the reason, professionals often don't recognize that the signs and symptoms for depression may be different for African-American patients than for white patients. These doctors don't see our distress because they aren't looking through the right lens. They see the *effects* of depression—broken homes, addiction, violence, anger—but not the depression itself.

Here are some truths, without the myths:

- African Americans are 12 percent of the population, but we account for only 2 percent of psychiatrists, 2 percent of psychologists, and 4 percent of social workers.
- According to the surgeon general's 1999 report on mental health, only a third of all Americans get care. That's bad enough; but of the Black Americans with mental illness, only one-sixth receive care. Yet according to that same study, we account for one-*quarter* of the mental health care needs in this country.
- Black people are less likely than whites to have ailments be treated with medication. When we do get medication, we're less likely to receive newer, more sophisticated, specific meds, and our dosages have been set using white people as the standard, not taking into account medical conditions that are specific to us. Often the highest dosage is prescribed first, and we don't get the follow-up treatments

we need to regulate the medication.

• A study of 19,000 people in 5 U.S. cities showed that a much higher rate of Black women than white women or men mistakenly believe that emotional pain is a physical symptom.

> The important thing is not to stop questioning.
>
> –ALBERT EINSTEIN, NOBEL PRIZE-WINNING THEORETICAL PHYSICIST AND AUTHOR

• Regardless of race, a person who has had two episodes of major depression has a 70 percent chance of experiencing a third. A person who has had three episodes has a 90 percent chance of experiencing a fourth.

• Of Black women suffering from depression, only 7 percent receive treatment. The figure for white women is 20 percent.

Take Donna: her lifelong belief that she is "short, dark, fat, and ugly" led her to feel socially and professionally worthless. Like many of us, she thinks of therapy as ". . . a hobby for rich white folks who don't have to earn a living." Despite her solid white-collar job and a decent salary, when her sleeplessness and anxiety got worse she went to her primary care physician instead of a therapist. Her white doctor prescribed Ambien and Klonopin, which reduced the symptoms but did nothing to address what caused them.

Donna's experience highlights an important fact. Depression can come and go, and without proper diagnosis and treatment the chances of it coming back are high. That's why most national guidelines recommend not only treatment of the current episode but also six months of treatment after it seems to have let up.

There's more: If patients took their prescribed drugs for five years, the burden of depression would be cut in half. Yet how realistic is it for patients, especially Black patients under the pressure of high medical costs that too often come out of pocket, to stick to a drug treatment for that long? It's not. Statistics show that 42 percent of patients discontinued their antidepressant treatment *during the first thirty days* and 72 percent had stopped within 90 days. Of the people who discontinue drugs in primary care, three-fifths have not informed their doctor three months later. (By the way, I stopped taking my meds for six months because, I admit, I just got tired of the morning routine of taking meds and vitamins.)

Every few minutes there's an antidepressant ad on TV, and all these ads have resulted in more folks asking primary care physicians to write prescriptions for them. This doesn't begin to include all of the Black folks who are underinsured or uninsured altogether and receiving care from emergency rooms. There are only about 40,000 psychiatrists nationwide, so more than half of the antidepressant prescriptions are written by family doctors. That's one reason some experts believe there is little follow-up care.

Dr. Darrel Regier, the American Psychiatric Association's director of research, claims that carrying out treatment the way the FDA recommends would push up costs more than 50 percent. Studies keep showing that prescription medication and talk therapy *together* make the most effective treatment of depression symptoms, but insurance companies find that paying for pills is considerably cheaper than paying therapists to address the root causes of suffering—especially because general physicians can and do write most of the prescriptions.

Dr. Roberto Lewis-Fernandez, a Massachusetts psychiatrist, makes a hard-hitting point: "After a certain amount of suffering for a certain amount of time, your brain reacts. The idea of mainstream psychiatry is that the pill will correct the chemical imbalance in the brain. But the imbalance keeps happening because of the situations people are in, and the pill can't correct situations."

One study I read about found that patients on antidepressants rarely get the psychiatric therapy they need right after they start the drugs, a time when risk of suicidal behavior can temporarily rise. What's more, according to Dr. Richard A. Friedman, director of the psychopharmacology clinic at Cornell University's medical school, "Ten percent of patients with severe depression will kill themselves." And a study published by *General Hospital Psychiatry* said that 44 percent of adults who are suicidal visit their primary care physicians regularly, and only about a quarter of suicidal adults ever receive care from a mental health professional. On top of this, less than 15 percent of Americans living with depression are currently receiving both talk therapy and drug treatment. And a third of working-age African Americans are estimated to be uninsured—meaning that more than 6 million adults had a gap in their coverage or were uninsured altogether. Is it any wonder folks are walking around in pain?

But let's return to Donna. Years later she's still on and off the drugs, but nowhere closer to getting the real help she needs. Still embarrassed by her looks and the general equivalency diploma (GED) she earned after a teen pregnancy prevented her from finishing high school, she suffers from a crippling shame that is doubled by the impact racism has on how she feels about her looks. If she sought the psychological help she needs, Donna might realize that her primary problem is depression and begin to sort out the complex relationship between the way her brain works and her own destructive beliefs so that she can deal with the stresses of daily life more effectively.

And then there are women like Cindy Jenkins, who was fired from her high-powered corporate job. After six months of binge eating and unemployment, her partner, Dionne, finally convinced her to go to a therapist. After several weeks of working together, the therapist confided to Cindy that she was her first Black patient. Something in Cindy shut down then. Before the comment, she discussed her feelings of apathy and her lack of energy. After it, Cindy focused more on dressing for sessions as she would for work, focusing on her accomplishments, and otherwise making sure to prove to her therapist that not all Black women are welfare moms.

"It's not that she said anything offensive, just that every once in a while I could tell that she had certain assumptions about how Black people live," Cindy said. The therapy ended when her six months of insurance ran out, and in their last session the therapist told her that given how well-groomed, articulate, and motivated Cindy was, there was no doubt about her future success. Can you imagine?! It took finding a Black psychiatrist for Cindy to be diagnosed with major depression and given medication to stabilize her feelings while undergoing therapy. Finally Cindy felt seen and heard.

Bad Blood:
Black Folks' Historical Mistrust of Medical Practice

Black folks' distrust of the health care system reaches as deep into our psyches as it does our history. That's no surprise, since "scientific reasoning" has long been used to justify our racial humiliation. I chose to share with you the below quotes, one from *Drylongso,* the masterpiece of African-American anthropology by John Langston Gwaltney, and the other from Chris Rock's 1999 HBO special, *Bigger and Blacker,* because they both speak to our suspicion and dread of the white health care institutions and imply that those institutions have no commitment to healing, or even helping Black people.

(There's a terrific new book on the subject called *Medical Apartheid: The Dark History of Medical Experimentation on Black Americans from Colonial Times to the Present* by Harriet A. Washington that I recommend if you'd like to go deeper into this sad history.) And so our community doesn't trust professionals, focusing on the horrors committed against us and doubting the lifesaving breakthroughs offered to us; so much so that often new FDA-approved drugs are viewed as a form of social control. We are so skeptical that many of us simply turn to illegal drugs as a way of self-medicating and turn drug dealers into our "street pharmacists."

> There may be times when we are powerless to prevent injustice, but there must never be a time when we fail to protest.
>
> —ELIE WIESEL, HOLOCAUST SURVIVOR, NOBEL PRIZE WINNER, AND AUTHOR

Take Debra, a twenty-five-year-old Ivy League graduate from a middle-class, West Indian family. In the middle of the spring semester of her sophomore year, she began to suffer from crippling bouts of emotional numbness. She was unable to get out of bed, let alone complete assignments or keep what used to be an intense study schedule. A friend reported Debra to the university's student health office after two weeks of this behavior. A counselor there gave Debra an ultimatum: She either had to agree to attend weekly sessions for an hour, or news of her condition would be reported home to her parents.

"It frightened me to death. I felt under enough pressure without my parents yelling at me about how I was throwing away an opportunity of a lifetime. I already constantly criticized myself about how I wasn't good enough. I could just hear my mother saying, 'Maybe you don't belong up there with all those smart, rich white kids.' Looking back, I guess I feared that was the case. Without her ever coming right out and saying it, I sent that same message to myself. Finally, I just started acting like it was true, like I didn't belong."

To avoid what Debra feared would be her parents' wrath, she started going to the college's counseling center. At the beginning of the second session, the university therapist diagnosed her as suffering from antisocial personality disorder (what most folks call "sociopathic"), even though at the time most studies on the disorder were over ten years old and about male prison inmates! This same therapist also wrote Debra a low-dose prescription for a drug called phenytoin, found to be useful in treating antisocial personality. Yeah, that's right: A college girl at a top school was given a prescription drug only researched on inmates in the dark days of prison drug trials!

Imagine something for a moment: Ten Black people come into an emergency room with ten different kinds of injuries. One person has a broken leg. Another has a cracked skull. Another has a broken finger, and so on. All ten of the patients are given the same-size Band-Aid and told they are going to be fine. Sounds crazy, right? Now, imagine ten more Black people, all suffering from depression in varying degrees and forms, being prescribed the same medication. The horror of this scenario is that it happens all the time. It's what happened to Debra!

"After I went on the drug, I was a total mess," Debra said. "Before, I laid around thinking about how I was fucking up my life. Then I couldn't think at all. Sure, I went to class because that's what I was supposed to do. Doing otherwise would have been breaking the rules. But it was just like someone stuck a vacuum in my brain and sucked me out."

You don't have to be a brain surgeon to figure out that a drug used on violent inmates might not be the best option for a peaceful young woman showing signs of depression. I can only imagine race played a large part. Did the color of Debra's skin transform a young, overwhelmed woman into an angry inmate? Or did her doctor truly believe that the prescribed course of action was in the best interest of the patient, since the patient happened to be Black? Whatever the case, the consequences of Debra's misdiagnosis were serious. Even though the drugs enabled her to remain in school, her inability to concentrate put her scholarship in danger—and there was no way to keep that from her parents.

"I understand now that I should have left school for the

> As Black people, we need to be very careful about being suspicious of medical technology. On the one hand we have been abused by medical research, but on the other hand we often do not get the benefit of modern medical technology. I am on a mission to see to it that Black folks get the benefit of prevention from psychiatry.
>
> —CARL C. BELL, MD, PROFESSOR OF PSYCHIATRY AND PUBLIC HEALTH, UNIVERSITY OF ILLINOIS AT CHICAGO, PRESIDENT AND CEO, COMMUNITY MENTAL HEALTH

duration of that semester . . . I was able to stay on because of the drug, but what good did that do me?" In the end, none.

Debra's story made me think about how few entries there are in the American Psychological Association's historical documents for people of African descent, as well as Robert Whitaker's *Mad in America* and its description of early psychiatric diagnoses for African Americans: "During the nineteenth century, the perceived mental health of African Americans was closely tied to their legal status as free men or slaves. Those who lived in free states, or those who were slaves and publicly exhibited a desire to be free, were at particular risk of being seen as insane." At one time in this country, it was an accepted belief that Black people who wanted to be free were, by definition, out of their minds. Why?

John C. Calhoun, South Carolina senator, vice president under both John Quincy Adams and Andrew Jackson, white supremacist, passionate advocate of slavery, and intellectual forefather of the Confederate States of America, had this to say: "The African is incapable of self-care and sinks into lunacy under the burden of freedom. It is a mercy to give him guardianship and protection from mental death." That's right, the lawmakers

---

Americans are confused, and I will tell you why. The answer has to do with how health information is generated and communicated and who controls such activities. Because I have been behind the scenes generating health information for so long, I have seen what really goes on—and I'm ready to tell the world what is wrong with the system. The distinctions between government, industry, science, and medicine have become blurred. The distinctions between making a profit and promoting health have become blurred. The problems with the system do not come in the form of Hollywood-style corruption. The problems are much more subtle and yet much more dangerous. The result is massive amounts of misinformation, for which average American consumers pay twice. They provide the tax money to do the research, and then they provide the money for their health care to treat their largely preventable diseases.

*—THE CHINA STUDY: THE MOST COMPREHENSIVE STUDY OF NUTRITION EVER CONDUCTED
AND THE STARTLING IMPLICATIONS FOR DIET, WEIGHT LOSS AND LONG-TERM HEALTH,
BY T. COLIN CAMPBELL, THOMAS M. CAMPBELL II, JOHN ROBBINS, AND HOWARD LYMAN*

of our newly formed country, besides being slaveholders, actually believed that freedom for our ancestors meant "mental death," while slavery equaled "protection." The so-called crazy desire of our foremothers and forefathers to be free was considered a disease with an actual name: *drapetomania.* (Google the term, you'll be amazed at what you find!)

History doesn't get more relevant than that. It explains so much to us about where our negative attitudes toward psychiatry and psychology come from. First, our desire for freedom was considered a mental illness. Then, the cure for this so-called disease was brutality, insofar as a good whipping could exorcise "the devil" from our bodies. If this was psychology, we'd have to have been crazy *not* to fear it! The sad fact is that for too long "science" served the interests of racism. Our so-called insanity was the product of policies used to either directly oppress us or at least "explain" how we were inferior.

At the point where white health care institutions fail altogether or ignore us, our journey toward healing ends, killing off the possibility of a better self and a better life. Today, most of us are not in jeopardy of disappearing from the record books of our cities or states. But we are dying, and we are at risk of being emotionally and spiritually unavailable to ourselves, as well as absent in meaningful ways from the lives of our families and communities.

Tuskegee Horror

In July 1972 when one of America's most outrageous medical studies finally became public on the front page of the *Washington Evening Star,* Associated Press reporter Jean Heller wrote, "For forty years, the U.S. Public Health Service (PHS) has conducted a study in which human guinea pigs, not given proper treatment, have died of syphilis and its side effects." Further, Heller explained that the experiments were not in pursuit of a cure for the venereal disease. Rather, "the study was conducted to determine from autopsies what the disease does to the human body."

More valuable to science dead than alive, between 1932 and 1972, 399 Black men in the late stages of syphilis were part of an experiment supervised by PHS. At the start of the study, there was no proven treatment for syphilis. But even after penicillin became the standard treatment for the disease in 1947, the medicine was withheld from the men, who were for the most part sharecroppers from one of the poorest counties in Alabama and could barely read. The men were never told what disease they were suffering from. They were informed that they were being treated for "bad blood" (also the title of James H. Jones's must-read book on the subject); the doctors had no intention of curing the men of syphilis at all. Again, the data for the experiment was to be collected for their autopsies, and they were thus left to die from the disease, which caused tumors, heart disease, paralysis, blindness, insanity, and death. "As I see it," one of the doctors involved explained, "we have no further interest in these patients until they die."

This horror exposes beyond a shadow of a doubt the racist attitudes of white government officials who ran the experiment—that data on the dead Black men was worth more to the United States Public Health Service than their humanity. It also shows us that the sharecroppers who were poor, Black, and uneducated made for easy subjects. Trusting the idea of free medical care—almost none of them had ever seen a doctor before—these unsophisticated and trusting men became victims of what James H. Jones calls "the longest nontherapeutic experiment on human beings in medical history."

By the end of the experiment, twenty-eight of the men had died directly of syphilis, one hundred were dead of related complications, forty of their wives had been infected, and nineteen of their children had been born with lifelong syphilis. The PHS, however, remained unapologetic, claiming the men had been "volunteers" who "were always happy to see the doctors." An Alabama state health officer who had been involved claimed "somebody is trying to make a mountain out of a molehill."

In 1973, the NAACP (National Association for the Advancement of Colored People) filed a class-action lawsuit. A $9 million settlement was reached and divided among the study's victims. Free health care was given to the men who were still living and to the infected wives, widows, and children who had been infected as a result of the experiment.

It wasn't until 1997, a quarter century after the experiment was exposed, that the government formally apologized for the immoral, horrific study. President Clinton delivered the apology, saying what the government had done was deeply, profoundly, and morally wrong. He addressed the victims directly: "We can stop turning our heads away. We can look you in the eye and finally say, on behalf of the American people: What the United States government did was shameful." However heartfelt the president's words may have been, they can't make up for what happened.

Don't get me wrong here, it's not that I found the apology to be insincere; I just can't help thinking about the appointments where white doctors ushered Black men to their painful deaths with no mercy. Is it any wonder that most Black people in this country have trouble trusting the medical establishment?

When Fiction Turns to Fact

Remember Dr. Charles Drew, blood plasma pioneer? After he died from injuries sustained in a car accident in North Carolina, rumors began circulating that Drew was left to bleed to death after being denied care at a whites-only hospital. That the lifesaving technique Drew himself had created was not used to save his life because of Jim Crow segregation, or so this story goes.

But that isn't the only myth of this kind whirling around in our psyches. It has been rumored for over sixty years now that genius blues singer Bessie Smith also bled to death after a whites-only hospital refused her admission! What was going on here? Were famous Black people bleeding to death all over the Jim Crow South? Not exactly. But there is something to these stories, even if that something is not what actually happened. Both stories come from Black pain and Black fear, from the powerful belief that the white medical establishment's racism is stronger than their commitment to saving lives—that white doctors let Black people die.

Broken Trust

It shouldn't surprise anyone that a 1990 survey found that 10 percent of African Americans believed that the U.S. government created AIDS as a plot to exterminate Blacks and another 20 percent could not rule out that the possibility might be true. As ridiculous as this may sound, the Tuskegee experiment more than explains how ideas like this can gain legitimacy in our community.

While on the road I spoke about these attitudes with Marie, a consulting care manager for a state agency. Marie never actually sees patients. She only evaluates individuals via their case folders, describing the main duty of her job as "watching hospitals and doctors drain money from the state at the cost of further deteriorating poor Black people's health." See, the cases Marie evaluates are overwhelmingly Title 19, which means that the patients have insufficient funds to effectively care for themselves. But a picked-up tab for Marie's clients doesn't necessarily mean better care.

I wish this wasn't the case, but as I see it in my job right now, physicians are in the business of recklessly prescribing medications to Black people. The drugs usually cause the patients other health problems in addition to whatever was wrong in the first place. You'd think this would be a dilemma for the doctors, since their job is to heal and repair. It's not. As long as they can send heftier bills to the state, they're in the clear. I *don't* mean to give all physicians a bad rap, but how they pay their bills a lot of the time, especially the folks dealing with the Title 19s, is by prescribing chemicals that are poisonous.

I've found that some of the most potentially harmful drugs are antipsychotic drugs prescribed for schizophrenia. There have been so many cases of this with a drug called Zyprexa. I've seen people's white blood cell count go through the roof on that drug. It can give patients respiratory issues. Another possible side effect of this same drug is enormous weight gain. Then, in a matter of months, the patients can become diabetics. When I said something about this once to a supervising physician, maybe two or three years ago now, that all the evidence pointed to the drug making people hypoglycemic, his response, and he was a white man, by the way, was, 'What's the matter? We can prescribe them insulin next.' God, I wanted to quit right then! But I'm a single parent with three kids. The truth is I can't go anywhere. And let's get real: With the whites in the white coats and it being mostly us getting sent to the loony bin, I don't have much of a choice—this is the setup of the public mental health field.

Marie's experiences are not unique, especially for the treatment of illnesses like schizophrenia, where Black and Hispanic patients are more than three times as likely to be diagnosed with the disease as whites—even though studies indicate that the rate of the disorder is the same in all groups. The effect of the drugs on our chemistry is complicated by yet another factor. We are underrepresented in the best available studies of psychiatric drugs for depression, bipolar disorder, schizophrenia, and attention deficit disorder. So we are both under- *and* overprescribed medications, a huge plus for the health care industry's financial bottom line.

Now take a minute to take in this next statistic. Sixty-three percent of poor, meaning living under the federal poverty level, African-American adults have either one or more of the following chronic diseases: hypertension, heart disease, diabetes, or asthma. I'm not saying that our poor health is a direct result of psychiatric medications, I am saying that there is a huge possibility that some of these drugs may aggravate already existing conditions. In all, just 8 percent of the patients studied for psychiatric drug trials were people of color. The only effective way to deal with this is to take strategic action.

> I found out that the things that hurt us the most can become the fuel and the catalyst that propel us toward our destiny. It will either make you bitter or it will make you better.
>
> —BISHOP T. D. JAKES,
> THE POTTER'S HOUSE, DALLAS, TEXAS

Nobody is helped if we just mistrust the whole mental health care profession any more than they would be if we were to mistrust the whole medical establishment; what we have to do is engage them critically. We have to monitor the medical establishment for racism, but we also have to participate in drug trials so we know how new drugs affect us.

A growing number of health care advocates, many of whom are people of color themselves, are warning that doctors are harming patients by ignoring evidence about the effects of ethnic background, sex, religious beliefs, social class, and birthplace on mental health and mental illness. In fact, Carl Bell, a psychiatrist at the University of Illinois at Chicago, has warned, "This thing called psychiatry—it is a European-American invention, and it largely has no respect for nonwhite philosophies of mental health and how people function."

Seconding this opinion is Michael Smith, a psychiatrist at the University of California, Los Angeles's research center for the psychobiology of ethnicity, who talks about the lack of information about drug metabolism and side effects among various groups and said, "The drug companies are thinking about the average Caucasian male patient." That some minorities distrust drug trials worsens the problem, he and other researchers said. Understandably so, in my opinion. But the health care establishment's disrespect of Black people reaches far beyond us as patients. It also applies to African-American medical professionals.

Take the case of brilliant Dr. Vivien Theodore Thomas, a Black surgeon who developed the procedures used to treat blue baby syndrome, a congenital heart disease in children, in the 1940s. Check out the great HBO movie about his life, *Something the Lord Made,* starring Mos Def.

After the Great Depression depleted the savings Thomas had collected working as a carpenter at Fisk University in the summer of 1929, his hopes of going to college and studying to become a doctor were dashed. Soon thereafter at the age of nineteen, Thomas was hired by Dr. Alfred Blalock at Vanderbilt University to work in his research laboratory as a janitor. In little more than ten years, Thomas went from sweeping the floors to creating and designing some of the surgical tools that Blalock used. And when Blalock was made chief of surgery at Johns Hopkins Hospital in 1941, he had Thomas join him.

Two years later, another doctor suggested to Blalock an idea for how to treat blue baby syndrome, involving an extremely delicate surgical procedure and requiring many new medical instruments to be created.

Thomas was set on the complicated task of first creating a blue baby–like condition in a dog and then remedying the condition. Two years and two hundred dogs later, Thomas developed the lifesaving procedure. On November 29, 1944, the procedure was tried for the first time on a human patient, a little girl whose heart was exhausted even by the effort of walking. Then check this out: Blalock had Thomas stand *behind* him in the surgery, like on a segregated bus, while walking him through the procedure, since Thomas had, after all, done the surgery on dogs many more times than Blalock himself had! The operation kept the girl alive for another two months, but she then died. The next operation, on an eleven-year-old girl, was a success (I wonder if the second time around Blalock took better direction from Thomas). In an article on the technique in the *Journal of the American Medical Association,* Blalock got full credit for the procedure. Thomas didn't get so much as a footnote.

Thomas eventually began to train others in the procedure, but he was still so poorly paid that he had to take part-time work to pay the bills. He occasionally worked as a bartender, sometimes finding himself making drinks for men who were his students in the operating theater. Talk about humiliation. Eventually Blalock got Thomas's pay boosted to the point where he was the best-paid technician at the university—although he was paid a tenth of what Blalock made!

In his late thirties, Thomas contemplated pursuing his dream of becoming a doctor but soon realized that no school would give him credit for what he had already done, and if he went through the entire education process, he would be fifty years old before he entered regular practice. He gave up the idea. Finally in 1976 Johns Hopkins University presented Thomas with an honorary doctorate, but due to certain restrictions, it was an honorary doctor of *laws* he received, not a medical doctorate!

Now, heaven knows that medical school is not an easy road to hoe! But for the health of our community, it is definitely worth turning over. Though not exactly discouraged to the extent Thomas was, Kaley, a sister in her late twenties, also found obstacles to her dreams.

For as long as Kaley can remember, she always wanted to be a doctor. Though not a gifted science student, she studied hard as an undergraduate and pulled off a biology major. She thought medical school would be the same, that with a strong work ethic she could make it. After getting a below-average score on her medical school test, she was told by a career counselor at her liberal arts college that it wouldn't be good enough to get into medical school.

"The woman pretty much told me that if I wanted to be a doctor then maybe I should think about getting a doctorate in public health. She said that *maybe* I could get into medical school because I was Black and a woman, but by the end of our conversation that wasn't anything I felt comfortable with or proud of."

Currently, Kaley is getting that doctorate in public health, but still feels angry at the white counselor's comment. She even admits that from time to time she whispers to herself, hauntedlike, while doing regular things like washing dishes or walking to the bus stop, "You could have been an MD by now . . . You could have been an MD by now . . ." Kaley's reflex to repeat to herself what a white person felt she couldn't accomplish, instead of reminding herself of everything that she has achieved, reflects the depth of her pain and disappointment in herself. She was made to feel like she didn't deserve an opportunity well within her grasp, and now she throws it up in her own face. She feels now that she should have just applied to med school and gone from there. Instead, she listened to the white woman and robbed herself of the possibility.

"I'm somewhere between laughing and crying," Kaley said, "when I think of how I was made to believe that affirmative action was a bad thing. If that woman had told me I wasn't smart enough, or that my grades weren't good enough, that would have been one thing. I might even have been motivated to prove her wrong. But I just felt so defeated."

It's just so sad. Many of our students are being steered away from medicine, while most aren't even considering it an option.

"Do I Look Crazy to You?"
Seeing a Therapist While Black

I read about a survey, sponsored by the National Alliance on Mental Illness (NAMI) and funded by Wyeth Pharmaceuticals, that said new findings show that people of color were just as likely as whites to self-report their depression. The good news of the study is that we're more aware of depression as an illness than we used to be (even though we have a *long* way to go). The bad news is we're not doing nearly enough with that awareness, and to throw fat on the fire, it's not easy to get good care even if we try. In a 2005 health survey researchers found that 17 percent of African Americans with health problems did not visit a doctor in the last year. In addition, 61 percent of African-American adults with no health insurance reported having medical bills or debt problems, while over a third of us (36 percent) visited an emergency room for a condition that could have been easily treated by a primary care physician.

Why is that? Because going to the doctor is not an easy thing for Black folks. Joyce, an elementary schoolteacher from California in her early thirties, knows where I'm coming from.

After my father died, I started seeing a therapist. I knew I needed to talk about it with someone who could give me some pointers on coping with loss. So I called up the first doctor listed on my insurance plan. I went to him and, of all the things I expected, I didn't expect to be freaked out; I was. Our first few sessions, he kept fumbling around on his desk with papers and whatnot. After that he just scribbled stuff on a pad. I was never under the impression, either, that anything he wrote was about me. I know this sounds crazy but I thought he thought it was okay to ignore me because I'm Black.

Joyce's example is classic. She felt entitled to search out help at a hard time, but not entitled enough to be choosy about it. When she felt uncomfortable in the first session, she didn't have to go back—she could have called the next doctor her insurance plan offered and made an appointment for a consultation. Instead, she stuck it out with someone who she immediately felt uncomfortable with. Why? Because her core belief that she was inferior and the white doctor superior went deeper than her desire to get help.

Now, we have no way of knowing what was going on in that therapist's head. What we do know is that, by continuing to see him, Joyce couldn't get the help she so desperately needed. And that inability to demand what she needed from a medical professional has everything to do with race. As a Black person, she didn't feel important enough to demand the attention from a white doctor—even though she was paying him! And there's more to it than that.

"One afternoon after school I worked out really hard, something I wouldn't have done if I'd remembered I had a therapy appointment. By the time I got home my hair was a damp, frizzy mess. I could have washed it and just worn it curly, but I didn't want the doctor to see me without my hair blown straight—not that he ever looked at me anyway. So since I didn't have time to blow dry *and* make it to the office, I canceled the appointment. It was same-day notice, so I had to pay for the session, but it was worth it to me."

Even though Joyce knew the therapist hardly looked at her, her need to look put together in front of him kept her from going to a session she'd paid for. For a Black woman, I don't think we can underestimate the particular importance of hair to our image. Running smack up against what felt like racism, Joyce's instinct to hide her natural hair from him was the same instinct that led her to mask her real self from him. I'm not saying that the therapist isn't to blame here—he seems unprofessional and maybe a little bit racist—but over the ten weeks that Joyce met with this man, she didn't get any closer to dealing with the pain of her father's death, and that *is* her fault because we're the only ones who can guarantee the quality of our own health care.

Another dangerous dynamic for Black people in therapy is what I call the "Do I look crazy to you?" syndrome. The most pronounced example of this I've come across has been in the experiences of a geriatric social worker married to a successful doctor named Linda.

From the outside it looks like Linda has it all. A huge home in a ritzy New Jersey suburb, a kind and supportive husband, and two beautiful, smart kids. But after her first child, things didn't feel as glowing to Linda as they looked to other people. She suffered for months from postpartum depression, something she didn't share with anyone besides her husband. And she didn't even tell him outright. He had to put the pieces together himself.

"I remember once I was at home alone in the kitchen writing checks, and the baby was sitting in her swing. The washer machine was going, and in the swish of the water I kept hearing, 'Kill the baby! Kill the baby!' The same thing with the hum of the refrigerator. I felt like I was going completely out of my mind. Yeah, I'm a social worker . . . so of course I've been trained in counseling, but that didn't make it easier to admit that I was hearing voices."

As the overachieving little sister of a drug addict who often displays erratic behavior, the most important thing in the world to Linda was to not look or seem crazy, to not look or act in any way like her sister, who'd had a breakdown with the birth of her first child.

"My husband told me to stop comparing myself to my sister, but I couldn't do it. Finally my husband got me a referral and pushed me into therapy. I thank him for that now, but the therapist I started seeing was a white woman who was a professional acquaintance of a colleague of mine. I understood that it would have been completely unethical for her to share any information from our sessions, but for about a month I was 100 percent positive that she was doing exactly that. I spent that whole month posturing, trying not to seem crazy. It's not that she *was* unethical, or even acted like she might be, but I believed the chances of her being unethical were higher because she was white."

> Man is born broken. He lives by mending. The grace of God is glue.
>
> —EUGENE O'NEILL, PLAYWRIGHT

Linda's not alone. For many of us, the idea of appearing crazy, especially to a white person, is enough to drive us mad. Our deep and insistent need to keep it together, even at the cost of our mental health, is a price worth paying for too many of us. Especially for someone like Linda, who had achieved all the trappings of an upwardly mobile life. She felt that she didn't have the right to be depressed, despite everything she knew about postpartum depression. Unlike her sister, she had escaped the pitfalls of the working-class neighborhood where she grew up. Her depression caused

QUICK FACTS

FACTORS THAT CONTRIBUTE TO POSITIVE MENTAL HEALTH:

- having social support
- being able to work and love
- feeling of well-being
- resilience
- connection with physical/spiritual self
- gratitude
- helping others
- reducing stress and depression

SELF-MANAGING YOUR MOODS:

- Check your stress levels and eliminate sources of chronic stress.
- Exercise on a regular basis.
- Eat healthy foods.
- Establish your support system.
- Remember, "No" is a complete sentence!
- Practice relaxation techniques.
- Be thankful.

—JANET TAYLOR, MD, HARLEM HOSPITAL

her to question whether she really had escaped. "So many of the people I knew growing up," Linda said, "got their minds turned out by drugs. I wasn't on drugs, but I felt strange after I had the baby."

When I asked Linda whether or not there were many other Black folks in her professional network of social workers, she said no. And the race of the colleague who had a relationship with her therapist was South Asian. As a trained social worker myself, I know just how white the field is, but when I asked Linda why she thought so few of us go into the mental health professions, she gave me an answer that rang absolutely true.

"The few of us interested in giving back to our communities," Linda said, "think that the problems are in the institutions, not within us. To a certain extent, I think they're right—the problems *are* in racist policies. But those racist policies infect us. If we work for city hall we can try to prevent problems in the future, but it doesn't really do anything about the problems people have in the here and now."

Linda is dead-on about the denial in our community. Too few of us go into the mental health field; what's worse is that, according to Linda, the few who do often go as researchers and the like into policy agencies (as Kaley plans to do), where they

> Not everything that is faced can be changed. But nothing can be changed until it is faced.
>
> —JAMES BALDWIN, AUTHOR

work on the big picture. That's important work and they deserve props for it, but where are the brothers and sisters addressing the tangible issues on the ground in our communities? They're there, but not in the numbers we need! Those of us who go into the field are, as my social worker friend Stephanie Dyre says, "on special assignment." We're called to do this hard work, and it's deeply meaningful to us, but it can also be spiritually draining and many of us are burned out and emotionally exhausted.

I think too many of us in these fields concentrate on issues like poverty and drug abuse, without connecting those dots to mental illness and depression. The story of Jessica, a childhood neighbor of Linda's, is a horrific example of how an untreated life can fall through the cracks.

Jessica's the youngest of five siblings. She was a beautiful teenager with large hazel eyes, sporting a Halle Berry nineties haircut, when she took a bus trip with a few friends one weekend to Washington, DC. Jessica doesn't remember anymore what they were headed down there to do. What she does know for certain is that she experimented with PCP for the first time; while she was tripping on the drug, she was gang-raped.

> Poetry can clear away the clutter, providing a tranquil space where thinking is possible.

The crime went unreported, and at the end of the weekend Jessica returned home. Only, when she did, her mind was lost. From that day on, without ever getting medical attention or any kind of counseling, Jessica continued to experiment with drugs and began having delusions, which made her more and more dangerous. After she attempted to stab her ten-year-old nephew in the leg, her parents threw her out of the house.

For the past fifteen years Jessica has been ping-ponging back and forth between jail and the streets. In that time she has given birth to two drug-addicted daughters. Currently, Jessica's serving a one-year prison sentence for assaulting her elderly father, who suffers from dementia.

Too many of us know a version of Jessica, someone who was the victim of sexual violence and never received proper treatment. Someone whose response to that violence was self-medicating, an illegal drug addiction being the result. Everyone on the street where Jessica grew up, including Linda, knows the details of her story. Her own mother, a registered nurse, admits that she should have tried to get Jessica help years ago but was unable to acknowledge just how bad her daughter's problems were for fear of admitting her own failure as a mother. Her reaction is all too common. When she thinks of one of her grandchildren in foster care, she shudders with regret, her gray-rimmed eyes welling up with tears. "I haven't only failed my child; I've sold *her* children down the river, too. Where that river leads, I don't know. The truth is, [it's] probably somewhere like where their mother ended up."

> The mere formulation of a problem is far more essential than its solution. . . . To raise new questions, new possibilities, to regard old problems from a new angle requires creative imagination and marks real advances.
>
> —ALBERT EINSTEIN, NOBEL PRIZE–WINNING THEORETICAL PHYSICIST AND AUTHOR

I don't buy that. Although I appreciate her honesty, I can't agree with Jessica's mother's conclusion about her grandchildren's fate, because I believe that, with the hard work treatment demands, hope and healing can be fought for and won. The thing that bothers me most about her comment, though, is her sense that a miserable fate for her grandchildren is inevitable.

For Jessica's mother, and for everyone who feels as she does, treatment is not an option they can see, even for children who are in desperate need of therapeutic tools that may literally save their lives. The only choices they can see are lives that are low functioning at best, and criminal and violent at worst. Why? Because they don't know or believe that therapy is an option! If you walk away from this chapter with only one thing, I hope it's a sense of the *necessity* of talking openly with our children about mental health issues, especially if there is mental illness in the family.

I've seen people's lives unfold like Jessica's and her children's more times than I care to count. Grief made more difficult by guilt creates a paralysis in Black life that foster care and the criminal justice system only

CHECK THIS OUT

If you are a person in a toxic environment, Dr. Carl Bell believes that education is not enough to overcome pain and trauma. Healing from pain and preventing pain means putting into effect the seven principles of resiliency:

1. Rebuilding the village: Activities that ensure there will be "villages" will ensure there will be social norms, rules—spoken and unspoken—and values that will guide and direct behavior.
2. Providing access to health care: If you are addicted to drugs you need the most modern method of getting treatment for drug abuse.
3. Improving bonding, attachment, and connectedness dynamics: Doing things that ensures people will be connected to one another; for example, one strategy we used in Chicago public schools was that we had neighborhood churches adopt local schools so the church members could provide mentorship for the local school students, thereby allowing the students to be "connected" to a responsible adult role model in addition to their parents.
4. Helping folks develop self-esteem: Helping folks develop a sense of power, a sense of models, a sense of uniqueness, and a sense of connectedness (overlap with connectedness above). For example, people who have a sense of the political process and understand how to get services for their community from politicians are in a better position. People who have a sense of power feel they are capable of dealing with bad and messy situations and so they are less vulnerable to stress because they believe they can handle it.
5. Helping folks develop social skills: Helping people improve their communication skills, their leadership skills, their parenting skills, their job skills, etc.
6. Reestablishing the adult protective shield: Like the metal detector when you get on a plane, it is your parent monitoring who your friends are so you will be less likely to get in risky situations like early sexual experiences, drug use, or gang involvement.
7. Minimize the effects of trauma: A lot of times people engage in unhealthy behaviors because they were traumatized (or really "stressed out"). So, when these folks find themselves under stress again, the ones who are obese eat, the ones who use drugs use more drugs, the ones who panic and get upset panic and get upset, and make their

situation worse. These people do not know how to soothe their trauma, they don't have faith in themselves and do not believe they can cope. Many of them have been traumatized before and were overwhelmed and fell apart, so when they find themselves under stress again they fall apart again. However, if they are taught to have a sense of power, if they are taught that they can take a negative situation and turn it into a positive situation (like using the negative energy of being raped and turning it into the positive healing energy of building a rape prevention program), then they have learned to minimize their trauma.

make worse. Like Jessica, so many of us in prison are there for crimes committed out of mental illness. It is one of my deepest beliefs, especially when I call on that part of myself that is and will always be a social worker, that prisons—filled way out of proportion with our brothers and sisters—are the biggest and worst example of the effects of misdiagnosis on our community. Misdiagnosis and its partner in crime, the lack of treatment (or altogether wrong treatment), are much more than an inconvenience to us; they are a quiet and subtle form of genocide.

To fight our own self-defeating agendas, as well as the harmful, racist ideas at work in society at large, we have to make insurance coverage a priority in our lives. I know it doesn't sound very sexy or exciting, but being underinsured or uninsured is the biggest obstacle between most of us and care. If you don't have coverage, you have to research city and state programs that offer care. If you do have coverage, find out how to get the most out of those benefits!

Covered or not, you have to be informed about the kind of care you're getting. As we've discussed in this chapter, not all care is good care—but not all care is bad, either. Terrible things have happened to us, but that's not a reason to assume that all health care

> It is not the strongest of the species that survive, nor the most intelligent, but the one most responsive to change.
>
> —CHARLES DARWIN, NATURALIST

professionals are out to get us or would happily see us suffer. Once you've educated yourself about mental health so you're not just a patient but an active participant, you'll have less to be distrustful about.

And who knows? Maybe you'll find out so much about the field that you'll be interested in pursuing a career in it. And then the number of Black health care professionals in this country will increase right along with our rates of health and productivity! Then, if a medical situation makes a friend nervous, or you anxious for that matter, you can either go as an advocate, or take an informed friend along. Let me share a quick example.

If you're out shopping with a friend, and you're not sure how a dress fits, you wouldn't hesitate to ask her opinion. Our relationship to our health care isn't any different. Just as you wouldn't feel obligated to buy the first dress you try on in the first store you visit, you should also feel entitled to shop around for health care whenever possible. Until, that is, you feel like you've found the perfect fit.

> I believe that doctors, like artists, need to draw upon the pain they see in the lives of others and in their own experiences. They need to observe, understand, and then transform the experience of suffering into a more general understanding that can, in turn, help patients and their families deal with what has been dealt them.
>
> —KAY JAMISON, AUTHOR OF
> *AN UNQUIET MIND*

Let's extend the shopping image a little further. If a salesperson follows you around a store, certain you're going to steal something because you're Black, is this a store you'll buy anything from? No. Is this a store you'll return to? No. Well, health care is no different. If you encounter a caregiver who seems racist or insensitive to your needs and issues, you shouldn't be afraid to call him or her on it. After all, you wouldn't be afraid to confront that sales associate who followed you around in the store. Keeping that in mind, you shouldn't be afraid to confront a physician or a therapist, either. Your health, unlike anything you'll find in a store, doesn't have a price tag on it. It's priceless!

Last and most important, we have to encourage those we care about to seek treatment. It's no exaggeration to say it could be the difference between life and death, happiness and hell.

Six Reasons I See a Therapist

- because I'm strong enough to ask for help
- to keep me real and honest with myself about how I'm doing
- to keep me from acting out my feelings
- to unburden myself freely
- so worries don't bring me down
- to talk to a caring yet objective person about things I can't talk to anyone else about

Chapter Nine

I WILL SURVIVE

Getting the Healing Done—
Therapy, Medication, Alternative Medicine, Exercise, and Spirituality

Admitting that my depression was out of control and that I would need medication to bring it under control so I could start to work on it with therapy was one of the hardest things I've ever done. I just never thought of myself as someone who would need medication to stabilize my moods. Now I realize that medication isn't a criticism of me or an inability to "handle it." It's just one of many resources I draw on to battle the illness called depression. I also use therapy, exercise, church, friends, family, and "helping while hurting."

I'm realizing more and more that wanting to be alone, to avoid my life when I feel overwhelmed, only makes my symptoms snowball. I'm learning to talk about how I feel, to reach out more, to set limits, to know what triggers my depression, and to put my own needs first. I've stopped giving myself a hard time for being depressed. I give talks all over the country about my condition, and that constant connection to other people keeps me grounded and connected, reassuring me that I'm not alone. I now know that it's critical to get support when you're depressed—that as much as we may want to show how tough we are, we must learn to accept help. One of the things I've learned is that it makes me who I am: compassionate because I know pain.

As we've seen in previous chapters, depression is a complicated diagnosis. The factors of race, gender, class, stress, and physical health make it even more complicated. However, depression has an 80 percent cure rate.

THE MEDICINE CABINET

African Americans don't like to admit having depression and anxiety because we consider these feelings a weakness of character. So we are less likely to report symptoms of sadness, fear, or worry when we go to the doctor; however, we will talk about bodily complaints.

Often patients come to me complaining of blurred vision, ringing in the ears, hot and cold flashes, chronic dermatitis, grinding their teeth, pains, aches, stiffness, headache, and muscle tension. Or they may notice rapid heartbeat and chest pain, shortness of breath, choking sensations, abdominal pain, nausea, looseness of bowels, constipation, feelings of fullness and heartburn, frequent urination, loss of sex drive, impotence, or menstrual irregularities.

Each of these symptoms may result in their seeing a specialist. Over the course of a year a number of primary care visits and specialty visits could result in an impressive and expensive array of medications in the patient's medicine cabinet. Muscle relaxants, pain medications, antacids, anti-inflammatory agents, over-the-counter sleep medications, herbal remedies, etc, etc. Just taking all those medicines would make me anxious! Imagine this occurring in a fifty-two-year-old lawyer with job stress and relationship trouble? The medicine cabinet becomes the secret indicator of pain, and trips to the doctor take the place of an appointment with a sympathetic therapist who might help relieve the stress that's causing all of these symptoms in the first place!

—DR. HENRY MCCURTIS, PRACTITIONER OF
ADDICTION PSYCHIATRY AND PSYCHIATRY IN NEW YORK CITY

That's very high! Therefore, there is no need for you to suffer alone or in silence. Help is out there. You just need to understand what your options are. The rest of this chapter is going to walk you through some of the most common treatments, including stories of folks just like you who have been helped.

Breaking the Silence:
Opening Pandora's Box

In chapter two, Yvette Hyater-Adams asked herself if having "my body, mind, and desires . . . ripped from me in order to acquiesce to the power of men" was "what it means to be a woman."

My answer to Yvette's question is "No." Being oppressed and powerless is *not* what being a woman is about. But it's very easy to feel that way when our less-than-ideal situations collide with our all-too-vulnerable selves. When Yvette's memories of a lifetime of traumatic violations came flooding back to her during a retreat, she was stunned by their power. She hadn't known what she was feeling, or that she hadn't yet processed these painful events in her life. Under so many unbearable memories, Yvette's emotional levees broke and threatened to wash away her sanity.

"I had held in all of this pain, all of this experience and told no one . . . And now, here I was in corporate America, curled up like a kitten on the floor. I was so overwhelmed by the experience, one of the facilitators had to come in and check on me later. I got myself upright, and just sat still for over an hour with no words. My two wise Black women colleagues put in the palm of my hand the name and phone number of an African-American woman therapist."

For Yvette, acknowledging that her issues had everything to do with her gender and race was a first step. Caring acquaintances, sisters like you and me, were able to recognize her pain and gave Yvette information that set her on the road to recovery via treatment.

However, when Yvette returned home to "one- and two-year-old babies and a husband who was having

> We are each other's harvest; we are each other's business; we are each other's magnitude and bond.
>
> —GWENDOLYN BROOKS, POET

difficulty transitioning from military to civilian life," she didn't want to do anything but sleep, stay in bed, and be "in my quiet and still." For Yvette to face her depression head-on, she had to sit still with it for a period so she could begin to understand the conditions of her life. That was when Yvette started to write.

"I wrote about the ache and pain of my new awareness . . .Writing helped me say what I was afraid to say. It made me face what I didn't want to see . . . Through writing, I opened Pandora's box where the fantasy jewels showed their real value. I knew that I wanted to claim my life on my terms." Pen in hand, Yvette discovered the transforming and healing power of sitting down to write.

Take it from me, I understand better than most the hard, often soul-changing work that writing can be—the bridge to thoughts and feelings you didn't even know you had, that words and solitude, together, can build. But writing is one of the ways we have been blessed by God with the power to create, the power to share our stories and transform our pain. For many of us, writing is hope.

Yvette now runs workshops for African-American women called Breaking Silences, Changing Lives where "creative writing, photography and textile art are used as a way for Black women to fully express themselves." Yvette's "self-help" not only constitutes personal expression but is a way she reaches out to others to help them heal. In a different context, Tanya Odums has done a similar thing. She started a social work agency called HYPE (Helping Young People Excel) in Brooklyn. Here she works with teens, often stepping in to provide caring support and guidance to kids who might otherwise be lost. Often she refers to herself as a coach because so many of her kids are scared of the word "therapist." Her amazing work points to the fact that it doesn't matter what you call it if you're offering the right kind of help.

Born and raised in a single-parent household in the Boulevard housing projects in Brooklyn's East New York neighborhood, Tanya was seventeen when her mother died of cancer. Desperate to avoid becoming another teen statistic, Tanya decided to attend college. This was no easy decision: "I was grieving the loss of my mom," Tanya said, "dodging drug dealers, bullets, peer pressure, and sexual predators." In search of love, stability, and support, Tanya entered several abusive relationships, eventually marrying a violent boyfriend when she was nineteen. Years later, after having earned her bachelor's degree from the City University of New York, she was confronted by another major decision as she registered for a graduate social work program at Hunter College. Her husband had been arrested and charged with a felony. Tanya's dilemma: "Do I take out a loan to pay for my husband's lawyer or my master's degree?" In June 1997 when Tanya graduated from her master's program, her husband was sentenced to twelve to thirty-six years in prison.

As a result of her painful experiences, Tanya has dedicated her career to transforming the lives of at-risk youth and their families. "I understand these angry teens, struggling single mothers, and the sense of hopelessness among families because I have been there."

I believe there are people in prison and in mental hospitals in part because they cannot give and receive touch. I try to touch the people I love, because a hug can change someone's whole day! Touch your children, make love (don't fuck) your partner, and if you're single and feeling isolated, get a massage! I know many of you think a massage is a luxury, but you could start a massage circle with your friends. The human touch is essential—like breathing!

Though she is a licensed mental health professional, Tanya does not refer to herself as a "therapist." Rather, she considers herself "a success coach," adding, "When people in my community hear the term 'therapy' they immediately think, 'I'm not crazy and I don't need help!' There is a stigma attached to the idea of seeking professional help to cope with life's problems. What is unique about HYPE is that it provides services to people who would not normally seek services from agencies because they have been victimized by existing organizations."

Our community has a long history of being treated badly by social workers and social services. That is why an organization like Tanya's is so important. Besides providing access to treatment and assistance with basic life skills, they are also a culturally sensitive ear for many of the challenges we face in both inner-city and rural communities.

Who Is a Therapist?
Psychologists, Psychiatrists, and MSWs

Let's begin by identifying some of the professions we've been talking about so far. As I'm sure you know, not all therapists receive the same training, and there are huge differences in education and orientation between a psychiatrist, a psychologist, and a social worker. I think a good place to start is with the term "psychologist."

Most commonly, a psychologist is a person with a doctorate in psychology who uses that training to work as a therapist, counselor, or coach. In this country, you can't call yourself a psychologist unless you have a doctorate in the field and you've passed the licensing requirements of whatever state you're practicing in. Social

> If I speak with the tongues of men and of angels, and have not love, I am like blaring brass or a clanging cymbal.

workers, on the other hand, require only a master's degree in clinical social work to practice. Remember Tanya Odums, CEO and founder of HYPE? Well, she's a social worker with an MSW (Master of Social Work), which is a type of master's degree you obtain after two years of graduate study beyond your degree, in combination with field experience. Most people with MSWs pursue a clinical track, focusing on direct practice with clients. But unlike psychiatrists and psychologists, social workers are also trained in community organizing, policy analysis, and human services management, which means that they may have a better handle on the issues that shape and influence mental health in our community. Psychologists have more formal education than social workers, but both can provide a great deal of help.

A psychiatrist is a medical doctor who specializes in mental illness. Just like pediatricians or allergists, they go to medical school for four years after college and then spend four years in psychiatric residency, which means they are practicing psychiatrists but still under supervision. In many places, if you go to a city or county hospital to work with a psychiatrist, you may be paired with someone in his or her third or fourth year of residency. (And if you are, don't panic—they're often very good!) Because they are medical doctors, they are qualified to prescribe medication, something that psychologists and social workers cannot do. Psychologists and social workers will refer you to a psychiatrist if they think you need meds, because only a psychiatrist can evaluate you medically and write a prescription. Through therapy, psychologists, psychiatrists, and social workers help people attain insight into themselves and their relationships with others so they can function better in their daily lives.

How Therapists Can Help

Let me tell you about a young woman named Valerie, a sweet high school science teacher in a Chicago suburb. Everyone she knows asks her for advice, often taking it to heart as if it were the Gospel. She's been in a healthy relationship for nearly three years. Attractive, fit, and cheerful, Valerie appears to be right with herself. But she wasn't always. "I didn't understand why people were always bringing their problems to me. Now I do. I didn't let on that I had any of my own. I might have two or three phone conversations in a week with friends. I'd spend most of these talks listening to people, trying to help them sort out their feelings. Meanwhile everything *I* was feeling was not even on the back burner. It wasn't on the stove at all." Valerie's experience is way too typical in the lives of Black women. Where do you go when you are the strong one? Often we're there for everyone but ourselves, playing the role of therapist when the truth is we're the ones in desperate need of counseling. After working in publishing for a year right out of college, Valerie abruptly quit that job with little more than fifty dollars in her checking account. She found another job quickly, so her friends and family weren't worried, but they should have been. Valerie was a chronic weed smoker, and she was at a crossroads. "There was nothing in my life then that gave me any joy. I went to work. I came home. I smoked because I couldn't bring myself to eat without being high. Then when I did eat, it was always cereal in bed. After that I would watch about two hours of *Sanford and Son* and *The Golden Girls*. Then I would read, mostly biographies of writers. All I can say now is that I wanted desperately to be living someone else's life."

The one positive thing that happened to Valerie during all this was that a family friend encouraged her to apply to graduate writing programs. She took the advice and began attending one the following fall—at the same time she was undergoing a painful breakup with a man she had fallen deeply in love with. He had absolutely no idea about her depression. "I started school and since I was writing regularly I was more in touch with my feelings than I had been—at least, I knew that I was having feelings. But I was going through this agonizing breakup with a guy I'd been friends with since college. My dependence on weed increased and there were some days I would just sit on the windowsill, smoke, and watch the cars go by. That's when I finally went to professional counseling at my school. The thing that pushed me over the edge was realizing that I was 'in love' with someone who didn't have a genuine clue as to what I was really like. I was tired of knowing people without them knowing me." Valerie was diagnosed as clinically depressed. She was lucky that her school had a number of psychiatry residents working as in-school psychotherapists. Valerie was assigned to one and found that over time she became more comfortable discussing her pent-up anxieties. For the first time, she wasn't in the role of therapist anymore; a professional was. For some people like Valerie, it's psychiatric therapy that works. For others it's writing, and for still others it's the help they find in a community organization like Tanya Odums's HYPE or my Stay Strong Foundation.

Treating What Ails You

Now, as you know, treatment for depression and mental illness often includes medication as well as a number of different types of therapy. It's very important that you understand that medication alone is unlikely to stop your depression. People who are successful at handling the illness take medication *while* attending regular therapy sessions. *The Washington Post* recently reported on the largest antidepressant study to date, where it was seen that antidepressants only alleviated symptoms in half the subjects. In addition, the subjects of the study were the recipients of the best care available, a situation that is not usually the case, especially not for Black people.

But some people are so depressed they need to be hospitalized. Being hospitalized for depression is a serious step and one that is usually taken when someone is considered a potential threat to themselves or others. For many Black folks, being hospitalized is their greatest fear. On one hand, many of us think it means we're now officially "crazy." On the other hand, we fear being victimized by racist institutions. For Renee, a woman whose mother underwent psychiatric care in the 1950s, the idea that she would somehow be submitted, like her mother, to electroshock therapy was a fear that kept her from getting the help she desperately needed.

Renee's father was an abusive alcoholic and his brutality drove her already fragile mother to the breaking point. By the time Renee was ten, her father had died of liver failure and her mother had been in and out of a state psychiatric institution for two years. Shuffled between the homes of relatives, Renee was molested a number of times by an uncle. As an adult she thought she was going out of her mind when she admitted she had been abused to a cousin. "I couldn't hardly believe it myself when I said it. But the worst was when I said that my only regret after having endured the abuse was that my aunt's husband didn't go all the way and have sex with me. The way my cousin looked at me when I said it was the same way that people looked at my mother when I was kid. It frightened me." Motivated by fear and prompted by her cousin's concern, Renee sought therapy, but because she had an irrational fear of being institutionalized, she couldn't express her true feelings during sessions. "I never saw my mother receive an electroshock treatment, but after I started seeing a shrink I had nightmares about it, only the electrodes were placed on *my* scalp from temple to temple, not my mother's. I was the one getting shocked."

The Reality of Your Existence

- Nothing can provide enduring, unshakable meaning, satisfaction, or security.
- Nothing is as we expect, hope, or believe it to be.
- Everything is constantly changing—there is no way to carve anything solid out of the flow of reality.

The Healing

- We develop gratitude for the beauty of life just as it is.
- We distinguish between our true feelings and the stories we tell ourselves about these feelings.
- We let go of the "inner judge" that tells us we are flawed, no good, never able to get it together, and that the world is cold and hard.
- We allow ourselves to feel our negative feelings—fear, anger, and uncertainty.
- We view depression as an opportunity to learn about ourselves.

–DR. DENESE SHERVINGTON, PROFESSOR OF CLINICAL PSYCHIATRY, COLUMBIA UNIVERSITY MEDICAL CENTER

Used commonly until the mid-twentieth century for treating severe cases of clinical depression and the manic side of bipolar disorder, electroshock treatment caused patients to have seizures by passing electricity through the brain. It is used much more selectively these days, and when it's used properly it can be effective for the right people.

"I don't know this for sure and my mother surely doesn't remember now, but once—I think not too long after she was shocked—me and my aunt showed up at the hospital to see her. She didn't know who we were. When she didn't recognize me, it was like I didn't exist. I was afraid that going to therapy and being honest would put me right back in that place." After months of sessions, Renee finally came clean with her therapist and revealed her mother's history of mental illness, as well as her own complicated feelings around her experiences of sexual abuse. "It's not a fear many people articulate to themselves or anyone else, because they don't have any reason to. But in therapy, I know for sure that I got over one major hurdle—the fear that if I admitted anything was wrong, I was going to be hospitalized, just like my mother." Nowadays, before psychiatric treatment in any hospital begins, a patient undergoes a complete physical examination to determine the overall state of his or her health. Once treatment begins, patients usually get individual therapy with a primary therapist, group therapy with peers, and sometimes family therapy with significant people in their lives. At the same time, patients are often (but not always) put on one or more psychiatric medications. As I've said earlier, the people who

---

Having been diagnosed with manic depression, it has been a marvelous discovery to know that it's not the end of the world. I've worked through the challenges of what this diagnosis means in my life, and it's led me to a closer relationship with God. What keeps me strong is thanking God every day that I awaken to see another day with all of its glorious possibilities: a wonderful family, supportive friends, a great therapist, medications, exercise, a walk taking in the sunny weather, listening to good music, involvement in civic and social activities, and the spirit of laughter. I no longer hide in my shell like a turtle. Life is truly worth living!

—GAIL HOLLIDAY, BOSTON, MASSACHUSETTS

are most successful in overcoming their depression undergo talk therapy while on medication. Statistics show again and again that medication alone is not enough to guard against a relapse! Speaking of talk therapy, psychiatric outpatients periodically visit their psychiatrist for appointments in an office, like both Renee and Valerie ended up doing. These consultations last anywhere from thirty to sixty minutes and involve the psychiatrist interviewing the patient to monitor their condition and the effectiveness of any medication.

Types of Therapy:
Psychoanalysis, Cognitive Behavioral Therapy, and EMDR

First, let me start out by saying that any therapist or counselor worth their salt doesn't use just one technique. Instead, they use a combination of techniques depending on the unique needs of the individual patient. Psychoanalysis, cognitive behavioral therapy, and EMDR (eye movement desensitization and reprocessing), to name a few, are kinds of psychodynamic therapies. "Psychodynamic" means that the goal of therapists using these types of treatments is to help their patients develop insight into the reasons behind their behavior by focusing on the patient's past experiences, including, of course, family dynamics. The assumption is that understanding your life will inspire personal change.

If I'm going to give you the most complete background of psychotherapy that I can, it's difficult to leave out Sigmund Freud, the father of analysis. I don't mean to bore you with images of old white guys sitting in big leather chairs and puffing on their pipes, but Freud's contribution is important and in a book like this it cannot be overlooked.

In Vienna in the 1880s, Freud, who was trained as a neurologist, began noticing neurological problems in patients that weren't biological in nature. Seeing blindness, paralysis, and anorexia with no apparent physical cause (disease, deformity, etc.), he began to look toward the mind for answers. Using tools like dream interpretation and free association (saying anything that comes into your head), psychoanalysts today believe that psychotherapy is most effective when it leads to increased self-knowledge on the part of the patient. Take Johnson Colley, a brother in his forties from Brooklyn. His depression, like that of the patients Freud saw, manifested first in the form of physical illness.

Johnson was the youngest of three. His brother got involved in drugs before finishing high school and his sister dropped out in the twelfth grade. Feeling immense pressure to succeed, Johnson had a dual career as a media consultant and a performer. When he first became ill he figured he had the flu. But after months of a steady fever along with swollen joints, Johnson went to a specialist. Still, no one could diagnose him. He went from weighing 240 pounds to 190 pounds, trying to keep his energy up by drinking freshly squeezed juices because his appetite had disappeared. Then he borrowed a book from a spiritual friend. "I only opened the book once, but I turned to the page with 'D' words and saw disease spelled 'disease.' I began to think right then and there that I was harboring something emotional that kept the doctors from diagnosing me. Then I began to look for someone to help me find out if I was harboring emotions that were keeping me from healing."

Soon after, Johnson met a healer with a "gift for prayer and touch" who recommended a number of psychotherapists. Johnson auditioned a few before he found the perfect fit for his needs. "I walked into her office and the first thing she said was, 'So, how is your soul?' Suddenly tears flowed out. I had no idea so many things were bothering me." After three weeks of therapy, Johnson had his third CAT scan of the year and he was immediately diagnosed with a rare condition called sarcoidosis. Johnson says now that he is a firm believer that people have to express their feelings. "Not expressing them," Johnson said, "was killing me emotionally and physically." Johnson has been seeing a therapist once a week now for almost nine years. He says that, next to marrying his wife, therapy "is the best thing that I have ever done." Then there's Farai Chideya, a beautiful young sister whose list of accomplishments is longer than that of most retirees. A Harvard graduate, she's most well known as a multimedia journalist, having worked in television, online, and on radio, as well as authoring several books, including *The Color of Our Future: Race in the 21st Century*. She had this to say about the role of therapy and medication in treating her depression.

I think that for me one thing that has become easier as I've gotten older is recognizing my triggers. I know that if I don't get enough sleep I'll get depressed. If I don't get enough light, I'll get depressed. If I don't give myself enough time to breathe and not always feel under the gun, I'll get depressed. I can take better care of myself because I know what to look out for. I'm also more assertive than I used to be because I take antidepressants, so I'm more willing to say what isn't working for me.

About four months ago I went to my doctor and I was like, "Well, you know, the Celexa is working for the sluggishness of the depression, that feeling like I can't finish anything and all that stuff, but now I'm feeling a bit of anxiety." And so he worked with me and we added Klonopin as an occasional antianxiety medication, which, as it turns out, I don't really need. I used it very briefly as an antianxiety medication, but then I started using it with his guidance as a sleeping pill. And so it went back to one of my fundamental physical symptoms, which is insomnia. And once we really dealt with the insomnia, the anxiety went away.

Sometimes you have to do a little check-in to know whether or not your medication and/or talk therapy is working. I think a lot of people get frustrated because they've been doing everything and it's still not working, but it's a process, it's like life. What's happening in your life changes. Then your body changes and your body chemistry changes. So for people who have depression and acknowledge it, it's always gonna be a struggle because there's always gonna be something new that comes up and you have to readjust the whole balance again.

Farai is a good example of what it looks like to feel entitled to good care. She's informed and not afraid to talk about her symptoms, so she knows when they're getting better or worse and is able to regulate her treatment to keep her feeling well.

But before we move on from psychoanalysis, let's revisit Sandra Goodridge. You'll remember Sandra from chapter four—her lifelong relationship with depression began after her best friend was shot in the face. For many years afterward, periods of prolonged depression for Sandra always began with sleeplessness, followed by feelings of "emptiness, fatigue, and a general indifference toward life." It was only when she was studying psychology in college that Sandra learned about depression and its biological dimensions. "I earned two master's degrees, one in psychology," Sandra said, "but it wasn't until my thirties, after entering psychotherapy with a brilliant psychiatrist, when I truly began viewing depression as an illness."

I think Sandra's story is a powerful one to share for a couple of reasons. At the end of the last chapter, we talked about how educating yourself about mental health equals personal empowerment. Well, Sandra discov-

---

Five *Sorry* Reasons I Don't Take My Meds

- I just don't feel like it.
- I feel better today.
- Missing one day won't really matter.
- I travel a lot and sometimes forget to bring them.
- I got up late for a meeting and didn't have time; I feel like I can do it on my own.

---

ered through formal study a kind of road map to her emotional life. And it's where this road map guided Sandra that I feel is particularly inspiring. "I am actively involved," Sandra said, "in developing programs to educate others. I developed the Mental Health Thought Leaders conference for the National Urban League, which brought together African-American clergy leaders, educators, and law enforcement officials to explore the impact of mental illness on our community."

For all of her good work, Sandra gets a huge "Go girl!" But amazing as she is, she's not unique. If you commit yourself to becoming informed about depression and its spiraling influence on our community, you can do amazing things, too, big and small! And get this: Besides helping yourself, in the process, you'll probably end up helping somebody else along the way.

> One of the few things I know . . . is this: spend it all, shoot it, play it, lose it all, right away, every time. Do not hoard what seems good for [later]; give it all, give it now. . . . Something more will arise for later. . . . Anything you do not give freely and abundantly becomes lost to you. You open your safe and find ashes.
>
> —ANNIE DILLARD, AUTHOR

You Are What You Think

That's what a young woman named Grace did. She hasn't started an organization, and she doesn't sit on the board of something-or-other. But she has spread the word on cognitive behavioral therapy. When Grace was four years old, her mother died of breast cancer; at six she was taken away from her alcoholic father. A gifted pianist and singer as well as a student, Grace was always an overachiever who never felt good enough about herself or anything she accomplished. She won numerous performing arts awards while attending boarding school, and she even earned an academic scholarship to an Ivy League college and eventually entered a graduate program in social work. But after growing up in the household of an aunt where she never felt wanted, let alone loved, and with the inheritance her mother left her spent on her fancy boarding school education, Grace sought counseling. "It just seemed to me that if I was serious about helping other people, it was time that I helped myself. Since I was going into social work, I began seeing an MSW who has her own practice. From the moment we met, we connected. And she knew right off the bat that cognitive behavioral therapy would work for me. She explained that it was how I thought about things and the kinds of things I think about that made me feel stifled and depressed. Within a few weeks—and I never would have believed this if it didn't actually happen to me—well, I wasn't a new person, but I thought like one." Cognitive behavioral therapy focuses on positively changing the way people think by highlighting how they can get caught up in negative thinking. The goal of this therapy, instead of focusing on past experiences, is to teach patients to challenge the kinds of thoughts that keep them depressed, showing them that their moods can be brought under control if they learn to identify the triggers of an emotional downswing in their *own* thoughts.

"What I learned in my therapy sessions that I tell almost everyone I know," Grace said, "is that when you experience a disappointment, it doesn't mean you *are* a disappointment. When you have a failure, that doesn't mean you *are* a failure. For most of my life, when any one thing was wrong, in spite of all the things that went right, I always identified myself with the mishap or the failure. I don't do that anymore and I don't want anyone I love to, either. It's funny, and so many of my friends laugh, but I just tell folks: Things happen that make any given day good, bad, or okay. How you feel walking away from that day has everything to do with sentence structure. And I'm not talking about the sentences we speak to other people. It's the stuff we say to ourselves that really matters."

The Eyes Have It

Beyond providing personal insight into behavior or helping folks undo their low self-esteem, there are newer types of therapy that deal exclusively with helping people recover from posttraumatic stress syndrome. One such therapy is called EMDR (eye movement desensitization and reprocessing). During this particular technique a therapist guides the patient through a visualization of the traumatic event while directing the patient's eye movement, thus directing a reprocessing of the trauma. There is evidence that this procedure leads to a lessening of posttraumatic stress syndrome symptoms. A book on this topic that means the world to me is *Emotional Healing at Warp Speed: The Power of EMDR* by David Grand, PhD. (Pick it up, if you get a chance. Believe me, you won't regret it.) But I'll let my good friend and coach, David Grand, speak for himself:

> Remember "diet" is a noun—not a verb.
>
> —SCOTLAND DAVIS,
> FASHION DESIGNER

My work is about no assumptions, no demands, just helping a person to be in the best place that they can be, so as to let the miracle of their brains and body do what it is supposed to do, which is to first, survive and second, thrive.

We have all been bumped around in life, and the experience is physical as well as emotional. Trauma is ubiquitous. Trauma is a part of life, but then there are the large traumas, the existential traumas that happen to us individually and together. They get imprinted on us. The good thing is that we learn from the experience. The bad part is that we get blocked. When our systems are overwhelmed they can't throw off the unnatural and go back to the natural state. That is really what the trauma symptoms are about. Whether you are afraid something will happen again, you are avoiding certain places, you can't sleep, you have nightmares, or you get flashbacks of images and sound—that is unnatural. Your system is just trying to go back to the natural, but it can't throw it off. A trauma therapist needs to understand not only the mind, but also the body and the spirit and the unity of the three of them and to know that you can not preordain a person's healing. You can put them in the best place for that healing to happen on its own. As the healing happens you observe it and you guide it, but you don't guide it to make it happen. You guide it as it is happening.

What I love about his book is that he speaks openly about his own pain. It's what makes him such an amazing healer.

Say Yes or No to Drugs? The Deal with Antidepressants

Now that I've told you about a few specific types of therapy and what they entail, let's talk about when medication is an appropriate treatment option. Let's say you're feeling down or suffering from life stresses or transitions like unemployment, a breakup, or the death of a loved one; medication may not necessarily make those kinds of situations easier. Life has difficult periods that can shake your very foundation, and even though you may feel sad and vulnerable, sitting with your feelings and talking to a therapist or a counselor may be a more effective way of coping with those kinds of situations. An antidepressant is not a miracle cure, and it won't make problems disappear. But let's say your feelings of sadness last all day, day after day, for several weeks; on top of that, you're unable to find pleasure in activities you used to enjoy, you're losing or gaining weight, having trouble sleeping, or feel suicidal. That's when medication may help you manage these feelings, *while* you're getting the psychological help you need. And if you're feeling this way, it's very important that you tell your doctor or make an appointment with a therapist who can evaluate your condition and refer you to a caring and knowledgeable physician who will prescribe the right medication for you (often it will be a psychiatrist, but more and more frequently it is a specialist in medication for mental illnesses, called a psychopharmacologist).

Antidepressants affect your mood by changing your brain chemistry. Let me explain them to you so you have a sense of what's out there and what your treatment options are. But remember, medication is not a sure science. Each individual is unique, and the right medication and the right dosage may take a few weeks or months to nail down. Make sure you're seeing a competent physician who is willing to take the time to make sure you're on the right medication at the right dosage and to make adjustments if necessary. A doctor who doesn't take your concerns seriously, or who ignores side effects, should not be treating you. Always remember, doctors work for *you*! You have the right to a second opinion at any time. If going on medication is an option, or if you are already on medication to treat your depression, here are a few questions you should be sure to ask your therapist or physician: What does this drug treat? What's the best way to take it (morning or night, with or without food)? What are the major side effects? Will it interact with other drugs I take?

In addition, be sure to do your homework on any drug you are prescribed. I'm going to go over the three major classes of antidepressants with you in the next few paragraphs, but since people continually do clinical trials and research on these medications, new information about them is always being released. So keep your eyes and ears open for any information pertaining to a drug you're taking or that a friend has been prescribed. (If you have Internet access you can always type the medication's name into www.google.com and see what comes up; it's one way to see if there have been any recent problems or press on the drug.)

Now that you have a few questions to ask your physician, here are the three classes of drugs that reduce depression: tricyclics, MAOIs (monoamine oxidase inhibitors), and SSRIs (selective serotonin reuptake inhibitors). Stay with me—I know this is a lot. We're going to discuss tricyclics first, because they are the oldest class of antidepressants. Tricyclics work by allowing the chemicals associated with emotions like joy and happiness (outstanding among them are serotonin and norepinephrine) to stay in the system longer than they normally would by blocking their reabsorption into brain cells. Tricyclics usually take between two to four weeks to kick in, and they are most often used to treat severe depression, ADHD (attention deficit hyperactivity disorder), and bulimia. Tricyclics have largely been replaced by SSRIs because they have a very narrow therapeutic index; the dose at which they are regularly prescribed comes close to being toxic. As you can imagine, both accidental and deliberate suicides on this class of drug are more likely. In addition, there are a number of side effects, including:

- low blood pressure
- weight gain
- dry mouth
- vomiting
- decreased sex drive
- constipation

> We who lived in concentration camps can remember the people who walked through the huts comforting others, giving away their last piece of bread. They may have been few in number, but they offer sufficient proof that everything can be taken from a person but one thing: the last of the human freedoms—to choose one's attitude in any given set of circumstances, to choose one's own way.
>
> —VIKTOR FRANKL, HOLOCAUST SURVIVOR AND AUTHOR OF
> *MAN'S SEARCH FOR MEANING*

Nowadays, tricyclics are used to treat depression when patients are unresponsive to SSRIs. Some drugs on the market that belong to this class are Endep and Tryptanol.

Next up are MAOIs (monoamine oxidase inhibitors). Like tricyclics, they work by blocking the processes responsible for breaking down serotonin and norepinephrine. MAOIs are used to treat depression and social anxiety. In addition, they have been proven to help smokers kick the habit. Unfortunately, they can combine very badly with certain foods and other medication, so MAOIs are often considered a last resort, when tricyclics and SSRIs don't work. If you're taking MAOIs, you want to be sure to read labels on any over-the-counter drugs

> Black people are often very resistant to Yoga because they believe there may be a religious conflict. There isn't. I have found that Yoga can benefit everyone [by] helping them to be more centered and balanced [and] providing them with tools to handle life's stresses.

you're taking or thinking of taking. (It's known, for example, that MAOIs interact with St. John's Wort, which a lot of people take as an herbal antidepressant.) Further, if you're on this class of antidepressant, it is suggested you carry around an MAOI card, which in an emergency situation alerts medical personnel as to what drugs they should *not* give you. If you're taking MAOIs, you don't want to eat foods with high levels of the chemicals tyramine or tryptophan, which are in cheese, milk, yogurt, turkey, chicken, fish, soy sauce, alcoholic beverages, and chocolate. MAOIs currently on the market include Marplan and Nardil.

Don't worry if tricyclics and MAOIs sound scary, because I've saved the best for last. The safest and most popular class of antidepressants is SSRIs (selective serotonin reuptake inhibitors). They work by allowing serotonin to persist longer than it might normally by blocking its reabsorption into brain cells. Tricyclics do a similar thing but they keep many chemicals from being reabsorbed by the brain, not just serotonin. SSRIs treat depression, anxiety disorder, and personality disorders. Their therapeutic index is wide, meaning that they are not toxic, like tricyclics; however, they do have a number of side effects, including:

> Too often we underestimate the power of a touch, a smile, a kind word, a listening ear, an honest compliment, or the smallest act of caring, all of which have the potential to turn a life around.
>
> —LEO BUSCAGLIA

- changes in weight and appetite
- decreased sex drive
- nausea
- drowsiness
- headache

Drugs currently on the market that fall into this class are Prozac, Wellbutrin, Zoloft, Lexapro (the one I'm on), and Paxil.

Mary Foster, whose mother died when she was five, has experienced low-level chronic depression most of her life. Zoloft works for her.

After her mother's death, Mary's family was too busy to address her needs. She was a child and therefore invisible. Until she was in her early twenties, her depression went undiagnosed and untreated. That's when she began seeing a therapist and taking medication, but she absolutely hated the way the drug made her feel, so she abruptly stopped seeing the doctor and dropped the meds; no surprise, her depression came creeping back. After her sister became ill five years ago, Mary's depression became crippling. "Though she is older than me," Mary said, "I am the alpha personality. Not being able to control what was happening to her made me feel defeated. I didn't care about my job, my church, or my life. I decided to go for treatment again after the tearfulness and anxiety became overwhelming."

Mary regularly sees a therapist now and is on Zoloft, which she says "helps tremendously." But Mary does "not expect to be on the drug forever. In fact, I think I can see the light at the end of the tunnel. The Zoloft gives me clarity so that I can address the issues that make me unhappy. I am being weaned off of it and I am working to build a better, happier life."

> Do you think that death will somehow fail to catch us all, no matter what we are doing? . . . What do you want to be doing when it catches you? . . . If you have anything you believe is more important to have done or be doing when death comes, get to work on that.
>
> —EPICTETUS, GREEK PHILOSOPHER

You Are What You Eat: Diet and Exercise

Medication is not the only therapy that is capable of changing our brain chemistry. The amount of exercise we get in conjunction with our diet has a tremendous impact not only on our physical health, but on our emotional health, too. Did you know that people who exercise regularly are less likely to become depressed than people who don't? Well, it's true. In addition, studies show that eating more saturated fats and sugars are linked to depression *and* to problems with memory. Dr. Andrew McCulloch, chief executive of the Mental Health Foundation, has said: "We are only beginning to understand how the brain as an organ is influenced by the nutrients it derives from the food we eat and how diets have an impact on our mental health." He also added that, in some cases, addressing mental health problems through changes in diet showed better results than using drugs!

After Jonell S. Clark's marriage deteriorated, what began as just months of loneliness turned into years. "I had been married all of my life and I was afraid suddenly of growing old alone," Jonell said. "I missed the sight, sound, smell, and comfort of having a man around. I missed the companionship . . . I missed loving someone and them loving me back." Using alcohol to unwind and leaving the television on all night for com-

> I expect to pass through this world but once; any good thing therefore that I can do, or any kindness that I can show to any fellow creature, let me do it now; let me not defer or neglect it, for I shall not pass this way again.
>
> —STEPHEN GRELLET, QUAKER

pany, Jonell began to realize that her methods of coping were a form of self-medication. "I ate all day and half of the night. I gained more weight than I could handle. I allowed my business to suffer as I just went through the motions." In need of someone to share her ideas, joys, and fears with, Jonell jump-started her own recovery by starting a community women's group. Putting a permanent end to internalizing her feelings of disappointment and despair, Jonell began an exercise program and stopped overeating. She had the women in her group as a backbone of support and encouragement. "After I began to do better because I was talking about my feelings, I decided I wanted to look and feel great. After a lot of hard work, I lost thirty-six pounds and I look fabulous. More important, though, I feel fabulous!" Jonell's recovered self-esteem is the norm for most people who overhaul their fitness and eating habits. Regular exercise, whether you work with a trainer, take an aerobics class, or play a sport, is a great way to gain confidence in your body—and it's also an excellent way to meet people. Besides lifting depression, exercise can motivate creativity, soothe jitters, build up your immune system, and put the heat back in your sex life. Susan Taylor, a dear friend, remains a constant encouraging presence by phone, even on a plane to foreign lands, making sure that I'm eating well and exercising. She'll even call me early in the morning to get me up and going! Kimi Timmons, a twenty-eight-year-old newspaper reporter in Philadelphia, has lived the truth of this. She lived alone, rarely went out except to attend class, smoked weed incessantly, and complained that she would never meet a man. Kimi wasn't surprised when a doctor at her school's clinic diagnosed her with depression. She refused most avenues of treatment. She didn't want to talk to a therapist, and she didn't want to take medication because she was afraid it would negatively interact with marijuana. Then the doctor proposed another plan. Kimi agreed to join a group of women who were recovering from depression who jogged in the morning. She did it because it seemed like a challenge. "I was twenty pounds overweight, I hadn't exercised since I was fourteen, and I smoked like a chimney. The last time I'd gone biking, I made it only ten minutes and thought I was going to die. I guess in a way, I thought exercising was a joke. But I was tired of feeling like the punch line."

The base goal of the group Kimi joined was to cover a mile. The time it took didn't matter. Kimi took the suggestions of women from the group, taking very small steps at the outset, trotting more than jogging. After four weeks at a rate of four times per week, Kimi was able to keep pace with

her group for two miles without any hardship. "First, I never thought that I would keep it up. Then I didn't think I would start to look forward not only to exercising but to hanging out on the track with these women I came to think of as friends. We were all going through some version of the same thing, and with them I didn't feel isolated anymore."

Kimi is a case study in the community-building, mood-lifting power of exercise. In 1999 researchers at Duke University published the results of a study that divided depressed patients, ages fifty to seventy-seven, into three groups. The first did thirty minutes of jogging or brisk walking three times a week. The second took Zoloft, and the third did both. After four months, patients in all three groups were doing equally well, the medication offering no particular advantage over the regular practice of working out, except in relieving the symptoms a little faster. When the researchers followed up six months later, however, they found a major difference. About a third of the patients who initially improved on Zoloft combined with exercise were depressed again, whereas 92 percent of those benefiting from just the exercise were still doing well. Are you thinking you want to put this book down and buy a pair of running shoes? I hope so. Because if you're suffering from anxiety or low-level chronic depression, you just might want to visit a gym before you head out to your doctor to receive a consultation.

> All human suffering must have an end; there is no wind that always blows a storm.
>
> —SOPHOCLES, PHILOSOPHER

Around 2000, Dr. Candace Cabbil moved to New York City, and without realizing it, she spiraled into depression. If it hadn't been for a powerful combination of friendship, school, *and* exercise, she might not have managed.

I had all the symptoms: crying spells, no appetite, effortless weight loss, poor self-esteem, little contact with family or friends. I talked to people just enough to let them know I was okay. If I had to do it all over again I would seek counseling. But at the time, this is what I did: In addition to talking to my best friend every day, I worked out for a minimum of one and a half to two hours per day. I figured that even if I didn't feel good about myself, the very act of working out

291

would be good for my body. I did cleansing fasts and paid attention to my diet. I also focused on my studies and completed my master of science degree in natural health. I created a mantra for myself that I said whenever I was feeling low or crying. I also said it first thing in the morning and all day long, whenever I thought of it. I took a course on the mind/body connection and I figured, even if I didn't believe it or feel it, eventually it would come true. My mantra is: I am calm, I am clear, I am happy, I am love, I am peace, I am power!

As I was coming out of my deep pit of depression, it felt like a rebirth. It was then that I realized I had been having a functional nervous breakdown. I'm still moved to tears when I think about that time because the pain was so real. I understood what it was to have a broken heart. My whole body ached. It was a pain that I wouldn't wish on my worst enemies. I had become a shell of my former self. Today, I can once again see all the possibilities for my life and I feel blessed.

And think about expanding your physical horizons. The gym isn't the only place to get structured exercise. The benefits of the five-thousand-year-old discipline called Yoga can also work wonders for your body, mind, and spirit.

Gayle Fleming is a Yoga therapist and the mother of Malaak, comedian Chris Rock's wife. At lunch one day she told me that she has a number of private Yoga clients who are dealing with depression. "Often what I find is that the depression is undiagnosed or the person is not willing to deal with it. As a Yoga therapist I work with individuals on a one-on-one basis. My training is not medical, but I am trained to look at the whole person from a holistic standpoint. My work is to go beyond the mere physical and work with mental and emotional issues. According to the principles of Ayurveda (a kind of medicine that's been practiced in India for thousands of years), every person has five layers of being, starting with the outward physical layer. I work to get people to go inward—so if you have back pain, I give you postures to relieve the pain but also to help identify and relieve the things that are causing the stress. By moving from the outside in, it is often possible to uncover in a gentle, systematic way deeply rooted emotional pain that manifests as physical discomfort and stress."

Having Each Other's Backs:

The Importance of Social Support

One of the most debilitating aspects of my depression was my tendency to isolate. And the more I isolated, the more depressed I became. Let me be clear about this: Talking about it with your coworkers and doing business over lunch is not the same thing as being connected. Many of us have such stressful jobs that we're forced to interact with dozens of folks every day. By the time we get home we just want to be left alone, and that's understandable. But let's talk about why. The kinds of interactions we have most typically at work are draining; they take us away from ourselves and make us hide parts of ourselves because we think people might hurt our fragile inner selves. Meaningful connection, on the other hand, is the opposite of this game face–driven life. Meaningful connection means spending quality time with someone or a group of people you trust and like. It's the space where you feel safe to share your real self. We need meaningful connection so that we can feel meaningful! Whether it's family, friends, a boyfriend, or a girlfriend, we need to create a circle of social support that lifts us out of ourselves and restores social meaning to our lives.

This is where support groups, including 12-step programs like Alcoholics Anonymous and Children of Addicted Parents, come in. A young woman I know shared with me that in college she had a support group of ten Black women. Every two weeks they would get together and exchange stories of hardship and joy. "Meeting to talk exclusively about our emotional and academic issues was very different from just hanging out with friends," she told me. "It was a sacred space because we knew that everything said was confidential, that we had each other's backs." Even now after college she and these other women have a special bond, a connection that allows them to pick up the phone and spill "the real deal" at a moment's notice.

Not all support groups necessarily involve talking. There are a number of meditation groups, prayer communities, and retreats that use silence and writing as therapy. Along those lines, I want to recommend a book to you by a powerful sister named Angel Kyodo Williams called *Being Black: Zen and the Art of Living with Fearlessness and Grace*. Besides giving thoughtful background information as to what, exactly, Zen Buddhism is (a form of Buddhism that uses meditation to focus on living in the present and seeing deeply into the nature of things by direct experience), Angel presents the principles and practices of Zen that emphasize healthy emotional lives for Black people in particular. Angel knows from personal experience how Zen

principles apply to our community. "People of color are especially in need of new ways and new answers to the separation and fear we face each day," Angel said. "It wouldn't be a stretch to say that as Black people, more than most groups in this country, we live our daily lives with the distinct taste of fear in our mouths."

Angel's words speak to the heart of what this chapter is about. Being educated about your treatment options, whether you're looking at medication, therapy, or both, is vital to recovering from depression without being victimized by the medical industry or by a single health care professional. Understanding that there are things you can do *without* the assistance of a doctor, like writing in a journal, meditating, or exercising—not to mention getting more green vegetables into your diet while cutting back on fast food—can all be huge steps toward increasing the quality of your life. I say this because all of the things I've just mentioned can help all of us, in either big or small ways, spit out what Angel called "the taste of fear" and put in its place the most satisfying flavor in the world. And that, my friend, is the taste of self-acceptance in a community that is meaningful and personally rewarding to you. Most of us tend not to eat foods we don't like the taste of. Why would you ever dream of living your life that way?

When I spoke with friend and noted African-American psychiatrist Annelle Primm, who is the director of Minority and National Affairs for the American Psychiatric Association and an associate professor of psychiatry at the Johns Hopkins School of Medicine, she reinforced these ideas.

People of African descent all over the world feel the hurtful force of racism in different ways. Black pain, often masked and ignored by the people who have it, is a common experience. It is caused by humiliation, [by] not having enough, [by] loss, and in some cases, by physical and emotional abuse. How can Black people cope with the pain and heal from it? They can reach inside themselves and harness their strengths, their spirit, their will to live, their inborn capacity to make do with the less-than-perfect, and thrive in spite of hard times. People can also cope by being creative and leaning on their family, their community, their pastors, and their healers. These supports are part of the "protective factors" that have held our communities together like "social glue." Transforming the negative energy of pain into positive action, helping and uplifting others, maintaining hope, using creative expression as an outlet to work through pain, is a strategy that has been used by Black people to cope with the most horrible circumstances. This paradigm of "flipping the script" on pain has been essential to our survival and resilience through one of the most terrible traumas in human history.

As for me, my story is not a "success story" in any conventional sense. I'm not over my depression; I haven't "kicked" it or "gotten all better." I take 30 mg of Lexapro a day, I see my therapist every week, and I'm exercising with Harry, my wonderfully patient and butt-kicking personal trainer. My issues haven't disappeared, it's just that I'm able to work on them, one day at a time. I no longer think I will wake up one morning and be free of every depressive feeling that has ever plagued me. I have not "snapped out" of depression—I no longer believe that's possible—but I am fully engaged, day by day, in the fight to feel, to have fear and sadness rather than anxiety, and to become reacquainted with calm, vibrancy, and joy. And I will not rest until you join me in that fight.

Because I am a woman on fire.

A Final Word
Making a Way Out of No Way

In the last several chapters I've shared many stories of pain. Some of them have been tragic, some of them uplifting. I would like to end the book on an unmistakably positive note. I talk here about the ways that depression is not only a curse, but also at times a blessing. Despite its debilitating nature, depression can give us a unique perspective, a deep sensitivity to the suffering of other people, a capacity for great humanity.

Several months ago I got this letter from my friend Denese Shervington, who is now my therapist. It's a powerful testimony to daring to live our life to the fullest, *now*!

One lonely night, six weeks after the death of my husband, Walter, I came to a fork in my life, "forward growth or regression." I remember thinking I would never see Walter again; he was never going to walk through that door and announce in his always vibrant voice, "I'm home!" The reality of his death, his being forever gone, was now upon me.

With that realization I fell into deep despair. My thoughts raced as I went through the kaleidoscope of my life with Walter. I wondered if I had loved Walter the way he deserved. Writhing in pain, the doctor in me suggested that I call a doctor friend and get a few sleeping pills, thinking at least sleep would temporarily numb my suffering. But then I thought, "If I take a pill now, I'll probably have to keep taking them for a long time, because the pain doesn't seem to be going anywhere."

And in that moment, knowing that I did not want to add addiction to my problems, a little voice inside whispered, "Denese, perhaps you are supposed to feel pain. You have just gone through the worst tragedy of your life. Whoever would have thought that Walter Shervington, the incredible psychiatrist, at the top of his career, president of the National Medical Association, your handsome, charming, youthful husband, and devoted father of your beautiful daughters, would die within six weeks of being diagnosed with lung cancer? And worse—that he would die on the night of your oldest child's birthday, two weeks before her graduation from high school?"

That realization allowed me to open up to my grief and set free the tears that were begging their release. I got out of bed and rolled on the floor and wailed for Walter and all those others I had lost, my mother, my father, my nephew. Laying myself bare, all the tears released for now, I gave myself permission to cry whenever I felt sad, no matter where or when.

And I took the big leap—I used my pain to teach me about myself and how I had positioned myself with others and the world around me. I forgave myself for not showing Walter (the depth of) my love—it had been there, but buried inside deep ego bruises from early childhood pain. (I therefore challenged myself to use this as a profound lesson that from henceforth any loving partnership that I engaged in would have mutual support for self-growth and actualization as the core mantra upon which the relationship was based.)

By experiencing and accepting the reality of the mystery of this thing called life, that the self is forever changing, that pain does not have to mean suffering, I opened myself to the dance of life. Sleep did eventually grace me. And when I awoke the next morning, I felt at peace, filled with curious joyfulness about starting anew, becoming more present with life. Looking back, that is when I slipped into the glorious afternoon of my life.

When I think of great leaders like Malcolm X, Harriet Tubman, W.E.B. DuBois, and Sojourner Truth, I see men and women who grappled at times with feelings that look an awful lot like what we now call depression. These folks suffered, but that suffering enabled them to feel injustice acutely, to advocate for the defenseless, and to inspire others. Although I don't believe in the mystique of the tortured artist—no one should have to suffer needlessly when there are alternatives—I think that suffering is one of life's great equalizers. Suffering makes us human, tests our faith, strengthens our belief, and, in an ironic twist, can give us the powerful will to hope and a burning desire to give life meaning.

My depression has caused me much suffering, but it has also brought me closer to God, closer to my family, and closer to my calling. I can't separate out those parts of me that are sick because I'm depressed, or bad because my brain can generate depression. I am forced every day to accept my fragility, to find the will to care for myself and others despite my pain, and to go on in the face of my fears. That strength is also part of my depression, and it is a gift I must look to every bit as much as I look to the removal or avoidance of pain. It is a gift that makes me who I am.

A Guide to Breaking Our Silence and Getting the Healing Started

We Heal by Sharing!

Now that you've finished the book you may be saying to yourself, "That's great, Terrie, but what do I do now?"

I've thought about that and come up with what I think is a powerful way for folks everywhere to begin the process of sharing their pain by sharing their story.

The most powerful thing you can do is start a sharing circle. Think of at least three friends (and more is even better) who you think might be hurting, too, and send them this note on nice stationery:

Dear _____,

I'm writing to you because I just read Terrie Williams's new book, Black Pain: It Just Looks Like We're Not Hurting. *I was so moved by the power of her story and the people who shared their stories in the book that I wanted to share my own story. I've been in pain and, instead of reaching out, I've kept that pain to myself. Something in me has sensed that you might feel pain, too. If that's the case I want to hear your story.*

Maybe we could get together once a month and talk about what's going on in our lives. I think Terrie's book would be a great starting place.

Terrie says "that no matter how difficult or embarrassing you think your situation is, (and believe me on this!) there are at least two or three others that have had the exact same experience or know some- one who has!" I believe what she says is true and I hope you're open to sharing your thoughts and feelings with me. It's time we came together and strengthened the bonds of our community by breaking our silence around being in pain. Let's reach out and hear one another so we can share and heal.

Stay Strong,

_____

Now, what do you do once a few people have agreed to come over and share their stories?

I suggest simply taking my book and working through it chapter by chapter. Talk about yourselves, about family members, about folks you know in the community who may be suffering or in pain. Ask one another questions like:

- How are you truly feeling right now? And don't be afraid to say how you *really* feel!
- How many times have you walked into work and said "Good morning" with a smile, knowing that you really feel like shit? Did you struggle to get out of bed? Was your stomach in knots? How do you get through the day when that happens?
- Do you worry all the time? Have you ever had an anxiety attack?
- What are small steps you can take to make yourself feel better? How do you cope?
- What makes you feel good? What takes you out of a good mood?
- What makes you feel down and out? How do you get out of that feeling?
- What is bothering you right now about someone else that you just can't say to them?
- Do you feel angry a lot?
- Is there someone you can call when you feel like the walls are closing in?

And remind one another to consider even the smallest step that you've taken to feel better to be a victory.

You can use the group to set up a buddy system, to create a space where, when things get rough, you can go and just be real. And think about inviting a friend who is a mental health professional to come over for the evening—or a sensitive pastor or healer in your area. He or she can share his or her knowledge, and your group can get more information to help each other heal.

Encourage one another to talk to a doctor, to find a sympathetic therapist, coach, or healer. (I've driven a friend to therapy when she felt afraid to begin the process—that's the kind of support you and your group can offer one another.)

But one of the most important things to remember is that a group or healing circle is sacred: *What's said in the group must stay in the group!* A healing circle is not a gossip session. In order to feel safe, the members of your group must feel like they can lay bare their hearts and know that what they say won't leave the group or come back to haunt them.

Creating a group is such a simple and powerful way to heal. It creates intimacy, stops isolation, and provides a safe space in a culture that can feel very lonely and cold at times. Think of your little group as a lifeline to mental health, as the first step to creating the blessed community we all want to live in.

And once you're done talking about the book you're holding right now, I have some others to stimulate conversation. When it comes to understanding pain and depression you might consider the following (see pages 299–308 for a full, comprehensive list of resources):

- *What Mama Couldn't Tell Us About Love: Healing the Emotional Legacy of Racism by Celebrating Our Light* by Brenda Richardson and Brenda Wade
- *Standing in the Shadows: Understanding and Overcoming Depression in Black Men* by John Head
- *Shifting: The Double Lives of Black Women in America* by Charisse Jones and Kumea Shorter-Gooden
- *I Don't Want to Talk About It: Overcoming the Secret Legacy of Male Depression* by Terrence Real
- *When Food Is Love: Exploring the Relationship Between Eating and Intimacy* by Geneen Roth
- *What the Blues Is All About: Black Women Overcoming Stress and Depression* by Angela Mitchell and Kennise Herring, PhD
- *Women Who Love Too Much: When You Keep Wishing and Hoping He'll Change* by Robin Norwood
- *The Rage of a Privileged Class: Why Do Prosperous Blacks Still Have the Blues?* by Ellis Cose
- *Lay My Burden Down: Unraveling Suicide and the Mental Health Crisis Among African-Americans* by Alvin F. Poussaint and Amy Alexander

• *Healing the Shame That Binds You* by John Bradshaw
• *The Road Less Traveled* by M. Scott Peck
• *He-Motions: Even Strong Men Struggle* by T. D. Jakes
• *Black Rage* by William Grier and Price Cobbs

My Invitation to You

If this book has touched you, please share your story with me. Tell me what your pain looks, sounds, and feels like. I would love to get your letter! Include your name and a return address and send them to me at:

Terrie M. Williams
Columbus Circle Station
P.O. Box 20227
New York, NY 10023

Or e-mail me at:

liftingeachotherup@yahoo.com

Resources
For Working Through
Your Pain and Staying Strong

Afua, Queen. *Sacred Woman: A Guide to Healing the Feminine Body, Mind, and Spirit.* New York: One World, 2000.

Anderson, Stanice. *I Say a Prayer for Me: One Woman's Life of Faith and Triumph.* West Bloomfield, MI: Warner Books, 2002.

Anderson-Tazi, Shellie. *Soul Beginnings: 8 Strategies for Overcoming Life's Challenges.* New York: Berkley Publishing Group, 2004.

Aron, Elaine N. *The Highly Sensitive Person: How to Thrive When the World Overwhelms You.* New York: Carol Publishing Group, 1996.

Barras, Jonetta Rose. *Whatever Happened to Daddy's Little Girl?: The Impact of Fatherlessness on Black Women.* New York: Ballantine Publishing Group, 2000.

Bassett, Angela, and Courtney B. Vance. *Friends: A Love Story.* New York: Harlequin, 2007.

Bazile, Ronald P., Sr., et. al. *"You Have Cancer.": A Death Sentence That Four African-American Men Turned into an Affirmation to Remain in the "Land of the Living."* New Orleans, LA: Domain Developers Inc., 2007.

Beck, Aaron T. *Depression: Causes and Treatment.* Philadelphia: University of Pennsylvania Press, 1967.

Booth, Father Leo. *When God Becomes a Drug: Breaking the Chains of Religious Addiction and Abuse.* New York: Jeremy P. Tarcher, 1991.

Boyd, Julia A. *In the Company of My Sisters: Black Women and Self-Esteem.* New York: Dutton, 1993.

Bradshaw, John. *Healing the Shame That Binds You.* Deerfield Beach, FL: Health Communications, 1988.

Brock, Rovenia M, PhD. *Dr. Ro's Ten Secrets to Livin' Healthy: America's Most Renowned African American Nutritionist Shows You How to Look Great, Feel Better, and Live Longer by Eating Right.* New York: Bantam Books, 2004.

Brown, Diane R., and Verna M. Keith, eds. *In and Out of Our Right Minds: The Mental Health of African American Women*. New York: Columbia University Press, 2003.

Bryant, Solliah. *SOLLIAH: She Only Looks Like It Ain't Hurtin*. http://www .solliah.com.

Burns, David D, MD. *Feeling Good: The New Mood Therapy*. Rev. ed. New York: Avon, 1999.

Campbell, Bebe Moore. *72 Hour Hold*. New York: Knopf, 2005.

————. *Sometimes My Mommy Gets Angry*. New York: G. P. Putnam's Sons, 2003.

Campbell, T. Colin, PhD, and Thomas M. Campbell II. *The China Study: The Most Comprehensive Study of Nutrition Ever Conducted and the Startling Implications for Diet, Weight Loss and Long-term Health*. Dallas, TX: Ben-Bella Books, 2005.

Canada, Geoffrey. *Fist, Stick, Knife, Gun: A Personal History of Violence in America*. Boston: Beacon Press, 1995.

Carter, William Lee, EdD. *It Happened to Me: A Teen's Guide to Overcoming Sexual Abuse*. Oakland, CA: New Harbinger Publications, 2002.

Cathcart, Christopher D. *The Lost Art of Giving Back: A Helpful Guide to Making a Difference*. Xlibris Corporation, 2006.

Chambers, Eric J. *The Love I Have for You*. Hollywood, CA: Who Dat? Publishing House, 2006.

Chapman, Audrey B. *Getting Good Loving: Seven Ways to Find Love and Make It Last*. 3rd ed., 1st Agate ed. Chicago: Agate, 2005.

Chödrön, Pema. *When Things Fall Apart: Heart Advice for Difficult Times*. Boston: Shambhala, 1997.

Cobbs, Price M, MD. *My American Life: From Rage to Entitlement*. New York: Atria Books, 2005.

Collins, Catherine Fisher, ed. *African American Women's Health and Social Issues*. 2nd ed. Westport, CT: Praeger Publishers, 2006.

Cook, Dr. Suzan Johnson. *Live Like You're Blessed: Simple Steps for Making Balance, Love, Energy, Spirit, Success, Encouragement, and Devotion Part of Your Life*. New York: Doubleday, 2006.

Cose, Ellis. *The Rage of a Privileged Class*. New York: HarperCollins, 1993.

Craddock, Maggie. *The Authentic Career: Following the Path of Self-Discovery to Professional Fulfillment*. Novato, CA: New World Library, 2004.

Cronkite, Kathy. *On the Edge of Darkness: Conversations About Conquering Depression*. New York: Doubleday, 2004.

Danquah, Meri Nana-Ama. *Willow Weep for Me: A Black Woman's Journey Through Depression*. New York: Norton, 1998.

Davis, Sampson, George Jenkins, and Rameck Hunt. *The Bond: Three Young*

Men Learn to Forgive and Reconnect with Their Fathers. New York: Riverhead Books, 2007.

———. *The Pact: Three Young Men Make a Promise and Fulfill a Dream.* New York: Riverhead Books, 2002.

———. *We Beat the Street: How a Friendship Pact Led to Success.* New York: Dutton, 2005.

Dortch, Thomas W., Jr. *The Miracles of Mentoring: The Joy of Investing in Our Future.* New York: Doubleday, 2000.

Durruthy, Stephanie S, MD. *The Pregnancy Decision Handbook for Women with Depression.* Ellicott City, MD: Mindsupport, LLC, 2005.

Ellis, Glenn, Sr. *Which Doctor?: What You Need to Know to Be Healthy.* Las Vegas: Long & Silverman Publishing, Inc., 2006.

Elmore, John V, Esq. *Fighting for Your Life: The African-American Criminal Justice Survival Guide.* Phoenix, AZ: Amber Books, 2004.

Evans, Dwight L., MD, and Linda Wasmer Andrews. *If Your Adolescent Has Depression or Bipolar Disorder: An Essential Resource for Parents.* New York: Oxford University Press, 2005.

Fanon, Frantz. *Black Skin, White Masks.* Translated by Richard Philcox. Rev. ed. New York: Grove Press, 2007.

Fassler, David G., MD, and Lynne S. Dumas. *"Help Me, I'm Sad": Recognizing, Treating, and Preventing Childhood and Adolescent Depression.* New York: Viking, 1997.

Frankl, Viktor E. *Man's Search for Ultimate Meaning.* New York: Perseus Publishing, 2000.

The Freedom Writers with Erin Gruwell. *The Freedom Writers Diary: How a Teacher and 150 Teens Used Writing to Change Themselves and the World Around Them.* New York: Broadway Books, 2001.

Friedrich, William N. *Psychotherapy With Sexually Abused Boys: An Integrated Approach.* Thousand Oaks, CA: Sage Publications, 1995.

Gandy, Debrena Jackson. *Sacred Pampering Principles: An African-American Woman's Guide to Self-care and Inner Renewal.* New York: William Morrow and Company, 1997.

Gaston, Marilyn Hughes, MD, and Gayle K. Porter, PsyD. *Prime Time: The African American Woman's Complete Guide to Midlife Health and Wellness.* Edited by Sheryl Hilliard Tucker. New York: One World, 2001.

Gil, Eliana. *Treating Abused Adolescents.* New York: Guilford Press, 1996.

Golant, Mitch, PhD, and Susan K. Golant. *What to Do When Someone You Love Is Depressed: A Self-Help and Help Others Guide.* New York: Villard Books, 1996.

Grand, David, PhD. *Emotional Healing at Warp Speed: The Power of EMDR.* New York: Harmony Books, 2001.

Green, Jacqualyn F., PhD. *Spiritual Resilience: Survival Strategies for African Americans.* Indianapolis, IN: Green Enterprizes Publications, 2005.

Gregory, Deborah. *The Cheetah Girls.* Series. New York: Hyperion Books for Children, 1999.

Grier, William H., MD, and Price M. Cobbs, MD. *Black Rage.* New York: BasicBooks, 1968.

Guitard, S. James. *Mocha Love: A Novel of Passion, Honesty, Deceit and Power.* Washington, DC: Literally Speaking Publishing House, 2004.

Hammond, Michelle McKinney. *Get Over It and On With It!: How to Get Up When Life Knocks You Down.* Colorado Springs, CO: WaterBrook Press, 2002.

———. *Release the Pain, Embrace the Joy: Help for the Hurting Heart.* Ventura, CA: Regal Books, 2005.

———. *The Power of Being a Woman: Embracing the Triumph of the Feminine Spirit.* Eugene, OR: Harvest House Publishers, 2004.

———. *The Real Deal on Overcoming Heartache: Learning to Live and Love Again.* Eugene, OR: Harvest House Publishers, 2007.

Harmon, Ruby M. *Poetic Moves While Doctoring.* New York: Jay Street Publishers, 2006.

Harper, Hill. *Letters to a Young Brother: Manifest Your Destiny.* New York: Gotham Books, 2006.

Harris, E. Lynn. *I Say a Little Prayer.* New York: Doubleday, 2006.

———. *What Becomes of the Brokenhearted.* New York: Doubleday, 2003.

Head, John. *Standing in the Shadows: Understanding and Overcoming Depression in Black Men.* New York: Broadway Books, 2004.

Heller, Fanya Gottesfeld. *Love in a World of Sorrow: A Teenaged Girl's Holocaust Memoirs.* New York: Devora Publishing, 2005.

Hendricks, Obery M. *Living Water.* San Francisco: HarperSanFrancisco, 2004.

———. *The Politics of Jesus: Rediscovering the True Revolutionary Nature of Jesus' Teachings and How They Have Been Corrupted.* New York: Doubleday, 2006.

Hopson, Darlene Powell, Dr., and Dr. Derek S. Hopson. *The Power of Soul: Pathways to Psychological and Spiritual Growth for African Americans.* New York: William Morrow and Company, 1998.

Hopson, Derek S., PhD, and Darlene Powell Hopson, PhD. *Friends, Lovers, and Soul Mates: A Guide to Better Relationships Between Black Men and Women.* New York: Simon & Schuster, 1994.

Huber, Cheri. *Being Present in the Darkness: Using Depression as a Tool for Self-Discovery.* New York: Perigee Books, 1996.

Jamison, Kay Redfield. *An Unquiet Mind: A Memoir of Moods and Madness.*

New York: Knopf, 1995.

Jampolsky, Gerald G, MD. *Love Is Letting Go of Fear.* Berkeley, CA: Celestial Arts, 1979.

Jeffers, Susan J., PhD. *Feel the Fear . . . and Do It Anyway.* New York: Ballantine Books, 2007.

Jones, Charisse, and Kumea Shorter-Gooden, PhD. *Shifting: The Double Lives of Black Women in America.* New York: HarperCollins, 2003.

Kashef, Ziba. *Like a Natural Woman: The Black Woman's Guide to Alternative Healing.* New York: Dafina Books, 2001.

Kunjufu, Jawanza. *Countering the Conspiracy to Destroy Black Boys.* Chicago, IL: African American Images, 1995.

———. *Keeping Black Boys Out of Special Education.* Chicago: African American Images, 2005.

———. *Motivating and Preparing Black Youth For Success.* Chicago: African American Images, 1986.

———. *To Be Popular or Smart: The Black Peer Group.* Chicago: African American Images, 1988.

Leary, Joy DeGruy, PhD. *Post Traumatic Slave Syndrome: America's Legacy of Enduring Injury and Healing.* Milwaukie, OR: Uptone Press, 2005.

Loehr, Jim, and Tony Schwartz. *The Power of Full Engagement: Managing Energy, Not Time, Is the Key to High Performance and Personal Renewal.* New York: Free Press, 2003.

Martin, Marilyn, MD, MPH. *Saving Our Last Nerve: The Black Woman's Path to Mental Health.* Roscoe, IL: Hilton Publishing, 2002.

Martin, Philip. *The Zen Path through Depression.* San Francisco: HarperSanFrancisco, 1999.

Mitchell, Angela, with Kennise Herring, PhD. *What the Blues Is All About: Black Women Overcoming Stress and Depression.* New York: Berkeley Books, 1998.

Morris, Dashaun "Jiwe." *War of the Bloods in My Veins.* New York: Simon & Schuster, forthcoming.

Morris, Leslie A. *How Ya Like Me Now!* http://howyalikemenow.com.

Mundy, Linus. *A Man's Guide to Prayer.* New York: Crossroad Publishing Company, 1998.

Murray, Victoria Christopher. *The Ex Files.* New York: Simon & Schuster, 2007.

Neal-Barnett, Dr. Angela. *Soothe Your Nerves: The Black Woman's Guide to Understanding and Overcoming Anxiety, Panic, and Fear.* New York: Simon & Schuster, 2003.

Nelson, John E., MD, and Andrea Nelson, PhD, eds. *Sacred Sorrows: Embracing and Transforming Depression.* New York: Putnam, 1996.

Acknowledgments

I owe a debt of gratitude to *Black Rage* for giving Black people such a loving model of personal and political understanding and transformation.

In Loving Memory

Bebe Moore Campbell, your special gifts and loving spirit wove a deep understanding for those of us who are broken. Thank you for casting a light on the dark path of despair, brightening the way toward hope and healing.

Tracey Mitchell, for reminding me that I do not stand on that ledge alone. It echoes in my spirit.

Shellie Anderson-Tazi, for your unconditional love and friendship.

Special Thanks

Mom and Dad, I owe everything to you. You lived during a time that is beyond my realm of comprehension, facing and overcoming obstacles with grace and dignity. I know that my survival in the world I grew up in would have been impossible had I not been blessed to be the daughter of Charles and Marie Williams. You are the embodiment of all that is gentle, determined, kind, powerful, and beautiful. In all my endeavors, big and small, I thank and love you both with all my heart.

Aunt Jo (Mom number two) and Uncle Floyd, Gene Gaddy, Tony Gaddy, Pat Perry, Earlene Williams, Bernice Symes (especially for your courage and ability to stand tall after going through the fire), **Wes Greene, Tom Johnson, Rocky Ephraim, and Sonya Ephraim.** They say you can't pick your family.

309

For the record, given the chance I would have chosen you. To all of you who helped me over the years, encouraged me, protected me, saved and believed in me . . . thank you.

Twanna Rose, in some of my darkest hours, your quiet, nurturing presence helped me breathe again. We are family. I love and admire you.

Linda Loewenthal, from the first moment we sat across from each other, I knew that our working together had been preordained. Every author dreams of having an agent whose spirit and passion for their work will light a fire beneath all other players . . . you are that agent. From the awesome proposal to the deadline, I thank you for your wisdom, guidance, professionalism, hard work, diligence, and, most of all, your friendship. (And thank you *again* Joann Davis for putting us together.)

Tanya McKinnon, I raise my glass to toast you. You are simply divine and original. I truly cannot fathom this book without your dedication, your counsel, your sense of organization, your extensive research, and your commitment. *Black Pain* would not have been possible without being deep in the trenches with you as my writing associate. Thank you for your sassiness, for fighting for me, and for putting so much of yourself into this work. I am forever grateful to you—and to Richard Simon.

Beth Wareham, my editor, you are special; your boundless energy and down-to-earth demeanor captivated me from the very beginning. Quite literally, you've made this incredible journey possible. You are a true visionary—I thank you for believing in me. Most important, I thank you for believing in the significance of the groundbreaking movement that is *Black Pain*.

My Scribner family: Susan Moldow, Nan Graham, and Roz Lippel, thank you for seeing this book for all that it could be when it came to you in its rawest form.

Whitney Frick, Kate Bittman, Brian Belfiglio, Tyler LeBlue, Stephanie Evans, and Julienne Regan, I greatly appreciate your part in making this work everything that it will be. Thanks for being there when my mental and creative accounts seemed low or overdrawn.

Madeline "Laurel" McCray, I don't even remember my life before you entered it. You have been such a powerful force. Your insight into the human spirit has helped me flesh out this work. You are a most amazing friend and road dawg. Thank you for being a kindred spirit and always helping me to complete what I can't seem to finish.

Susan L. Taylor, I am so proud to call you my sister. You have always been there for me, encouraging me, guiding me, and loving me. I cannot thank you enough nor can I imagine a day without your gentle and prodding ways. Over the years your healing words have uplifted and inspired me right along with the masses of people whose lives you have touched. You are one in a million and I love you dearly.

Xavier Artis, your ability to dream dreams without walls is a constant reminder to me that all things are possible when we truly believe with all our heart. When I see so many people in pain, I sometimes become a bit weary, but your philosophy always gives me the strength and courage to keep pushing forward: *"I can't be all that I'm supposed to be, until you become who you are supposed to be."* In friendship and love I thank you for sharing your eloquence and your spirit with me.

Dashaun "Jiwe" Morris and Jason "Jay" Davis, not a day goes by that I don't recall the first time we met. You have both given me a rare glimpse into the pain-filled lives of young people who join gangs. You've trusted me with your souls, and I want you to know how incredibly special that makes me feel. Because of your honesty I was able to add layers of information that will create greater awareness and healing for our youth. I love you.

Vernon Slaughter, my attorney, thank you for being a wonderful friend and for your wisdom, courage, and perseverance . . . and for being a living and breathing example of what it means to stand tall and strong in the face of adversity. You are so necessary.

Shanene Pinder, thank you for being a big part of this entire process. Your ability to always capture what I am trying to put into words has been a Godsend. Your spirit and presence in this movement is necessary and is a blessing. Thank you for being one with me and for always holding it down.

Scotland Davis, that you've been able to stand by me with grace and patience these past two years is nothing short of a miracle. Your warm spirit and unshakable calm during my stormy hours have been the blessing and balance I needed to complete this critical work. From my heart I will always be thankful for your support.

Uhuru McCray, my fellow curmudgeon, you are an extraordinary artist, and I thank you for always being there to use your gift and to bring my visions to life. I truly appreciate your friendship . . . you are God sent.

Alile Eldrige, Jourdan Cha-Taun Atkinson, Jasmine Velazquez, and Veronica Marshall, thanks so much, ladies, for your patience and consistency. Because of your diligence and hard work, this mission has flourished. Each of you is a blessing and a joy to know.

Dr. Carl Bell, you are an amazing human being. I will never forget your willingness to make yourself available when I reached out for answers. Your genuine concern for the well-being of Black people in pain and your commitment to the work that will help to heal them are inspiring. Your wisdom encouraged me to look deeper within myself, and I'm deeply grateful to you for everything.

Dr. Annelle Primm, thank you for introducing and embracing me into your community. Your guidance has enabled me to affect so many lives by spreading the word about our pain—giving arms to lift our people out of despair.

Reggie Hatchett, "When you dance with me, the rhythm's only for you." I celebrate the friendship and the love.

Special thanks to those who have kindly, and perhaps cautiously, consented to lay out their lives to an unfamiliar and scrutinizing public—many for the first time—to encourage and guide those who still search for someone with whom to identify, who can inspire better health and healing. Thank you for your faith in me and your bold courage: Marie Kearney Williams, my amazing mother, I know all that your contribution to this work meant—and I love you for your courage and for always having my back; Malaika Adero; John Amos; Solliah Bryant; Candace Cabbil; Gloria Arnau; Geoffrey Canada; Farai Chideya; Marcia Dyson; Mama DeBarge; Alicia Evans; Rita Ewing; Gayle Fleming; David Grand; Derek Hopson; Sandra Goodridge; Obery Hendricks; Heavy D; Deborah Gregory; Nina Hickson; Lucille O'Neal; Gail Holliday; Evans Hopkins; Karin Grant Hopkins; Noah Hopkins; Yvette Hyater-Adams; Dr. Joy DeGruy Leary; George Fraser; Ellin LaVar; Sean Longmire; Bill Lynch; Bernice McFadden; Victoria Christopher Murray; Tanya Odums; Charles Ogletree; Pam Perry; Denise Reed; Matty Rich; Tony Rose; Jackie Rowe; Ilyasah Shabazz; Set Shakur; Denese Shervington; Khalid Sumner; Dr.

Janet Taylor; Glenn Townes; Mike Tyson; Marilyn Underwood; Blair Underwood; Joyce Walker Joseph; Mathew Knowles; Rev. Dr. Barbara King; Tonja Ward; Diane Weathers; Sheila Evans-Tranum; Mary Pender Greene; Dr. Sampson Davis; Erich Williams; Kathryn Wilson-Duprey; Nadine Thompson; Westina Matthews; Veronica Jones.

Much love and thanks to those whose trust and faith endorse this book. I am eternally grateful for your support. Your dedication to our people inspires me. Thank you for offering words of wisdom that will help us reach the masses: Mary J. Blige, Bishop T. D. Jakes, Sean Combs, Dr. Cornel West, E. Lynn Harris, Patti LaBelle, Rev. Al Sharpton, Iyanla Vanzant, Danny Glover, Roland Martin, Jamie Hector, Butch Lewis, Rev. Frank M. Reid III, Zane, Andrew Solomon, Dr. Alvin Poussaint, Dr. Price Cobbs, Eddie Levert, Felicia "Snoop" Pearson.

You understood I was a woman "on fire" when it came to expanding the territory of this movement to save the countless lives of our people. You dreamt with me, cajoled me, conferred with me, answered questions, and gave feedback and priceless assistance. Thank you for your time, energy, and faith: Carole Hall; Ellis Gordon; Adrienne Ingrum; Linda Wharton-Boyd; Vickee Jordan Adams; Courtney Hill; Jacqueline Rowe; Priscilla Clarke; Alita Carter; Eustace Collins; Dia Banks; Charlotte Floyd-Pruitt; Sondra Roberts; Patti Webster; Sharon Harris; Kendu Isaacs; Aliya Crawford; Linda Duggins—you are always on time, girl! Jerri DeVard; Dennis Scott; Darryl Green; Dion Clarke; the members of the winning team of Clark Atlanta University public relations class, True PR, who designed a campaign for the book under the amazing guidance of Professor Tinlyn Graham: Caralynn Hampton, Kasheyna McDonald, Apria Brown, Shayla Simmons, Chiquita Hartage, Malene Ferguson, Patrick McCullough, Antonia Mills, Aftan Williams. Appreciation is also extended to the work of the members of the Winner's Circle team.

To those who saw me at my most fragile and spoke up, know that I am profoundly grateful for your care and strengthening words. Your advice for mental respite and your constant, loving counsel helps me stay in the trenches. I love you: Doug Brown—for the twenty-plus years of extraordinary and unconditional love; Cheryl Duncan—for your honor and integrity, and for relentlessly nudging me to step out of my comfort zone and into the world of technology and, finally, into peace and joy; Jim Kelly; Cicely Tyson; Ramon Hervey; Pat Kabore; Charlie Ward; Terry McMillan; Brenda Blackmon; Alex

English; Ed Dowdy—for the daily reminders that I am loved; Warrington Hudlin; Cynthia Diaz—for your friendship and for introducing me to God's Mouthpieces; Wanda Lundy—for your loving and caring boldness; Dr. Deborah Simmons; Dr. Gayatri Devi; Dr. Carolyn Britton Bailey; Dr. Jean Chin; Dr. Lynne Perry-Bottinger; Dr. Roberta Shapiro; Dr. Michael Hickson; Harry Jonassaint—for your patience in helping me get to where I need to be; Glenn Ellis—you are always on time! Chris Cathcart; Mark Jones; Ken Carter; Tracey Rico; Gerald Peart; Stephanie Dyre; Bridget Isaac; Jennifer Warnken; Becky Gatlin; Jennifer Holliday; Bob Law; Delroy Lindo; Tamara Monosoff; Ruth Clark; Eric Adams; Sue Annetts; Bikbaye Inejnema; Karen Roache; Betty Walker; Susan Toepfer; Jane Kendall; Helen Goss; Wiley Woodard; Roxanne Johnson; Carol Mackey; Margaret E. Shorter; Tonya Cannon; Leah Wilcox; Dr. Yolanda Brooks; Jade Kirby; Shirlee Strother; Carole Temple Phillips, Paula Banks.

I thank those of you in the media who joined me in partnership and provided welcoming forums to get out the wake-up call. Thank you for joining me in this movement to enlighten Black America: Michelle Burford, Stanley Crouch, Mark Thompson, Keith Murphy, Elinor Tatum, Rodney Reynolds, Pat Coulter, Angelo Henderson, Kay Byrd, Celeste Terry, Janet Shields, Lorna Owens, Easy Klein, Fatiyne Muhammad, David Dahmer, Demetrius Patterson, Jean Wells, Adrienne Lopez, Milton Allimadi, Brenda J. Wyche, Sylvia Flanagan, Dana Slagle, Curtis Taylor, George Kilpatrick, Carolyn Butts, Nyja Green, Linda Stasi, Kim Riley, Dr. Teresa Taylor Williams, Toya Beasley, Walter Leavy, Anita S. Lane, Joe Parisi, Audrey Bernard, Kate Ferguson, Lynnette Holloway, Gatsby Melodi.

I am also grateful to those throughout the country who joined in partnership by providing the platform to declare the cause of healing and enlightenment for the greater good of our brothers and sisters: Sharon Haynes and the Sisters Sippin' Tea, Tulsa, OK; Michelle Miller; Marilyn French Hubbard; Natatia Griffith; Khalilah Abdul-Baqi; Richard McCoy Jr.; Dr. Karen Daughtry; Wendy Brennan; Carol Jones; Caryn Curry; Penny Doyle; Hakim Hasan; Doyle Laudry; Jeff Burns; Dawn Walker; Carrie Mobley; Patricia Butts; Marcia Mayne; Alex Boone Johnson; Dell Hamilton; Sonya Alleyne; Alyssa Fant; Dr. Trevellya Ford-Ahmed; Ruth Fuller; Maurice Cox; Dawn Kelly; Andrew Carr; Juliann "Jewelz" Weston; Michelle Drayton-Martin; Wynona Redmond; Yvonne Davis; David Elwell; LiRon Anderson-Bell; Christopher "Kid" Reid; Dr. Linda Burke-Holloway; Rev. Thedora N. Brooks; Rev. Robert Waterman; Katasha Harley; Dorothy Rick; Anthony Istrico; Antoinette Forbes; Carolyn Ashford; Stacy Holman; Dr. Norman J. Goodman; Sandra

Baxter; Henry Louis Gates.

I thank all of you who, with your encouragement, words, prayers, advice, and financial support, helped get this critical work done.

> *And who Sometimes, when I was*
> *lifeless, loveless*
> *brought the paints*
> *N said*
> *Go on now*
> *Make your rainbows*

—DEBORAH REYNOLDS

Loreen Arbus; Regina Kulik-Scully; John Scully; Alan Gansberg; Courtney Lang; Joy Thomas Moore; Larry Yates; Vashta Dunlap; Tracy Richards; Cecile Cross Plummer; Pam Moore; Lisa Cash; Renee Gilbert; Ed Goldberg; Tom Zapf; Lauren Price; Floyd Townsend; Jeanne Ashe; John Elmore; Carol Salter; Carmen George; Heather Covington; Ulysses Bell; Ruxton McDougald; Clerenda McGrady; Bishop Nathan and Denise Edwers; Rev. Dr. Lester Taylor; Maggie Craddock; Abigail Disney; Francine LeFrak; Richie and Danielle Harmon Parker; Rev. Rae Brown; Frank Fraley; Iris Register; Lori Adams; Carol Van Atten; Carol Ross; C. Vernon Mason; Curtis Bunn; Wes Moore; Loretta Thomas; Chrisette Hudlin; Marty, Monique, and Elian Berg; Aldora Dunham; Tawana Tibbs; Joann Davis; Ally Roberson; Rev. Richard H. Dixon; Michael Robinson; Reese Stone; Sir Shadow; Ken Smikle; Dianne Hayes; Debra Nelson; Holly Blackmon; Lena Williams; Chet Burger; Toya White; Dotty Anderson; Raina Bundy; Marie Jackson; Andrew Morrison; Monique Fortune; James Mtume; Bruce Meyer; Kendal Whitlock Hart; Susan Nowak; Jacqueline Adams; Elaine Brown; Teri Williams Smith; Michelle Gadsden-Williams; Kim Cooper; David Burstine; David Charles; Steve Groom; Richard McKoy Jr.; Yvonne Pointer; Ericka Jackson; Seitu Orinde; Carol O'Gilvie; Angela Edwards; Lynne Edwards; Deborah Baron Ellis; Monique Clyburn; Chris Curry; Joe Cooney; Marilyn Artis; Stephanie Irace; Carolyn Wright Lewis; Leon Carter—the best damn sports editor, ever; Tara Douglas; Darius Baptiste; Feteroff Colen; Enid Nemy; Ruth Hirsch; Carol Phillips Johnson; Marcella Maxwell; James Powell; Lynnette Velasco; Yvonne Rose; Tim Richardson; Monica Bella Bragg; Regina Darby; Jill Devers; Teri Agins; Felicia Polk; Derek Anderson; Alex Blankson; the amazing Center for Creative Leadership team: Lily Kelly-Radford, Roger Conway, Gayle Magee, Candice Frankovelgia, John and Lynne Alexander; 382 CREW—who go above and beyond: Joann O'Neil, Frank Rizzo, Charlie O'Neil, James Madero, and Anthony Contento . . . and also Donnie, Sean, Chris, Song, Danny, Richard, Alexis, and Dario.

For those whose lives are public record—who have been through the storm or through the fire and endured to stand tall and strong—I thank you for your witness that if we can keep the faith through the night, everything will be all right. You gave us something we could "feel": Ntozake Shange, Jenifer Lewis, Dominic Carter, Sharon Robinson, Nadine Thompson, Cheryl James, Samuel Jackson, Stanley Jefferson, LL Cool J, The Game, Janet Jackson, Oprah Winfrey, Richard Cowan, Charles Bracey, Ray Alvarez, Rhonda Ross, Tina Turner, Whoopi Goldberg, Mariah Carey, Fantasia Barrino, Tyra Banks, Todd Bridges, Laveraneus Coles, John Head, Sybil Clark-Amuti, Kwaku Amuti, DeWayne Wickham, Lenny Kravitz, Bryan Monroe, Alma Powell, Harry Carson, Charlie Wilson, Duquina J. Johnson, Korbi G. Kelly, Andrea Morris, Marsha Kelly, Gladys Knight, Natalie Cole, Carly Simon, Joel Martin, Angie Bofill, Donnie McLurkin, Dr. Monica Coleman, Diane Stevens, Tavis Smiley, Laverne Ballard, Sandra LaDay, Judge Lynn Toler, Loretta Dixon-Castle, Diane Patrick, Karen Gormandy, Donna Chavous, Kitty Dukakis, Isis Sapp-Grant, Halle Berry, Wendy Williams Hunter, Mary Jo Codey.

I am grateful to my friends in the publishing world who saw the potential of this work. Thank you for your enthusiasm and for bidding encouragingly for it, especially: Rachel Kahan, Ivan Held, Marilyn Ducksworth, Heather Jackson, Donna Passannante, Kristen Kiser, Tammy Blake, Judith Kerr, Toni Burbank, Nita Taublib, Barb Burg, Beth Rashbaum, Lisa Considine, Caryn Karmatz Rudy, Jamie Raab.

Words cannot fully express my appreciation of those of you who shared your heart and soul with me and whose bold stories are unable to appear in this work. Thank you for lending an ear and for supporting the movement: Tracy Truitt, Diane Harris, Alexis Page Sprewell, Lisa Davis, Patricia Hodges, Evelyn L. Polk, Deborah "Sojourner" Edwards, Carline Balan, Leslie Morris, Judge Glenda Hatchett, Leon Ellis, Theodore Moye, Saundra Parks, Courtnei Evans, Judith Singer, Hilary Beard, Darryl Dawkins, Todd Averyhart, Helen Mashburn, Mathew St. Patrick, Angela Crockett, Myrna Gale, Robin Kearse, Marcia Ann Gillespie, Charles Rogers, Carla Owens, Julieanna Richardson, Randreta Ward Evans, Tevin Campbell, Kevin Powell, Dr. Altha Stewart, Wendy Anderson, Dikembe Mutombo, Anthony Hamilton, Arlivia Gamble, Helena Washington, Cassaundra Williams, Jeff Stetson, Gus Bennett Jr., Judith Killen, Belinda Anderson, Justine Simmons, Howard Bingham,

Ravi Windom, Jonathan Ortiz, Christopher D. Cathcart, Nadine Comeau, Stephanie L. Dyer, Marita Green, Eisa Nefertari Ulen, Ruby Harmon, Rev. Run, Natara Sampson, Darbi Alexander, Dana Dane, Vikki Pryor, Burgess Harrison.

In Memoriam—an old song talks of precious memories and how even in the midnight hour they come back and comfort the soul. Below are names of those whose spirit and very presence come, unbidden, to sustain me still: Phyllis Hyman, Mildred Ray, Arthur Ashe, Johnnie L. Cochran Jr., Josephine Premice, Emma Bowen, Ossie Davis, Gordon Parks, Miles Davis, Gregory Hines, Vernon Lynch Sr., Jim Moore, DeWitt Johnson, David Bradley—for showing us how to live and make the transition with grace, courage, and dignity.

To God Be the Glory

Index